Traveler's Language Guides:
German

Rupert Livesey

All inquiries should be addressed to:
Barron's Educational Series, Inc.
250 Wireless Boulevard
Hauppauge, NY 11788
http://www.barronseduc.com

ISBN-13: 978-0-7641-3206-3
ISBN-10: 0-7641-3206-7
Library of Congress Control Number 2005921550

Printed in China
9 8 7 6 5 4 3 2 1

Photos
Bundesverband Selbsthilfe Körperbehinderter, Krautheim: 77;
Cycleurope, Bergisch-Gladbach: 60; Deutsche Telekom AG, Bonn:
181; Fordwerke AG: 58; H. Geißel, Stuttgart: 9, 15, 49, 83, 121,
139, 145; Ifa, Stuttgart: 19, 129; U. Messelhäuser, Salem: 73;
Österreich Werbung, Frankfurt/M. (L. Hirnsl): 93; G. Reinboth,
Stuttgart: 31; Wolpert Fotodesign, Stuttgart: 41, 104–110, 165, 167
Cover: Getty Images/Imagebank (Werner Bokelberg; Werner
Dietrich); Getty Images/Stone (Rohan)

Vowels		
phonetic	sound in English	in German
[a]	short "a" – somewhere between "fan" and "fun"	danke, Land
[aː]	"ar"/"ah" - as in "hard," "calm"	Abend
[ɐ]	somewhere between "er" and "air"	Vater
[ɛ]	"e" – as in "net"	wenn
[ɛː]	somewhere between the vowel sound in "day" and "fair"	fährt, spät
[eː]	close to the long "a" in "bathe"	geht
[ə]	like first syllable of "alive"	bitte, viele
[ɪ]	"i" – as in "fit"	mit
[iː]	"ee" – as in "seen," "deal"	Ziel
[ɔ]	short "o" – as in "hot"	Gott
[oː]	somewhere between "loan" and "lawn"	Lohn
[ʊ]	as in "put," "look"	Mutter
[uː]	as in "fool," "rule"	Stuhl, Fuß

Special German Vowels		
[œ]	as in "Kent," but with rounded "kissing" lips	könnte
[øː]	almost as in "bird," "learn"	schön
[ʏ]	as in "fill," with "kissing" lips	füllen
[yː]	as in "feel," with "kissing" lips	fühlen

Diphthongs		
[aɪ]	as in "by"	bei
[aʊ]	as in "house"	Haus
[ɔɪ]	as in "boy"	neu

Consonants		
[b]	as in "ball"	Ball
[ç]	the "h" sound at the beginning of "hymn" or "humor"	mich, zwanzig, Honig
[d]	as in "down"	danke
[f]	as in "fine"	fein
[g]	as in "give" (never as in "George")	geben
[h]	as in "house"	Haus
[j]	the "y" sound at the beginning of "yes"	ja
[k]	as in "kindly"	Kind

[l]	as in "love"	Liebe
[m]	as in "mister"	Mädchen
[n]	as in "no"	nein
[ŋ]	the "ng" sound as in "longing"	lang
[p]	as in "pair"	Paar
[ʀ]	UVular as in French or trilled as in Spanish	warum
[s]	as in "missing"	missen, Maß
[ʃ]	"sh" - as in "show"	schon, Stein
[t]	as in "table"	Tisch
[v]	as in "very"	wo
[x]	as in "Loch (Ness)"	Loch
[z]	as in "zero"	sehr
[ʒ]	"zh" - as in "massage," "treasure," "Zhivago"	Massage
[ts]	as in "cats," "its"	Zeit, Blitz
[tʃ]	"ch" – as in "check"	deutsch
	Other Symbols	
[']	main stress	
[ˌ]	secondary stress	
[:]	long vowel	
[ʔ]	glottal stop	

More detailed information about German pronunciation may be found in "A Short Guide to German Pronunciation" on page 202.

The Alphabet

A	a	[aː]	J	j	[jot]	S	s	[ɛs]
B	b	[beː]	K	k	[kaː]	T	t	[teː]
C	c	[tseː]	L	l	[ɛl]	U	u	[uː]
D	d	[deː]	M	m	[ɛm]	V	v	[fau]
E	e	[eː]	N	n	[ɛn]	W	w	[veː]
F	f	[ɛf]	O	o	[oː]	X	x	[iks]
G	g	[geː]	P	p	[peː]	Y	y	[ʔˈʏpzilɔn]
H	h	[haː]	Q	q	[kuː]	Z	z	[tsɛt]
I	i	[iː]	R	r	[ɛr]			

Abbreviations

adj	adjective
adv	adverb
conj	conjunction
el	electricity
f	feminine gender

7

fam		familiar, colloquial
fig		figurative
m		masculine gender
n		neuter gender
pl		plural
poss prn		possessive pronoun
prp		preposition
rel		religious
sing		singular
s.o.		someone
s.th.		something
tele		telecommunications
vb		verb

Common Abbreviations

A	Österreich	Austria
ADAC	Allgemeiner deutscher Automobilclub	German automobile association
BRD	Bundesrepublik Deutschland	Federal Republic of Germany
bzw.	beziehungsweise	or, respectively
°C	(Grad) Celsius	(degrees) Celsius/Centigrade
CH	Schweiz (Helvetia)	Switzerland
CHF	Schweizer Franken	Swiss francs
D	Deutschland	Germany
DB	Deutsche Bahn	German railroad
etw.	etwas	something
EU	Europäische Union	European Union
H	Haltestelle	bus or streetcar stop
jdm.	jemandem	for, to someone
jdn.	jemand	someone
Jh.	Jahrhundert	century
JH	Jugendherberge	youth hostel
n. Chr.	nach Christus	A.D.
ÖBB	Österreichische Bundesbahnen	Austrian railroad
PKW	Personenkraftwagen	car/auto
PS	Pferdestärke	horsepower
s.	siehe	see
SB	Selbstbedienung	self-service
SBB	Schweizerische Bundesbahnen	Swiss railroad
Std.	Stunde	hour
Str.	Straße	street
StVO	Straßenverkehrsordnung	traffic regulations
tgl.	täglich	daily
v. Chr.	vor Christus	B.C.
z. B.	zum Beispiel	e.g.

8

Different Countries, Different Customs

Intercultural Tips

General

German is spoken not only in Germany but also in Austria and Switzerland. There are, however, numerous differences. In general, people in Austria and Switzerland speak more slowly than they do in Germany; their intonation is softer, so that it is sometimes difficult to differentiate between a "**b**" and a "**p**." Only the context would show whether an Austrian was talking about a cake or a case when (s)he said "**Gepäck.**"

In contrast to German and Austrian regional dialects, Swiss German is treated as a separate language and is spoken on TV and radio, and at school. Some words are derived from French, although stress is often placed on the first syllable of a word. Like the Germans, the Swiss also use a lot of English words, especially those for sports, e.g. "**goal**" instead of "**Tor,**" or "**corner**" instead of "**Eckball.**"

There is no "**ß**" in Swiss German; all words that are written with "**ß**" in German – even after the recent spelling reforms – are written with "**ss**" in Swiss German: e.g. "**Grüsse**" instead of "**Grüße,**" or "**Füsse**" instead of "**Füße.**"

Some nouns in Swiss German are also different in gender from their counterparts in German: thus the Swiss say "**der Butter**" and "**das Tram.**"

Forms of Address

Until you become closely acquainted, you should use the formal "**Sie**" when speaking to an adult. On meeting someone for the first time, it is usual to shake hands and say your surname; only when you have gotten to know each other well and have exchanged first names, should you use the informal "**du.**" Between children and young people it is normal to use "**du.**" A short handshake is also common when meeting someone, and young people often give each other a kiss on the cheek.

In Austria it is normal for work colleagues and people of the same age to use "**du**" to each other and, especially in rural areas, "**du**" is sometimes even used between strangers.

Although "**Fräulein**" ("*Miss*") is no longer used as a form of address in Germany, it is still fairly common in Austria. In Vienna, women can expect to be addressed as "**Gnädige Frau,**" usually shortened to "**Gnä Frau,**" meaning "*madame.*"

Titles are important in Germany and Austria. For example, someone with a doctorate (Ph.D.) would be addressed as "**Frau/Herr Doktor.**" Titles are less important in Switzerland.

Greetings

The most general form of greeting in German-speaking countries is "**Guten Tag**" or the more informal "**Hallo;**" in the morning you could say "**Guten Morgen,**" in the afternoon "**Guten Tag**" (<u>not</u> "*Guten Nachmittag*") and in the evening "**Guten Abend.**" In southern Germany and Austria it is common to hear "**Grüß Gott,**" and in northern Germany "**Moin, Moin!,**" both of which just mean "*Hello!*" If you know someone well, you could say "**Grüß dich!**" and then "**Wie geht's?,**" meaning "*How are things?*" or "*How are you doing?*"; more formally, you would use "**Wie geht es Ihnen/dir?**", meaning "*How are you?*" In reply, you could say "**Danke, gut. Und Ihnen/dir?**" = "*Fine, thanks. And you?*"

The Swiss greet each other with "**Grüezi,**" or more informally "**Hoi**" or "**Sali.**" In Austria they say "**Servus**" or more rarely "**Habe die Ehre.**"

Farewells

The most common way of saying goodbye is "**Auf Wiedersehen!**" or informally "**Tschüs(s)**" or "**Mach's gut!**" = "*See you!*", or "**Bis morgen**" = "*See you tomorrow.*" Among friends you could hear the Italian "**Ciao,**" and on parting late at night, you might also say "**Gute Nacht!**"

In Austria and parts of Bavaria, rather than "**Tschüs(s),**" you are likely to hear "**Pfiat' di**" (which roughly means "*May God be with you*"). In Switzerland they say "**Auf Wiederluege**" or "**Adieu.**"

Please and Thank You

In Germany it is not nearly as common as in the US to use "*please*" and "*thank you,*" so don't take it as a sign of impoliteness or curtness if you don't hear a "**bitte**" or "**danke**" where you might expect to hear one in English. It is common in Germany, however, to reply to someone who says "*thank you*" to you. So if someone says "**Vielen Dank**" or "**Danke schön,**" you could reply "**Bitte schön**" or "**Bitte sehr**" or "**Gern geschehen**" = "*Not at all*" or "*You're welcome*" or "*It's a pleasure/My pleasure.*" In Austria you reply "**Gerne.**" A Swiss is more likely to say "**Merci**" or "**Merci vielmals**" rather than "**Danke.**"

Mealtimes

At mealtimes it is common to say "**Guten Appetit!**" or "**Mahlzeit!**" and to reply "**Danke, gleichfalls!**" = "*Thank you, and the same to you!*" There are numerous expressions for "*Cheers!*" when having a drink with someone, but the most common is "**Prost!**" or more formally "**Zum Wohl!**"

In Switzerland, you wish each other "**Guten Appetit!**" or "**En Guete.**" Breakfast is called "**Morgenessen**" or "**Zmorge,**" lunch is "**Zmittag**" and dinner/supper is "**Nachtessen**" or "**Znacht.**"

Telephone

When answering the telephone in Germany it is usual to give your surname or to say "**Hallo**" or "**Ja, bitte?**" if you prefer to stay anonymous – rather than to state your phone number. When saying goodbye on the phone, you say "**(Auf) Wiederhören**" rather than "**(Auf) Wiedersehen.**"

Numbers

To make a clear distinction between 1 and 7, Germans put a short horizontal line through the stem of the seven. One billion (1.000.000.000: a thousand million) = "**eine Milliarde**" in German; "**eine Billion**" in German = "*one trillion*" in English (= a million million). Decimal points are written with a comma in German: "**3,14**" and you should say: "**drei Komma eins vier**" although it is also common to hear "**drei Komma vierzehn.**"

Time

Use of the 24-hour clock is widespread, but beware! – "**halb zwei**" does <u>NOT</u> mean "*half two*" but "*half past one.*" In southern Germany you could also hear "**viertel zwei**" = "*(a) quarter past one*" or "**drei viertel zwei**" = "*(a) quarter to two.*"

Speed Limits

The speed limit on expressways ("**Autobahnen**") in Switzerland is 120 km/h (75 mph) and in Austria 130 km/h. Although there is no official speed limit on German expressways, there are numerous places (such as exits and interchanges) where speed <u>is</u> restricted and these are often quite strictly controlled. In built-up areas the speed limit is 50 km/h (c. 30 mph) and in residential "housing zones" actual walking speed.

Interspersed with the expressway service stations ("**Raststätte**"), you will also find numerous places to pull off and take a break ("**Rastplatz**").

Stamps

In Germany, the basic price of a stamp for a letter or postcard to anywhere in the EU is the same as the price within Germany.

School

Most schoolchildren wear a satchel or backpack (for older children) to school; pupils do not wear a school uniform and there are usually no classes in the afternoons. Those who perform extremely poorly and do not achieve the required grades at the end of the year have to repeat the year.

Military Service

A system of compulsory military service operates in Germany. Every young man must do either 9 months of military service or, if he objects on conscientious grounds, 10 months of community service, "**der Zivildienst.**"

Bars/Restaurants

Buying a round of drinks is not common practice in Germany. Drinks are brought directly to your table and a mark is made on your coaster or beer mat. At the end of the evening these marks are counted up and you are asked if you want to pay "**zusammen**" (all together) or "**getrennt**" (individually). Tipping is normal, but in smaller amounts than in the US; more than 10% of the bill would be considered excessive unless the service had been absolutely wonderful.

In the wine-growing regions of Austria you are likely to find a "**Heurige**," an inn selling new local wine, accompanied by a "**Jause**" (snack) or "**Hausmannskost**" (traditional fare). In Switzerland, an inn is called a "**Beiz**"; the waitress is called a "**Serviertochter**" and you can order such things as a "**Panaschee**" (beer and lemon-lime soda), a "**Stange**" (small beer) or a "**Jus**" (fruit juice). The phrase "**à discrétion**" on a menu means that you can help yourself to as much as you like for a set price.

Tea

Tea in Germany is invariably made with a teabag and is very weak. It is also served without milk but occasionally with lemon. It is far more common to have "**Kaffee und Kuchen**" (*coffee and cake*) in the afternoon rather than tea.

Domestic Matters

Expect to pay for plastic bags in supermarkets and in Germany to pay a refundable deposit ("**Pfand**") on all bottles and cans of mineral water, soft drinks, and beer. Household trash is sorted into sometimes 5 different containers: one for glass, one for paper, one for plastic, foil, cartons, and cans, one for organic waste, and one for everything else.

There is a collection for bulky household waste on demand, called "**Sperrmüll,**" which is simply placed in piles by the roadside. It is quite acceptable to take anything from these piles that takes your fancy – thus many items are recycled rather than just thrown away.

Christmas, New Year, & Easter

In German-speaking countries the most important day of the Christmas season is Christmas Eve ("**Heiliger Abend**"), during the evening of which most children are allowed to unwrap their presents.

The biggest excuse for a big fireworks party is New Year's Eve ("**Silvester[abend]**").

The Easter bunny ("**Osterhase**") comes at Easter and hides brightly decorated hard-boiled eggs (in their shells), chocolate Easter eggs and chocolate bunnies, and other presents around the house and garden for the children to find.

And Finally ...

There are many more dedicated bicycle lanes than in the US, and some are integrated into the normal street surface – so watch out where you walk!

Travel Preparations

Reserving a Hotel Room by E-Mail

Dear Sir or Madam,

I would like to reserve a single/double/twin-bed room for 2
nights on the 24th and 25th of June. Please let me know if you
have any vacancies and the total cost per night (plus dinner).

Yours sincerely,

Sehr geehrte Damen und Herren,

am 24. und 25. Juni benötige ich für zwei Nächte ein Einzel-/
Doppel-/Zweibettzimmer. Bitte teilen mir mit, ob Sie ein
Zimmer frei haben und was es pro Nacht (einschließlich
Abendessen) kostet.

Mit freundlichen Grüßen

Renting a Car by E-Mail

Dear Sir / Madam,

I would like to rent a small / mid-range / luxury sedan /
7-seater van from July 20–25 from Munich Airport.
I depart from Frankfurt Airport, so I wish to leave the car there.
Please inform me of your rates and what documents I require.

Yours sincerely,

Sehr geehrte Damen und Herren,

für den Zeitraum vom 20.–25. Juli möchte ich am Flughafen
München einen Kleinwagen / Mittelklassewagen / eine Luxus-
limousine / eine 7-sitzige Großraumlimousine mieten. Ich fliege
von Frankfurt ab und möchte deshalb dort den Leihwagen
abgeben. Bitte teilen Sie mir Ihre Tarife mit und welche Unter-
lagen ich benötige.

Mit freundlichen Grüßen

General Questions

I am planning to spend my vacation in … . Can you give me details on accommodations in the area?
Ich habe vor, meinen Urlaub in … zu verbringen. Können Sie mir bitte Informationen über Unterkünfte in der Gegend geben? [ˀɪç haːbə 'foɐ maɪnn ˀuɐlaʊp ˀɪn … tsʊ fɛ'bʀɪŋŋ kœnn zi miɐ 'bɪtə ˀɪnfɐma'tsjoːnn ˀyːbɐ ˀʊntɐkʏnftə ˀɪn dɐ geːgŋt geːbm]

Where is the best place to go on a boating vacation?
Welche Gegend empfiehlt sich für Ferien auf einem Boot?
['vɛlçə geːgŋt ˀɛmp'fiːlt zɪç fyɐ 'feːʀɪən ˀaʊf ˌˀaɪnəm 'boːt]

What sort of accommodations are you looking for?
An welche Art von Unterkunft haben Sie gedacht?
[ˀan 'vɛlçə ˀaːt fɔn ˀʊntɐkʊnft haːbm zi gə'daxt]

  a hotel
  ein Hotel [ˀaɪn ho'tɛl]
  pension/small hotel
  eine Pension [ˌˀaɪnə paŋ'zjoːn]
  bed and breakfast
  ein Fremdenzimmer [ˀaɪn 'fʀɛmdntsɪmɐ]
  vacation apartment
  eine Ferienwohnung [ˌˀaɪnə 'feːʀɪənˌvoːnʊŋ]

Questions About Accommodations

Hotel – Pension – Bed & Breakfast

I'd like to stay in a hotel, but nothing too expensive – something in the mid-price range.
Ich suche ein Hotel, jedoch nicht zu teuer – etwas in der mittleren Preislage. [ˀɪç 'zuːxə ˀaɪn ho'tɛl je'dɔx nɪçt tsʊ 'tɔjɐ ˀɛtvas ˀɪn dɐ 'mɪtlərən 'pʀaɪslaːgə]

I'd like to stay in a hotel with a swimming pool / a golf course / tennis courts.
Ich suche ein Hotel mit Hallenbad / Golfplatz / Tennisplätzen.
[ˀɪç 'zuːxə ˀaɪn ho'tɛl mɪt 'halnbaːt / 'gɔlfplats / 'tɛnɪsplɛtsn]

Can you recommend a good bed-and-breakfast?
Können Sie mir ein schönes Fremdenzimmer mit Frühstück empfehlen?
[kœnn zi miɐ ˀaɪn 'ʃøːnəs 'fʀɛmdntsɪmɐ mɪt 'fʀyːʃtʏk ˀɛmp'feːln]

How many people does it sleep?
Für wie viele Leute soll es sein? [fyɐ 'viːɫfiːlə 'lɔɪtə zɔl əs 'zaɪn]

Are dogs allowed?
Sind dort Hunde erlaubt? [zɪnt dɔɐt 'hʊndə ˀɐ'laʊpt]

17

Vacation Cottages and Apartments

I'm looking for a vacation apartment or cottage.
Ich suche eine Ferienwohnung oder einen Bungalow.
[ʔɪç 'zu:xə ˌʔaɪnə 'fe:ʀɪənˌvo:nʊŋ ˌʔo:dɐ ˌʔaɪnn 'bʊŋgalo]

Can you recommend a farmhouse suitable for children?
Können Sie mir einen kinderfreundlichen Ferienbauernhof
empfehlen?
[kœnn zi miɐ ˌʔaɪnn 'kɪndɐˌfʀɔɪntlɪçn 'fe:ʀɪənˌbaʊɐnho:f ʔɛmp'fe:ln]

Is there ...?
Gibt es ...? [gɪpt əs]

  a baby crib
  ein Kinderbett [ʔaɪn 'kɪndɐbɛt]
  high chair
  einen Hochstuhl [ʔaɪnn 'ho:xʃtu:l]
  TV
  einen Fernseher [ʔaɪnn 'fɛɐnze.ɐ]
  telephone
  ein Telefon [ʔaɪn 'te:ləfo:n]
  washing machine
  eine Waschmaschine [ˌʔaɪnə 'vaʃmaˌʃi:nə]
  dishwasher
  eine Spülmaschine [ˌʔaɪnə 'ʃpy:lmaˌʃi:nə]
  microwave
  eine Mikrowelle [ˌʔaɪnə 'mɪkʀoˌvɛlə]

Is electricity included in the price?
Sind die Stromkosten im Preis eingeschlossen?
[zɪnt di 'ʃtʀo:mkɔstn ʔɪm pʀaɪs ˈʔaɪngəʃlɔsn]

Are bed linen and towels provided?
Werden Bettwäsche und Handtücher gestellt?
[veɐdn 'bɛtvɛʃə ʔʊnt 'hanty:çɐ gəˈʃɛlt]

How much deposit do you require and how long in advance?
Wie viel muss ich anzahlen und wann ist die Anzahlung fällig?
['vi:_fi:l mʊs ɪç ˈʔantsa:ln ʔʊnt 'van ʔɪst di ˈʔantsa:lʊŋ 'fɛlɪç]

Where and when should I pick up the keys?
Wo und wann kann ich die Schlüssel abholen?
['vo: ʔʊnt 'van kan ɪç di ʃlʏsl ˈʔapho:ln]

Camping

I'm looking for a small campground in .... Is there anything you can recommend?
Ich suche einen kleinen Campingplatz in ... Können Sie mir irgend etwas empfehlen? [ʔɪç 'zu:xə ʔaɪnn 'klaɪnn 'kɛmpɪŋplats ʔɪn ... kœnn zi miɐ ˈʔɪʀgnt ˌʔɛtvas ʔɛmp'fe:ln]

A regular language

For the most part German is very regular in pronunciation. Most words are spoken with stress on the first syllable: *danke, Deutschland.* Important exceptions are words beginning with *ge-, ver-, ent-* (*gegessen, verboten, Entschuldigung* – these are stressed on the second syllable) – and words borrowed from other languages. In general, words borrowed from French and English retain their original pronunciation – to the extent that German speakers can imitate this. Borrowings from English have been increasing explosively for the last half century, particularly in "modern" areas such as computer technology, high-tech, business, and entertainment. You will run into countless English words in German; your best bet is simply to rely on your own familiar way of saying these.

Basic Phrases

Yes.
Ja. [jaː]

No.
Nein. [naɪn]

Please.
Bitte. [ˈbɪtə]

Thank you.
Danke! [ˈdaŋkə]

Many thanks! / Thanks a lot!
Vielen Dank! [fiːln daŋk]

Thanks, (and) the same to you!
Danke, gleichfalls! [ˈdaŋkə ˈglaɪçfals]

You're welcome! / Not at all!
Bitte! / Gern geschehen! [ˈbɪtə / ˈgɛrn gəˈʃeːn]

Not at all! / Don't mention it!
Nichts zu danken! [ˈnɪçts tsʊ ˈdaŋkn̩]

Pardon? / Excuse me?
Wie bitte? [ˈviː bɪtə]

Of course.
Selbstverständlich! [zɛlpstfɛˈʃtɛntlɪç]

Agreed!
Einverstanden! [ˈʔaɪnfɛʃtandn̩]

Okay! / OK!
Okay! [ˈʔoˈke], In Ordnung! [ˈʔɪn ˈʔɔɐtnʊŋ]

20

Excuse me.
Verzeihung! [fɐˈtsaɪʊn]

Just a minute, please.
Einen Augenblick, bitte. [ˈʔaɪnn ˈʔaʊɡn̩ˈblɪk ˈbɪtə]

All right, that's enough!
Das reicht jetzt! [das ˈʀaɪçt jɛtst]

Help!
Hilfe! [ˈhɪlfə]

Who?
Wer? [veɐ]

What?
Was? [vas]

Which?
Welcher?/Welche?/Welches? [ˈvɛlçɐ/ˈvɛlçə/ˈvɛlçəs]

Where?
Wo? [voː]

Where is ...? / Where are ...?
Wo ist ...? / Wo sind ...? [voː ˈʔɪst .../voː zɪnt ...]

Why?
Warum? [vaˈʀʊm] / Weshalb? [vɛsˈhalp] / Wozu? [voˈtsuː]

How much? / How many?
Wie viel? / Wie viele?
[viˈ_ˈfiːl / viˈ_ˈfiːlə]

How long?
Wie lange? [viˈ_ˈlaŋə]

When?
Wann? [van]

When? / (At) what time?
Um wie viel Uhr? [ʔʊm ˈviː_fiːl ˈʔuɐ]

I'd like ...
Ich möchte ... [ʔɪç ˈmœçtə ...]

Is there ...?/Are there ...?
Gibt es ...? [ɡɪpt əs]

0	null [nʊl]
1	eins [ʔaɪns]
2	zwei [tsvaɪ]

"Zwo" [tsvoː] is sometimes used in speaking, to distinguish "zwei" from "drei."

3	drei [dʀaɪ]
4	vier [fiɐ]
5	fünf [fʏnf]
6	sechs [zɛks]
7	sieben ['ziːbm]
8	acht [axt]
9	neun [nɔɪn]
10	zehn [tseːn]
11	elf [ɛlf]
12	zwölf [tsvœlf]
13	dreizehn ['dʀaɪtseːn]
14	vierzehn ['fɪʀtseːn]
15	fünfzehn ['fʏnftseːn]
16	sechzehn ['zɛçtseːn]
17	siebzehn ['ziːptseːn]
18	achtzehn ['axtseːn]
19	neunzehn ['nɔɪntseːn]
20	zwanzig ['tsvantsɪç]
21	einundzwanzig ['aɪnʊn͵tsvantsɪç]
22	zweiundzwanzig ['tsvaɪʊn͵tsvantsɪç]
23	dreiundzwanzig ['dʀaɪʊn͵tsvantsɪç]
24	vierundzwanzig ['fiɐʊn͵tsvantsɪç]
30	dreißig ['dʀaɪsɪç]
40	vierzig ['fɪʀtsɪç]
50	fünfzig ['fʏnftsɪç]
60	sechzig ['zɛçtsɪç]
70	siebzig ['ziːptsɪç]
80	achtzig ['axtsɪç]
90	neunzig ['nɔɪntsɪç]
100	(ein)hundert ['(aɪn)hʊndet]
101	hundert(und)eins [͵hʊndet(ʔʊnt)ʔaɪns]
200	zweihundert ['tsvaɪhʊndet]
300	dreihundert ['dʀaɪhʊndet]
1000	(ein)tausend [(͵aɪn)'taʊznt]
2000	zweitausend ['tsvaɪtaʊznt]
10,000	zehntausend (10.000) ['tseːntaʊznt]

22

100,000	hunderttausend (100.000) ['hʊndɛttaʊznt]
1,000,000	eine Million (1.000.000) [aɪnə mɪ'ljoːn]
first	erster ['eestə]
second	zweiter ['tsvaɪtə]
third	dritter ['dʀɪtə]
fourth	vierter ['fietə]
fifth	fünfter ['fʏnftə]
sixth	sechster ['zɛkstə]
seventh	siebter ['ziːptə]
eighth	achter ['ʔaxtə]
ninth	neunter ['nɔɪntə]
tenth	zehnter ['tseːntə]
1/2	einhalb [aɪnhalp]
1/3	ein Drittel [aɪn 'dʀɪtl]
1/4	ein Viertel [aɪn 'fɪrtl]
3/4	drei Viertel ['dʀaɪ 'fɪrtl]
3.5 %	drei Komma fünf Prozent (3,5 %) ['dʀaɪ 'kɔma 'fʏnf pʀo'tsɛnt]

Note that for numbers, the use of the comma and the decimal point is reversed: "1,200,500 people" becomes "1.200.500 Menschen" and "3.5 percent" becomes "3,5 Prozent."

27 °C	siebenundzwanzig Grad Celsius ['ziːbmʊn,tsvantsɪç gʀaːt 'tsɛlzɪʊs]
–5 °C	minus 5 Grad ['miːnʊs fʏnf gʀaːt]
1999	neunzehnhundertneunundneunzig ['nɔɪnts(e)n,hʊndet,nɔɪn(ʊ)n'nɔɪntsɪç]
2003	zweitausenddrei ['tsvaɪtaʊznt'dʀaɪ]
millimeter	der Millimeter [de 'mɪli,meːtə]
centimeter	der Zentimeter [de ,tsɛnti'meːtə]
meter	der Meter [de 'meːtə]
kilometer	der Kilometer [de ,kilo'meːtə]
liter	der Liter [de 'liːtə]
gram(s)	das Gramm [das gʀam]
kilogram(s)	das Kilo [das 'kiːlo]
pound(s)	das Pfund [das (p)fʊnt]

23

Weights and measures

All German-speaking countries use the metric system. An inch is about 2.5 centimeters, a meter is a bit more than a yard, a mile is about 1.6 kilometers, and a liter is roughly a quart.

1 Zentimeter (cm)	$\cong$ 0.39 inches
1 Meter (m) = 100 cm	$\cong$ 3.28 feet /
	39.3 inches
1 Kilometer (km) = 1000 m	$\cong$ 0.62 miles
1 Liter (l) ['liːtɐ]	$\cong$ 1.75 pints (UK)/
	2.11 pints (US)/
	0.87 quarts (UK)/
	1.05 quarts (US)/
	0.22 gallons (UK)/
	0.26 gallons (US)
1 Gramm (g) ['gʀam]	$\cong$ 0.03 ounces
1 Kilogramm (kg) = 1000 g	$\cong$ 35.2 ounces /
	2.20 pounds
1 Zentner = 50 kg ['tsɛntnɐ]	$\cong$ 110 lbs.

Telling the Time

Time

What time is it, please?
Wie viel Uhr ist es bitte? ['viː_fil ʔuɐ ʔɪst əs 'bɪtə]

It's (exactly/about) ...
Es ist (genau/ungefähr) ... [ʔəs ɪst gə'nau/ʔʊngə'fɛɐ]

three o'clock.
drei Uhr. [dʀaɪ ʔuɐ]

five past three.
fünf nach drei. [fynf nax 'dʀaɪ]

ten past three.
drei Uhr zehn. [dʀaɪ ʔuɐ tseːn]

quarter past three.
Viertel nach drei. ['fɪʀtl nax dʀaɪ]

half past three.
halb vier. [halp fiɐ]

quarter to four.
Viertel vor vier. ['fɪʀtl fɔɐ fiɐ]

five to four.
fünf vor Vier. [fʏnf fɔɐ fiɐ]

twelve noon.
zwölf Uhr Mittag. [tsvœlf ʔuɐ ˈmɪtaːk]

midnight.
Mitternacht. [ˈmɪtɐnaxt]

What time?/When?
Um wie viel Uhr?/Wann? [ʔʊm ˈviː_fiːl ʔuɐ / van]

At one o'clock.
Um ein Uhr. [ʔʊm ʔaɪn ʔuɐ]

At two o'clock.
Um zwei Uhr. [ʔʊm tsvaɪ ʔuɐ]

At about four o'clock.
Gegen vier Uhr. [ˈgeːgŋ fiɐ ʔuɐ]

In an hour.
In einer Stunde. [ʔɪn ʔaɪnɐ ˈʃtʊndə]

In two hours.
In zwei Stunden. [ʔɪn tsvaɪ ʃtʊndn]

Not before nine A.M.
Nicht vor neun Uhr morgens. [nɪçt foɐ ˈnɔɪn uɐ ˈmɔɐgŋs]

Between three and four.
Zwischen drei und vier. [ˈtsvɪʃn dʀaɪ ʔʊnt fiɐ]

After eight P.M.
Nach acht Uhr abends/zwanzig Uhr.
[nax ʔaxt uɐ ʔaːbms/ˈtsvantsɪç ʔuɐ]

> Germans like to use the 24-hour time system. 10 A.M. is *zehn Uhr* and 10 P.M. is *zweiundzwanzig Uhr*.

How long?
Wie lange? [vi_ˈlaŋə]

For two hours.
Zwei Stunden (lang). [tsvaɪ ʃtʊndn laŋ]

From ten to eleven.
Von zehn bis elf. [fɔn tseːn bɪs ʔɛlf]

Until five o'clock.
Bis fünf/siebzehn Uhr. [bɪs fʏnf/ˈziːptseːn ʔuɐ]

Since when?
Seit wann? [zaɪt van]

Since eight A.M.
Seit acht Uhr morgens. [zaɪt ʔaxt uɐ ˈmɔɐgŋs]

For half an hour.
Seit einer halben Stunde. [zaɪt ˀaɪnɐ ˈhalbm̩ ˈʃtʊndə]

For a week.
Seit acht Tagen. [zaɪt ˀaxt taːgn̩]

about noon	gegen Mittag [ˈgeːgn̩ ˈmɪtaːk]
in the afternoon	nachmittags [ˈnaxmɪtaːks]
daily	täglich [tɛːklɪç]
during the day	tagsüber [ˈtaːksˀyːbɐ]
during the morning	vormittags [ˈfɔɐmɪtaːks]
in the evening	abends [ˀaːbm̩ts]
every day	jeden Tag [jeːdn̩ taːk]
every hour, hourly	stündlich [ˈʃtʏntlɪç]
now and then	ab und zu [ˀap ˀʊn ˈtsuː]
in two weeks	in 14 (vierzehn) Tagen [ˀɪn ˈfɪɐtseːn ˈtaːgn̩]
at lunch time	mittags [ˈmɪtaːks]
last Monday morning	letzten Montagmorgen [lɛtstn̩ moːntaːkˈmɔɐgn̩]
ten minutes ago	vor zehn Minuten [fɔɐ tseːn mɪˈnuːtn̩]
in the morning	morgens [ˈmɔɐgn̩s]
never	nie [niː]
next year	nächstes Jahr [ˈnɛːçstəs ˈjaː]
at night	nachts [naxts]
now	jetzt [jɛtst]
on Sunday	am Sonntag [ˀam ˈzɔntaːk]
recently	kürzlich [ˈkʏɐtslɪç]
sometimes	manchmal [ˈmançmaːl]
soon	bald [balt]
the day before yesterday . . .	vorgestern [ˈfɔɐgɛstɐn]
the day after tomorrow	übermorgen [ˈˀyːbɐmɔɐgn̩]
this morning/this evening . .	heute Morgen/heute Abend [hɔɪtə ˈmɔɐgn̩/hɔɪtə ˀaːbm̩t]
this week	diese Woche [ˈdiːzə ˈvɔxə]
today	heute [ˈhɔɪtə]
tomorrow	morgen [ˈmɔɐgn̩]
tomorrow morning/	morgen früh/morgen Abend
tomorrow evening	[mɔɐgn̩ ˈfʀyː/mɔɐgn̩ ˀaːbm̩t]
on the weekend	am Wochenende [ˀam ˈvɔxn̩ˀɛndə]
yesterday	gestern [ˈgɛstɐn]

The Days of the Week

Monday .... Montag ['mo:nta:k]
Tuesday .... Dienstag ['di:nsta:k]
Wednesday .... Mittwoch ['mɪtvɔx]
Thursday .... Donnerstag ['dɔnɛsta:k]
Friday .... Freitag ['fʀaɪta:k]
Saturday .... *(southern Germany)* Samstag ['zamsta:k]
(northern Germany) Sonnabend
['zɔna:bmt]
Sunday .... Sonntag ['zɔnta:k]

The Months of the Year

January .... Januar ['janʋa:], *(Austria)* Jänner ['jɛnɐ]
February .... Februar ['fe:bʀʋa:]
March .... März [mɛɛts]
April .... April ['ʔa'pʀɪl]
May .... Mai [maɪ]
June .... Juni ['ju:ni]
July .... Juli ['ju:li]
August .... August [ʔaʊ'ɡʊst]
September .... September [zɛp'tɛmbɐ]
October .... Oktober ['ɔk'to:bɐ]
November .... November [no'vɛmbɐ]
December .... Dezember [de'tsɛmbɐ]

The Seasons

spring .... der Frühling [dɐ 'fʀy:lɪŋ]
summer .... der Sommer [dɐ 'zɔmɐ]
fall .... der Herbst [dɐ 'hɛɐpst]
winter .... der Winter [dɐ 'vɪntɐ]

Holidays

In addition to the holidays mentioned below, there are various local religious holidays.

New Year's Day .... Neujahr [nɔɪ'ja:]
Swiss Holiday (2.1.) ...... Berchtoldstag ['bɛɛçtɔldsta:k]
Epiphany (6.1.) .... Erscheinungsfest [ʔe'ʃaɪnʊŋsfɛst]
Monday before Shrove ... Rosenmontag [ʀo:zn'mo:nta:k],
Tuesday   *(Switzerland)* Fastnachtmontag
[ˌfasnaxt'mo:nta:k]
Shrove Tuesday .... Faschingsdienstag [ˌfaʃɪŋs'di:ns ta:k],
Fas(t)nachtdienstag [ˌfasnaxt'di:ns ta:k]

27

Good Friday	Karfreitag [kaˈfʀaɪtaːk]
Easter Sunday	Ostersonntag [ˌʔoːstɐˈzɔntaːk]
Easter Monday	Ostermontag [ˌʔoːstɐˈmoːntaːk]
Labor Day	Tag der Arbeit (Erster Mai) [taːk de ˈʔaʀbaɪt (ˈʔeɐstɐ ˈmaɪ)]
Whit Sunday/Pentecost	Pfingstsonntag [ˌpfɪŋstˈzɔntaːk]
Whit Monday	Pfingstmontag [ˌpfɪŋstˈmoːntaːk]
Ascension Day	Christi Himmelfahrt [ˌkʀɪsti ˈhɪmlˌfaːt]
Corpus Christi	Fronleichnam [fʀɔnˈlaɪçnaːm]
German Unification Day ... (October 3rd)	Tag der deutschen Einheit [taːk de dɔɪtʃn ˈaɪnhaɪt]
Austrian National Day	26. (Sechsundzwanzigster) Oktober [ˈzɛksʊnˌtsvantsɪçstɐ ˈʔɔkˈtoːbɐ]
Swiss National Day	Erster August [ˈʔeɐstɐ ˈʔaʊˈɡʊst]
All Saints' (Nov. 1st)	Allerheiligen [ˈʔalɐˈhaɪlɪɡn]
Christmas Eve	Heiliger Abend [ˈhaɪlɪɡɐ ˈʔaːbmt], Heiligabend [ˌhaɪlɪç ˈʔaːbmt]
Christmas	Weihnachten [ˈvaɪnaxtn]
Christmas Day	Erster Weihnachts(feier)tag [ˈʔeɐstɐ ˈvaɪnaxtsˌ(faɪɐ)taːk]
Day After Christmas	Zweiter Weihnachts(feier)tag [ˈtsvaɪtɐ ˈvaɪnaxtsˌ(faɪɐ)taːk]
New Year's Eve	Silvester [sɪlˈvɛstɐ]

The Date

Can you tell me what today's date is, please?
Können Sie mir bitte sagen, den Wievielten wir heute haben?
[kœnn zi miɐ ˈbɪtə zaːɡn den ˈviːfiːltn viɐ ˌhɔɪtə ˈhaːbm]

Today's the fourth of August.
Heute ist der vierte August. [ˈhɔɪtə ˈʔɪst de ˈfiɐtə ˈʔaʊˈɡʊst]

The Weather

What wonderful/awful weather!
Was für ein herrliches/schreckliches Wetter!
[ˈvas fyɐ ˈʔaɪn ˈhɛɐlɪçəs/ˈʃʀɛklɪçəs vɛtɐ]

It's very cold/hot/humid.
Es ist sehr kalt/heiß/schwül. [ˈʔəs ɪst zeɐ kalt/haɪs/ʃvyːl]

It's foggy/windy..
Es ist neblig/windig. [ˈʔəs ɪst ˈneːblɪç/ˈvɪndɪç]

It's going to stay nice.
Es bleibt schön. [ˈʔəs blaɪpt ʃøːn]

28

It's going to get warmer/colder.
Es wird wärmer/kälter. [ˀəs vɪɐt ˈvɛɐmɐ/ˈkɛltə]

It's going to rain/snow.
Es wird regnen/schneien. [ˀəs vɪɐt ˈʀeːknən/ˈʃnaɪən]

It's stormy.
Ein Sturm tobt. [ˀaɪn ʃtʊɐm toːpt]

The roads are icy.
Die Straßen sind glatt. [di ˈʃtʀaːsn zɪnt ˈglat]

Visibility is only 20 meters.
Die Sicht beträgt nur zwanzig Meter.
[di ˈzɪçt bəˈtʀɛkt nuɐ ˈtsvantsɪç ˈmeːtə]

You need snow chains.
Schneeketten sind erforderlich. [ˈʃneːkɛtn zɪnt ˀeˈfɔɐdəlɪç]

air	die Luft [di lʊft]
black ice	das Glatteis [das ˈglataɪs]
changeable	wechselhaft [ˈvɛkslhaft]
cloud	die Wolke [di ˈvɔlkə]
cloudy	bewölkt [bəˈvœlkt]
cold	kalt [kalt]
fog	der Nebel [dɐ ˈneːbl]
frost	der Frost [dɐ fʀɔst]
gale	der Sturm [dɐ ʃtʊɐm]
gust of wind	die Bö [di bøː]
hail(stones)	der Hagel [dɐ ˈhaːgl]
heat	die Hitze [di ˈhɪtsə]
high tide	die Flut [di fluːt]
hot	heiß [haɪs]
humid	schwül [ʃvyːl]
ice	das Eis [das ˀaɪs]
lightning	der Blitz [dɐ blɪts]
low tide	die Ebbe [di ˀɛbə]
rain	der Regen [dɐ ˈʀeːgn]
rainy	regnerisch [ˈʀeːknəʀɪʃ]
shower	der Regenschauer [dɐ ˈʀeːgnʃaʊɐ]
snow	der Schnee [dɐ ʃneː]
storm	der Sturm [dɐ ʃtʊɐm]
sun	die Sonne [di ˈzɔnə]
sunny	sonnig [ˈzɔnɪç]
temperature	die Temperatur [di ˌtɛmpəʀaˈtuɐ]
thunder	der Donner [dɐ ˈdɔnɐ]
warm	warm [vaːm]
weather forecast	die Wettervorhersage [di ˈvɛtɐfoˌheːzaːgə]
weather report	der Wetterbericht [dɐ ˈvɛtɐbəʀɪçt]

GENERAL

wet . . . . nass [nas]
wind . . . . der Wind [dɐ vɪnt]
wind velocity . . . . die Windstärke [di 'vɪntʃtɛɐkə]

Colors

beige . . . . beige [beːʃ]
black . . . . schwarz [ʃvaːts]
blue . . . . blau [blaʊ]
brown . . . . braun [bʀaʊn]
colored . . . . farbig ['faʀbɪç]
green . . . . grün [gʀyːn]
grey . . . . grau [gʀaʊ]
pink . . . . rosa ['ʀoːza]
plain . . . . einfarbig [ˀaɪnfaʀbɪç]
purple . . . . lila ['liːla]
red . . . . rot [ʀoːt]
turquoise . . . . türkisfarben [tʏɐ'kiːsfaːbm]
white . . . . weiß [vaɪs]
yellow . . . . gelb [gɛlp]

dark blue/dark green . . . . . . dunkelblau [dʊŋkl'blaʊ]/
                                                 dunkelgrün [dʊŋkl'gʀyːn]
light blue/light green . . . . . hellblau [hɛl'blaʊ]/hellgrün [hɛl'gʀyːn]

Personal Contacts

Greetings and Farewells

Saying Hello

Good morning!
Guten Morgen! ['gu:tn 'mɔɐɡn̩]

Good afternoon!
Guten Tag! ['gu:tn ta:k]

Good evening!
Guten Abend! ['gu:tn 'a:bmt]

Hello!/Hi!
Hallo!/Grüß dich! ['halo:/'ɡʀy:s dɪç]

What's your name? (*formal*) / (*familiar*)
Wie ist Ihr Name? [vi: ʔɪst ʔiɐ 'na:mə] / Wie heißt du? [vi 'haist du]

My name's ...
Mein Name ist ... [main 'na:mə ʔɪst]

I'm called ...
Ich heiße ... [ʔɪç 'haisə]

How are you? (*formal*) / (*familiar*)
Wie geht es Ihnen? [vi 'ge:t əs ʔi:nn] / Wie geht's? [vi 'ge:ts]

Fine, thanks. And you? (*formal*) / (*familiar*)
Danke. Und Ihnen/dir? ['daŋkə. ʔʊnt 'diɐ]

Introductions

May I introduce you?
Darf ich bekannt machen? ['da:f ɪç bə'kant maxn]

This is ...
Das ist ... [das ʔɪst]
  Mrs./Ms. ...
  Frau ... [fʀaʊ ...]
  Mr. ...
  Herr ... [hɛɐ ...]

32

my husband.
mein Mann. [maɪn 'man]
my wife.
meine Frau. [ˌmaɪnə 'fʀaʊ]
my son.
mein Sohn. [maɪn 'zoːn]
my daughter.
meine Tochter. [ˌmaɪnə 'tɔxtɐ]
my girlfriend.
meine Freundin. [maɪnə 'fʀɔɪndɪn]
my boyfriend.
mein Freund. [maɪn 'fʀɔɪnt]

Nice to meet you.
Es freut mich, Sie kennen zu lernen.
[ʔəs 'fʀɔɪt mɪç zi 'kɛnn tsʊ lɛɐnn]

Saying Goodbye

Auf Wiedersehen is the German way of saying "goodbye." But
you will often hear it shortened to *Wiederseh'n* ['viːdɐzeːn]. Less
formal variations are *Ciao* [tʃaʊ] (from Italian) or *Tschüs*
[tʃy(ː)s]. Use *bis dann* [bɪs 'dan] to say "see you later."

Goodbye!
Auf Wiedersehen! [ʔaʊf 'viːdɐzeːn]

See you soon!
Bis bald! [bɪs 'balt]

See you later!
Bis später! [bɪ_'ʃpɛːtɐ]

See you tomorrow!
Bis morgen! [bɪs 'mɔɐgn̩]

All the best!
Mach's gut! [maxs 'guːt]

Good night!
Gute Nacht! [ˌguːtə 'naxt]

Bye!
Tschüs! [tʃyːs]

Have a good trip!
Gute Reise! [ˌguːtə 'ʀaɪzə]

33

Requesting and Thanking

Please.
Bitte. ['bɪtə]

Yes, please.
Ja, bitte. [ja: 'bɪtə]

Thank you.
Danke. ['daŋkə]

Thank you very much.
Vielen Dank. [fi:ln 'daŋk]

You're welcome.
Bitte sehr. ['bɪtə zeɐ]

No, thank you.
Nein, danke. [naɪn 'daŋkə]

Yes, thank you.
Danke, sehr gern. ['daŋkə zeɐ 'gɛɐn]

That's very kind, thank you.
Das ist nett, danke. [das ɪst 'nɛt 'daŋkə]

Don't mention it.
Gern geschehen. ['gɛɐn gəʃeːn]

Do you mind?
Gestatten Sie? [gəʃtatn zi]

Please forgive the interruption.
Entschuldigen Sie bitte die Störung.
[ˀɛntʃʊldɪgŋ zi 'bɪtə di 'ʃtøːʀʊŋ]

Excuse me, may I ask you something?
Entschuldigen Sie bitte, dürfte ich Sie etwas fragen?
[ˀɛntʃʊldɪgŋ zi 'bɪtə 'dʏɐftə ˀɪç zi ˌˀɛtvas 'fʀaːgŋ]

Can /Could I ask you a favor?
Darf /Dürfte ich Sie um einen Gefallen bitten?
[daːf/'dʏɐftə ˀɪç zi ʊm ˀaɪnn gə'faln bɪtn]

Would you mind just ...?
Würden Sie bitte so freundlich sein und ...?
['vʏɐdn zi 'bɪtə zo 'fʀɔɪntlɪç zaɪn ˀunt ...]

Thank you very much /Thanks a million, you've been a great help.
Vielen /Tausend Dank, Sie haben mir sehr geholfen. [fi:ln/'taʊznt 'daŋk zi haːbm miɐ 'zeɐ gə'hɔlfn]

That was very nice of you.
Das war sehr lieb von Ihnen. [das vaː zeɐ liːp fɔn ˀiːnn]

Can you tell me..., please?
Können Sie mir bitte sagen, ...? [kœnn zi miɐ ˈbɪtə zaːgn]

Can you recommend ...?
Können Sie mir bitte ... empfehlen?
[kœnn zi miɐ ˈbɪtə ... ʔɛmpˈfeːln]

Could you help me, please?
Können Sie mir bitte helfen? [ˈkœnn zi miɐ ˈbɪtə ˈhɛlfn]

Every *danke* should be followed up by the response *bitte* or *gerne* in Austria. This may seem almost like a ritual, but it's a sign of elementary politeness. *Bitte* has basically two meanings: (1) "You're welcome" when used after *danke*; (2) "please" when added to requests such as above, *Können Sie mir bitte helfen?* But be careful: if someone offers you something and you reply with *danke*, this will be interpreted as meaning "no, thank you." If you want to accept something, say *ja, bitte*.

Apologies

I'm sorry!
Entschuldigung! [ʔɛntˈʃʊldɪgʊŋ]

I'm very sorry!
Das tut mir sehr Leid! [das tuːt miɐ zeɐ ˈlaɪt]

I didn't mean it that way.
Es war nicht so gemeint. [ʔəs vaː nɪçt zo gəˈmaɪnt]

That's all right! / It doesn't matter!
Keine Ursache! / Macht nichts! [ˈkaɪnə ʔuɐzaxə / maxt nɪçts]

Congratulations/Wishes

Congratulations!
Herzlichen Glückwunsch! [ˌhɛɐtslɪçn ˈglʏkvʊnʃ]

All the best!
Alles Gute! [ʔaləs ˈguːtə]

Good luck!
Viel Glück! [fiːl glʏk] / Viel Erfolg! [fiːl ʔeˈfɔlk]

I'll keep my fingers crossed for you.
Ich drück' Ihnen die Daumen. [ʔɪç ˈdRʏk ʔiːnn di ˈdaʊmm]

Bless you! *(after sneezing)*
Gesundheit! [gəˈzʊnthaɪt]

Get well soon!
Gute Besserung! [ˌguːtə ˈbɛsəRʊŋ]

Agreement and Conversational Responses

Good.
Gut. [guːt]

Right.
Richtig. [ˈrɪçtɪç]

Agreed! / It's a deal!
Einverstanden! / Abgemacht! [ˈʔaɪnfɛʃtandn / ˈʔapɡəmaxt]

That's all right!
Geht in Ordnung! [geːt ɪn ˈʔɔɐtnʊŋ]

Okay! / O.K.! / OK!
Okay! / o.k.! / O.K.! [ˈʔoˈkeː]

Exactly!
Genau! [ɡəˈnaʊ]

Oh!
Ach! [ʔax]

Oh, I see!
Ach, so! [ʔax ˈzoː]

Really?
Wirklich? [ˈvɪrklɪç]

How interesting!
Interessant! [ˈʔɪntʀəˈsant]

How nice!
Wie schön! [vi ˈʃøːn]

I understand.
Ich verstehe. [ˈʔɪç fɐˈʃteː(ə)]

That's how it is.
So ist es eben. [zoː ˈʔɪst əs ˈʔeːbm]

I agree with you entirely.
Ganz Ihrer Meinung. [ˈɡants ˌʔiːʀɐ ˈmaɪnʊŋ]

That's right.
Das stimmt. [das ʃtɪmt]

I think that's a good idea.
Das finde ich gut. [das fɪndə ˈʔɪç ɡuːt]

With pleasure. / Gladly.
Mit Vergnügen! [mɪt fɐˈɡnyːɡŋ]

That sounds good to me.
Das hört sich gut an. [das høɐt zɪç ˈɡuːt an]

Refusal

I don't want to.
Ich will nicht. [ˀɪç ˈvɪl nɪçt]

I don't feel like it.
Dazu habe ich keine Lust. [ˈdaːtsu habə ɪç ˈkaɪnə lʊst]

I can't agree to that.
Damit bin ich nicht einverstanden.
[ˈdaːmɪt bɪn ɪç nɪçt ˈˀaɪnfeʃtandn]

That's out of the question.
Das kommt nicht in Frage. [das kɔmt ˈnɪçt ˀɪn ˈfʀaːɡə]

Certainly not!/No way!
Auf gar keinen Fall! [ˀaʊf ˈɡaː kaɪnn fal]

Count me out!
Ohne mich! [ˌˀoːnə ˈmɪç]

I don't like this at all.
Das gefällt mir gar nicht. [das ɡəˈfɛlt miɐ ˈɡaː nɪçt]

Preferences

I like it.
Das gefällt mir. [das ɡəˈfɛlt miɐ]

I don't like it.
Das gefällt mir nicht. [das ɡəˈfɛlt miɐ nɪçt]

I'd rather ...
Ich möchte lieber ... [ˀɪç ˈmœçtə ˈliːbɐ]

I'd really like ...
Am liebsten wäre mir ... [ˀam ˈliːpstn ˈvɛːʀə miɐ]

I'd like to find out more about it.
Darüber würde ich gerne mehr erfahren.
[ˈdaːʀyːbɐ ˈvʏɐdə ˀɪç ˌɡɛɐnə ˈmeɐ ˀeˈfaːʀən]

Expressing Ignorance

I don't know (that).
Das weiß ich nicht. [das ˈvaɪs ɪç nɪçt]

No idea!
Keine Ahnung! [ˈkaɪnə ˈˀaːnʊŋ]

Indecision

I don't care.
Das ist mir egal. [das ɪst miɐ eˈɡal]

I don't know yet.
Ich weiß noch nicht. [ˀɪç ˈvaɪs nɔx nɪçt]

Perhaps. / Maybe.
Vielleicht. [fɪˈlaɪçt]

Probably.
Wahrscheinlich. [vaˈʃaɪnlɪç]

Delight—Enthusiasm

Great!
Großartig! [ˈɡʁoːsaːtɪç]

Fine!
Prima! [ˈpʁiːma]

Fantastic!
Toll! [tɔl]

Contentment

I'm completely satisfied.
Ich bin voll und ganz zufrieden. [ˈʔɪç bɪn ˈfɔl ʊnt ɡants tsuˈfʁiːdn̩]

I can't complain.
Ich kann mich nicht beklagen. [ˈʔɪç kan mɪç nɪçt bəˈklaːɡŋ]

That worked out extremely well.
Das hat hervorragend geklappt. [das hat hɛˈfoɐʁaːɡn̩t ɡəˈklapt]

Boredom

How boring! / What a bore!
Wie langweilig! / So was von langweilig!
[vi ˈlaŋvaɪlɪç / ˈzoːvas fɔn ˈlaŋvaɪlɪç]

... is totally boring.
... ist total öde. [ˈʔɪst toˈtaːl ˈʔøːdə]

Astonishment – Surprise

Oh, I see!
Ach so! [ˈʔax ˈzoː]

You don't say!
Ach nein! [ˈʔax ˈnaɪn]

Really?
Wirklich? [ˈvɪʁklɪç]

Incredible!
Unglaublich! [ˈʔʊnˈɡlaʊplɪç]

Relief

It's lucky that...!
Ein Glück, dass ...! [ˈʔaɪn ˈɡlʏk das]

Thank God!
Gott sei Dank! [ˌɡɔt zaɪ ˈdaŋk]

At last!
Endlich! [ˈʔɛntlɪç]

Composure

Don't panic!
Nur keine Panik! [ˈnuɐ ˌkaɪnə ˈpaːnɪk]

Don't get excited!
Nur keine Aufregung! [ˈnuɐ ˌkaɪnə ˈʔaʊfʀeːɡʊŋ]

Don't you worry about a thing.
Machen Sie sich keine Sorgen. [maxn̩ zi zɪç ˈkaɪnə ˈzɔɐɡn̩]

Annoyance

How annoying!
Das ist aber ärgerlich! [das ʔɪst ˈʔaːbɐ ˈʔɛɐɡəlɪç]

Darn!
Verflixt! [fɛˈflɪkst]

What a nuisance!
So ein Mist! [zo ˈʔaɪn mɪst]

That's enough!
Jetzt reicht's! [jɛtst ˈʀaɪçts]

... is getting on my nerves.
... geht mir auf den Geist / Wecker / Keks.
[ɡeːt miɐ ˈʔaʊf den ˈɡaɪst / ˈvɛkɐ / ˈkeːks]

That's outrageous! / What a nerve!
Eine Unverschämtheit ist das! / So eine Frechheit!
[ˈʔaɪnə ˈʔʊnfɛʃɛːmthaɪt ʔɪst das / ˈzoː ˌʔaɪnə ˈfʀɛçhaɪt]

That can't be true!
Das darf doch wohl nicht wahr sein!
[das daːf dɔx voːl nɪçt ˈva: zaɪn]

Rebuking

What do you think you're doing!
Was fällt Ihnen ein! [vas ˈfɛlt ˈʔiːnn̩ ˈʔaɪn]

Don't you dare come near me!
Kommen Sie mir bloß nicht zu nahe!
[kɔmm̩ zi miɐ ˈbloːs nɪçt tsʊ ˈnaː]

That's completely out of the question.
Das kommt gar nicht in Frage. [das kɔmt ˈɡaː nɪçt ɪn ˈfʀaːɡə]

Regret – Disappointment

I'm (so) sorry!
Es tut mir Leid! [ˀɛs tuːt miɐ laɪt]

I feel really sorry for ...
Es tut mir richtig Leid für ... [ˀɛs tuːt miɐ ˈʀɪçtɪç ˈlaɪt fyɐ]

Oh dear!
Oh je! [ˀoˈjeː]

What a shame!
Schade! [ˈʃaːdə]

Body Language

Most German gestures can be easily understood by English-speaking people as they differ only marginally from ones we use ourselves. There are, however, one or two that may need further explanation.

- The German expression for good luck is not "I'll keep my fingers crossed," but "I'll press my thumbs for you – Ich drück' dir die Daumen," thus the corresponding gesture involves wrapping the four fingers of one hand around the thumb of the same hand and pressing firmly.
- Tapping one's index finger against one's temple does **not** indicate that you think someone has been really clever – on the contrary, in Germany it indicates that you think they're crazy.
- If people start rapping loudly on the table with their knuckles in Germany, it means that they either agree with what you have said or are expressing their thanks. If this happens in a bar, it's a form of welcome.

Good luck!

Excellent!

Maybe?

Can't help it!

Idiot!

No idea!/Don't know!

How nice! / That's lovely!
Wie schön! [viː ʃøːn]

That is very kind / nice of you.
Das ist sehr nett von Ihnen/dir. [das ʔɪst zeɐ 'nɛt fɔn ʔiːnn/diɐ]

I think you're very nice.
Ich finde Sie sehr sympathisch /nett.
[ʔɪç 'fɪndə zi zeɐ zɪm'paːtɪʃ / nɛt]

That meal was really excellent!
Das Essen war ausgezeichnet! [das ʔɛsn va ʔaʊsgə'tsaɪçnət]

We've seldom had such a good meal.
Wir haben selten so gut gegessen wie bei Ihnen.
[viɐ 'haːbm 'zɛltn soː guːt gə'gɛsn viː baɪ ʔiːnn]

It really is lovely here!
Es ist wirklich traumhaft hier! [ʔəs ɪst 'vɪɐklɪç 'traʊmhaft hiɐ]

Well, you speak very good English.
Sie sprechen aber sehr gut Englisch.
[zi ʃpʀɛçn ʔaːbɐ 'zeɐ guːt ʔɛnglɪʃ]

We felt very welcome here.
Wir haben uns bei Ihnen sehr wohl gefühlt.
[viɐ 'haːbm ʊns baɪ ʔiːnn zeɐ voːl gə'fyːlt]

That looks good!
Das sieht gut aus! [das ziːt 'guːt ʔaʊs]

The dress suits you.
Das Kleid steht Ihnen/dir gut. [das klaɪt ʃteːt ʔiːnn/diɐ 'guːt]

cozy	gemütlich [gə'myːtlɪç]
delicious	köstlich ['kœstlɪç]
excellent	ausgezeichnet [ʔaʊsgə'tsaɪçnət]
friendly	freundlich ['fʀɔɪntlɪç]
glorious, splendid	herrlich ['hɛɐlɪç]
gorgeous	hinreißend ['hɪnʀaɪsnt]
impressive	beeindruckend [bəʔ'aɪndʀʊknt]
kind	liebenswürdig ['liːbmsvvɐdɪç]
lovely	schön [ʃøːn]
pleasant	angenehm [ʔ'angəneːm]
pretty	hübsch [hypʃ]
tasty	lecker ['lɛkɐ]

Personal information

Where are you from?
Woher kommen Sie? [ˌvoheɐ ˈkɔmm ziː]

I'm from ...
Ich bin aus ... [ˈʔɪç bɪn aʊs ...]

Have you been here long?
Sind Sie schon lange hier? [ˈzɪnt zi ʃon ˈlaŋə hiɐ]

I've been here since ...
Ich bin seit ... hier. [ˈʔɪç bɪn zaɪt ... hiɐ]

How long are you staying?
Wie lange bleiben Sie? [vi ˈlaŋə ˈblaɪbm ziː]

Is this your first time here?
Sind Sie zum ersten Mal hier? [ˈzɪnt zi tsʊm ˈɛɐstn maːl hiɐ]

Do you like it here?
Gefällt es Ihnen hier? [gəˈfɛlt əs ˈʔiːnn hiɐ]

How old are you?
Wie alt sind Sie? [vi ˈʔalt zɪnt ziː]

I'm thirty-nine.
Ich bin neununddreißig. [ˈʔɪç bɪn ˌnɔɪnʊnˈdraɪsɪç]

What do you do for a living?
Was machen Sie beruflich? [vas maxn zi bəˈʀuːflɪç]

I'm a ...
Ich bin ... [ˈʔɪç bɪn]

I work for ...
Ich arbeite bei ... [ˈʔɪç ˈʔaːbaɪtə baɪ]

I'm retired.
Ich bin Rentner/Rentnerin. [ˈʔɪç bɪn ˈʀɛntnɐ/ ˈʀɛntnəʀɪn]

I'm still in school.
Ich gehe noch zur Schule. [ˈʔɪç geː nɔx tsʊɐ ˈʃuːlə]

I'm a college student.
Ich bin Student/Studentin. [ˈʔɪç bɪn ʃtʊˈdɛnt/ ʃtʊˈdɛntɪn]

43

Family

Are you married?
Sind Sie verheiratet? ['zɪnt zi fɐ'haɪʀaːtət]

Do you have any children?
Haben Sie Kinder? ['haːbm zi 'kɪndɐ]

Yes, but they're all grown up.
Ja, aber sie sind schon erwachsen. [jaː ꞏ²abɐ zi zɪnt ʃoːn ²ɛ'vaksn]

How old are your children?
Wie alt sind Ihre Kinder? [viː ²alt zɪnt '²iːʀə 'kɪndɐ]

My daughter is 8 (years old) and my son is 5.
Meine Tochter ist acht (Jahre alt) und mein Sohn ist fünf.
[maɪnə 'tɔxtɐ ²ɪst ²axt ('jaːʀə ²alt) ²ʊnt maɪn 'zoːn fynf]

Hobbies

➢ also "Active Vacations" and "Creative Vacations"

Do you have a hobby?
Haben Sie / Hast du ein Hobby? [haːbm zi/hast du ²aɪn 'hɔbi]

I spend a lot of time with my children.
Ich verbringe viel Zeit mit meinen Kindern.
['²ɪç fɐ'bʀɪŋə fiːl tsaɪt mɪt maɪnn 'kɪndɐn]

I surf the Internet a lot.
Ich surfe viel im Internet. ['²ɪç 'səːfə fiːl ɪm '²ɪntɛnɛt]

I do a little painting.
Ich male ein wenig. ['²ɪç 'maːlə ²aɪn 'veːnɪç]

I collect antiques/stamps.
Ich sammle Antiquitäten/Briefmarken.
['²ɪç 'zamlə ²antɪkviꞏ'tɛːtn/'bʀiːfmaːkn]

What are you interested in?
Wofür interessieren Sie sich so? ['voːfyɐ ²ɪntʀə'siːʀən zi zɪç zoː]

I'm interested in ...
Ich interessiere mich für ... ['²ɪç ²ɪntʀə'siːʀə mɪç fyɐ ...]

I'm active in ...
Ich bin bei ... aktiv. ['²ɪç bɪn baɪ ... ak'tiːf]

... is one of my favorite pastimes.
... ist eine meiner Lieblingsbeschäftigungen.
['²ɪst '²aɪnə ˌmaɪnɐ 'liːplɪŋsbəʃɛftɪgʊŋŋ]

44

cooking	kochen ['kɔxn]
doing handicrafts	basteln [bastln]
drawing	zeichnen ['tsaɪçnn]
learning languages	Sprachen lernen ['ʃpraːxn lɛɛnn]
listening to music	Musik hören [muˈziːk 'høːrən]
making music	musizieren [muzɪˈtsiːrən]
making pottery	töpfern ['tœpfɐn]
playing cards/chess	Karten/Schach spielen ['kaːtn/ʃax ʃpiːln]
reading	lesen [leːzn]
surfing the Internet	im Internet surfen ['ʔɪntɐnɛt səːfn]
traveling	reisen [raɪn]
watching television	fernsehen ['fɛɐnzeːn]
writing	schreiben [ʃraɪbm]

You can also say, *ich koche gern - I like to cook* (literally: "I cook gladly") or *ich arbeite gern im Garten – I like gardening*, etc.

Fitness

➤ also Active Vacations

How do you keep fit?
Wie halten Sie sich fit? [viː haltn zi zɪç fɪt]

I jog/swim/ride a bike.
Ich jogge/schwimme/fahre Rad. ['ɪç 'dʒɔgə/'ʃvɪmə/'faːrə raːt]

I play squash/tennis/golf once a week.
Ich spiele einmal die Woche Squash/Tennis/Golf.
['ɪç 'ʃpiːlə 'ʔaɪnmaːl di 'vɔxə skvɔʃ/'tɛnɪs/gɔlf]

I go to a fitness center regularly.
Ich gehe regelmäßig ins Fitnesscenter.
['ɪç geːə 'reːglmɛːsɪç 'ʔɪns 'fɪtnəs,tsɛntɐ]

I work out twice a week.
Ich trainiere zweimal die Woche. ['ɪç treˈniːrə 'tsvaɪmaːl diː 'vɔxə]

I lead a healthy life.
Ich lebe gesund. ['ɪç leːbə gəˈzʊnt]

What kind of sports do you do?
Welchen Sport treiben Sie? [vɛlçn ʃpɔɐt traɪbm ziː]

I play ...
Ich spiele ... ['ɪç 'ʃpiːlə]

I'm a ... fan.
Ich bin ein Fan von ... ['ɪç bɪn ʔaɪn fɛːn fɔn ...]

I like going to ...
Ich gehe gern ... [ˈɪç ˈgeː gɛɛn]

Can I play too?
Kann ich mitspielen? [kan ɪç ˈmɪtʃpiːln]

Making a Date

Do you have any plans for tomorrow evening?
Haben Sie/Hast du morgen Abend schon etwas vor?
[ˈhaːbm ziː/hast dʊ ˈmɔɛgŋ ˈʔaːbmt ʃɔn ˌʔɛtvas ˈfoɐ]

Do you want to go together?
Wollen wir zusammen hingehen? [ˈvɔln viɐ tsʊˈzamm ˈhɪngeːn]

Do you want to go out together this evening?
Wollen wir heute Abend miteinander ausgehen?
[ˈvɔlən viɐ ˈhɔɪtə ˈabɛnt ˈmɪtaɪnˈandɐ ˈaʊsgeːn]

Can I take you out for dinner tomorrow evening?
Darf ich Sie/dich morgen Abend zum Essen einladen?
[ˈdaːf ɪç ziː/dɪç mɔɛgŋ ˈʔaːbmt tsʊm ˈʔɛsn ˈʔaɪnlaːdn]

When should we meet?
Wann treffen wir uns? [van ˈtʀɛfn viɐ ˈʔʊns]

Let's meet at 9 o'clock in front of ...
Treffen wir uns um neun Uhr vor ...
[ˈtʀɛfn viɐ ˈʔʊns ˈʔʊm nɔɪn uɐ foɐ ...]

I'll pick you up.
Ich hole Sie/dich ab. [ˈɪç hoːlə ziː/dɪç ˈʔap]

Can I see you again?
Kann ich dich wieder sehen? [ˈkan ɪç dɪç ˈviːdeze:n]

That was really a nice evening!
Das war wirklich ein netter Abend! [das va ˈvɪɛklɪç ˈʔaɪn ˈnɛtɐ ˈʔaːbmt]

Flirting

You have beautiful eyes.
Du hast wunderschöne Augen. [du hast ˈvʊndɐʃøːnə ˈʔaʊgŋ]

I like the way you laugh.
Mir gefällt, wie du lachst. [mɪɐ gəˈfɛlt vi du laxst]

I like you.
Du gefällst mir. [du gəˈfɛlst mɪɐ]

46

I like you a lot.
Ich mag dich. [ʔɪç maːk dɪç]

I think you're great.
Ich finde dich ganz toll! [ʔɪç ˈfɪndə dɪç gants tɔl]

I'm crazy about you.
Ich bin verrückt nach dir. [ʔɪç bɪn feˈʀʏkt nax diɐ]

I'm in love with you.
Ich bin in dich verliebt. [ʔɪç bɪn ɪn dɪç feˈliːpt]

I love you.
Ich liebe dich. [ʔɪç ˈliːbə dɪç]

Do you have a steady boyfriend / a steady girlfriend?
Hast du einen festen Freund / eine feste Freundin?
[hast duː ʔaɪnn ˈfɛstn fʀɔɪnt / ʔaɪnə ˈfɛstə ˈfʀɔɪndɪn]

Do you live with someone?
Lebst du mit jemandem zusammen? [ˈleːpst duː mɪt ˈjeːmandəm tsuˈzamm]

I'm divorced.
Ich bin geschieden. [ʔɪç bɪn gəˈʃiːdn]

We're separated.
Wir leben getrennt. [viɐ leːbm gəˈtʀɛnt]

Let's snuggle.
Wir können kuscheln. [viɐ kœnn ˈkʊʃln]

Please go now.
Bitte geh jetzt! [ˈbɪtə geː jɛtst]

Please leave me alone.
Lassen Sie mich bitte in Ruhe! [lasn ziː mɪç ɪn ˈʀuə]

Stop that right now!
Hören Sie sofort damit auf! [høɐn ziː zoˈfɔɐt ˌdamɪt ˈʔaʊf]

Communication Problems

Pardon me? / Excuse me?
Wie bitte? [ˈviː bɪtə]

I can't understand you.
Ich verstehe Sie nicht. [ʔɪç feˈʃteː ziː nɪçt]

Could you repeat that, please?
Könnten Sie das bitte wiederholen? [kœntn ziː das ˈbɪtə viːdeˈhoːln]

Could you speak more slowly, please?
Könnten Sie bitte etwas langsamer sprechen?
[kœntn ziː ˈbɪtə ˌʔɛtvas ˈlaŋzameɐ ʃpʀɛçn]

Yes, I understand/see.
Ja, ich verstehe. [ja: ˀɪç feˈʃteː]

Do you speak ...
Sprechen Sie ... [ˈʃpʀɛçn̩ zi]
  German?
  Deutsch? [ˈdɔɪtʃ]
  English?
  Englisch? [ˈˀɛŋlɪʃ]
  French?
  Französisch? [fʀanˈtsøːzɪʃ]

I speak only a little German.
Ich spreche nur wenig Deutsch. [ˀɪç ˈʃpʀɛçə nuɐ ˈveːnɪç ˈdɔɪtʃ]

Primary roads and public transportation

Travelers in the German-speaking countries profit from excellent road systems and reliable public transportation. IC and ICE trains provide the fastest and most convenient connections between city centers. Reservations on trains are easy to make and will make your trip more pleasant. If you prefer to go by car, you will have the advantage of flexibility in getting to destinations outside city centers. Be ready, however, for rather aggressive driving behavior by American standards. Tailgating is a national sport, and many drivers seem oblivious to speed limits. These are well-posted on freeways/expressways and highways. Be advised that there are radar checks and police who may stop speeders. This can be quite expensive.

Asking for Directions

Useful Words

left	links [lɪŋks]
right	rechts [ʀɛçts]
straight ahead	geradeaus [gʀaːdəˀʔaʊs]
in front of	vor [foɐ]
behind	hinter ['hɪntɐ]
next to	neben ['neːbm̩]
in the vicinity (of)	in der Nähe (von) [ɪn de 'nɛːə fɔn]
opposite	gegenüber [geːgn̩ˀʔyːbɐ]
here	hier [hiɐ]
there	dort [dɔɐt]
near	nah [naː]
far	weit [vaɪt]
after	nach [naːx]
street/road	die Straße [di ʃtʀaːsə]
curve	die Kurve [di 'kʊɐvə]
intersection/junction	die Kreuzung [di 'kʀɔɪtsʊŋ]
traffic light	die Ampel [di ˀʔampl̩]
the street corner	die Straßenecke [di ʃtʀaːsn̩ˀʔɛkə]

Directions

Excuse me, how do I get to ...?
Entschuldigen Sie bitte, wie komme ich nach ...?
[ˀʔɛntʃʊldɪgn̩ zi 'bɪtə viː kɔmə ɪç naːx]

Straight ahead until you get to ...
Immer geradeaus bis ... [ˀʔɪmɐ gʀaːdəˀʔaʊs bɪs ...]

50

Then turn left/right at the traffic light.
Dann bei der Ampel links/rechts abbiegen.
[dan baɪ dɐ ʔampl lɪŋks/ʀɛçts ˈapbiːgn̩]

Follow the signs.
Folgen Sie den Schildern. [ˈfɔlgn̩ zɪ den ˈʃɪldɐn]

How far is it?
Wie weit ist das? [viː vaɪt ʔɪst das]

It's very near here.
Es ist ganz in der Nähe. [ʔəs ʔɪst gants ɪn dɐ ˈnɛːə]

Excuse me, is this the road to ...?
Bitte, ist das die Straße nach ...? [ˈbɪtə ʔɪst ˈdas di ˈʃtʀaːsə nax]

Excuse me, where's ..., please?
Bitte, wo ist ...? [bɪtə voː ʔɪst ...]

I'm sorry, I don't know.
Tut mir Leid, das weiß ich nicht. [tut miɐ laɪt das ˈvaɪs ɪç nɪçt]

I'm not from around here.
Ich bin nicht von hier. [ʔɪç ˈbɪn nɪçt fɔn hiɐ]

Go straight ahead.
Gehen Sie geradeaus. [geːn zi graːdəˈʔaʊs]

Turn left/right.
Gehen Sie nach links/nach rechts. [geːn zi nax lɪŋks/nax ʀɛçts]

The first street on the left.
Erste Straße links. [ˈʔeɐstə ˈʃtʀaːsə lɪŋks]

The second street on the right.
Zweite Straße rechts. [ˈtsvaɪtə ˈʃtʀaːsə ʀɛçts]

Cross ...
Überqueren Sie ... [ʔyːbɐˈkveɐn zi ...]
  the bridge.
  die Brücke. [di ˈbʀʏkə]
  the square.
  den Platz. [den ˈplats]
  the street.
  die Straße. [di ˈʃtʀaːsə]

The best thing would be to take the number ... bus.
Sie nehmen am besten den Bus Nummer ...
[zi ˈneːmm̩ am ˈbɛstn̩ den bʊs ˈnʊmɐ ...]

Passport Check

Your passport, please.
Ihren Pass, bitte! [ˈʔiͤn pas ˈbɪtə]

Do you have a visa?
Haben Sie ein Visum? [haːbm̩ zi ʔaɪn ˈviːzʊm]

Can I get the visa here?
Kann ich das Visum hier bekommen?
[ˈkan ɪç das ˈviːzʊm ˈhiͤ bəˈkɔmm̩]

Customs

Do you have anything to declare?
Haben Sie etwas zu verzollen? [ˈhaːbm̩ zi ˈʔɛtvas tsʊ fɛˈtsɔln]

Pull over to the right/the left, please.
Fahren Sie bitte rechts/links heran!
[ˈfaːʁən zi ˈbɪtə ʁɛçts/lɪŋks həˈʁan]

Open the trunk, please.
Öffnen Sie bitte den Kofferraum! [ˈʔœfnən zi ˈbɪtə den ˈkɔfeʁaʊm]

Open this suitcase, please.
Öffnen Sie bitte diesen Koffer! [ˈʔœfnən zi ˈbɪtə diːzn̩ ˈkɔfe]

Do I have to pay duty on this?
Muss ich das verzollen? [ˈmʊs ɪç das fɛˈtsɔln]

Personal Data

Christian name/first name . .	der Vorname [de ˈfoͤnaːmə]
date of birth	das Geburtsdatum [das gəˈbʊetsdaːtʊm]
maiden name	der Geburtsname [de gəˈbʊetsnaːmə]
marital status	der Familienstand [de faˈmiːljənʃtant]
married	verheiratet [fɛˈhaɪʁaːtət]
single	ledig [ˈleːdɪç]
widowed	verwitwet [fɛˈvɪtvət]
nationality	die Staatsangehörigkeit [di ˈʃtaːts̩ʔangehøːʁɪçkaɪt]
place of birth	der Geburtsort [de gəˈbʊetsʔɔet]
place of residence	der Wohnort [de ˈvoːnʔɔet]
surname/last name	der Familienname [de faˈmiːljənnaːmə]

At the Border

border crossing	der Grenzübergang [de ˈgʁɛntsʔyːbegaŋ]

customs	der Zoll [de 'tsɔl]
driver's license	der Führerschein [de 'fy:ʀeʃaɪn]
duties	die Zollgebühren *f pl* [di 'tsɔlgəby:ʀən]
duty-free	zollfrei ['tsɔlfʀaɪ]
entering (a country)	die Einreise [di ʔaɪnʀaɪzə]
green card	die grüne Versicherungskarte [di 'gry:nə fe'zɪçəʀʊŋska:tə]
identity card	der Personalausweis [de p(ɛ)ezo'na:l,ʔaʊsvaɪs]
international car index mark	das Nationalitätskennzeichen [das natsjonalɪ'tɛ:tskɛntsaɪçn]
international vaccination certificate	der internationale Impfpass [de ʔɪntenatsjona:lə ʔɪmpfpas]
leaving (a country)	die Ausreise [di 'aʊsraɪzə]
license plate	das Nummernschild [das 'nʊmenʃɪlt]
subject to duty	zollpflichtig ['tsɔl(p)flɪçtɪç]
passport	der Reisepass [de 'ʀaɪzəpas]
passport check	die Passkontrolle [di 'paskɔntʀɔlə]
US citizen	US-Bürger/US-Bürgerin [ʔu:ʔɛs byege/ʔe:ʔu: byegəʀɪn]
valid	gültig ['gʏltɪç]
visa	das Visum [das 'vi:zʊm]

Cars and Motorcycles

In German-speaking countries people drive on the right side of the road and pass on the left. There are three main categories of roads: *Landstraßen* (ordinary roads), *Bundesstraßen* (highways) and *Autobahnen* (expressways/freeways).
On Swiss and Austrian expressways drivers have to pay a toll. Safety belts (*Sicherheitsgurte*) and special child seats for small children are mandatory.

country road	die Landstraße [di 'lantʃtra:sə]
divided highway	die Schnellstraße [di 'ʃnɛlʃtra:sə]
expressway/freeway	die Autobahn [di ʔaʊtoba:n]
expressway toll	die Autobahngebühren [di ʔaʊtoba:ngə,by:ʀən]
fine	das Bußgeld [das 'bu:sgɛlt]
highway service area	die Raststätte [di 'ʀastʃtɛtə]
to hitchhike	trampen [tʀɛmpm]
hitchhiker	der Anhalter [der ʔanhalte]
legal blood alcohol limit	die Promillegrenze [di pʀo'mɪləˌgʀɛntsə]
main street	die Hauptstraße [di 'haʊptʃtra:sə]

radar check	die Radarkontrolle [di ʀaˈda:kɔnˌtʀɔlə]
side street	die Nebenstraße [di ˈne:bmʃtʀa:sə]
sign (*directions*)	der Wegweiser [dɐ ˈve:kvaɪzɐ]
street/road	die Straße [di ˈʃtʀa:sə]
traffic jam	der Stau [dɐ ʃtaʊ]

At the Gas Station
> also At the Garage

Where's the nearest gas station, please?
Wo ist bitte die nächste Tankstelle?
[vo: ʔɪst ˈbɪtə di ˈnɛ:çstə ˈtaŋkʃtɛlə]

I'd like ... liters of ...
Ich möchte ... Liter ... [ʔɪç ˈmœçtə ... ˈlɪtɐ]
  regular gasoline.
  Normalbenzin. [nɔˈma:lbɛntsi:n]
  super/premium.
  Super. [ˈzu:pɐ]
  diesel.
  Diesel. [ˈdi:zl]
  leaded.
  verbleit. [fɐˈblaɪt]
  unleaded.
  bleifrei. [ˈblaɪfʀaɪ]

Super/premium, please. For 50 euros.
Super bitte, für fünfzig Euro. [ˈzu:pɐ ˈbɪtə fyɐ ˈfʏnftsɪç ˈʔɔɪro]

Fill it up, please.
Volltanken, bitte. [ˈfɔltaŋkŋ ˈbɪtə]

Would you mind checking the oil?
Würden Sie bitte den Ölstand prüfen?
[vvɐdn zi ˈbɪtə den ˈʔø:lʃtant pʀy:fn]

I'd like a road map of this area, please.
Ich hätte gern eine Straßenkarte dieser Gegend.
[ʔɪç ˈhɛtə gɛɐn ʔaɪnə ˈʃtʀa:snka:tə dizɐ ˈge:gŋt]

Parking

Parking can be a problem in inner cities. As elsewhere, you'll
have to live with parking meters (*Parkuhren*), or you'll need a
parking disc (*Parkscheibe*) for restricted zones. Find a parking
garage (*Parkhaus* – look for a sign with a large "P" on it), or
park on the outskirts of town and take the bus. In either case,
make sure you have enough small change.

Excuse me, is there a place to park near here?
Entschuldigen Sie bitte, gibt es hier in der Nähe eine
Parkmöglichkeit? [ʔɛntˈʃʊldɪɡn̩ zi ˈbɪtə ɡɪpt əs hie ʔɪn dɐ ˈnɛːə ʔaɪnə ˈpaːkmøːklɪçkaɪt]

Can I park my car here?
Kann ich den Wagen hier abstellen? [ˈkan ɪç den ˈvaːɡn̩ hie ʔapʃtɛln]

Is there an attendant?
Ist der Parkplatz bewacht? [ʔɪst dɐ ˈpaːkplats bəˈvaxt]

How much is it by the hour?
Wie hoch ist die Parkgebühr pro Stunde?
[viː hoːx ʔɪst di ˈpaːkɡəbyɐ pʀo ˈʃtʊndə]

Is the parking garage open all night?
Ist das Parkhaus die ganze Nacht geöffnet?
[ʔɪst das ˈpaːkhaʊs di ˈɡantsə naxt ɡəˈʔœfnət]

A Breakdown

My car's broken down.
Ich habe eine Panne. [ʔɪç ˈhaːbə ʔaɪnə ˈpanə]

Is there a garage near here?
Ist hier in der Nähe eine Werkstatt?
[ʔɪst hie ʔɪn dɐ ˈnɛːə ʔaɪnə ˈvɛɐkʃtat]

Would you call the emergency road service, please?
Würden Sie bitte den Pannendienst anrufen?
[vʏɐdn zi ˈbɪtə den ˈpanndiːnst ʔanʀuːfn]

Could you let me have some gas, please?
Könnten Sie mir mit Benzin aushelfen?
[ˈkœntn zi mie mɪt bɛnˈtsiːn ʔaʊshɛlfn]

Could you help me change the tire?
Könnten Sie mir beim Reifenwechsel helfen?
[ˈkœntn zi mie baɪm ˈʀaɪfnvɛksl ˈhɛlfn]

Could you help me jump-start my car?
Könnten Sie mir Starthilfe geben? [ˈkœntn zi mie ˈʃtaːthɪlfə ɡeːbm]

Could you give me a lift to the nearest garage?
Würden Sie mich bis zur nächsten Werkstatt mitnehmen?
[ˈvʏɐdn zi mɪç bɪs tsʊɐ nɛːçstn ˈvɛɐkʃtat ˈmɪtneːmm]

Three main automobile associations, the *ADAC* in Germany, the *ÖAMTC* in Austria, and the *TCS* in Switzerland, will assist you if your car breaks down. You can call from emergency telephones on all expressways and on many main roads. Simple repair jobs are free, but you'll have to pay for towing service. There may also be reciprocal agreements if you're a member of an automobile association in your own country.

breakdown	die Panne [di 'panə]
emergency flashers	die Warnblinkanlage [di 'vaːnblɪŋkʔanlaːgə]
emergency road service	der Pannendienst [dɐ 'panndiːnst]
emergency telephone	die Notrufsäule [di 'noːtʀufzɔɪlə]
flat (tire)	die (Reifen)Panne [di '(ʀaɪfn)panə]
gasoline can	der Benzinkanister [dɐ bɛn'tsiːnkaˌnɪstɐ]
jack	der Wagenheber [dɐ 'vaːɡnheːbɐ]
jumper cables	das Starthilfekabel [das 'ʃtaːthɪlfəkaːbl]
spare tire	der Ersatzreifen [dɐ ʔɛ'zatsʀaɪfn]
tools	das Werkzeug [das 'vɛɐktsɔɪk]
to tow (away)	abschleppen [ʔapʃlɛpm]
towing service	der Abschleppdienst [dɐ ʔapʃlɛpdiːnst]
tow rope	das Abschleppseil [das ʔapʃlɛpzaɪl]
tow truck	der Abschleppwagen [dɐ ʔapʃlɛpvaːɡn]
warning triangle	das Warndreieck [das 'vaːndʀaɪɛk]

At the Garage

The engine won't start.
Der Motor springt nicht an. [dɐ 'moːtoɐ ʃpʀɪŋt nɪçt ʔan]

There's something wrong with the engine.
Mit dem Motor stimmt was nicht. [mɪt dem 'moːtoɐ ʃtɪmt vas nɪçt]

The brakes don't work.
Die Bremsen funktionieren nicht. [di 'bʀɛmzn fʊŋktsjo'niːen nɪçt]

It's losing oil.
Der Wagen verliert Öl. [dɐ 'vaːɡn fɐ'liːɐt ʔøːl]

When will the car be ready?
Wann ist der Wagen fertig? ['van ʔɪst dɐ 'vaːɡn 'fɛɐtɪç]

Roughly how much will it cost?
Was wird es ungefähr kosten? [vas vɪɐt əs 'ʔʊngəfɛɐ 'kɔstn]

accelerator/gas pedal	das Gaspedal [das 'ga:speda:l]
air filter	der Luftfilter [dɐ 'lʊftfɪltɐ]
alarm system	die Alarmanlage [di ʔa'la:manla:gə]
antifreeze	das Frostschutzmittel [das 'fʀɔstʃʊtsmɪtl]
automatic (transmission) ...	das Automatikgetriebe [das ʔaʊto'ma:tɪkgə,tʀi:bə]
brake fluid	die Bremsflüssigkeit [di 'bʀɛmsflʏsɪçkaɪt]
brake lights	die Bremslichter [di 'bʀɛmslɪçtɐ]
clutch	die Kupplung [di 'kʊplʊŋ]
cooling water	das Kühlwasser [das 'ky:lvasɐ]
dimmed headlights	das Abblendlicht [das ʔapblɛntlɪçt]
engine/motor	der Motor [dɐ 'mo:toɐ]
fault	der Defekt [dɐ de'fɛkt]
garage	die Werkstatt [di 'vɛɐkʃtat]
gas pump	die Benzinpumpe [di bɛn'tsi:npʊmpə]
gas tank	der Tank [dɐ taŋk]
gear	der Gang [dɐ gaŋ]
first/low gear	erster Gang ['ʔeɐstɐ gaŋ]
neutral	der Leerlauf [dɐ 'leɐlaʊf]
reverse gear	der Rückwärtsgang [dɐ 'ʀʏkvɛɐtsgaŋ]
generator	die Lichtmaschine [di 'lɪçtmaʃi:nə]
hand brake/emergency brake	die Handbremse [di 'hantbʀɛmzə]
high beams	das Fernlicht [das 'fɛɐnlɪçt]
hood	die Motorhaube [di 'mo:tɔˌhaʊbə]
horn	die Hupe [di 'hu:pə]
ignition	die Zündung [di 'tsʏndʊŋ]
left-hand-drive car	der Linkslenker [dɐ 'lɪŋkslɛŋkɐ]
motorbike/motorcycle	das Motorrad [das mo'to:ʀat]
oil	das Öl [das ʔø:l]
oil change	der Ölwechsel [dɐ 'ʔø:lvɛksl]
right-hand-drive car	der Rechtslenker [dɐ 'ʀɛçtslɛŋkɐ]
screw	die Schraube [di 'ʃʀaʊbə]
short-circuit	der Kurzschluss [dɐ 'kʊɐtʃlʊs]
sidelights	das Standlicht [das 'ʃtantlɪçt]
spark plug	die Zündkerze [di 'tsʏntkɛɐtsə]
speedometer	der Tacho(meter) [dɐ ˌtaxo('me:tɐ)]
starter	der Anlasser [dɐ 'ʔanlasɐ]
tail light	das Rücklicht [das 'ʀʏklɪçt]
transmission	das Getriebe [das gə'tʀi:bə]
wheel	das Rad [das ʀa:t]
winter tire	der Winterreifen [dɐ 'vɪntɐʀaɪfn]

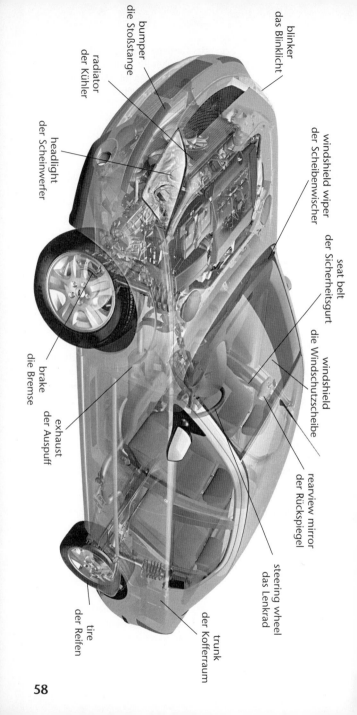

blinker
das Blinklicht

bumper
die Stoßstange

radiator
der Kühler

headlight
der Scheinwerfer

windshield wiper
der Scheibenwischer

seat belt
der Sicherheitsgurt

windshield
die Windschutzscheibe

rearview mirror
der Rückspiegel

brake
die Bremse

exhaust
der Auspuff

steering wheel
das Lenkrad

trunk
der Kofferraum

tire
der Reifen

58

Accident

There's been an accident.
Es ist ein Unfall passiert. [ˀɛs ˀɪst aɪn ˈˀʊnfal paˈsiet]

Quick! Please call ...
Rufen Sie bitte schnell ... [ˈʀuːfn zi ˈbɪtə ʃnɛl ...]
  an ambulance.
  einen Krankenwagen. [ˀaɪnn ˈkʀaŋkn̩vaːgn]
  the police.
  die Polizei. [di pɔlɪˈtsaɪ]
  the fire department.
  die Feuerwehr. [di ˈfɔjɐveɐ]

Do you have a first-aid kit?
Haben Sie Verbandszeug? [haːbm zi fɛˈbantstsɔɪk]

> It is mandatory in Germany, Austria, and Switzerland to carry a
> first-aid kit and a warning triangle in your vehicle. If you're
> involved in an accident, do not move your car or allow the
> other party to leave until the police come.

You ...
Sie haben ... [zi ˈhaːbm]
  didn't yield (observe the right of way).
  die Vorfahrt nicht beachtet. [di ˈfoɐfaːt nɪçt bəˈˀaxtət]
  didn't signal your turn.
  nicht geblinkt. [nɪçt gəˈblɪŋkt]

You ...
Sie sind ... [zi zɪnt]
  were speeding (driving too fast).
  zu schnell gefahren. [tsʊ ˈʃnɛl gəˈfaːʀən]
  were too close behind/tailgating.
  zu dicht aufgefahren. [tsʊ dɪçt ˈˀaʊfgəfaːʀən]
  went through a red light.
  bei Rot über die Kreuzung gefahren.
  [baɪ ʀoːt ˈˀyːbɐ di ˈkʀɔɪtsʊŋ gəˈfaːʀən]

Please give me your name and address.
Geben Sie mir bitte Ihren Namen und Ihre Anschrift.
[geːbm zɪ miɐ ˈbɪtə ˀien ˈnaːmm ʊnt ˌiʀə ˈˀanʃʀɪft]

We should call the police.
Wir sollten die Polizei holen. [viɐ zɔltn di pɔlɪˈtsaɪ hoːln]

Can we settle this ourselves, without the police?
Können wir uns so einigen, ohne die Polizei?
[kœnn viɐ ˀʊns ˈzoː ˈˀaɪnɪgn oːnə di pɔlɪˈtsaɪ]

Thank you very much for your help.
Vielen Dank für Ihre Hilfe! [fiːln ˈdaŋk fyɐ ˈˀiːʀə ˈhɪlfə]

Car/Motorcycle/Bicycle Rental

handlebars
der Lenker

saddle
der Sattel

gears
die Gangschaltung

front light
das Vorderlicht

pump
die Luftpumpe

rear light,
tail light
das Rücklicht

brake
die Bremse

(inner) tube
der Schlauch
(Reifen)

tire
der Mantel
(Reifen)

chain
die Kette

pedal
das Pedal

wheel
das Rad

spoke
die Speiche

hub
die Nabe

I'd like to rent ... for two days/for a week.
Ich möchte für zwei Tage / für eine Woche ... mieten.
[ʔɪç 'mœçtə fʏɐ tsvaɪ 'taːgə / fʏɐ ʔaɪnə 'vɔxə ... miːtn̩]

a car
einen Wagen / ein Auto [ʔaɪnn 'vaːgŋ / ʔaɪn ʔaʊto]

a jeep
einen Geländewagen [ʔaɪnn gə'lɛndəvaːgŋ]

a motorcycle
ein Motorrad [ʔaɪn mo'toːʀat]

a scooter
einen Roller [ʔaɪnn 'ʀɔlɐ]

a bike/bicycle
ein Fahrrad [ʔaɪn 'faːʀat]

How much does it cost per week?
Wie hoch ist die Wochenpauschale? [vi hoːx ʔɪst di 'vɔxnpaʊʃaːlə]

Does that include unlimited mileage?
Ist das einschließlich unbegrenzter Kilometerzahl?
[ʔɪst das ʔaɪnʃliːslɪç ʔʊnbəgʀɛntstɐ kɪlo'meːtɐtsaːl]

What do you charge per kilometer?
Wie viel verlangen Sie pro gefahrenen Kilometer?
['viː_fiːl fɐ'laŋŋ zi pʀo gə'faː(ʀə)nn kɪlo'meːtɐ]

60

> Conversion factor for kilometers: 1 mile = 1.6 km; 1 km = 0.6
> mile. Cut the kilometers in half, add 10 percent of the original,
> and you'll have it in miles. 40 km = 20 + 4 = 24 miles.

How much is the deposit?
Wie hoch ist die Kaution? [vi 'ho:x ʔɪst di kaʊ'tsjo:n]

Does the vehicle have comprehensive insurance/full coverage?
Ist das Fahrzeug vollkaskoversichert?
[ʔɪst das 'fa:tsɔɪk 'fɔlkaskofɐˌzɪçɛt]

Is it possible to leave the car in ...?
Ist es möglich, das Fahrzeug in ... abzugeben?
[ʔɪst əs 'mø:klɪç das 'fa:tsɔɪk ʔɪn ... ʔaptsʊge:bm̩]

child seat	der Kindersitz [dɐ 'kɪndɐzɪts]
crash helmet	der Sturzhelm [dɐ 'ʃtʊɐtshɛlm]
to deposit *(money)*	Geld hinterlegen [gɛlt hɪntɐ'le:gn̩]
deposit	die Kaution [di kaʊ'tsjo:n]
driver's license	der Führerschein [dɐ 'fy:ʁɐʃaɪn]
full insurance coverage ...	die Vollkasko [di 'fɔlkasko]
green card	die grüne Versicherungskarte
	[di 'gʁy:nə fɛ'zɪçəʁʊŋska:tə]
ignition key	der Zündschlüssel [dɐ 'tsʏntʃlʏsl̩]
papers	die Papiere *n pl* [di pa'pi:ʁə]
safety belt	der Sicherheitsgurt [dɐ 'zɪçɐhaɪtsgurt]
sunroof	das Schiebedach [das 'ʃi:bədax]
third party, fire, and theft	
coverage	die Teilkasko [di 'taɪlkasko]
weekend rate	die Wochenendpauschale
	[di 'vɔxn̩ʔɛntpaʊʃa:lə]

Signs and Notices

Achtung	look out, danger
Anlieger frei	residents only
Anfänger	learner, beginner
Ausfahrt	exit
Ausfahrt freihalten	keep exit clear
... ausgenommen	except for ...
Autofähre	car ferry
Behelfsausfahrt	temporary exit
Bis zur Haltelinie vorfahren	drive up to line
Bitte einordnen	get in lane
Bushaltestelle	bus stop
Einbahnstraße	one-way street
Einfahrt	entrance
Fahrbahn wechseln	change lane
Fahrbahnverengung	road narrows
Feuerwehrzufahrt	fire department access

Frauenparkplätze	parking spaces for women only
Fußgängerzone	pedestrian zone
Gefahr	danger
Gefährliche Kurve	dangerous curve
Gegenverkehr	two-way traffic
Geschwindigkeitsbegrenzung	speed limit
Gesperrt (für Fahrzeuge aller Art)	closed (to all vehicles)
Gewichtsgrenze	weight limit
Glatteis	black ice
Haarnadelkurve	hairpin curve
Hochwasser	flooding
Industriegebiet	industrial area
Innenstadt	city center, downtown
Keine Einfahrt	no entry
Krankenhaus	hospital
Kreisverkehr	traffic circle
Kreuzung	intersection
Kurzparkzone	limited parking zone
Ladezone	loading zone
Langsam fahren	reduce speed
Licht	headlights
Nebel	fog
Notruf	emergency phone
Ölspur	oil slick
Parken verboten	no parking
Parkhaus	parking garage
Parkplatz	parking lot
Parkscheinautomat	ticket machine
Rechts (Links) fahren	keep right (left)
Rechtsabbiegen verboten	no right turn
Rutschgefahr	slippery road
Sackgasse	dead end
Schritt fahren	drive at walking speed
Schule	school
Schulkinder überqueren	children crossing
Seitenwind	sidewind
Spielstraße	children playing
Starkes Gefälle	steep hill
Stau	traffic jam
Steinschlag	falling rocks
Straßenarbeiten	construction
Tunnel	tunnel
Überholverbot	no passing
Umleitung	detour
Unbeschrankter Bahnübergang	crossing – unprotected crossing
Unfall	accident
Verschmutzte Fahrbahn	muddy road surface
Vorfahrt beachten	yield
Vorsicht	caution
Wenden verboten	no U-turn
Wildwechsel	deer crossing
Zebrastreifen	zebra crossing
Zentrum	city center, downtown

Making a Flight Reservation

Can you tell me when the next flight to ... is, please?
Können Sie mir bitte sagen, wann die nächste Maschine nach ...
fliegt? [k'ænn zi miɐ 'bɪtə zaːgn van di 'nɛːçstə ma'ʃiːnə nax ... fliːkt]

Are there any seats left?
Sind noch Plätze frei? [zɪnt nɔx 'plɛtsə fʀaɪ]

I'd like a one-way ticket to ...
Ich möchte einen einfachen Flug nach ... buchen.
[ʔɪç 'mœçtə ʔaɪnn ʔaɪnfaxn fluːk nax ... buːxn]

I'd like a round-trip ticket to ...
Ich möchte einen Hin- und Rückflug nach ... buchen.
[ʔɪç 'mœçtə ʔaɪnn hɪn ʊnt 'ʀʏkfluːk nax ... buːxn]

How much is an economy-class/a first-class ticket?
Was kostet bitte der Flug Touristenklasse/ erste Klasse?
[vas 'kɔstət bɪtə deɐ 'fluːk tʊ'ʀɪstnklasə/'ʔeɐstə 'klasə]

Smoking or non-smoking?
Raucher oder Nichtraucher? ['ʀaʊxɐ 'ʔoːdɐ 'nɪçtʀaʊxɐ]

I'd like ...
Ich möchte ... [ʔɪç 'mœçtə ...]
   a window seat.
   einen Fensterplatz. [ʔaɪnn 'fɛnstɐplats]
   an aisle seat.
   einen Platz am Gang. [ʔaɪnn plats am gaŋ]

I'd like to cancel my flight.
Ich möchte diesen Flug stornieren. [ʔɪç 'mœçtə 'diːzn fluːk ʃtɔ'niɐn]

I'd like to change the reservation.
Ich möchte diesen Flug umbuchen.
[ʔɪç 'mœçtə 'diːzn fluːk 'ʔʊmbuːxn]

At the Airport

Where's the ... counter, please?
Wo ist bitte der Schalter der ...-Fluggesellschaft?
[voː ʔɪst bɪtə deɐ 'ʃaltɐ deɐ ...'fluːkgəˌzɛlʃaft]

Could I see your ticket, please?
Könnte ich bitte Ihren Flugschein sehen?
['kœntə ɪç 'bɪtə 'ʔiːʀən 'fluːkʃaɪn zeːn]

Can I take this as carry-on baggage?
Kann ich das als Handgepäck mitnehmen?
[kan ɪç das ʔals 'hantgəpɛk 'mɪtneːmm]

63

On Board

Could you bring me a glass of water, please?
Könnten Sie mir bitte ein Glas Wasser bringen?
['kœntn zi miɐ 'bɪtə ʔaɪn glaːs 'vasɐ brɪŋŋ]

Could I have another pillow/blanket, please?
Könnte ich bitte noch ein Kissen/ eine Decke haben?
['kœntə ɪç 'bɪtə nɔx ʔaɪn kɪsn/ʔaɪnə 'dɛkə haːbm]

Would it be possible for us to switch seats?
Wäre es möglich, dass wir den Platz tauschen?
[vɛːRə ʔəs 'møːklɪç das viɐ den plats taʊʃn]

Arrival ➤ also Lost-and-Found Office

My baggage is missing.
Mein Gepäck ist verloren gegangen.
[maɪn gə'pɛk ʔɪst fɐ'loɐn gə'gaŋŋ]

My suitcase has been damaged. Mein Koffer ist beschädigt worden. [maɪn 'kɔfɐ ʔɪst bə'ʃɛːdɪkt vɔɐdn]

Where does the bus to ... leave from?
Wo fährt der Bus in Richtung ... ab?
[voː feɐt dɐ bʊs ʔɪn 'ʀɪçtʊŋ ... ʔap]

➤ also Train

accompanying adult	die Begleitperson [di bə'glaɪtpɛ(ɛ)zoːn]
airline	die Fluggesellschaft [di 'fluːkgə‚zɛlʃaft]
airport	der Flughafen [dɐ 'fluːkhaːfn]
airport bus	der Flughafenbus [dɐ 'fluːkhaːfn‚bʊs]
airport tax	die Flughafengebühr [di 'fluːkhaːfngə‚byɐ]
arrival	die Ankunft [di 'ankʊnft]
baggage	das Gepäck [das gə'pɛk]
baggage cart	der Gepäckwagen [dɐ gə'pɛkvaːgŋ]
baggage claim	die Gepäckausgabe [di gə'pɛkʔaʊsgaːbə]
boarding card	die Bordkarte [di 'bɔɐtkaːtə]
to cancel	stornieren [ʃtɔ'niɐn]
to change the reservation	umbuchen [ʔʊmbuːxn]
to check in	einchecken [ʔaɪntʃɛkn]
connection	der Anschluss [dɐ ʔanʃlʊs]
delay	die Verspätung [di fɐ'ʃpɛːtʊŋ]
departure	der Abflug [dɐ ʔapfluːk]
domestic flight	der Inlandsflug [dɐ ʔɪnlantsfluːk]
duty-free shop	zollfreier Laden ['tsɔlfRaɪɐ laːdn]
emergency chute	die Notrutsche [di 'noːtRʊtʃə]
emergency exit	der Notausgang [dɐ 'noːtʔaʊsgaŋ]

emergency landing	die Notlandung [di ˈnoːtlandʊŋ]
excess baggage	das Übergepäck [das ˈʔyːbɐɡəpɛk]
flight	der Flug [dɐ fluːk]
gate	der Flugsteig [dɐ ˈfluːkʃtaɪɡ]
international flight	der Auslandsflug [dɐ ˈʔaʊslantsfluːk]
landing	die Landung [di ˈlandʊŋ]
life jacket	die Schwimmweste [di ˈʃvɪmvɛstə]
luggage	das Gepäck [das ɡeˈpɛk]
passenger	der Passagier [dɐ pasaˈʒiɐ]
pilot	der Pilot [dɐ piˈloːt]
scheduled time of departure	planmäßiger Abflug [ˈplaːnmɛːsɪɡɐ ˈʔapfluːk]
security charge	die Sicherheitsgebühr [di ˈzɪçɐhaɪtsɡəˌbyɐ]
security control	die Sicherheitskontrolle [di ˈzɪçɐhaɪtskɔnˌtrɔlə]
steward/stewardess	der Steward/die Stewardess [dɐ ˈstjuaːt/di ˈstjuadɛs]
stopover	die Zwischenlandung [di ˈtsvɪʃnˌlandʊŋ]
take-off	der Abflug [dɐ ˈʔapfluːk]
terminal	das Terminal [das ˈtəːmɪnəl]
time of arrival	die Ankunftszeit [di ʔankʊnftˌtsaɪt]

Train

Intercity trains (IC) connect most cities on an hourly basis. *EuroCity* (EC) trains connect European cities. The fastest trains are the *InterCity Express* (ICE), but they connect fewer places. In addition, there are *InterRegio* (IR) trains and *D-Zug*/*Schnell-zug* (express) trains. For a small fee it is possible to reserve seats in advance. If you travel less than 50 km, you have to pay an extra fee for express trains.

Buying Tickets

A one-way ticket to Frankfurt, please.
Eine einfache Fahrt nach Frankfurt, bitte.
[ˈʔaɪnə ˈʔaɪnfaxə faːt nax ˈfrankfʊɐt ˈbɪtə]

Two round-trip tickets to Stuttgart, please.
Zweimal Stuttgart hin und zurück, bitte.
[ˈtsvaɪmal ˈʃtʊtgaːt hɪn ʊnt tsuˈrʏk ˈbɪtə]

first-class
erster Klasse [ˈʔeɐstɐ ˈklasə]

Is there a reduced fare for children/students/senior citizens?
Gibt es eine Ermäßigung für Kinder/ Studenten/Senioren?
[gɪpt əs ʔaɪnə ʔeˈmɛːsɪgʊn fye ˈkɪndɐ/ ʃtʊˈdɛntn/zenˈjoːʀən]

I'd like to reserve two non-smoking seats, please,
Ich möchte gern zwei Nichtraucherplätze reservieren:
[ʔɪç ˈmœçtə gɛɐn tsvaɪ ˈnɪçtʀaʊxɐˌplɛtsə ʀezɐˈviːʀən]

for the EC to ...
für den EC nach ... [fye den ʔeˈtse: nax]
on ... at ... (o'clock)
am ... um ...Uhr [ʔam ... ʔʊm ... ʔuɐ]
in the couchette car
im Liegewagen [ʔɪm ˈliːgəvaːgn]
in the sleeping car
im Schlafwagen [ʔɪm ˈʃlaːfvaːgn]
in the restaurant car
im Speisewagen [ʔɪm ˈʃpaɪzəvaːgn]

Is there an auto-train to ...?
Gibt es einen Autoreisezug nach ...?
[gɪpt əs ʔaɪnn ʔʔaʊtoˌʀaɪzetsuːk nax]

Is there a connection to Leipzig at Fulda?
Habe ich in Fulda Anschluss nach Leipzig?
[haːb ɪç ʔɪn ˈfʊlda ʔʔanʃlʊs nax ˈlaɪptsɪç]

How many times do I have to change?
Wie oft muss ich da umsteigen? [viː ʔɔft mʊs ɪç da ʔʔʊmʃtaɪgn]

I'd like to check this suitcase.
Ich möchte diesen Koffer als Reisegepäck aufgeben.
[ʔɪç ˈmœçtə diːzn ˈkɔfɐ ʔals ˈʀaɪzəgəpɛk ʔʔaʊfgeːbm]

Where can I check in my bicycle?
Wo kann ich mein Fahrrad aufgeben?
[ˈvoː kan ɪç maɪn ˈfaːʀaːt ʔʔaʊfgeːbm]

Excuse me, which platform does the train to Heidelberg leave from?
Entschuldigen Sie bitte, von welchem Gleis fährt der Zug nach Heidelberg ab?
[ʔɛntˈʃʊldɪgn zi ˈbɪtə fɔn vɛlçm glaɪs feɐt dɐ tsuːk nax ˈhaɪdlbɛɐk ʔap]

The intercity ... from Hamburg is running 10 minutes late.
Der Intercity ... aus Hamburg hat voraussichtlich zehn Minuten Verspätung.
[dɐ ʔɪntɐˈsɪti ʔaʊs ˈhambʊɐk hat foˈʀaʊsɪçtlɪç ˈtseːn mɪˈnuːtn fɐˈʃpɛːtʊn]

On the Train

All aboard, please!
Bitte einsteigen! ['bɪtə ˈʔaɪnʃtaɪgn̩]

Is this seat taken/free?
Ist dieser Platz noch frei? [ʔɪst 'diːzɐ plats nɔx fʀaɪ]

Excuse me, I think that's my seat.
Entschuldigen Sie, ich glaube das ist mein Platz.
[ʔɛntˈʃʊldɪgn̩ ziː ʔɪç ˈglaʊbə das ɪst 'maɪn plats]

Here is my seat reservation.
Hier ist meine Platzreservierung. [hiɐ ʔɪst ˌmaɪnə 'platsʀezeviːʀʊŋ]

May I open/shut the window?
Darf ich bitte das Fenster aufmachen/schließen?
[daf: ɪç ˈbɪtə das ˈfɛnstɐ ˈʔaʊfmaxn̩/ʃliːsn̩]

Tickets, please.
Die Fahrkarten, bitte. [di ˈfaːkaːtn̩ 'bɪtə]

➢ **also Airplane**

arrival	die Ankunft [di ˈʔankʊnft]
auto-train	der Autoreisezug [dɐ ˈʔaʊtoˌʀaɪzətsuːk]
baggage	das Gepäck [das geˈpɛk]
baggage counter	der Gepäckschalter [dɐ gəˈpɛkʃaltɐ]
baggage deposit	die Gepäckaufbewahrung [di gəˈpɛkˌʔaʊfbəvaːʀʊŋ]
baggage locker	das Schließfach [das ˈʃliːsfax]
car number	die Wagennummer [di ˈvaːgn̩nʊmɐ]
children's ticket	die Kinderfahrkarte [di ˈkɪndɐˈfaːkaːtə]
compartment	das Abteil [das ʔapˈtaɪl]
conductor	der Zugbegleiter/die Zugbegleiterin [dɐ ˈtsuːkbəˌglaɪtɐ/di ˈtsuːkbəˌglaɪtəʀɪn]
corridor	der Gang [dɐ gaŋ]
departure	die Abfahrt [di ˈʔapfaːt]
to get on	einsteigen [ˈʔaɪnʃtaɪgn̩]
to get off	aussteigen [ˈʔaʊʃtaɪgn̩]
luggage	das Gepäck [das geˈpɛk]
main station	der Hauptbahnhof [dɐ ˈhaʊptbaːnhoːf, ˈhaʊpbaːnof)]
no-smoking compartment	das Nichtraucherabteil [das ˈnɪçtʀaʊxɐˈʔapˌtaɪl]
open seating area car	der Großraumwagen [dɐ ˈgʀoːsʀaʊmvaːgn̩]
platform	das Gleis [das glaɪs]
railcard	die Bahncard [di ˈbaːnkaːt]
reduction	die Ermäßigung [di ɐˈmɛːsɪgʊŋ]

GETTING AROUND

67

reservation	die Reservierung [di ʀezeˈviːʀʊŋ]
restaurant car	der Speisewagen [dɐ ˈʃpaɪzəvaːɡn̩]
round-trip ticket	die Rückfahrkarte [di ˈʀʏkfaːˌkaːtə]
seat reservation	die Platzreservierung [di ˈplatsʀezeˌviːʀʊŋ]
severely handicapped person	der/die Schwerbehinderte [dɐ/di ˈʃveɐbəhɪndɐtə]
smoking compartment	das Raucherabteil [das ˈʀaʊxɐʔapˌtaɪl]
station	der Bahnhof [dɐ ˈbaːnhoːf]
stop	der Aufenthalt [dɐ ˈʔaʊfn̩talt]
supplementary charge	der Zuschlag [dɐ ˈtsuːʃlaːk]
track	das Gleis [das ɡlaɪs]
train fare	der Fahrpreis [dɐ ˈfaːpʀaɪs]
ticket	die Fahrkarte [di ˈfaːkaːtə]
ticket check/inspection	die Fahrkartenkontrolle [di ˈfaːkaːtnkɔnˌtʀɔlə]
ticket collector/conductor ..	der Schaffner/die Schaffnerin [dɐ ˈʃafnɐ/di ˈʃafnəʀɪn]
ticket office	der Fahrkartenschalter [dɐ ˈfaːkaːtnʃaltɐ]
timetable	der Fahrplan [dɐ ˈfaːplaːn]
train	der Zug [dɐ tsuːk]
waiting room	der Wartesaal [dɐ ˈvaːtəzaːl]
wheelchair user	der Rollstuhlfahrer/die Rollstuhlfahrerin [dɐ ˈʀɔlʃtuːlˌfaːʀɐ/di ˈʀɔlʃtuːlˌfaːʀəʀɪn]
window seat	der Fensterplatz [dɐ ˈfɛnstɐplats]

Ship

Information

**Can you tell me when the next ship/ the next ferry leaves for ...,
please?**
Können Sie mir bitte sagen, wann das nächste Schiff/die nächste Fähre nach ... abfährt?
[kœnn zi miɐ ˈbɪtə zaːɡn̩ van das ˈnɛːçstə ʃɪf/di: ˈnɛːçstə ˈfeːʀə ... ˈʔapfeɐt]

How long does the crossing take?
Wie lange dauert die Überfahrt? [vi_ˈlaŋə ˈdaʊɐt di ˈʔyːbɐfaːt]

When do we land at ...?
Wann legen wir in ... an? [van ˈleɡn̩ viɐ ˈʔɪn ... an]

How long do we stop in ...?
Wie lange haben wir in ... Aufenthalt?
[vi laŋə haːbm̩ viɐ ˈʔɪn ... ˈʔaʊfn̩talt]

I'd like ..., please.
Ich möchte bitte ... [ˀɪç 'mœçtə 'bɪtə]

a ticket to ...
eine Schiffskarte nach ... [ˀaɪnə 'ʃɪfskaːtə nax]

first class
erste Klasse [ˀeɐstə 'klasə]

tourist class
Touristenklasse [tuˈʀɪstnklasə]

a single cabin
eine Einzelkabine [ˀaɪntslkabiːnə]

a double cabin
eine Zweibettkabine ['tsvaɪbɛtkabiːnə]

I'd like a ticket for the circular tour at ... o'clock.
Ich möchte eine Karte für die Rundfahrt um ... Uhr.
[ˀɪç 'mœçtə ˀaɪnə 'kaːtə fyɐ diː 'ʀʊntfaːt ˀʊm ... ˀuɐ]

Where's the restaurant/lounge, please?
Wo ist bitte der Speisesaal/der Aufenthaltsraum?
[voː ˀɪst 'bɪtə dɐ 'ʃpaɪzəzaːl/dɐ ˀaʊfntalts‚ʀaʊm]

I don't feel well.
Ich fühle mich nicht wohl. [ˀɪç 'fyːlə mɪç nɪçt voːl]

Could you call the ship's doctor, please.
Könnten Sie bitte den Schiffsarzt rufen?
[kœntn zɪ bɪtə den 'ʃɪfsˀaːtst ʀuːfn]

Could you give me something for seasickness, please?
Könnten Sie mir bitte ein Mittel gegen Seekrankheit geben?
[kœntn zi miɐ 'bɪtə ˀaɪn 'mɪtl geːgn 'zeːkʀaŋkaɪt geːbm]

cabin	die Kabine [di kaˈbiːnə]
captain	der Kapitän [dɐ kapiˈtɛːn]
car ferry	die Autofähre [di ˀaʊtofɛːʀə]
coast	die Küste [di ˈkʏstə]
deck	das Deck [das dɛk]
to dock at	anlegen in [ˀanleːgn ˀɪn]
excursion	der Landausflug [dɐ 'lantˀaʊsfluːk]
ferry	die Fähre [di 'fɛːʀə]
harbor	der Hafen [dɐ 'haːfn]
hovercraft	das Luftkissenboot [das 'lʊftkɪsnboːt]
to land at	anlegen in [ˀanleːgn ˀɪn]
life belt/life preserver	der Rettungsring [dɐ 'ʀɛtʊŋsʀɪŋ]
lifeboat	das Rettungsboot [das 'ʀɛtʊŋsboːt]
life jacket	die Schwimmweste [di 'ʃvɪmvɛstə]
port	der Hafen [dɐ 'haːfn]
quay	der Kai [dɐ kaɪ]

GETTING AROUND

reservation	die Buchung	[di 'buːxʊŋ]
round trip	die Rundfahrt	[di 'ʀʊntfaːt]
seasick	seekrank	['zeːkʀaŋk]
ticket	die Fahrkarte	[di 'faːkaːtə]

Take advantage of the excellent public transportation found in Germany. There will often be different providers, one for the city area, another for the surrounding area. These providers are usually integrated into a network, and you will be able to buy tickets valid for all vehicles. Ask for help if you're not sure. A good place to start is the local tourist office. Within a municipal area, you will find buses, streetcars, and even a *U-Bahn* (subway). Rural areas are almost always served by buses. Normally, you can buy a ticket from the driver, but it may be cheaper to buy one from a vending machine. Multiple tickets, family tickets (*Familienkarte*), and day passes for all routes (*Netzkarte*) are usually available. Make sure the ticket has a date and time stamped on it, otherwise you will be expected to have it stamped by a separate machine, labeled *entwerten*. There are no longer conductors on German buses or streetcars, but you may run into a *Kontrolleur* (inspector) who fines people without valid stamped tickets.

Excuse me, where's the nearest ...
Bitte, wo ist die nächste ... ['bɪtə voː ʔɪst di nɛçstə ...]
bus stop?
Bushaltestelle? ['bʊshaltəʃtɛlə]
streetcar stop?
Straßenbahnhaltestelle? ['ʃtʀaːsnbaːn,haltəʃtɛlə]
subway station?
U-Bahnstation? ['ʔuːbaːnʃta,tsjoːn]

Which line goes to ... ?
Welche Linie fährt nach ...? ['vɛlçə 'liːnjə feːt nax ...]

When's the last (subway) train to ...?
Wann fährt die letzte U-Bahn nach ...?
['van feːt di 'lɛtstə 'ʔuːbaːn nax]

Excuse me, does this bus go to ...?
Entschuldigen Sie, ist das der Bus nach ...?
[ʔɛntʃʊldɪgn zi ʔɪst das dɐ bʊs nax]

How many stops is it?
Wie viele Haltestellen sind es? ['viː_fiːlə 'haltəʃtɛln ˌzɪnt əs]

Excuse me, where do I have to get out?
Entschuldigen Sie, wo muss ich aussteigen?
[ʔɛntˈʃʊldɪgŋ zi voː mʊs ɪç ˈʔaʊʃtaɪgŋ]

Excuse me, will I have to change?
Entschuldigen Sie, muss ich umsteigen?
[ʔɛntˈʃʊldɪgŋ zi mʊs ɪç ˈʔʊmʃtaɪgŋ]

Could you let me know when I have to get off, please?
Könnten Sie mir bitte Bescheid geben, wann ich aussteigen
muss? [kœntn zi miɐ 'bɪtə bəˈʃaɪt geːbm vɛn ɪç ˈʔaʊʃtaɪgŋ mʊs]

A ticket to ..., please.
Bitte, einen Fahrschein nach ... ['bɪtə ʔaɪnn 'faːʃaɪn nax]

The ticket machine is broken.
Der Fahrkartenautomat ist kaputt/defekt.
[dɐ 'faːkaːtnʔaʊtoˌmaːt ʔɪst kaˈpʊt/deˈfɛkt]

The machine doesn't accept bills.
Der Automat nimmt keine Geldscheine an.
[dɐ ʔaʊtoˈmaːt nɪmt ˈkaɪnə ˈgɛltʃaɪnə ʔan]

bus	der Bus [dɐ bʊs]
bus station	der Busbahnhof [dɐ ˈbʊsˌbaːnhoːf]
cable car	die Zahnradbahn [di ˈtsaːnʀatˌbaːn]
conductor/ticket collector . .	der Schaffner [dɐ ˈʃafnɐ]
day ticket (pass)	die Tageskarte [di ˈtaːgəskaːtə]
departure	die Abfahrt [di ˈʔapfaːt]
direction	die Richtung [di ˈʀɪçtʊŋ]
fare	der Fahrpreis [dɐ ˈfaːpʀaɪs]
to get on	einsteigen [ˈʔaɪnʃtaɪgŋ]
inspector	der Kontrolleur [dɐ kɔntʀoˈløɐ]
local train	der Nahverkehrszug [dɐ ˈnaːfɐˌkeːɐstsuːk]
stop	die Haltestelle [di ˈhaltəʃtɛlə]
streetcar	die Straßenbahn [di ˈʃtʀaːsnbaːn]
suburban train	die S-Bahn [di ˈɛsbaːn]
subway	die U-Bahn [di ˈʔuːbaːn]
terminus/end of the line . . .	die Endstation [di ˈʔɛntʃtatsjoːn]
ticket	der Fahrschein [dɐ ˈfaːʃaɪn]
ticket machine	der Fahrkartenautomat [dɐ ˈfaːkaːtnʔaʊtoˌmaːt]
timetable	der Fahrplan [dɐ ˈfaːplaːn]
weekly season ticket/	die Wochenkarte [di ˈvɔxnkaːtə]
one-week pass	

Excuse me, where's the nearest taxi stand?
Entschuldigen Sie bitte, wo ist der nächste Taxistand?
[ʔɛntʃʊldɪgn̩ zi ˈbɪtə ˈvoː ʔɪst dɐ ˈnɛːçstə ˈtaksiʃtant]

To the train station, please.
Zum Bahnhof, bitte. [tsʊm ˈbaːnhoːf ˈbɪtə]

To the ... Hotel, please.
Zum ... Hotel, bitte. [tsʊm ... hoˈtɛl ˈbɪtə]

To ... Street, please.
In die ...-Straße, bitte. [ʔɪn di ... ʃtʀaːsə ˈbɪtə]

To (name of a town)..., please.
Nach ..., bitte. [nax ... ˈbɪtə]

How much will it cost to ...?
Wie viel kostet es nach ...? [ˈviː_fil ˈkɔstət əs nax]

Could you stop here, please?
Halten Sie bitte hier. [ˈhaltn̩ zi ˈbɪtə hiɐ]

That's for you.
Das ist für Sie. [das ʔɪst fyɐ ˈziː]

Keep the change.
Behalten Sie das Restgeld. [bəˈhaltn̩ zi das ˈʀɛstgɛlt]

fasten one's seat belt	anschnallen [ˈʔanʃnaln̩]	
flat rate	der Pauschalpreis [dɐ pauˈʃaːlpʀaɪs]	
house number	die Hausnummer [di ˈhausnʊmɐ]	
price per kilometer	der Kilometerpreis [dɐ kiloˈmeːtɐpʀaɪs]	
receipt	die Quittung [di ˈkvɪtʊŋ]	
seat belt	der Sicherheitsgurt [dɐ ˈzɪçɐhaɪtsˌgʊɐt]	
to stop	anhalten [ˈʔanhaltn̩]	
taxi driver	der Taxifahrer/die Taxifahrerin [dɐ ˈtaksifaːʀɐ/di ˈtaksifaːʀəʀɪn]	
taxi stand	der Taxistand [dɐ ˈtaksiʃtant]	
tip	das Trinkgeld [das ˈtʀɪŋk(g)ɛlt]	

Traveling with Children

Adequate facilities
If you are traveling with small children, you will find adequate facilities almost everywhere. Playgrounds are easy to find, the larger department stores usually have baby-care rooms, and almost all restaurants have high chairs for the asking. If you are driving, you will find rest areas at regular intervals along the autobahn with play areas and child-friendly restaurants.

Useful Questions

Could you tell me if there is a children's playground here, please?
Könnten Sie mir bitte sagen, ob es hier einen Kinderspielplatz gibt? [kœnn zi miɐ 'bɪtə za:gŋ ʔɔp əs hiɐ ʔaınn 'kındeʃpi:lplats gıpt]

Is there a baby-sitting service here?
Gibt es hier eine Kinderbetreuung?
[gıpt əs hiɐ ,ʔaınə 'kındebətrɔıʊŋ]

From what age up?
Ab welchem Alter? [ab 'vɛlçm ʔ'altɐ]

Do you know anyone who could babysit for us?
Kennen Sie jemanden, der bei uns babysitten kann?
['kɛnn zi 'je:mandn dɐ baı ʔʊns 'be:bisɪtn kan]

Do you have a baby monitor?
Haben Sie ein Babyfon? ['ha:bm zi ʔaın 'be:bifo:n]

Is there a reduced rate for children?
Gibt es eine Ermäßigung für Kinder?
[gıpt əs ,ʔaınə ʔɐ'mɛ:sıgʊŋ fyɐ 'kındɐ]

On the Road

We're traveling with a young child.
Wir reisen mit einem Kleinkind. [viɐ 'ʀaızn mɪt ,ʔaınəm 'klaınkɪnt]

Can we get seats right at the front?
Können wir Plätze ganz vorn bekommen?
[kœnn viɐ 'plɛtsə gants 'fɔɐn bə'kɔmm]

Do you rent child seats for the car?
Verleihen Sie Kinderautositze? [fɐ'laın zi 'kındɐ,ʔautozıtsə]

Do you possibly have some crayons and a coloring book for our child?
Haben Sie vielleicht Stifte und ein Malbuch für unser Kind?
['ha:bm zi fı'laıçt ʃtıftə ʔʊnt aın 'ma:lbu:x fyɐ ʔʊnsɐ 'kınt]

74

In a Restaurant

Could you bring us a high chair, please?
Könnten Sie bitte noch einen Kinderstuhl bringen?
[kœntn zi 'bɪtə nɔx ʔaɪn 'kɪndeʃtu:l bʀɪŋn]

Do you also have children's portions?
Gibt es auch Kinderportionen? [gɪpt əs aʊx 'kɪndepɔ'tsjo:nn]

Could you warm up the baby bottle, please?
Könnten Sie mir bitte das Fläschchen warm machen?
['kœntn zi miɐ 'bɪtə das 'flɛʃçn va:m maxn]

Could you tell me where I can breastfeed my baby?
Könnten Sie mir bitte sagen, wo ich hier stillen kann?
[kœntn zi miɐ 'bɪtə za:gn vo: ɪç hiɐ 'ʃtɪln kan]

adventure playground	der Abenteuerspielplatz [de 'a:bmtɔɪɐʃpi:lplats]
baby bonnet	die Schildmütze [di 'ʃɪltmytsə]
baby bottle	die Trinkflasche [di 'tʀɪŋkflaʃə]
baby carriage	der Kinderwagen [de 'kɪndeva:gn]
baby food	die Kindernahrung [di 'kɪndena:ʀʊŋ]
baby monitor	das Babyfon [das 'be:bifo:n]
baby seat	die Babyschale [di 'be:biʃa:lə]
babysitter	der Babysitter [de 'be:bisɪte]
babysitting service	die Kinderbetreuung [di 'kɪndebətʀɔjʊŋ]
changing table	der Wickeltisch [de 'vɪkltɪʃ]
child seat	der Kindersitz [de 'kɪndezɪts]
child seat cushion	das Kindersitzkissen [das 'kɪndezɪtskɪsn]
children's bed	das Kinderbett [das 'kɪndebɛt]
children's clothing	die Kinderkleidung [di 'kɪndeklaɪdʊŋ]
children's club	der Miniclub [de 'mɪniklʊp]
children's playground	der Kinderspielplatz [de 'kɪndeʃpi:lplats]
children's pool	das Kinderbecken [das 'kɪndebɛkn]
coloring book	das Malbuch [das 'ma:lbu:x]
crib	das Kinderbett [das 'kɪndebɛt]
diapers	die Windeln *f pl* [di vɪndln]
feeding bottle	die Saugflasche [di 'zaʊkflaʃə]
high chair	der Kinderstuhl [de 'kɪndeʃtu:l]
inner tube	der Schwimmring [de 'ʃvɪmʀɪŋ]
nipple	der Sauger [de 'zaʊge]
pacifier	der Schnuller [de 'ʃnʊle]
reduced rate for children . .	die Kinderermäßigung [di 'kɪnde'e'mɛ:sɪgʊŋ]
sand castle	die Sandburg [di 'zantbuek]
sunscreen	der Sonnenschutz [de 'zɔnnʃʊts]
swimming lessons	der Schwimmkurs [de 'ʃvɪmkuɐs]

toys	die Spielsachen *f pl* [di ˈʃpiːl zaːxn]
wading pool	das Planschbecken [das ˈplanʃbɛkn]
water wings	die Schwimmflügel *m pl* [di ˈʃvɪmflyːgl]

Health

Could you tell me if there's a pediatrician here?
Könnten Sie mir bitte sagen, ob es hier einen Kinderarzt gibt?
[kœntn ziː miɐ ˈbɪtə zaːgn ɔp əs hiɐ ˀaɪnn ˈkɪndɐˀaːtst gɪpt]

My child has ...
Mein Kind hat ... [maɪn ˈkɪnt hat]

My child is allergic to ...
Mein Kind ist allergisch gegen ... [maɪn ˈkɪnt ɪst ˀaˈlɛɐgɪʃ geːgn ...]

He/She has been sick.
Er/Sie hat erbrochen. [ˀeɐ/ziː hat ˀɛˈbʀɔxn]

He/She has (got) diarrhea.
Er/Sie hat Durchfall. [ˀeɐ/ziː hat ˈdʊɐçfal]

He/She has been stung.
Er/Sie ist gestochen worden. [ˀeɐ/ziː ɪst gəˈʃtɔxn vɔɐdn]

allergy	die Allergie [di ˀal(ɛ)ɐˈgiː]
chicken pox	die Windpocken *f pl* [di ˈvɪntpɔkn]
childhood disease	die Kinderkrankheit [di ˈkɪndɐˌkʀaŋkhaɪt]
cold	die Erkältung [di ˀɛˈkɛltʊŋ], der Schnupfen [dɐ ʃnʊpfn]
fever	das Fieber [das ˈfiːbɐ]
fungal infection	der Pilz [dɐ pɪlts]
German measles	die Röteln *f pl* [di ˈʀøːtln]
health food	die Heilnahrung [di ˈhaɪlnaːʀʊŋ]
inflammation of the middle ear	die Mittelohrentzündung [di ˈmɪtlˀoɐˀɛnˌtsʏndʊŋ]
insect bite	der Insektenstich [dɐ ˀɪnˈzɛktnʃtɪç]
measles	die Masern *f pl* [ˈmaːzɐn]
mumps	der Mumps [dɐ mʊmps]
pediatric hospital	das Kinderkrankenhaus [das ˈkɪndɐˌkʀaŋknhaʊs]
rash	der Ausschlag [dɐ ˈʔaʊʃlaːk]
scarlet fever	der Scharlach [dɐ ˈʃaːlax]
temperature	das Fieber [das ˈfiːbɐ]
vaccination record	der Impfpass [dɐ ˈʔɪm(p)fpas]
wind	die Blähungen *f pl* [di ˈblɛːʊŋŋ]

Travelers with Disabilities

Problematic buildings, helpful people

Although most German cities are trying very hard to improve conditions, disabled people will encounter a number of problems. Historical sections of towns present obvious problems such as narrow streets with cobblestones. Older buildings usually have steps, and even if you get in, there may not be an elevator inside. Much work has been done in larger cities to level curbs and make public transportation accessible. Large department stores are almost always accessible and have suitable toilet facilities. It is possible to travel by train, but wheelchair users should try to travel by *IC* or *ICE* (express) trains and avoid older passenger trains marked *E-Zug* or those printed in black on schedules. Larger hotels and modern restaurants are usually fully prepared for the disabled. Information will be essential, so the tourist information office should be one of your first stops. Ask if there is a *Stadtführer für Behinderte*, a guide to the city for the disabled. Most people are very willing to help if you run into trouble.

I have a disability.
Ich habe eine Behinderung. [ˀɪç ˈhaːbə ˀaɪnə bəˈhɪndəʀʊŋ]

I'm ...
Ich bin ... [ˀɪç bɪn ...]
  a paraplegic.
  querschnittsgelähmt. [ˈkveeʃnɪtsgəlɛːmt]
  partially sighted / visually impaired.
  sehbehindert. [ˈzeːbəhɪndɐt]

I have ...
Ich habe ... [ˀɪç ˈhaːbə]
  a physical handicap.
  eine körperliche Behinderung. [ˀaɪnə ˈkœepəlɪçə bəˈhɪndəʀʊŋ]
  multiple sclerosis.
  Multiple Sklerose. [mʊlˈtiːplə skleˈʀoːzə]

Can you help me ...
Können Sie mir helfen, ... [ˈkœnn ziː miɐ hɛlfn]
  cross this street.
  die Straße zu überqueren. [di ˈʃtʀaːsə tsʊ ˀybeˈkveen]
  get on the bus.
  in den Bus zu kommen. [ɪn den bʊs tsʊ kɔmm]

Can you help me up these steps?
Können Sie mir helfen, die Treppen hinaufzukommen?
[ˈkœnn ziː miɐ hɛlfn di tʀɛpm hɪnˈaʊftsʊkɔmm]

We have to go up backwards.
Wir müssen rückwärts hinauf. [viɐ mʏsn ˈʀʏkvɛɐts hɪnˈaʊf]

We'll need one more person to help.
Wir brauchen noch jemanden, der hilft.
[viɐ brauxn nɔx ˈjeːmandn deɐ hɪlft]

Tilt the wheelchair back first.
Zuerst den Rollstuhl kippen. [tsuˈʔeɐst den ˈʀɔlʃtuːl kɪpm]

Could you put the wheelchair in the back of the car?
Könnten Sie den Rollstuhl hinten ins Auto stellen?
[ˈkœntn zi den ˈʀɔlʃtuːl ˈhɪntn ɪns ˈʔauto ˈʃtɛln]

Do you have a bathroom/a toilet for disabled people?
Haben Sie ein Bad/eine Toilette für Behinderte?
[ˈhaːbm zi ˈʔaɪn baːt/ˈʔaɪnə toˈlɛtə fyɐ bəˈhɪndɐtə]

Getting Around

Can I take a folding wheelchair with me on the plane?
Kann ich einen faltbaren Rollstuhl im Flugzeug mitnehmen?
[kan ɪç ˈʔaɪnn ˈfaltbaʀən ˈʀɔlʃtuːl ɪm ˈfluːktsɔɪk ˈmɪtneːmm]

Will a wheelchair be provided at the airport?
Wird ein Rollstuhl am Flughafen bereitgestellt?
[vɪɐd ˈʔaɪn ˈʀɔlʃtuːl am ˈfluːkhaːfn bəˈʀaɪtgəʃtɛlt]

I'd like an aisle seat.
Ich möchte einen Sitz am Gang. [ˈʔɪç ˈmœçtə ˈʔaɪnn zɪts am ˈgaŋ]

Is there a toilet for the disabled?
Gibt es eine Behindertentoilette? [gɪpt əs ˈʔaɪnə bəˈhɪndɐtntoˈlɛtə]

Is there a washroom for the disabled?
Gibt es einen Behindertenwaschraum?
[gɪpt əs ˈʔaɪnn bəˈhɪndɐtn͜ˌvaʃʀaʊm]

Could someone help me change trains?
Könnte mir jemand beim Umsteigen behilflich sein?
[ˈkœntə miɐ ˈjeːmant baɪm ˈʔumʃtaɪgŋ bəˈhɪlflɪç zaɪn]

Are the doors of the train at ground level?
Ist der Einstieg in den Wagen ebenerdig?
[ˈʔɪst dɐ ˈʔaɪnʃtiːk ɪn den vaːgŋ ˈʔeːbmˈʔeɐdɪç]

Are there low-floor buses?
Gibt es Niederflurbusse? [gɪpt əs ˈniːdɐfluɐˌbusə]

Do the platforms have ramps for wheelchair users?
Gibt es Rampen zu den Bahnsteigen für Rollstuhlfahrer?
[gɪpt əs ˈʀampm tsu den ˈbaːnʃtaɪgŋ fyɐ ˈʀɔlʃtuːlˌfaːʀɐ]

Are there rental cars with hand controls for the disabled?
Gibt es für Körperbehinderte Leihwagen mit Handbetrieb?
[gɪpt əs fyɐ ˈkœɐpɐbəˌhɪndɐtə ˈlaɪvaːgŋ mɪt ˈhantbətʀiːb]

Do you rent RVs suitable for wheelchair users?
Vermieten Sie rollstuhlgerechte Wohnmobile?
[fɐˈmiːtn̩ ziː ˈʀɔlʃtuːlgəˌʀɛçtə ˈvoːnmobiːlə]

Is it possible to rent hand-operated bikes here?
Kann man hier Handbikes leihen? [kan man hiɐ ˈhɛntbaɪks laɪn]

Accommodations

Do you have information about hotels suitable for wheelchair users?
Haben Sie Informationen über Hotels, die für Rollstuhlfahrer geeignet sind? [ˈhaːbm̩ ziː ɪnfɔmaˈtsjoːnn̩ ʔyːbɐ hoˈtɛls diː fyɐ ˈʀɔlʃtuːlˌfaːʀɐ gəˈʔaɪknət zɪnt]

What hotels can you recommend for disabled people?
Welche Hotels können Sie Behinderten empfehlen?
[ˈvɛlçə hoˈtɛls ˈkœnn̩ ziː bəˈhɪndɐtn̩ ʔɛmˈpfeːln]

Could you tell me which hotels and campgrounds have special facilities for the disabled?
Könnten Sie mir bitte sagen, welche Hotels und Campingplätze behindertengerechte Einrichtungen haben?
[ˈkœntn̩ ziː miɐ ˈbɪtə zaːgn̩ ˈvɛlçə hoˈtɛls ʊnt ˈkɛmpɪŋplɛtsə bəˈhɪndɐtngəˌʀɛçtə ˈʔaɪnʀɪçtʊŋn haːbm̩]

Museums, Sights, Theater ...

Is there an elevator to the exhibition?
Gibt es einen Aufzug zu der Ausstellung?
[gɪpt əs ʔaɪnn̩ ˈʔaʊftsuːk tsʊ dɐ ˈʔaʊʃtɛlʊŋ]

I'm a wheelchair user. How do I get up there?
Ich bin Rollstuhlfahrer. Wie komme ich da hoch?
[ʔɪç bɪn ˈʀɔlʃtuːlˌfaːʀɐ viː ˈkɔmə ʔɪç da ˈhoːx]

Are there guided tours (of the city) for the disabled?
Gibt es (Stadt)führungen für Behinderte?
[gɪpt əs (ˈʃtat)ˌfyːʀʊŋn fyɐ bəˈhɪndɐtə]

Do you have an induction loop?
Haben Sie eine Induktionsschleife?
[ˈhaːbn̩ ziː ʔaɪnə ʔɪndʊkˈtsjoːnsˌʃlaɪfə]

Are there museum tours for the blind?
Gibt es Museumsführungen für Blinde?
[gɪpt əs muˈzeʊmsˌfyːʀʊŋn fyɐ ˈblɪndə]

access	der Zugang [dɐ ˈtsuːgaŋ]
accessible	zugänglich [ˈtsuːgɛŋlɪç]
accompanying person	die Begleitperson [di bəˈglaɪtp(ɛ)ɐˌzoːn]

aid to walking	die Gehhilfe [di 'ge:hɪlfə]
amputated	amputiert [ampu'tiet]
at ground level	ebenerdig ['ʔe:bmʔeedɪç]
automatic door	die automatische Tür [di ʔauto'ma:tɪʃə tyɐ]
blind	blind [blɪnt]
blind person	der Blinde [dɐ 'blɪndə]
Braille	die Blindenschrift [di 'blɪndnʃʀɪft]
cane	der Taststock [dɐ 'tastʃtɔk]
care	die Betreuung [di bə'tʀɔɪʊŋ]
crutch	die Krücke [di 'kʀvkə]
deaf	gehörlos [gə'høɐloːs], taub [taup]
deaf person	der/die Gehörlose [dɐ/dɪ gə'høɐloːzə]
deaf-mute	taubstumm ['taupʃtum]
deaf-mute (person)	der/die Taubstumme [dɐ/dɪ taupʃtumə]
disability	die Behinderung [di bə'hɪndəʀʊŋ]
disability identification	der Behindertenausweis [dɐ bə'hɪndetnʔausvaɪs]
disabled	behindert [bə'hɪndɐt]
disabled person	der/die Behinderte [dɐ/dɪ bə'hɪndetə]
door opener	der Türöffner [dɐ tyɐʔœfnə]
door width	die Türbreite [di tyɐbʀaɪtə]
doorstep	die Türschwelle [di tyɐʃvɛlə]
elevator	der Lift [dɐ lɪft]
epilepsy	die Epilepsie [di epilɛp'si]
good clearance	unterfahrbar ['ʊntɐfa:baː]
gradient	die Steigung [di 'ʃtaɪɡʊŋ]
guide dog	der Blindenhund [dɐ 'blɪndnhʊnt]
hall width	die Flurbreite [di 'fluebʀaɪtə]
hand throttle (car)	das Handgas [das 'hantgaːs]
hand-operated bike	das Handbike [das 'hɛntbaɪk]
handicap	die Behinderung [di bə'hɪndəʀʊŋ]
handle	der Haltegriff [dɐ 'haltəgʀɪf]
handrail	der Handlauf [dɐ 'hantlaʊf]
hard of hearing	schwerhörig ['ʃveɐhøːʀɪç]
headphones	der Kopfhörer [dɐ 'kɔpfhøːʀɐ]
height	die Höhe [di høːə]
hydraulic ramp	die Hebebühne [di 'he:bəbyːnə]
in need of care	pflegebedürftig ['pfleːgəbədyɐftɪç]
induction loop	die Induktionsschleife [di ɪndʊk'tsjoːnʃlaɪfə]
keyboard telephone	das Schreibtelefon [das 'ʃʀaɪpteləfoːn]
lift	der Lift [dɐ lɪft]
mentally handicapped	geistig behindert ['gaɪstɪç bə'hɪndet]
mute	stumm [ʃtʊm]
out-patient	ambulant [ambʊ'lant]

paraplegic, quadriplegic . . .	querschnittsgelähmt ['kveeʃnɪtsgə,lɛ:mt]
parking space for disabled .	der Behindertenparkplatz [der bə'hɪndetnpa:kplats]
partially sighted	sehbehindert ['se:bəhɪndet]
passable	befahrbar [bə'fa:ba:]
ramp	die Rampe [di 'rampə]
seeing-eye dog	der Blindenhund [de 'blɪndnhʊnt]
shower seat	der Duschsitz [de 'du:ʃzɪts]
sign language	die Zeichensprache [di 'tsaɪçnʃpra:xə]
stairs	die Treppen *f pl* [di trɛpm]
steering knob	der Lenkrad-Drehknopf [de 'lɛŋkrat,dre:knɔpf]
step	die Stufe [di 'ʃtu:fə]
suitable for the disabled . . .	behindertengerecht [bə'hɪndetngə,rɛçt]
suitable for wheelchair users	rollstuhlgerecht ['rɔlʃtu:lgə,rɛçt]
toilet for the disabled	die Behindertentoilette [di bə'hɪndetnto,lɛtə]
transport service	das Fahrdienst [das 'fa:di:nst]
visually impaired	sehbehindert ['se:bəhɪndet]
wheelchair	der Rollstuhl [de 'rɔlʃtu:l]
battery-driven	batteriebetrieben [batə'ri: bə'tri:bm]
electric wheelchair	der E-Rollstuhl [de 'ʔe:,rɔlʃtu:l]
folding wheelchair	der Faltrollstuhl [de 'falt,rɔlʃtu:l]
wheelchair cabin (*ship*)	die Rollstuhlkabine [di 'rɔlʃtu:lka,bi:nə]
wheelchair hiking	das Rollstuhlwandern [das 'rɔlʃtu:l,vanden]
wheelchair user (*man*)	der Rollstuhlfahrer [de 'rɔlʃtu:l,fa:re]
wheelchair user (*woman*) . .	die Rollstuhlfahrerin [di 'rɔlʃtu:l,fa:rərɪn]
width	die Breite [di 'braɪtə]

Accommodations

A good night's sleep

Finding a place to stay is easy enough in Germany. If you want to save money or get more of a "German feel" to your stay, time your overnight stops so you'll be in smaller towns or even rural areas. Hotels, especially in cities, are international in character. *Gasthaus* means basically a small hotel and will be more local in character. *Gasthof* is about the same thing, but in a rural area. A *Pension* is a bed-and-breakfast place, often your best value, and usually the most personal in character. *Hotel Garni* means they only serve breakfast. *Fremdenzimmer* means accommodation in a private house. Look for the sign *Zimmer frei* (vacancies).

Information

Can you recommend ..., please?
Können Sie mir bitte ... empfehlen?
['kœnn zi miɐ 'bɪtə ... ʔɛm'pfeːln]

a good hotel
ein gutes Hotel [ʔaɪn 'guːtəs ho'tɛl]
a simple hotel
ein einfaches Hotel [ʔaɪn ʔaɪnfaxəs ho'tɛl]
a bed-and-breakfast/boarding house
eine Pension [ʔaɪnə paŋ'zjoːn]

Is it central/quiet/near the beach?
Ist es zentral/ruhig/in Strandnähe gelegen?
['ɪst əs tsɛn'traːl/ʁuɪç/ʔɪn 'ʃtrantnɛːə gə'leːgn̩]

Is there ... here too?
Gibt es hier auch ... [gɪpt əs hiɐ ʔaʊx]
a youth hostel
eine Jugendherberge? [ʔaɪnə 'juːgnthɛɐ̯bɛɐgə]
a campground
einen Campingplatz? [ʔaɪnn 'kɛmpɪŋplats]

At the Hotel

At the Reception Desk

I've reserved a room. My name's ...
Ich habe ein Zimmer reserviert. Mein Name ist ...
[ʔɪç 'haːbə aɪn 'tsɪmɐ rezɛɐ'viet maɪn 'naːmə ʔɪst ...]

Do you have any vacancies?
Haben Sie noch Zimmer frei? ['haːbm zi nɔx 'tsɪmɐ fraɪ]
... for one night
... für eine Nacht [... fyɐ ʔaɪnə naxt]

... for two days
... für zwei Tage [... fye tsvaɪ 'taːgə]

... for a week
... für eine Woche [... fye ˈʔaɪnə ˈvɔxə]

No, I'm afraid not.
Nein, leider nicht. [naɪn ˈlaɪdɐ ˈnɪçt]

Yes, what sort of room would you like?
Ja, was für ein Zimmer wünschen Sie?
[jaː vas fye ˈʔaɪn ˈtsɪmɐ ˈvʏnʃn ziː]

I'd like ...
Ich hätte gern ... [ˈʔɪç ˈhɛtə gɛɐn]

  a single room
  ein Einzelzimmer [ˈʔaɪn ˈʔaɪntsltsɪmɐ]

  a double room
  ein Doppelzimmer [ˈʔaɪn ˈdɔpltsɪmɐ]

  a quiet room
  ein ruhiges Zimmer [ˈʔaɪn ˈʀuɪgəs ˈtsɪmɐ]

  with a shower
  mit Dusche [mɪt ˈduːʃə]

  with a bath
  mit Bad [mɪt baːt]

  with a balcony/terrace
  mit Balkon/Terrasse [mɪt balˈkɔn/teˈʀasə]

  with a view of the mountains
  mit Blick auf die Berge [mɪt blɪk aʊf di ˈbɛɐgə]

Can I see the room?
Kann ich das Zimmer ansehen? [kan ɪç das ˈtsɪmɐ ˈʔanzeːn]

Can I see a different one, please.
Kann ich bitte noch ein anderes sehen?
[kan ɪç ˈbɪtə nɔx aɪn ˈʔandərəs zeːn]

I'll take this room.
Dieses Zimmer nehme ich. [ˈdiːzəs ˈtsɪmɐ ˈneːmə ɪç]

Can you put a third bed/a crib in the room?
Können Sie noch ein drittes Bett/ein Kinderbett dazustellen?
[ˈkœnn zi nɔx aɪn bɛt/aɪn ˈkɪndɐbɛt daˈtsuːʃtɛln]

Beds usually have a duvet/comforter instead of a top sheet and
blankets. There will be an extra blanket in the wardrobe/cab-
inet. Don't expect to find tea- or coffee-making facilities in the
room.

How much is the room with ...
Was kostet das Zimmer mit ..., bitte?
[vas ˈkɔstət das ˈtsɪmɐ mɪt ... bɪtə]

breakfast?
Frühstück ['fʀy:ʃtʏk]

half-board (breakfast and dinner)?
Halbpension ['halpaŋzjo:n]

full board (all meals)?
Vollpension ['fɔlpaŋzjo:n]

Could you fill out the registration form, please?
Wollen Sie bitte den Anmeldeschein ausfüllen?
[vɔln zi 'bɪtə den ʔanmɛldəʃaɪn ʔaʊsfʏln]

May I see your passport?
Darf ich Ihren Ausweis sehen? [daːf ɪç 'iːʀən/ʔiən ʔaʊsvaɪs zeːn]

Where can I park the car?
Wo kann ich den Wagen abstellen? [voː kan ɪç den 'vaːgŋ ʔapʃtɛln]

In our garage.
In unserer Garage. [ʔɪn ˌʊnzəʀe gaˈʀaːʒə]

In our parking lot.
Auf unserem Parkplatz. [ʔaʊf ˌʊnzem 'paːkplats]

Asking for Service
➢ also Breakfast

When is breakfast served?
Ab wann gibt es Frühstück? [ʔap 'van gɪpt əs 'fʀy:ʃtʏk]

When are the meals served?
Wann sind die Essenszeiten? [van zɪnt die ʔɛsnstsaɪtn]

Where's the restaurant?
Wo ist der Speisesaal? [voː ʔɪst de 'ʃpaɪzəzaːl]

Where's the breakfast room?
Wo ist der Frühstücksraum? [voː ʔɪst de 'fʀy:ʃtʏksʀaʊm]

Could you wake me at seven o'clock tomorrow morning, please.
Könnten Sie mich bitte morgen früh um sieben Uhr wecken?
[kœntn zi mɪç 'bɪtə 'mɔəgŋ fʀy: ʊm 'zi:bm ʔue 'vɛkŋ]

How does ... work?
Wie funktioniert ...? [vi: fʊŋktsjoˈniet]

Room 24, please!
Zimmernummer vierundzwanzig, bitte!
['tsɪmenʊme 'fie(ʊ)n'tsvantsɪç 'bɪtə]

Is there any mail for me?
Ist Post für mich da? [ʔɪst pɔst fye mɪç da:]

Where can I ...
Wo kann ich ... [voː kan ɪç]

get something to drink?
hier etwas trinken? [hie ˌʔɛtvas 'tʀɪŋkŋ]

rent a car?
ein Auto mieten? [ʔaɪn ˈʔaʊto miːtn]

telephone from (here)?
hier telefonieren? [hiɐ teləfoˈniːʀən/-ˈniɐn]

Can I leave my valuables in your safe?
Kann ich meine Wertsachen bei Ihnen in den Safe geben?
[kan ɪç ˌmaɪnə ˈveɐtzaxn baɪ ʔiːnn ʔɪn den ˈsɛɪf/seːf geːbm]

Can I leave my baggage here?
Kann ich mein Gepäck hier lassen? [kan ɪç maɪn gəˈpɛk ˈhiɐ_lasn]

The room hasn't been cleaned today.
Das Zimmer ist heute nicht geputzt worden.
[das ˈtsɪmə ʔɪst ˈhɔɪtə nɪçt gəˈpʊtst vɔɐdn]

The air-conditioning doesn't work.
Die Klimaanlage funktioniert nicht.
[di ˈkliːmaʔanˌlaːgə fʊŋktsjoˈniɐt nɪçt]

The faucet drips.
Der Wasserhahn tropft. [de ˈvaseˌhaːn tʀɔpft]

There's no (hot) water.
Es kommt kein (warmes) Wasser. [ʔəs kɔmt kaɪn (vaːməs) ˈvasɐ]

The toilet/sink is stopped up.
Die Toilette/Das Waschbecken ist verstopft.
[di tɔ(ɪ)ˈlɛtə/das ˈvaʃbɛkŋ ʔɪst feˈʃtɔpft]

I'd like to have a different room.
Ich hätte gern ein anderes Zimmer.
[ʔɪç ˈhɛtə gɛɐn ʔaɪn ˈʔandərəs ˈtsɪmə]

I'm leaving tomorrow at ... o'clock.
Ich reise morgen um ... Uhr ab. [ʔɪç ˈʀaɪzə mɔɐgŋ ʊm ... ʔuɐ ˈʔap]

Could you prepare the bill, please?
Könnten Sie bitte die Rechnung fertig machen?
[kœntn zi ˈbɪtə di ˈʀɛçnʊŋ ˈfɛɐtɪç maxn]

Can I pay by credit card?
Kann ich mit Kreditkarte bezahlen?
[ˈkan ɪç mɪt kʀeˈdiːtˌkaːtə bəˈtsaːln]

Would you call a taxi for me, please.
Könnten Sie mir bitte ein Taxi rufen?
[kœntn zi miɐ ˈbɪtə ʔaɪn ˈtaksi ʀuːfn]

Thank you very much for everything. Goodbye!
Vielen Dank für alles! Auf Wiedersehen!
[ˈfiːln daŋk fyɐ ˈʔaləs ʔaʊf_ˈviːdəzeːn]

adapter	der Zwischenstecker [de ˈtsvɪʃnʃtɛkɐ]
air-conditioning	die Klimaanlage [di ˈkliːmɐʔanˌlaːɡə]
ashtray	der Aschenbecher [de ˈʔaʃnbɛçɐ]
balcony	der Balkon [de balˈkɔn]
bath	die Badewanne [di ˈbaːdəvanə]
bath towel	das Badetuch [das ˈbaːdətuːx]
bathroom	das Badezimmer [das ˈbaːdətsɪmɐ]
bed	das Bett [das bɛt]
bed linen	die Bettwäsche [di ˈbɛtvɛʃə]
bedside table	der Nachttisch [de ˈnaxttɪʃ]
bidet	das Bidet [das biˈdeː]
blanket	die Bettdecke [di ˈbɛtdɛkə]
breakfast	das Frühstück [das ˈfʁyːʃtʏk]
breakfast room	der Frühstücksraum [de ˈfʁyːʃtʏksʁaʊm]
buffet breakfast	das Frühstücksbüfett [das ˈfʁyːʃtʏksbʏˌfeː]
chair	der Stuhl [de ˈʃtuːl]
to clean	reinigen [ˈʁaɪnɪɡn]
clothes closet	der Kleiderschrank [de ˈklaɪdɐʃʁaŋk]
coat hanger	der Kleiderbügel [de ˈklaɪdɐbyːɡl]
cover/place (for breakfast)	das Gedeck (für das Frühstück) [das ɡəˈdɛk fyɐ (da)s ˈfʁyːʃtʏk]
dining room	der Speisesaal [de ˈʃpaɪzəzaːl]
dinner	das Abendessen [das ˈʔaːbmtʔɛsn]
door	die Tür [di tyɐ]
door code	der Türcode [de ˈtyɐkoːt]
elevator	der Aufzug [de ˈʔaʊftsuːk]
extra week	die Verlängerungswoche [di fɐˈlɛŋəʁʊŋsˌvɔxə]
fan	der Ventilator [de vɛntiˈlaːtoɐ]
faucet	der Wasserhahn [de ˈvasɐhaːn]
floor	die Etage [di ʔeˈtaːʒə]
garage	die Garage [di ɡaˈʁaːʒə]
glass	das Wasserglas [das ˈvasɐɡlaːs], das Glas [das ɡlaːs]
handheld shower	die Handbrause [di ˈhantbʁaʊzə]
heating	die Heizung [di ˈhaɪtsʊŋ]
high season	die Hauptsaison [di ˈhaʊptzɛˌzɔŋ]
key	der Schlüssel [de ˈʃlʏsl]
lamp	die Lampe [di ˈlampə]
lavatory	die Toilette [di toˈlɛtə]
light	das Licht [das lɪçt]
lightbulb	die Glühbirne [di ˈɡlyːbɪʁnə]
lounge	der Aufenthaltsraum [de ˈʔaʊfnthalts‚ʁaʊm]
low season/off-season	die Vorsaison [di ˈfoɐzɛˌzɔŋ]; die Nachsaison [di ˈnaːxzɛˌzɔŋ]

lunch	das Mittagessen [das 'mɪtak,ʔɛsn]
maid	das Zimmermädchen [das 'tsɪmemɛ:tçn]
mattress	die Matratze [di ma'tʀatsə]
motel	das Motel [das mo'tɛl]
mug	der Becher [dɐ 'bɛçɐ]
notepad	der Notizblock [dɐ no'ti:tsblɔk]
overnight stay	die Übernachtung [di ʔybɐ'naxtʊŋ]
pillow	das Kopfkissen [das 'kɔpfkɪsn]
plug	der Stecker [dɐ 'ʃtɛkɐ]
porter	der Portier [dɐ pɔɐ'tje:]
price list (*e.g. for the minibar*)	die Preisliste (*z.B. für die Minibar*) [di 'pʀaɪslɪstə (tsʊm 'baɪʃpi:l fyɐ di 'mɪniba:)]
radio	das Radio [das 'ʀa:djo]
reception desk	die Rezeption [di ʀetsɛp'tsjo:n]
registration	die Anmeldung [di 'ʔanmɛldʊŋ]
to repair	reparieren [ʀɛpa'ʀi:ʀən/-'ʀiɐn]
reservation	die Reservierung [di ʀezeɐ'vi:ʀʊŋ]
restroom	die Toilette [di to'lɛtə]
room	das Zimmer [das 'tsɪmɐ]
room service	der Zimmerservice [dɐ 'tsɪmɐɕœsə:vɪs]
room telephone	das Zimmertelefon [das 'tsɪmɐteləˌfo:n]
safe	der Safe [dɐ sɛɪf/se:f]
shoe cleaning kit	das Schuhputzzeug [das 'ʃu:pʊts,tsɔɪk]
shower	die Dusche [di 'du:ʃə]
shower curtain	der Duschvorhang [dɐ 'du:ʃfoɐhaŋ]
showerhead	der Brausekopf [dɐ 'bʀaʊzəkɔpf]
sink	das Waschbecken [das 'vaʃbɛkn]
sliding door	die Schiebetür [di 'ʃi:bətyɐ]
socket	die Steckdose [di 'ʃtɛkdo:zə]
table	der Tisch [dɐ tɪʃ]
tap	der Wasserhahn [dɐ 'vasɐha:n]
television lounge	der Fernsehraum [dɐ 'fɛɐnze:,ʀaʊm]
television, TV	der Fernseher [dɐ 'fɛɐnzeɐ]
terrace	die Terrasse [di te'ʀasə]
toilet	die Toilette [di to'lɛtə]
toilet paper	das Toilettenpapier [das to'lɛtnpaˌpiɐ]
towel	das Handtuch [das 'hantu:x]
trash can	der Abfalleimer [dɐ 'ʔapfal,ʔaɪmɐ]
tumbler	das Wasserglas [das 'vasɐgla:s]
wardrobe	der Kleiderschrank [dɐ 'klaɪdɐʃʀaŋk]
water	das Wasser [das 'vasɐ]
cold water	kaltes Wasser ['va:məs 'vasɐ]
hot water	warmes Wasser ['kaltəs 'vasɐ]
water glass	das Wasserglas [das 'vasɐgla:s]

| window | das Fenster [das ˈfɛnstɐ] |
| writing paper | das Briefpapier [das ˈbʀiːfpapiɐ] |

Vacation Cottages and Apartments

Is electricity/water included in the price?
Ist der Stromverbrauch/Wasserverbrauch im Mietpreis
enthalten?
[ˈʔɪst dɐ ˈʃtʀoːmfɛbʀaʊx /ˈvasɐfɛbʀaʊx ˈʔɪm ˈmiːtpʀaɪs ˈʔɛntˈhaltn̩]

Are pets allowed?
Sind Haustiere erlaubt? [zɪnt ˈhaʊstiːʀə ˈʔɛˈlaʊpt]

Clean up thoroughly before you leave.
Machen Sie gründlich sauber, bevor Sie abreisen.
[maxn̩ ziː ˈgʀʏntlɪç ˈzaʊbɐ bəˈfoɐ ziː ˈʔapʀaɪzn̩]

Do we have to clean the place ourselves before we leave?
Müssen wir die Endreinigung selbst übernehmen?
[mʏsn̩ viɐ diː ˈʔɛntʀaɪnɪgʊŋ ˈzɛlpst ˈʔybɐˈneːmm̩]

> Hikers and mountain climbers have a large choice of mountain
> huts, usually run by the national alpine clubs. Many serve
> meals, but otherwise you can bring your own food.

> also At the Hotel

additional costs	die Nebenkosten [di ˈneːbmkɔstn̩]
apartment	die Wohnung [di ˈvoːnʊŋ]
bedroom	das Schlafzimmer [das ˈʃlaːftsɪmɐ]
bungalow	der Bungalow [dɐ ˈbʊŋɡaloː]
bunk bed	das Etagenbett [das ˈʔeˈtaːʒnbɛt]
coffee machine	die Kaffeemaschine [di ˈkafemaʃiːnə]
crockery	das Geschirr [das ɡəˈʃɪʀ]
day of arrival	der Anreisetag [dɐ ˈʔanʀaɪzəˌtaːk]
day of departure	der Abreisetag [dɐ ˈʔapʀaɪzəˌtaːk]
dishes	das Geschirr [das ɡəˈʃɪʀ]
dishwasher	die Geschirrspülmaschine [di ɡəˈʃɪʀʃpyːlmaˌʃiːnə]
electricity	der Strom [dɐ ʃtʀoːm]
farm	der Bauernhof [dɐ ˈbaʊɐnhoːf]
flat rate for electricity	die Strompauschale [di ˈʃtʀoːmpaʊˌʃaːlə]
fridge/refrigerator	der Kühlschrank [dɐ ˈkyːlʃʀaŋk]
garbage	der Müll [dɐ mʏl]
kitchenette	die Kochnische [di ˈkɔxniːʃə]
landlord/landlady	der Hausbesitzer/die Hausbesitzerin [dɐ ˈhaʊsbəzɪtsɐ/di ˈhaʊsbəzɪtsəʀɪn]

to let	vermieten [fɛˈmiːtn̩]
living room	das Wohnzimmer [das ˈvoːntsɪmɐ]
microwave	die Mikrowelle [di ˈmiːkʁovɛlə]
pets	die Haustiere *n pl* [di ˈhaʊstiːʁə]
range	der Herd [dɐ heːɐt]
to rent	vermieten [fɛˈmiːtn̩]
rent	die Miete [di ˈmiːtə]
sleeper sofa	die Schlafcouch [di ˈʃlaːfkaʊtʃ]
stove	der Herd [dɐ heːɐt]
studio apartment	das Apartment [das ʔaˈpaːtmənt]
tea towel	das Geschirrtuch [das gəˈʃɪʁtuːx]
toaster	der Toaster [dɐ ˈtoːstɐ]
trash	der Müll [dɐ mʏl]
vacation house	das Ferienhaus [das ˈfeːʁiənhaʊs]
vacation property	die Ferienanlage [di ˈfeːʁiənʔanlaːgə]
voltage	die Stromspannung [di ˈʃtʁoːmʃpanʊŋ]
water consumption	der Wasserverbrauch [dɐ ˈvasɐfɛbʁaʊx]

Camping

Could you tell me if there's a campground nearby?
Könnten Sie mir bitte sagen, ob es in der Nähe einen Campingplatz gibt?
[kœntn̩ zi miɐ ˈbɪtə zaːgn̩ ʔɔp əs ɪn dɐ ˈnɛːə ʔaɪnn̩ ˈkɛmpɪŋplats gɪpt]

Do you have room for another trailer/tent?
Haben Sie noch Platz für einen Wohnwagen/ein Zelt?
[ˈhaːbm̩ zi nɔx plats fyɐ ʔaɪnn̩ ˈvoːnvaːgn̩/ʔaɪn ˈtsɛlt]

How much does it cost per day and person?
Wie hoch ist die Gebühr pro Tag und Person?
[vi hoːx ʔɪst di gəˈbyɐ pʁo taːk ʊnt pɛˈzoːn]

What's the charge for ...
Wie hoch ist die Gebühr für ... [vi hoːx ɪst di gəˈbyɐ fyɐ ...]
  the car?
  das Auto? [das ˈʔaʊto]
  the motor home/RV?
  das Wohnmobil? [das ˈvoːnmoˌbiːl]
  the trailer?
  den Wohnwagen? [den ˈvoːnvaːgn̩]
  the tent?
  das Zelt? [das ˈtsɛlt]

We'll be staying for ... days/weeks.
Wir bleiben ... Tage/Wochen. [viɐ blaɪbm̩ ... ˈtaːgə/ˈvɔxn̩]

Where are ...
Wo sind ...? [vo: zɪnt]
  the toilets?
  die Toiletten? [di toˈlɛtn]
  the washrooms?
  die Waschräume? [di ˈvaʃʁɔɪmə]
  the showers?
  die Duschen? [di ˈduːʃn]

Are there electrical outlets here?
Gibt es hier Stromanschluss? [gɪpt əs hiɐ ˈʃtʁoːmanʃlʊs]

Is the campground guarded at night?
Ist der Campingplatz bei Nacht bewacht?
[ˈʔɪst dɐ ˈkɛmpɪŋplats baɪ ˈnaxt bəˈvaxt]

to camp	zelten [ˈtsɛltn]
campground	der Campingplatz [dɐ ˈkɛmpɪŋplats]
camping	das Camping [das ˈkɛmpɪŋ]
camping guide	der Campingführer [dɐ ˈkɛmpɪŋfyːʁɐ]
camping stove	der Kocher [dɐ ˈkɔxɐ]
drinking water	das Trinkwasser [das ˈtʁɪŋkvasɐ]
dryer	der Wäschetrockner [dɐ ˈvɛʃətʁɔknɐ]
electrical outlet	die Steckdose [di ˈʃtɛkdoːzə]
electricity	der Strom [dɐ ʃtʁoːm]
gas canister	die Gasflasche [di gaːsflaʃə]
gas cartridge	die Gaskartusche [di ˈgaːskaˌtʊʃə]
kerosene lantern	die Petroleumlampe
	[di peˈtʁoːleʊmˌlampə]
lavatory	der Waschraum [dɐ ˈvaʃʁaʊm]
plug	der Stecker [dɐ ˈʃtɛkɐ]
propane (gas)	das Propangas [das pʁoˈpaːngaːs]
reservation	die Voranmeldung [di ˈfoɐʔanmɛldʊŋ]
sink	das Geschirrspülbecken
	[das gəˈʃɪʁspyːlbɛkn]
tent	das Zelt [das tsɛlt]
tent peg	der Hering [dɐ ˈheːʁɪŋ]
washroom	der Waschraum [dɐ ˈvaʃʁaʊm]
water	das Wasser [das ˈvasɐ]
water canister	der Wasserkanister [dɐ ˈvasɐkanˌɪstɐ]

Eating and Drinking

Good eating and drinking

In Austria, Germany, and Switzerland you have a number of different kinds of eating and drinking establishments to choose from:

- **Restaurant** – as elsewhere
- **Café** – a coffee house
- **Gasthaus** – a small hotel with a restaurant
- **Gasthof** – a *Gasthaus* in a rural area
- **Biergarten** – outdoor pub/tavern
- **Gartenwirtschaft** – an outdoor restaurant, usually with a limited menu
- **Ratskeller** – a restaurant in the cellar of the *Rathaus* (town hall)
- **Bistro** – a trendy pub or small restaurant, usually with a bar
- **Kneipe** – bar
- **Imbissstube** – fast-food place
- **Konditorei** – pastry shop, usually with a café

In Austria you also encounter simple restaurants called *Beisl*.

Eating Out

Is there ... here?
Gibt es hier ... ? [gɪpt əs hiɐ]

a good restaurant
ein gutes Restaurant [ˀaɪn 'guːtəs ʀɛstoˈʀaŋ]

an inexpensive restaurant
ein preiswertes Restaurant [ˀaɪn 'pʀaɪsveɐtəs ʀɛstoˈʀaŋ]

a gourmet restaurant
ein Feinschmeckerlokal [ˀaɪn 'faɪnʃmɛkɐloˌkaːl]

a fast-food place
einen Schnellimbiss [ˀaɪnn 'ʃnɛlɪmbɪs]

The restaurant business in Germany is rapidly falling into "exotic" hands. In cities and larger towns you'll easily find Italian, Greek, Chinese, and even Indian restaurants. The Italians and Greeks are often your best bet for tasty, inexpensive food. There are numerous Turkish fast-food places as a good alternative to the international fast-food chains. If you insist on getting "typical German food," find a *Gasthof* outside town or go to a fancy hotel.

Where's a good place to eat near here?
Wo kann man hier in der Nähe gut essen?
[vo: kan man hie ʔɪn de 'nɛːə guːt ʔɛsn]

Is there a good, inexpensive restaurant here?
Gibt es hier ein preiswertes Restaurant? [gɪpt əs hie ʔaɪn
'praɪsveetəs ʀɛsto'ʀaŋ]

In a Restaurant

Would you reserve us a table for a party of four for this evening, please?
Reservieren Sie uns bitte für heute Abend einen Tisch für vier Personen. [ʀɛzɐ'viːʀən zi ʔʊns 'bɪtə fyɐ 'hɔɪtə ʔaːbmt ʔaɪnn tɪʃ fyɐ fiɐ pe'zoːnn]

Is this table free?
Ist dieser Tisch noch frei? [ʔɪst 'diːzɐ tɪʃ nɔx 'fʀaɪ]

> In most restaurants you simply pick out your own table. It is also quite common, if the restaurant is crowded, to sit down with people who are strangers to you. You ask if there are seats "free" (not taken).

Are these seats taken?
Sind hier noch Plätze frei? [zɪnt hie 'plɛtsə nɔx 'fʀaɪ]

A table for three, please.
Einen Tisch für drei Personen, bitte.
[ʔaɪnn tɪʃ fyɐ dʀaɪ pe'zoːnn 'bɪtə]

Where are the toilets?
Wo sind die Toiletten? [vo: zɪnt di to'lɛtn]

Is it okay if I smoke?
Darf ich rauchen? [daːf ɪç 'ʀaʊxn]

Ordering

May we have the menu/beverage list, please?
Können wir bitte die Speisekarte/Getränkekarte haben?
[kœnn vie 'bɪtə di 'ʃpaɪzəkaːtə/gə'tʀɛŋkəkaːtə haːbm]

95

Traditionally, you address a waiter with *Herr Ober*, a waitress with *Fräulein*. This is going out of fashion, and most people simply say *Hallo!* in a clear and resonant voice, depending how classy the restaurant is. If it's a high-class eating establishment, a discreet raising of hand and arm should do.

Are you ready to order?
Haben Sie schon gewählt? ['ha:bm zi ʃon gə'vɛ:lt]

What can you recommend?
Was können Sie mir empfehlen? [vas kœnn zi miɐ ˀɛm'fe:ln]

I'll have ... to start with.
Als Vorspeise nehme ich ... [ˀals 'foɐʃpaɪzə 'ne:mə ˀɪç]

I'll have ... for the main course.
Als Hauptgericht nehme ich ... [ˀals 'haʊptgəʀɪçt 'ne:mə ˀɪç]

I don't want any dessert, thank you.
Ich möchte keinen Nachtisch, danke.
[ˀɪç 'mœçtə ˌkaɪnn 'na:xtɪʃ 'daŋkə]

I'm afraid we've run out of ...
Wir haben leider kein ... mehr. [viɐ ha:bm 'laɪdɐ 'kaɪn ... meɐ]

We only serve this dish if it's been pre-ordered.
Dieses Gericht servieren wir nur auf Bestellung.
['di:zəs gə'ʀɪçt zɐ'vi:ʀən viɐ nuɐ ˀaʊf bə'ʃtɛlʊŋ]

Could I have chicken instead of fish?
Könnte ich statt Fisch Huhn haben? ['kœntə ˀɪç ʃtat fɪʃ hu:n ha:bm]

I'm allergic to ...
Ich vertrage kein ... [ˀɪç fɐ'tʀa:gə kaɪn ...]

Could you make this dish without ...?
Könnten Sie das Gericht ohne ... zubereiten?
['kœntn zi das gə'ʀɪçt o:nə ... 'tsu:bəʀaɪtn]

Do you have children's portions?
Gibt es auch Kinderportionen? [gɪpt əs aʊx 'kɪndɐpɔ'tsjo:nn]

How would you like your steak?
Wie möchten Sie Ihr Steak haben? [vi mœçtn zi ˀiɐ 'ste:k ha:bm]
  well-done
  gut durch [gu:t dʊɐç]
  medium
  halb durch [halp dʊɐç]
  rare
  englisch [ˀɛŋlɪʃ]

What would you like to drink?
Was möchten Sie trinken? [vas mœçtn zi 'tʀɪŋkŋ]

A glass of ..., please.
Bitte ein Glas ... ['bɪtə ʔaɪn glaːs]

A bottle of/Half a bottle of ..., please.
Bitte eine Flasche/eine halbe Flasche ...
['bɪtə ʔaɪnə 'flaʃə/ʔaɪnə 'halbə 'flaʃə]

With ice, please.
Mit Eis, bitte. [mɪt ʔaɪs 'bɪtə]

Enjoy your meal!
Guten Appetit! ['guːtn ʔapə'tiːt]

Would you like anything else?
Haben Sie sonst noch einen Wunsch?
[haːbm̩ zi 'zɔnst nɔx aɪnn vʊnʃ]

Bring us ..., please.
Bitte bringen Sie uns ... ['bɪtə brɪŋŋ zi ʔʊns]

Could we have some more bread/water/wine, please?
Könnten wir noch etwas Brot/ Wasser/Wein bekommen?
['kœntn viɐ nɔx ˌɛtvas 'broːt/'vasɐ/'vaɪn bə'kɔmm]

Cheers!
Zum Wohl! [tsʊm 'voːl]

Complaints

We need another ...
Wir brauchen noch ein ... [viɐ braʊxn nɔx ʔaɪn]

Have you forgotten my ...?
Haben Sie mein ... vergessen? [haːbm̩ zi ˌmaɪn ... fɐ'gɛsn]

I didn't order that.
Das habe ich nicht bestellt. [das haːb ɪç nɪçt bə'ʃtɛlt]

The food is cold.
Das Essen ist kalt. [das ʔɛsn ʔɪst kalt]

There's too much salt in the soup.
Die Suppe ist versalzen. [di 'zʊpə ʔɪst fɐ'zaltsn]

The meat's tough/too fatty.
Das Fleisch ist zäh/zu fett. [das flaɪʃ ɪst 'tsɛː/tsʊ 'fɛt]

The fish is not fresh.
Der Fisch ist nicht frisch.
[deɐ fɪʃ ʔɪst nɪçt frɪʃ]

I'm afraid the wine is corked.
Es tut mir Leid, aber der Wein schmeckt nach Korken.
[ʔəs tuːt miɐ laɪt ʔabɐ deɐ vaɪn ʃmɛkt nax 'kɔɐkŋ]

Take it back, please.
Nehmen Sie es bitte zurück. ['ne:mm zi əs 'bɪtə tsʊ'ʀʏk]

Send the manager over, please.
Holen Sie bitte den Chef. ['ho:ln zi 'bɪtə den 'ʃɛf]

> Don't confuse German *Chef* (= manager) with English "chef"
> (= *Koch*).

Paying the Bill

Could I have the check, please?
Die Rechnung, bitte. [di 'ʀɛçnʊŋ 'bɪtə] /
Bezahlen, bitte. [bə'tsa:ln 'bɪtə]

All together, please.
Bitte alles zusammen. ['bɪtə ˀaləs tsʊ'samm]

Separate checks, please.
Getrennte Rechnungen, bitte. [gə'tʀɛntə 'ʀɛçnʊŋŋ 'bɪtə]

There seems to be a mistake on the bill.
Die Rechnung scheint mir nicht zu stimmen.
[di 'ʀɛçnʊŋ ʃaɪnt miɐ nɪçt tsʊ 'ʃtɪmm]

I didn't have that. I had ...
Das habe ich nicht gehabt. Ich hatte ...
[das 'ha:bə ɪç nɪçt gə'hapt ˀɪç 'hatə ...]

Did you enjoy your meal?
Hat es geschmeckt? [hat ˀɛs gə'ʃmɛkt]

The food was excellent.
Das Essen war ausgezeichnet. [das ˀɛsn va: ˀaʊsgə'tsaɪçnət]

That's for you.
Das ist für Sie. [das ɪst fyɐ 'zi:]

Keep the change.
(Es) Stimmt so. [(ˀəs) 'ʃtɪmt zo:]

> Drinks will be included on the bill with food. A service charge
> of 10% is included and it is customary to round up the total
> by about 10%.

Zum Weißen Adler – Meeting People

After arriving at the airport or driving through downtown, you may be wondering what became of the German-speaking Old World. To find that and real-time natives, head to the nearest *Gasthaus*. They usually have a name beginning with *zum* or *zur: Zum Weißen Adler* – at the white eagle, *Zum Roten Ochsen* – at the red ox, or *Zur Post* – at the post office. The *Gasthaus* was traditionally an inn for travelers and anyone else looking for a place to eat or sleep. They also became good places to drink beer or wine, meet people, and socialize. This they have remained to the present day.

Even if they appear often quite reserved, Germans, Austrians, and the Swiss pride themselves on being open and willing to exchange ideas. Furthermore, in any regular eating-and-drinking establishment any seat not taken is yours to sit down in for the asking: *„Ist hier noch frei?"* You can now strike up a conversation by asking about tomorrow's weather, satisfaction with the government, or what happened today in soccer. Sitting together with strangers is normal, unless you run into a couple who insist on being by themselves.

Don't be turned off if there aren't cuckoo clocks and alpine horns hanging from every wall. Some of these places can be very simple in decoration. There'll always be a small bar with beer on tap and dozens of bottles of schnapps and other forms of liquor above and below the bar. Somewhere not far away you'll also see that quintessence of Germanic drinking culture, the *Stammtisch* regulars' table. That means a no-go area for any stranger.

Good evening.
Guten Abend! ['guːtn ʔaːbmt]

Can I sit here?
Ist hier noch frei? [ʔɪst hiɐ nɔx fʀaɪ]

Where are you from?
Wo kommen Sie her? [voː kɔmm zi 'heɐ]

I come from the States.
Ich komme aus den USA.
[ʔɪç kɔmə aʊs den uːɛsʔaː]

What'll it be?
Was darf es sein? [vas da:f əs zaɪn]

I'd like a beer/a wine/a schnapps.
Ich hätte gern ein Bier/einen Wein/ einen Schnaps.
[ˀɪç ˈhɛtə gɛɛn ˀaɪn biɐ/ˀaɪnn vaɪn/ˀaɪnn ʃnaps]

What flavor?
Welche Geschmacksrichtung? [ˈvɛlçə gəˈʃmaksˌʀɪçtʊŋ]

A pint of dark beer.
Ein großes Dunkles. [ˀaɪn ˈgʀoːsəs dʊŋkləs]

A half-pint of light beer.
Ein kleines Helles. [ˀaɪn ˈklaɪnəs ˈhɛləs]

Would you like another drink?
Möchten Sie noch etwas trinken? [ˈmœçtn zi nɔx ˀɛtvas ˈtʀɪŋkŋ]

Same again.
Das Gleiche noch einmal. [das ˈglaɪçə nɔx ˀaɪnmaːl]

Here's to your health!
Zum Wohl! [tsʊm voːl]

Cheers!
Prost! [pʀoːst]

What do you drink where you're from?
Was trinkt man bei Ihnen zu Hause?
[vas ˈtʀɪŋkt man baɪ ˀiːnn tsʊ haʊzə]

Did you see that game on TV between ... and ...?
Haben Sie das Spiel im Fernsehen zwischen ... und ... gesehen?
[ˈhaːbm zi das ʃpiːl ˀɪm ˈfɛɐnzeːn ˈtsvɪʃn ... ˀʊnt ... gəˈzeːn]

What's your opinion of ...?
Was halten Sie von ...? [vas ˈhaltn zi fɔn]

I don't understand politics. I only pay taxes.
Ich verstehe nichts von Politik. Ich zahle nur Steuern.
[ˀɪç fɛˈʃteː nɪçts fɔn pɔliˈtiːk ˀɪç ˈtsaːlə nuɐ ˈʃtɔjen]

I'd like the check, please.
Die Rechnung, bitte. [di ˈʀɛçnʊŋ ˈbɪtə]

This round is on me.
Diese Runde übernehme ich. [ˈdiːzə ˈʀʊndə ˀybɐˈneːmə ˀɪç]

➤ also Groceries

alcohol-free	alkoholfrei [ˀalkoˈhoːlfʀaɪ]
appetizer	die Vorspeise [di ˈfoɐʃpaɪzə]
ashtray	der Aschenbecher [dɐ ˀaʃnbɛçɐ]
bone	der Knochen [dɐ knɔxn]
bowl	die Schüssel [di ʃʏsl]
breakfast	das Frühstück [das ˈfʀyːʃtʏk]

children's portion	der Kinderteller [dɐ ˈkɪndɛtɛlɐ]
cook	der Koch [dɐ kɔx]
corkscrew	der Korkenzieher [dɐ ˈkɔɐkntsiːɐ]
course	der Gang [dɐ gaŋ]
cover (setting)	das Gedeck [das gəˈdɛk]
cup	die Tasse [di ˈtasə]
cutlery	das Besteck [das bəˈʃtɛk]
dessert	der Nachtisch [dɐ ˈnaːxtɪʃ]
diabetic	diabetisch [diaˈbeːtɪʃ]
diabetic (person)	der Diabetiker/die Diabetikerin [dɐ diaˈbeːtɪkɐ/dɪ diaˈbeːtɪkərɪn]
diet	die Schonkost [di ˈʃoːnkɔst]
dinner	das Abendessen [das ˈʔaːbmtˀɛsn]
dish	das Gericht [das gəˈrɪçt]
dish of the day	das Tagesgericht [das ˈtaːgəsgərɪçt]
dressing	das Dressing [das ˈdrɛsɪŋ]
drink	das Getränk [das gəˈtrɛŋk]
fishbone	die Gräte [di ˈgrɛːtə]
fork	die Gabel [di ˈgaːbl]
glass	das Glas [das glaːs]
gourmet restaurant	das Feinschmeckerlokal [das ˈfaɪnʃmɛkɐloˌkaːl]
gravy	die (Braten)Soße [di (ˈbraːtn)zoːsə]
grill	der Rost [dɐ rɔst]
hard-boiled	hart gekocht [ˈhaːt gəˌkɔxt]
homemade	hausgemacht [ˈhaʊsgəmaxt]
hors d'œuvre	die Vorspeise [di ˈfoɐʃpaɪzə]
hot (spicy)	scharf [ʃaːf]
hot (temperature)	heiß [haɪs]
hungry	hungrig [ˈhuŋrɪç]
ketchup	das Ketschup [das ˈkɛtʃap]
knife	das Messer [das ˈmɛsɐ]
lunch	das Mittagessen [das ˈmɪtakˌʔɛsn]
main course	die Hauptspeise [di ˈhaʊptʃpaɪzə]
mayonnaise	die Mayonnaise [di majoˈnɛːzə]
menu	die Speisekarte [di ˈʃpaɪzəkaːtə]
mustard	der Senf [dɐ zɛnf (zɛmf)]
napkin	die Serviette [di zɛˈvjɛtə]
oil	das Öl [das ˀøːl]
on draft	vom Fass [fɔm fas]
on tap	vom Fass [fɔm fas]
order	die Bestellung [di bəˈʃtɛlʊŋ]
pepper	der Pfeffer [dɐ ˈpfɛfɐ]
plate	der Teller [dɐ ˈtɛlɐ]
portion	die Portion [di pɔˈtsjoːn]
salad bar	das Salatbüfett [das zaˈlaːtbʏˈfeː]
salt	das Salz [das zalts]

sauce	die Soße [di 'zo:sə]
saucer	die Untertasse [di ʔʊntɐtasə]
to season	würzen [vvɐtsn]
seasoning	das Gewürz [das gə'vvɐts]
set meal	das Menü [das me'ny:]
slice	die Scheibe [di 'ʃaɪbə]
soup	die Suppe [di 'zʊpə]
soup plate	der Suppenteller [dɐ 'zʊpmtɛlɐ]
special (of the day)	das Tagesmenü [das 'ta:gəsme,ny:]
specialty	die Spezialität [di ʃpetsjali'tɛ:t]
spice	das Gewürz [das gə'vvɐts]
spoon	der Löffel [dɐ lœfl]
stain	der Fleck [dɐ flɛk]
starter	die Vorspeise [di 'foɐʃpaɪzə]
straw	der Strohhalm [dɐ 'ʃtʀo:halm]
sugar	der Zucker [dɐ 'tsʊkɐ]
sweet	der Nachtisch [dɐ 'na:xtɪʃ]
sweetener	der Süßstoff [dɐ 'zy:ʃtɔf]
tablecloth	das Tischtuch [das 'tɪʃtu:x]
teaspoon	der Teelöffel [dɐ 'te:lœfl]
tip	das Trinkgeld [das 'tʀɪŋkgɛlt]
toothpick	der Zahnstocher [dɐ 'tsa:nʃtɔxɐ]
tumbler	das Wasserglas [das 'vasɐgla:s]
vegetarian	vegetarisch [vegə'ta:ʀɪʃ]
vegetarian (person)	der Vegetarier/die Vegetarierin [dɐ vegə'ta:ʀɪɐ/dɪ vegə'ta:ʀɪəʀɪn]
vinegar	der Essig [dɐ ʔɛsɪç]
waiter/waitress	der Kellner/die Kellnerin [dɐ 'kɛlnɐ/di 'kɛlnəʀɪn]
water	das Wasser [das 'vasɐ]
water glass	das Wasserglas [das 'vasɐgla:s]
wineglass	das Weinglas [das 'vaɪngla:s]

Preparation/Cooking Style

au gratin	überbacken [ʔybɐˈbakŋ]
baked	gebacken [gəˈbakn̩]
boiled	gekocht [gəˈkɔxt]
braised	geschmort [gəˈʃmoɐt]
broiled	gegrillt [gəˈgʀɪlt]
cooked/done	gar [gaː]
fried	in der Pfanne gebraten [ʔɪn dɐ ˈpfanə gəˈbʀaːtn̩]
grilled	vom Grill [fɔm ˈgʀɪl]
hot (spicy)	scharf [ʃaːf]
juicy	saftig [ˈzaftɪç]
lean	mager [ˈmaːgɐ]
raw	roh [ʀoː]
roasted	gebraten [gəˈbʀaːtn̩]
smoked	geräuchert [gəˈʀɔɪçɐt]
soft-boiled	weich gekocht [ˈvaɪç gəˌkɔxt]
sour	sauer [ˈzaʊɐ]
spit-roasted	am Spieß gebraten [am ʃpiːs gəˈbʀaːtn̩]
steamed	gedämpft [gəˈdɛmpft], gedünstet [gəˈdʏnstət]
stuffed	gefüllt [gəˈfʏlt]
sweet	süß [zyːs]
tender	zart [tsaːt]
tough	zäh [tsɛː]
well-done	durchgebraten [ˈdʊɐçgəbʀaːtn̩]

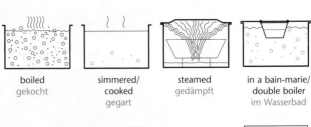

boiled
gekocht

simmered/ cooked
gegart

steamed
gedämpft

in a bain-marie/ double boiler
im Wasserbad

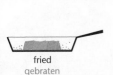

fried
gebraten

deep-fried
frittiert

grilled
gegrillt

EATING AND DRINKING

garlic
der Knoblauch
[d ˈkno:blaʊx]

onion
die Zwiebel
[di tsvi:bl]

dill
der Dill [d dɪl]

bay leaves
die Lorbeerblätter *n pl*
[di ˈlɔ be ˌblɛt]

rosemary
der Rosmarin
[d ˈʀo:smaʀi:n]

marjoram
der Majoran
[d ˈma:joʀa:n]

cilantro/coriander
der Koriander
[d ko:ri:ˈandə]

parsley
die Petersilie
[di pe:t ˈzi:ljə]

basil
das Basilikum
[das baˈzi:lɪkʊm]

nutmeg die Muskatnuss [di mʊsˈkaːtnʊs]

chili pepper
der Chili
[dɐ ˈtʃɪli]

hot pepper
die Peperoni
[di pɛpəˈroːni]

chives
der Schnittlauch
[dɐ ˈʃnɪtlaʊx]

sage
der Salbei
[dɐ ˈzalbaɪ]

chervil
der Kerbel
[dɐ ˈkɛɐbl]

thyme
der Thymian
[dɐ ˈtyːmiaːn]

savory
das Bohnenkraut
[das ˈboːnnkʁaʊt]

lovage
der/das Liebstöckl
[dɐ /das ˈliːpʃtˌkl]

I'd like ...
Ich hätte gern ...

I'd like ...
Ich hätte gern ...

Speisekarte   Menu

Frühstück   Breakfast

Schwarzer Kaffee [ʃvaːtsɐ ˈkafeː] .... black coffee
Kaffee mit Milch [ˈkafe mɪt ˈmɪlç] .... coffee with milk
Koffeinfreier Kaffee .... decaffeinated coffee
[kɔfeˈʔiːnfʀaɪɐ ˈkafeː]
Tee mit Milch/Zitrone .... tea with milk/lemon
[teː mɪt ˈmɪlç/tsɪˈtʀoːnə]
Schokolade [ʃokoˈlaːdə] .... hot chocolate
Fruchtsaft [ˈfʀʊxtzaft] .... fruit juice
Weiches Ei [vaɪçəs ʔaɪ] .... soft-boiled egg
Rühreier [ˈʀyːʔaɪɐ] .... scrambled eggs
Brot/Brötchen [bʀoːt/bʀøːtçn] .... bread/rolls
Toast [toːst] .... toast
Butter [ˈbʊtɐ] .... butter
Honig [ˈhoːnɪç] .... honey
Marmelade [mamәˈlaːdə] .... jam
Orangenmarmelade .... orange marmalade
[oˈʀaŋznmaməˌlaːdə]
Müsli [ˈmyːsli] .... muesli
Jogurt [ˈjoːgʊɐt] .... yogurt
Obst [ʔoːpst] .... fruit

> Most hotels have a breakfast buffet with a large selection of cheese, sausage, fruit, breakfast cereal, and juice. Bacon-and-eggs style breakfast can only be found in large international hotels. Smaller hotels may still offer "continental breakfast" – bread rolls, cheese, and jam. Tea is usually served with a slice of lemon; if you take milk, ask for it.

Vorspeisen   Hors d'œuvres

Austern f pl [ˈʔaʊstɐn] .... oysters
Avocado [ʔavoˈkaːdo] .... avocado
Garnelencocktail [gaˈneːlnˌkɔktɛɪl] .... prawn cocktail
Hummer [ˈhʊmɐ] .... lobster
Krabbencocktail [ˈkʀabmˌkɔktɛɪl] ..... shrimp cocktail
Melone mit Schinken .... melon with ham
[meˈloːnə mɪt ˈʃɪŋkŋ]
Muscheln f pl [mʊʃln] .... mussels
Räucherlachs [ˈʀɔɪçɐlaks] .... smoked salmon

Schinken [ˈʃɪŋkn̩] . . . . ham
Weinbergschnecken [ˈvaɪnbɛɐkʃnɛkn̩] . . snails in garlic butter

Salate   Salads

Bohnensalat [ˈboːnnzalaːt] . . . . bean salad
Gemischter Salat [gəˈmɪʃtɐ zaˈlaːt] . . . . . mixed salad
Gurkensalat [ˈgʊɐknzalaːt] . . . . cucumber salad
Karottensalat [kaˈrɔtnzalaːt] . . . . carrot salad
Kartoffelsalat [kaˈtɔflzalaːt] . . . . potato salad
Krautsalat [ˈkraʊtzalaːt] . . . . coleslaw

Suppen   Soups

Bouillon [bʊlˈjɔn] . . . . clear soup/consommé
Champignoncremesuppe . . . . cream of mushroom soup
[ˈʃampɪnjɔn͵krɛːmzʊpə]
Erbsensuppe [ˈʔɛɐpsn͵zʊpə] . . . . pea soup
Fleischbrühe [ˈflaɪʃbryə] . . . . clear soup/consommé
Französische Zwiebelsuppe . . . . French onion soup
[franˈtsøːzɪʃə ˈtsviːblzʊpə]
Gemüsesuppe [gəˈmyːzəzʊpə] . . . . vegetable soup
Gulaschsuppe [ˈgʊlaʃzʊpə] . . . . goulash soup
Hühnersuppe [ˈhyːnɐzʊpə] . . . . chicken soup
Ochsenschwanzsuppe . . . . oxtail soup
[ˈʔɔksnʃvants͵zʊpə]
Spargelcremesuppe . . . . cream of asparagus soup
[ˈʃpaːglkrɛːm͵zʊpə]
Tomatencremesuppe . . . . cream of tomato soup
[toˈmaːtnkrɛːm͵zʊpə]

Eierspeisen   Egg Dishes

(Käse-/Champignon-/Tomaten-) . . . . . . (cheese/mushroom/tomato)
Omelett [(ˈkɛːzə-/ˈʃampɪnjɔn/   omelet
toˈmaːtn)͵ʔɔmlɛt]
Rühreier [ˈryɐʔaɪɐ] . . . . scrambled eggs
Spiegeleier [ˈʃpiːglʔaɪɐ] . . . . fried eggs
Spiegeleier mit Schinken . . . . ham and eggs
[ˈʃpiːglʔaɪɐ mɪt ˈʃɪŋkn̩]
Verlorene Eier [vɛˈloːrənə ʔaɪɐ] . . . . poached eggs

Fisch	Fish
Aal [ʔaːl]	eel
Austern [ˈʔaʊstɐn]	oysters
Bückling [ˈbʏklɪŋ]	smoked herring
Forelle [foˈʀɛlə]	trout
Garnelen [gaˈneːln]	prawns
Hummer [ˈhʊmɐ]	lobster
Kabeljau [ˈkaːbljaʊ]	cod
Karpfen [kaːpfn]	carp
Krabben [kʀabm]	shrimp
Krebs [kʀeːps]	crab
Lachs [laks]	salmon
Makrele [maˈkʀeːlə]	mackerel
Matjesfilet [ˈmatçəsfɪˌleː]	salted young herring
Muscheln [mʊʃln]	mussels
Räucherhering [ˈʀɔɪçəheːʀɪŋ],	smoked herring
Scholle [ˈʃɔlə]	plaice
Schwertfisch [ʃveːtfɪʃ]	swordfish
Seezunge [ˈzeːtsʊŋə]	sole
T(h)unfisch [ˈtuːnfɪʃ]	tuna
Tintenfisch [ˈtɪntnfɪʃ]	squid

Geflügel	Poultry
Ente [ˈʔɛntə]	duck
Fasan [faˈzaːn]	pheasant
Gans [gans]	goose
Hähnchen/Huhn [ˈhɛːnçn/huːn]	chicken
Pute [ˈpuːtə]	turkey
Rebhuhn [ˈʀeːphuːn]	partridge
Truthahn [ˈtʀuːthaːn]	turkey
Wachtel [vaxtl]	quail

Fleisch	Meat
Filet(steak) [fɪˈleːsteːk]	filet (steak)
Frikadellen [fʀɪkaˈdɛln]	meatballs
Hackfleisch (vom Rind) [ˈhakflaɪʃ (fɔm ʀɪnt)]	ground beef
Hamburger [ˈhambʊɐgɐ]	hamburger
Hirsch [hɪɐʃ]	venison (red deer)
Kalbfleisch [ˈkalpflaɪʃ]	veal
Kaninchen [kaˈniːnçn]	rabbit
Kotelett [ˈkɔtlɛt]	chop/cutlet

EATING AND DRINKING

113

Kutteln [kʊtln]	tripe
Lamm [lam]	lamb
Leber ['leːbɐ]	liver
Nieren ['niːʀən]	kidneys
Reh [ʀeː]	venison (roe deer)
Rindfleisch ['ʀɪntflaɪʃ]	beef
Rumpsteak ['ʀʊmpsteːk]	rump steak
Schinken [ʃɪŋkn]	ham
Schweinefleisch ['ʃvaɪnəflaɪʃ]	pork
Spanferkel ['ʃpaːnfɛɛkl]	suckling pig
Wildschwein ['viltʃvaɪn]	wild boar
Würstchen ['vvɛstçn]	sausages
Zunge ['tsʊŋə]	tongue

Gemüse — Vegetables

Blumenkohl ['bluːmmkoːl]	cauliflower
Bratkartoffeln ['bʀaːtkaˌtɔfln]	fried potatoes
Brokkoli ['bʀɔkoli]	broccoli
Champignons ['ʃampɪnjɔns]	mushrooms
Chicorée ['ʃɪkoʀe]	chicory
Erbsen [ˀɛɐpsn]	peas
Fenchel [fɛnçl]	fennel
Folienkartoffel ['foːljənkaˌtɔfl]	baked potato
Frühlingszwiebeln ['fʀyːlɪŋstsviːbln]	green onions
grüne Bohnen [ˌgʀyːnə 'boːnn]	French beans
Gurke ['gʊekə]	cucumber
Karotten [ka'ʀɔtn]	carrots
Kartoffelbrei [ka'tɔflbʀaɪ]	mashed potato(es)
Kartoffeln [ka'tɔfln]	potatoes
Knoblauch ['knoːblaʊx]	garlic
Kresse ['kʀɛsə]	cress
Kürbis ['kvebɪs]	pumpkin
Lauch [laʊx]	leek
Maiskolben ['maiskɔlbm]	corn-on-the-cob
Möhren ['møːʀən]	carrots
Ofenkartoffel [ˀoːfnkaˌtɔfl]	baked potato
Paprikaschoten ['papʀɪkaˌʃoːtn]	peppers
Pommes frites [pɔm'fʀɪts]	French fries
Rosenkohl ['ʀoːznkoːl]	Brussels sprouts
Rösti ['ʀœsti]	hash brown potatoes
Rote Bete [ˌʀoːtə 'beːtə]	beets
Rotkohl ['ʀoːtkoːl]	red cabbage
Salzkartoffeln ['zaltskaˌtɔfln]	boiled potatoes
Schwenkkartoffeln ['ʃvɛŋkaˌtɔfln]	sauté(ed) potatoes
Spargel [ʃpaːgl]	asparagus

Spinat [ʃpɪ'na:t]	spinach
Stangensellerie ['ʃtaŋŋˌzɛləʀi]	celery
Tomaten [to'ma:tn]	tomatoes
Weißkohl ['vaɪsko:l]	cabbage
Zucchini [tsʊ'ki:ni]	zucchini
Zwiebeln [tsvi:bln]	onions

Some vegetable names vary from region to region, for example *Karfiol* ("cauliflower" in Austria) and *Erdäpfel* ("potatoes" in Austria and Switzerland); "carrots" are *Möhren* and *Mohrrüben* in northern Germany, and *Karotten* elsewhere.

Käse   Cheese

Blauschimmelkäse ['blaʊʃɪmlˌkɛ:zə]	blue cheese
Frischkäse ['fʀɪʃkɛ:zə]	cream cheese
Hüttenkäse ['hʏtnkɛ:zə]	cottage cheese
Schafskäse ['ʃa:fskɛ:zə]	sheep's milk cheese
Ziegenkäse ['tsi:gŋkɛ:zə]	goat's milk cheese

The German-speaking countries are also becoming important producers of cheese. Typical hard cheeses are *Emmentaler* or, more tasty, *Appenzeller, Greyerzer (Gruyère),* and *Bergkäse.* Particularly pungent are *Harzer, Limburger,* and *Handkäse.* Soft cheeses from France (*Camembert, Brie*) have become very popular and are also being produced domestically. A traditional dish of cheese is *Handkäse mit Musik,* served with caraway seeds, onions, and vinegar.

Nachtisch / Obst   Dessert / Fruit

Ananas ['ʔananas]	pineapple
Birnen [bɪʀnn]	pears
Eis [ʔaɪs]	ice cream
Eisbecher ['ʔaɪsbɛçɐ]	sundae
Erdbeeren ['ʔeɐtbeːʀən]	strawberries
Gebäck [gə'bɛk]	pastries
Kirschen [kɪʀʃn]	cherries
Kompott [kɔm'pɔt]	stewed fruit
Obstsalat ['ʔo:pstzaˌla:t]	fruit salad
Pfannkuchen ['pfanku:xn]	pancakes
Pfirsiche ['pfɪʀzɪçə]	peaches

Pflaumen [pflaʊmm]	plums
Rhabarber [ʀaˈbaːbɐ]	rhubarb
Schlagsahne [ˈʃlaːkzaːnə];	whipped cream
(Austria) Schlagobers [ˈʃlagobɐs]	
Stachelbeeren [ˈʃtaxlbeːʀən]	gooseberries
Vanillesoße [vaˈnɪlzoːsə]	custard

Germany, Switzerland, and Austria are a cake-eater's paradise. The range of cakes and pastries is overwhelming. As well as different types of fruit cakes such as *Apfelkuchen* and *Käsekuchen* (cheesecake), there are many *Torten* (with layers of cream), e.g. *Schwarzwälder Kirschtorte* (Black Forest Cake). People like to go to a Café for their cake, or buy some to bring back home for coffee. In a restaurant, on the other hand, the choice of desserts may seem limited – ice cream or fruit salad, but also typical desserts, such as *Rote Grütze,* stewed red summer fruit served cold with cream or custard.

Getränke — Beverages

Alkoholische Getränke — Alcoholic Drinks

Apfelwein [ˈʔapflvaɪn]	cider
Bier [biɐ]	beer

There are many different types of beer, and the names can vary, depending on the region. The most popular ones are *Export* or *Helles* (lager), *Pils* (a strong lager), *Alt* or *Bockbier* (dark beer) and *Weizenbier* (a light summer beer made from wheat). *Radler* or *Alsterwasser* is beer diluted with lemon soda.

Wein [vaɪn]	wine
Champagner [ʃamˈpanjɐ]	champagne (from France)
Sekt [zɛkt]	champagne-style wine
	(from outside France)
leicht [laɪçt]	light
lieblich [ˈliːplɪç]	sweet
rosé [ʀoˈzeː]	rosé
rot [ʀoːt]	red

trocken [tʀɔkn̩]	dry
weiß [vaɪs]	white
Weinschorle sauer ['vaɪnʃɔːlə 'zaʊɐ]	wine diluted with mineral water
Weinschorle süß ['vaɪnʃɔːlə 'zyːs]	wine diluted with lemon soda
Weinbrand ['vaɪnbʀant]	brandy
Most [mɔst]	cider
Kognak ['kɔnjak]	cognac
Likör [lɪ'køɐ]	liqueur
Gin [dʒɪn]	gin
Rum [ʀʊm]	rum
Whisky ['vɪski]	whiskey
Wodka ['vɔtka]	vodka

After a meal you may be offered a *Schnaps*, a spirit often distilled from pears, cherries, or plums. A sweeter variation is *Obstler,* a mixed-fruit schnapps.

Germany is famous for its white wines. The red wines and rosé tend to be light. There are two basic wine categories: *Tafelwein* (table wine) and *Qualitätswein* (quality wine). *QbA (Qualitätswein besonderer Anbaugebiete)* means that the wine comes from one of eleven special regions. Further designations are: *Kabinett* (premium quality), *Spätlese* (late harvest, with a richer flavor), *Auslese* (from selected grapes). A rare specialty is *Eiswein* (ice wine), made from frost-bitten grapes.

Alkoholfreie Getränke	**Alcohol-free Beverages**
Alkoholfreies Bier ['ʔalko'hoːlfʀaɪəs biɐ]	alcohol-free beer
Apfelsaft ['ʔapflzaft]	apple juice

Apple juice is often drunk diluted with mineral water *(eine Apfelsaftschorle* or *ein gespritzter Apfelsaft)*. Another popular drink is *Spezi* (a mixture of cola and orange). American children will be disappointed that lemonade as in the US is unknown.

Cola ['koːla]	Coke
Eistee ['ʔaɪsteː]	iced tea
Fruchtsaft ['fʀʊxtzaft]	fruit juice

Limonade [lɪmoˈnaːdə]	soda pop
Mineralwasser [mɪnəˈʀaːlvasə]	mineral water
mit Kohlensäure [mɪt ˈkoːlnzɔɪʀə]	carbonated
ohne Kohlensäure [ˈʔoːnə ˈkoːlnzɔɪʀə]	still
Orangensaft [ʔoˈʀaŋʒnzaft/ʔoˈʀaːʒnzaft]	orange juice
Tomatensaft [toˈmaːtnzaft]	tomato juice
Tonic [ˈtɔnɪk]	tonic water
Eiskaffee [ˈʔaɪskafeː]	iced coffee
Früchtetee [ˈfʀʏçtəteː]	fruit tea
(eine Tasse) Kaffee [(ˈʔaɪnə ˈtasə) kaˈfeː]	(a cup of) coffee
Koffeinfreier Kaffee [kɔfeˈʔiːnfʀaɪɐ kaˈfeː]	decaffeinated coffee
Kräutertee [ˈkʀɔɪtəteː]	herbal tea
Milch [mɪlç]	milk
Pfefferminztee [ˈpfɛfɛmɪntsteː]	peppermint tea
Sahne [ˈzaːnə]	cream
(eine Tasse/ein Glas) Tee [(ˈʔaɪnə ˈtasə/ˈʔaɪn glaːs) ˈteː]	(a cup/glass of) tea

Coffee is usually served with evaporated milk, normal milk, or cream. In Germany, when sitting outside, often you can only order *ein Kännchen,* a small pot for two cups. *Schümli* is Swiss-style frothy coffee. Italian coffees such as *Cappuccino* and *Espresso* are very popular. Austrian coffee houses offer a wide range of specialties such as *Melange* (milk coffee), *Schwarzer* (black coffee), or *kleiner Brauner* (small cup of coffee with milk or cream).

Österreichische Spezialitäten
Austrian Specialties

G'spritzter [ˈkʃpʀɪtstɐ]	1/8 liter of wine diluted with the same amount of mineral water
Heuriger [ˈhɔɪʀɪgɐ]	young wine less than a year old
Backhendl [ˈbakhendl]	whole roast chicken
Brettljause [ˈbʀɛtljaʊzə]	a selection of cheeses and sliced cold meat

Cevapcici [tʃeˈvaptʃitʃi]	spicy, grilled ground meat sausages
Dampfnudeln [ˈdampfnuːdln]	yeast dumplings often eaten with custard
Erdäpfel [ˈʔeɐdepfl]	potatoes
Faschiertes [faˈʃiɐtəs]	ground meat
Frittatensuppe [frɪˈdaːtnsupːe]	clear soup with strips of pancake
Germknödel [ˈgɛɐmkneːdl]	a yeast dumpling filled with plum jam
Geselchtes [ˈkselçtes)]	smoked meat
Haxe [haksə]	pork knuckles
Jause [ˈjauzə]	afternoon snack
Kaiserschmarren [ˈkɛːzeʃmoɐn]	Austrian pancakes with almonds and raisins
Kren [kʀeːn]	horseradish
Marillen [maˈʀɪln]	apricots
Nockerl [ˈnɔkel]	dumpling
Schlagobers [ˈʃlagobɛs]	whipped cream
Palatschinken [ˈpalatʃɪŋkn]	pancakes
Paradeiser [paʀaˈdaɪzə]	tomatoes
Sachertorte [ˈzaxɛtɔɐtə]	rich chocolate cake with a thin layer of apricot jam
Schwammerl [ˈʃvaməl]	mushrooms
Semmel [semːl]	bread roll
Surstelze [ˈsuːrstəltsə]	pork knuckle
Tafelspitz [ˈtaːflʃpɪts]	boiled beef served with horseradish
Topfen [ˈtɔpfn]	*Quark:* thick, creamy dairy product
Topfenstrudel [ˈtɔpfnʃtʀuːdl]	similar to apple strudel, but filled with *Topfen*

Schweizer Spezialitäten
Swiss Specialties

Café crème [kaˈfe: ˈkʀɛːm]	coffee with cream
Schale [ˈʃaːlə]	coffee with milk
Berner Platte [ˈbærnər ˈplatːe]	platter with different kinds of meat, boiled tongue, sausages, and beans
Bündner Fleisch [ˈbyndnər flaɪʃ]	paper-thin slices of air-dried beef
Bürli [ˈbyrli]	bread rolls
Fladen [flaːdn]	cake

Fondue [fɔn'dy:]	small pieces of filet of pork/beef on skewers dipped in hot oil, served with various sauces
Glacé [gla'se:]	ice cream
Kabis ['xabis)]	cabbage
Käsefondue ['kɛzəfɔndy:]	cheese fondue: hot melted cheese into which pieces of bread are dipped
Raclette ['raxlet)]	slices of melted raclette cheese served with potatoes
Rahm [ʀaːm]	whipped cream
Rösti ['røʃti)]	hash brown potatoes
Rübli ['ʀyːbli]	carrots
Züricher Rahmgeschnetzeltes ['tsyrxər 'ʀaːmgʃnɛtsltəs]	strips of veal in a creamy wine and mushroom sauce

Sightseeing and Excursions

Tourists love it here

The German-speaking countries are in many ways a tourist's dream. The countries are filled with old, romantic castles and other wonders of bygone days; the countryside is very pretty and remarkably varied; there is an abundance of cultural attractions such as festivals and concerts. Connecting all of this is an excellent system of roads and public transportation. Only the weather can be somewhat disappointing at times. Tourist high-season is the summer, of course. If you come earlier, the crowds of tourists will be smaller, but the weather more unpredictable. The crowds also get smaller starting in September, and the weather is usually quite good on into October – but the days will be shorter.

For information about interesting sights, festivals, and events follow the L-sign to the *Fremdenverkehrsamt* (tourist office). There is one in nearly every town. Before you leave, you can also check ahead by looking at a city's web page. Frankfurt, for example, is {www.frankfurt.de}.

Tourist Information

Where's the tourist office?
Wo ist das Fremdenverkehrsamt? [vo: ʔɪst das frɛmdnfɐˈkeɐsʔamt]

I'd like a map of ..., please.
Ich hätte gern einen Stadtplan von ...
[ˈɪç ˈhɛtə gɛɐn ʔaɪnn ˈʃtatplaːn fɔn]

Do you have a calendar of events for this week?
Haben Sie einen Veranstaltungskalender für diese Woche?
[haːbm zi ʔaɪnn fɐˈʔanʃtaltʊŋskaˌlɛndɐ fyɐ ˈdiːzə ˈvɔxə]

Are there sightseeing tours of the town?
Gibt es Stadtrundfahrten? [gɪpt əs ˈʃtatʀʊntfaːtn]

Cultural Attractions

Opening Hours, Guided Tours, Admission

Can you tell me what special attractions there are here?
Können Sie mir bitte sagen, welche Sehenswürdigkeiten es hier gibt? [kœnn zi miɐ ˈbɪtə zaːgn ˈvɛlçə ˈzeːnsvʏɐdɪçkaɪtn əs hiɐ gɪpt]

You really must visit ...
Sie müssen unbedingt ... besichtigen.
[zi mʏsn ˈʔʊnbədɪŋt ... bəˈzɪçtɪgn]

When's the museum open?
Wann ist das Museum geöffnet? ['van ɪst das muˈzeʊm gəˈʔœfnət]

Most museums and art galleries are closed on Mondays.

When does the tour start?
Wann beginnt die Führung? [van bəˈgɪnt di ˈfyːʀʊŋ]

Is there a tour in English, too?
Gibt es auch eine Führung auf Englisch?
[gɪpt əs aʊx ˈʔaɪnə ˈfyːʀʊŋ ˈʔaʊf ˈʔɛŋlɪʃ]

Two tickets, please.
Zwei Eintrittskarten, bitte! [tsvaɪ ˈʔaɪntʀɪtskaːtn ˈbɪtə]

Two adults and one child.
Zwei Erwachsene und ein Kind. [tsvaɪ ˈʔeˈvaksənə ˈʔʊnt ˈʔaɪn ˈkɪnt]

Are there discounts for ...
Gibt es Ermäßigungen für ... [gɪpt əs ˈʔeˈmɛːsɪgʊŋ fyɐ]

  children?
  Kinder? [ˈkɪndɐ]
  students?
  Studenten? [ʃtʊˈdɛntn]
  senior citizens?
  Senioren? [zenˈjoːʀən]
  groups?
  Gruppen? [ˈgrʊpm]

Is there an exhibition catalog?
Gibt es einen Katalog zur Ausstellung?
[gɪpt əs aɪnn kataˈloːk tsʊɐ ˈʔaʊʃtɛlʊŋ]

What? Who? When?

Is this/that ...?
Ist das ...? [ˈʔɪst das]

When was the church built?
Wann wurde die Kirche erbaut? ['van ˌvʊɐdə diː ˈkɪɐçə ˈʔeˈbaʊt]

When was this building restored?
Wann wurde dieses Gebäude restauriert?
[van ˌvʊɐdə ˈdiːzəs gəˈbɔɪdə ʀɛstaʊˈʀiet]

Who painted this picture?
Von wem ist dieses Bild? [fɔn veːm ˈʔɪst ˈdiːzəs bɪlt]

Do you have a poster of this picture?
Haben Sie das Bild als Poster? [ˈhaːbm ziː das bɪlt ˈʔals ˈpoːstɐ]

Cultural Attractions

alley	die Gasse [di ˈgasə]
art	die Kunst [di kʊnst]
city center	das Stadtzentrum [das ˈʃtattsɛntʁʊm]
district	der Stadtteil [dɐ ˈʃtataɪl]
downtown	das Stadtzentrum [ˈʃtattsɛntʁʊm]
emblem	das Wahrzeichen [das ˈvaːtsaɪçn]
emperor/empress	der Kaiser/die Kaiserin [dɐ ˈkaɪzɐ/di ˈkaɪzəʁɪn]
findings	die Funde *m pl* [di fʊndə]
folklore museum	das Volkskundemuseum [das ˈfɔlkskʊndəmuˌzeʊm]
guide	der Fremdenführer/die Fremdenführerin [dɐ ˈfʁɛmdnfyːʁɐ/ˈfʁɛmdnfyːʁəʁɪn]
guided tour	die Führung [di ˈfyːʁʊŋ]
history	die Geschichte [di gəˈʃɪçtə]
home town	die Geburtsstadt [di gəˈbʊɐtʃtat], die Heimatstadt [di ˈhaɪmaːtʃtat]
house	das Haus [das haʊs]
king	der König [dɐ ˈkøːnɪç]
lane	die Gasse [di ˈgasə]
market	der Markt [dɐ maːkt]
museum	das Museum [das muˈzeːʊm]
park	der Park [dɐ paːk]
pedestrian zone	die Fußgängerzone [di ˈfuːsgɛŋɐˌtsoːnə]
queen	die Königin [di ˈkøːnɪgɪn]
to reconstruct	rekonstruieren [ʁekɔnstʁʊˈʔiːʁən]
religion	die Religion [di ʁeliˈgjoːn]
remains	die Überreste *m pl* [di ˈʔyːbɐʁɛstə]
to restore	restaurieren [ʁɛstaʊˈʁiːʁən]
road	die Straße [di ˈʃtʁaːsə]
sights	die Sehenswürdigkeiten *f pl* [di ˈzeːnsvvɐdɪçkaɪtn]
sightseeing tour of the town/city	die Stadtrundfahrt [di ˈʃtatʁʊntfaːt]
street	die Straße [di ˈʃtʁaːsə]
suburb	der Vorort [dɐ ˈfoɐˀɔɐt]
symbol	das Wahrzeichen [das ˈvaːtsaɪçn]
tour	die Besichtigung [di bəˈzɪçtɪgʊŋ]

Architecture

abbey	die Abtei [di ʔapˈtaɪ]
altar	der Altar [dɐ ʔalˈtaː]
arch	der Bogen [dɐ ˈboːgn]
archaeology	die Archäologie [di ʔaˌçeoloˈgiː]
architect	Architekt/Architektin [ʔaːçɪˈtɛkt/ʔaːçɪˈtɛkt ɪn]

architecture	die Architektur [di ʔaːçitɛkˈtuɐ]
bay	der Erker [dɐ ˈʔɛɐkɐ]
bay window	das Erkerfenster [das ˈʔɛɐkɐfɛnstɐ]
bridge	die Brücke [di ˈbʀʏkə]
building	das Gebäude [das gəˈbɔɪdə]
castle (*fortress*)	die Burg [di buɐk]
castle (*palace*)	das Schloss [das ʃlɔs]
cathedral	die Kathedrale [di kateˈdʀaːlə]
ceiling	die Decke [di ˈdɛkə]
cemetery	der Friedhof [dɐ ˈfʀiːtoːf]
chapel	die Kapelle [di kaˈpɛlə]
church	die Kirche [di ˈkɪʀçə]
cloister	der Kreuzgang [dɐ ˈkʀɔɪtsgaŋ]
column	die Säule [di ˈzɔɪlə]
convent	das(Nonnen)Kloster [das (ˈnɔnn)ˌkloːstɐ]
covered market	die Markthalle [di ˈmaːkthalə]
crypt	die Krypta [di kʀʏpta]
dome	die Kuppel [di kʊpl]
excavations	die Ausgrabungen *f pl* [di ˈʔausgʀaːbuŋŋ]
façade	die Fassade [di faˈsaːdə]
fortress	die Festung [di ˈfɛstuŋ]
fountain	der (Spring)Brunnen [dɐ (ˈʃpʀɪŋ)bʀunn]
gable	der Giebel [dɐ giːbl]
gate	das Tor [das toɐ]
grave	das Grab [das gʀaːp]
graveyard	der Friedhof [dɐ ˈfʀiːtoːf]
inner courtyard	der Innenhof [dɐ ˈʔɪnnhoːf]
inscription	die Inschrift [di ˈʔɪnʃʀɪft]
mausoleum	das Mausoleum [das mauzoˈleum]
memorial	die Gedenkstätte [di gəˈdɛŋkʃtɛtə]
monastery	das (Mönchs)Kloster [das (ˈmœnçs)ˌkloːstɐ]
monument (*memorial edifice*)	das Denkmal [das ˈdɛŋkmaːl]
monument (*tomb*)	das Grabmal [ˈgʀaːbmaːl]
the old town	die Altstadt [di ˈʔaltʃtat]
opera	die Oper [di ˈʔoːpɐ]
palace	der Palast [dɐ paˈlast]
pilgrimage church	die Wallfahrtskirche [di ˈvalfaːtsˌkɪʀçə]
pillar	die Säule [di ˈzɔɪlə], der Pfeiler [dɐ ˈpfaɪlɐ]
portal	das Portal [das pɔ(ɐ)ˈtaːl]
pulpit	die Kanzel [di kantsl]
to rebuild	wieder aufbauen [viːdɐ ˈʔaufbauən]
roof	das Dach [das dax]
ruin	die Ruine [di ʀuˈʔiːnə]
square	der Platz [dɐ plats]

steeple	der Kirchturm [dɐ ˈkɪʁçtʊɐm]
temple	der Tempel [dɐ tɛmpl̩]
theatre	das Theater [das teˈʔaːtɐ]
tomb	das Grab [das gʁaːp]
tower	der Turm [dɐ tʊɐm]
town center	die Innenstadt [di ˈʔɪnnʃtat]
town hall	das Rathaus [das ˈʁaːthaʊs]
town walls	die Stadtmauern *f pl* [di ˈʃtatmaʊɐn]
treasure chamber	die Schatzkammer [di ˈʃatskamɐ]
triumphal arch	der Triumphbogen [dɐ tʁiˈʊmpfboːgn̩]
university	die Universität [di ʔunivɛɐziˈtɛːt]
vault(s)	das Gewölbe [das gəˈvœlbə]
wall (*inside partition of house*)	die Wand [di vant]
wall (*supportive structure*)	die Mauer [di ˈmaʊɐ]
window	das Fenster [das ˈfɛnstɐ]
wing	der Flügel [dɐ flyːgl̩]

Visual Arts

arts and crafts	das Kunstgewerbe [das ˈkʊnstɡəvɛɐbə]
bronze	die Bronze [di ˈbʁɔnsə]
carpet	der Teppich [dɐ ˈtɛpɪç]
ceramics	die Keramik [di keˈʁaːmɪk]
china	das Porzellan [das pɔɐtsəˈlaːn]
copperplate	der Kupferstich [dɐ ˈkʊpfɐʃtɪç]
copy	die Kopie [di koˈpiː]
cross	das Kreuz [das ˈkʁɔɪts]
crucifix	das Kruzifix [das ˈkʁʊtsifɪks]
drawing	die Zeichnung [di ˈtsaɪçnʊŋ]
etching	die Radierung [di ʁaˈdiːʁʊŋ]
exhibit	das Exponat [das ʔɛkspoˈnaːt]
exhibition	die Ausstellung [di ˈʔaʊʃtɛlʊŋ]
gallery	die Galerie [di galəˈʁiː]
glass painting	die Glasmalerei [di ˈglaːsmaːləˌʁaɪ]
gold work	die Goldschmiedekunst [di ˈgɔltʃmiːdəˌkʊnst]
graphic arts	die Grafik [di ˈgʁaːfɪk]
lithograph; lithography	die Lithografie [di litogʁaˈfiː]
model	das Modell [das moˈdɛl]
mosaic	das Mosaik [das mozaˈʔiːk]
nude (*painting*)	der Akt [dɐ ʔakt]
original (*version*)	das Original [das ʔɔʁigiˈnaːl]
painter	der Maler/die Malerin [dɐ ˈmaːlɐ/di maːləʁɪn]
painting (*picture or portrait*)	das Gemälde [das gəˈmɛːldə]
painting (*type of art*)	die Malerei [di maːləˈʁaɪ]
photography	die Fotografie [di fotogʁaˈfiː]
picture	das Bild [das bɪlt]

porcelain	das Porzellan [das pɔ(ɐ)tsə'la:n]
portrait	das Porträt [das pɔ(ɐ)'trɛ:]
poster	das Plakat [das pla'ka:t]
pottery	die Töpferei [di tœpfə'raɪ]
sculptor	der Bildhauer/die Bildhauerin [dɐ 'bɪlthaʊə/di 'bɪlthaʊəʀɪn]
sculpture	die Skulptur [di skʊlp'tuɐ]
silk-screen print	der Siebdruck [dɐ 'zi:pdrʊk]
statue	die Statue [di 'ʃta:tuə]
still life	das Stillleben [das 'ʃtɪle:bm]
tapestry	der Wandteppich [dɐ 'vanttɛpɪç]
terracotta	die Terrakotta [di tɛʀa'kɔta]
torso	der Torso [dɐ 'tɔʀzo]
vase	die Vase [di 'va:zə]
water-color (picture)	das Aquarell [das ʔakva'ʀɛl]
wood carving	die Schnitzerei [di ʃnɪtsə'ʀaɪ]
woodcut	der Holzschnitt [dɐ 'hɔltʃnɪt]

Styles and Periods

ancient	antik [ʔan'ti:k]
art nouveau	der Jugendstil [dɐ 'ju:gŋtsti:l]
baroque	barock [ba'ʀɔk]
Bronze Age	die Bronzezeit [di 'bʀɔŋsətsaɪt]
Celtic	keltisch ['kɛltɪʃ]
century	das Jahrhundert [das ja'hʊndet]
Christianity	das Christentum [das 'kʀɪstntu:m]
classicism	der Klassizismus [dɐ klasɪ'tsɪsmʊs]
dynasty	die Dynastie [di dʏnas'ti:]
epoch	die Epoche [di ʔe'pɔxə]
expressionism	der Expressionismus [dɐ ʔɛkspʀɛsjo'nɪsmus]
Gothic	die Gotik [di 'go:tik]
Greek	griechisch ['gʀi:çɪʃ]
heathen	heidnisch ['haɪtnɪʃ]
impressionism	der Impressionismus [dɐ ʔɪmpʀɛsjo'nɪsmus]
mannerism	der Manierismus [dɐ ˌmani'ʀɪsmus]
Middle Ages	das Mittelalter [das 'mɪtl̩ʔaltɐ]
modern	modern [mo'dɛɐn]
pagan	heidnisch ['haɪtnɪʃ]
prehistoric	vorgeschichtlich ['foɐgəʃɪçtlɪç]
prime	die Blütezeit [di 'bly:tətsaɪt]
Renaissance	die Renaissance [di ʀənɛ'sa):s]
rococo	das Rokoko [das 'ʀɔkoko]
Romanesque style/period	die Romanik [di ʀo'ma:nɪk]
Romanticism	die Romantik [di ʀo'mantɪk]
Stone Age	die Steinzeit [di 'ʃtaɪntsaɪt]

Excursions

When do we meet?
Wann treffen wir uns? [van 'trɛfn viɐ ʔʊns]

Where do we leave from?
Wo fahren wir los? [vo: 'faːrən viɐ loːs]

Will we pass by ...?
Kommen wir an ... vorbei? [kɔmm viɐ ʔan ... fɔ'baɪ]

Are we going to see ..., too?
Besichtigen wir auch ...? [bə'zɪçtɪgŋ viɐ ʔaʊx ...]

amusement park	der Freizeitpark [dɐ 'fraɪtsaɪt,paːk]
botanical gardens	der botanische Garten
	[dɐ bo'tanɪʃə 'gaːtn]
cave	die Höhle [di 'høːlə]
cliff	die Klippe [di 'klɪpə]
country(side)	das Land [das 'lant]
day trip	der Tagesausflug [dɐ 'taːgəs,ʔaʊsfluːk]
dripstone cave	die Tropfsteinhöhle [di 'trɔpfʃtaɪn,høːlə]
excursion	der Ausflug [dɐ 'ʔaʊsfluːk]
fishing port	der Fischerhafen [dɐ 'fɪʃɐhaːfn]
forest	der Wald [dɐ valt]
island	die Insel [di ʔɪnzl]
lake	der See [dɐ zeː]
market	der Markt [dɐ maːkt]
mountain village	das Bergdorf [das 'bɛɐkdoɐf]
mountains	das Gebirge [das gə'bɪrgə]
national park	der Nationalpark [dɐ natsjo'naːlpaːk]
nature reserve	das Naturschutzgebiet
	[das na'tuɐʃʊtsgəbiːt]
observatory	die Sternwarte [di 'ʃtɛɐnvaːtə]
open-air museum	das Freilichtmuseum
	[das 'fraɪlɪçtmʊ,zeʊm]
place of pilgrimage	der Wallfahrtsort [dɐ 'valfaːts,ʔɔɐt]
ravine	die Schlucht [di 'ʃlʊxt]
scenery	die Landschaft [di 'lantʃaft]
surroundings	die Umgebung [di ʔʊm'geːbʊŋ]
tour	die Rundfahrt [di 'rʊntfaːt]
trip	der Ausflug [dɐ 'ʔaʊsfluːk]
valley	das Tal [das taːl]
vantage point	der Aussichtspunkt [dɐ 'ʔaʊsɪçtspʊŋt]
view	die Aussicht [di 'ʔaʊsɪçt]
waterfall	der Wasserfall [dɐ 'vasefal]
wildlife park	der Wildpark [dɐ 'vɪltpaːk]
woods	der Wald [dɐ valt]
zoo	der Zoo [dɐ tsoː]

8

Active Vacations

Lots of opportunities

Germany is a very popular country. It offers fine scenery, from high mountains to beaches on the sea, and noteworthy cultural attractions. The weather in the summer is usually mild, although there can be rather high humidity in some areas. Regardless of the time of year, you'll have a lot to choose from, and you can take advantage of numerous sports and cultural opportunities, from swimming and hiking to taking a language course to improve your German.

Swimming

Excuse me, is there a (an) ... here?
Entschuldigen Sie bitte, gibt es hier ein ...
[ˀɛntˈʃʊldɪgn̩ zi ˈbɪtə gɪpt ɛs hiɐ ˀaɪn ...]

swimming pool
Schwimmbad? [ˈʃvɪmbaːt]

outdoor pool
Freibad? [ˈfʀaɪbaːt]

indoor pool
Hallenbad? [halnbaːt]

A/One ticket, please.
Eine Eintrittskarte, bitte! [ˀaɪnə ˀaɪntʀɪtskaːtə ˈbɪtə]

Can you tell me where the ... are, please?
Können Sie mir bitte sagen, wo die ... sind?
[kœnn zi miɐ ˈbɪtə zaːgn̩ voː di ... zɪnt]

showers
Duschen [ˈduːʃn̩]

changing rooms
Umkleidekabinen [ˀʊmklaɪdəkaˌbiːnn̩]

Is the beach ...
Ist der Strand ... [ˀɪst dɐ ʃtʀant ...]

sandy?
sandig? [ˈzandɪç]

pebbled/stony?
steinig? [ˈʃtaɪnɪç]

Are there any sea urchins/jellyfish here?
Gibt es hier Seeigel/Quallen? [gɪpt əs hiɐ ˈzeːˀiːgl̩/ˈkvaln]

Is the current strong?
Ist die Strömung stark? [ˀɪst di ˈʃtʀøːmʊŋ ʃtaːk]

Is it dangerous for children?
Ist es für Kinder gefährlich? [ˀɪst əs fyɐ ˈkɪndɐ gəˈfɛɐlɪç]

When's low tide/high tide?
Wann ist Ebbe/Flut? [van ɪst 'ʔɛbə/'flu:t]

I'd like to rent ...
Ich möchte ... mieten. [ʔɪç 'mœçtə ... mi:tn]

a deck chair.
einen Liegestuhl [ʔaɪnn 'li:gəʃtu:l]

a beach umbrella.
einen Sonnenschirm [ʔaɪnn 'zɔnnʃɪɐm]

a boat.
ein Boot [ʔaɪn 'bo:t]

a pair of water skis.
ein Paar Wasserski [ʔaɪn pa: 'vaseʃi:]

How much is it per hour/day?
Was kostet das pro Stunde/Tag? [vas 'kɔstət das pʀo 'ʃtʊndə/ta:k]

air mattress	die Luftmatratze [di 'lʊftma,tʀatsə]
boat rental	der Bootsverleih [dɐ 'bo:tsfɛlaɪ]
children's pool	das Kinderbecken [das 'kɪndɐbɛkn]
lifeguard	der Bademeister/die Bademeisterin [dɐ 'ba:dəmaɪstɐ/'ba:dəmaɪstəʀɪn]
non-swimmer	der Nichtschwimmer [dɐ 'nɪçtʃvɪmɐ]
nudist beach	der FKK-Strand [dɐ 'ʔɛfka'ka:ʃtʀant]
pedal boat	das Tretboot [das 'tʀe:tbo:t]
to swim	schwimmen [ʃvɪmm]
swimmer	der Schwimmer/die Schwimmerin [dɐ 'ʃvɪmɐ/di 'ʃvɪmərɪn]
volleyball	der Volleyball [dɐ 'vɔlɪbal]
to go water skiing	Wasserski fahren ['vaseʃi: 'fa:ʀən]
water wings	die Schwimmflügel *m pl* [di 'ʃvɪmfly:gl]
windbreak	der Windschirm [dɐ 'vɪntʃɪɐm]

Other Activities and Sports

Popular sports are soccer, tennis, and biking in summer and skiing in winter. Golf is becoming quite popular now, although golf courses are usually for members only.
The national pastime-sport is *Wandern,* something between hiking and walking. In almost any larger wooded area there'll be a parking area *(Wanderparkplatz),* complete with a map on a signboard showing possible routes and walking time.

What sports facilities are there here?
Welche Sportmöglichkeiten gibt es hier?
['vɛlçə 'ʃpɔʀtmø:klɪçkaɪtn gɪpt əs hiɐ]

Is there ... here?
Gibt es hier ... [gɪpt əs hiɐ ...]
  a golf course
  einen Golfplatz? [ˈʔaɪnn ˈgɔlfplats]
  a tennis court
  einen Tennisplatz? [ˈʔaɪnn ˈtɛnɪsplats]

Where can I go ... here?
Wo kann man hier ... [voː kan man hiɐ ...]
  fishing
  angeln? [ˈʔaŋln]
  hiking
  wandern? [ˈvandɐn]

Where can I rent ...?
Wo kann ich ... ausleihen? [voː ˈkan ɪç ... ˈʔaʊslaɪn]

I'd like to take a beginner's course/an advanced course.
Ich möchte einen Kurs für Anfänger/ Fortgeschrittene machen.
[ˈʔɪç ˈmœçtə ʔaɪnn kʊɐs fyɐ ˈʔanfɛŋɐ/ ˈfɔɐtgəʃrɪtənə maxn]

Water Sports

canoe	das Kanu [das ˈkaːnu]
inflatable boat	das Schlauchboot [das ˈʃlaʊxboːt]
motorboat	das Motorboot [das ˈmoːtɔboːt]
pick-up service	der Rückholservice [dɐ ˈrʏkhoːlœsœevɪs]
regatta	die Regatta [di rɛˈgata]
to row	rudern [ˈruːdɐn]
rowboat	das Ruderboot [das ˈruːdɐboːt]
rubber boat	das Schlauchboot [das ˈʃlaʊxboːt]
to sail	segeln [ˈzeːgln]
sailboat	das Segelboot [das ˈzeːglboːt]
to surf	surfen [ˈsœɐfn]
surfboard	das Surfbrett [das ˈsœɐfbrɛt]
wind conditions	die Windverhältnisse n pl [di ˈvɪntfɐˌhɛltnɪsə]
windsurfing	das Windsurfen [das ˈvɪntsœɐfn]

Diving

to dive	tauchen [taʊxn]
diving equipment	die Taucherausrüstung [di ˈtaʊxɐˈʔaʊsrʏstʊŋ]
diving goggles	die Taucherbrille [di ˈtaʊxɐbrɪlə]
snorkel	der Schnorchel [dɐ ʃnɔɐçl]
to go snorkeling	schnorcheln [ʃnɔɐçln]
wetsuit	der Neoprenanzug [dɐ neoˈpreːnˌʔantsuːk]

132

Fishing

bait	der Köder [de 'køːde]
fishing license	der Angelschein [de ˀaŋlʃaɪn]
fishing rod	die Angel [di ˀaŋl]
fresh water	das Süßwasser [das 'zyːsvase]
off season	die Schonzeit [di 'ʃoːntsaɪt]
salt water	das Salzwasser [das 'zaltsvase]
to go fishing	angeln ['ˀaŋln]

Ball Games

ball	der Ball [de bal]
basketball	der Basketball [de 'baːskətbal]
goal	das Tor [das toe]
goalkeeper	der Torwart [de 'toevaːt]
half-time	die Halbzeit [di 'halptsaɪt]
handball	der Handball ['hantbal]
soccer ball	der Fußball [de 'fuːsbal]
soccer field	der Fußballplatz [de 'fuːsbal,plats]
soccer match/game	das Fußballspiel [das 'fuːsbal,ʃpiːl]
team	die Mannschaft [di 'manʃaft]
volleyball	der Volleyball [de 'vɔlɪbal]

Tennis and Badminton

badminton	das Badminton [das 'bɛtmɪntn]
doubles	das Doppel [das dɔpl]
floodlight(s)	das Flutlicht [das fluːtlɪçt]
racquet	der Schläger [de 'ʃlɛːge]
shuttlecock	der Federball [de 'feːdebal]
singles	das Einzel [das ˀaɪntsəl]
squash	das Squash [das skvɔʃ]
table tennis/Ping-Pong	das Tischtennis [das 'tiʃtɛnɪs]
tennis	das Tennis [das 'tɛnɪs]
tennis racquet	der Tennisschläger [de 'tɛnɪʃlɛːge]

Physical Fitness and Weight Training

aerobics	das Aerobic [das ˀɛ'ʀɔbɪk]
body-building	das Bodybuilding [das 'bɔdɪbɪldɪŋ]
fitness center	das Fitnesscenter [das 'fɪtnəs,tsɛnte]
fitness training	das Konditionstraining [das kɔndɪ'tsjoːnstʀɛːnɪŋ]
gymnastics	die Gymnastik [di gɪm'nastɪk]
jazz aerobics	die Jazzgymnastik [di 'dʒɛsgɪm,nastɪk]
jogging	das Jogging [das 'dʒɔgɪŋ]
to jog	joggen ['dʒɔgn]
weight training	das Krafttraining [das 'kʀaftʀɛːnɪŋ]

Wellness

jacuzzi	der Whirlpool [dɐ ˈvœlpuːl]
massage	die Massage [maˈsaːʒə]
sauna	die Sauna [di ˈzaʊna]
solarium	das Solarium [das zoˈlaːʀɪʊm]
swimming pool	das Schwimmbad [das ˈʃvɪmbaːt]
Turkish bath	das Dampfbad [das ˈdampfbaːt]

Biking

bicycle/bike	das Fahrrad [das ˈfaːrat]
bike path	der Fahrradweg [dɐ ˈfaːratveːk]
bike tour	die Radtour [di ˈraːttuɐ]
crash helmet	der Fahrradhelm [dɐ ˈfaːratˌhɛlm]
cycling	der Radsport [dɐ ˈraːtʃpɔɐt]
flat tire	die Panne [di ˈpanə]
mountain bike	das Mountainbike [das ˈmaʊntnbaɪk]
pump	die Luftpumpe [di ˈlʊftpʊmpə]
racing bike	das Rennrad [das ˈʀɛnʀaːt]
repair kit	das Flickzeug [das ˈflɪktsɔɪk]
to ride a bike	Rad fahren [ˈʀaːt ˈfaːʀən]
touring bike	das Tourenrad [das ˈtuːʀənʀaːt]
trekking bike	das Trekkingrad [das ˈtʀɛkɪŋʀaːt]

Hiking and Mountain Climbing

I'd like to go for a hike in the mountains.
Ich möchte eine Bergtour machen.
[ˀɪç ˈmœçtə ˌˀaɪnə ˈbɛɐktuɐ maxn]

Can you show me an interesting route on the map?
Können Sie mir eine interessante Route auf der Karte zeigen?
[kœnn zi miɐ ˌˀaɪnə ˀɪntʀəˈsantə ˈʀuːtə ˀaʊf dɐ ˈkaːtə tsaɪgn]

day trip	die Tagestour [di ˈtaːgəstuɐ]
freeclimbing	das Freeclimbing [das ˈfʀiːklaɪmbɪŋ]
to hike	wandern [ˈvandɐn]
hiking map	die Wanderkarte [di ˈvandɐkaːtə]
hiking trail	der Wanderweg [dɐ ˈvandɐveːk]
mountain climbing, mountaineering	das Bergsteigen [das ˈbɛɐkʃtaɪgn]
path	der Pfad [dɐ pfaːt]
shelter	die Schutzhütte [di ˈʃʊtshʏtə]

Horseback Riding

horse	das Pferd [das pfeɐt]
to ride	reiten [ˈʀaɪtn]
ride, horseback ride	der Ausritt [dɐ ˈaʊsʀɪt]

riding school	die Reitschule [ˈʀaɪt͡ʃuːlə]
riding vacation	die Reiterferien pl [di ˈʀaɪtɐˌfeːʀiən]
saddle	der Sattel [dɐ zatl]

Golf

18-hole course	der 18-Loch-Platz [dɐ ˈaxtseːn lɔx plats]
club member	das Clubmitglied [das ˈklʊpˌmɪtgliːt]
clubhouse	das Clubhaus [das ˈklʊphaʊs]
day guest	der Tagesbesucher [dɐ ˈtaːgəsbəzuːxɐ]
golf	das Golf [das gɔlf]
golf club (implement)	der Golfschläger [dɐ ˈgɔlf͡ʃlɛːgɐ]
golf course	der Golfplatz [dɐ ˈgɔlfplats]
to play a round of golf	eine Runde Golf spielen [ˈaɪnə ˈʀʊndə gɔlf ˈ͡ʃpiːln]
tee	das Tee [das tiː]
tee-off	der Abschlag [dɐ apʃlaːk]

Gliding

glider	das Segelflugzeug [das ˈzeːglˌfluːktsɔɪk]
gliding	das Segelfliegen [das ˈzeːglfliːgn̩]
hang-gliding	das Drachenfliegen [das ˈdʀaxnfliːgn̩]
parachute	der Fallschirm [dɐ ˈfalʃɪʀm]
parachuting	das Fallschirmspringen [das ˈfalʃɪʀmʃpʀɪŋŋ]
paraglider	der Gleitschirm [dɐ ˈglaɪtʃɪʀm]
take-off area	der Startplatz [dɐ ˈʃtaːtplats]

Winter Sports

A one-day ski pass, please.
Eine Tageskarte, bitte. [ˈaɪnə ˈtaːgəskaːtə ˈbɪtə]

How many points does this ski lift cost?
Wie viele Punkte kostet dieser Skilift?
[ˈviː_filə ˈpʊŋktə ˈkɔstət diːzɐ ˈʃiːlɪft]

What time is the last trip up the mountain?
Um wie viel Uhr ist die letzte Bergfahrt?
[ˈʊm ˈviː_fil ˈuɐ ˈɪst di ˈlɛtstə ˈbɛɐkfaːt]

bottom station, base terminal	die Talstation [di ˈtaːlʃtaˌtsjoːn]
bunny lift	Babylift [ˈbeːbilɪft]
cable car	die Seilbahn [di ˈzaɪlbaːn]
cable railway	die (Stand)Seilbahn [di (ˈʃtant)ˌzaɪlbaːn]
chairlift	der Sessellift [dɐ ˈzɛsllɪft]
cross-country ski course	die Loipe [di ˈlɔɪpə]
cross-country skiing	der Langlauf [dɐ ˈlaŋlaʊf]
curling	das Curling [das ˈkəːlɪŋ]

day pass	der Tagespass [dɐ 'ta:gəspas]
downhill skiing	Ski alpin [ʃi: ʔal'pi:n]
funicular	die (Stand)Seilbahn [di (ʃtant)ˌzaɪlba:n]
ice hockey	das Eishockey [das ʔaɪshɔke:]
ice rink	die Eisbahn [di ʔaɪsba:n]
ice skates	die Schlittschuhe m pl [di ʃlɪtʃu:ə]
to go ice skating	Schlittschuh laufen [ʃlɪtʃu: laʊfn]
middle station	die Mittelstation [di mɪtlʃtaˌtsjo:n]
ski	der Ski [dɐ ʃi:]
ski bindings	die Skibindungen f pl [di ʃi:bɪndʊŋŋ]
ski course	der Skikurs [dɐ ʃi:kʊɐs]
ski goggles	die Skibrille [di ʃi:bʀɪlə]
to go skiing	Ski laufen [ʃi: laʊfn]
ski instructor	der Skilehrer/die Skilehrerin [dɐ ʃi:le:ʀɐ/ʃi:le:ʀərɪn]
ski poles	die Skistöcke m pl [di ʃi:ʃtœkə]
ski slope	die Skipiste [di ʃi:pɪstə]
sled	der Schlitten [dɐ ʃlɪtn]
snowboard	das Snowboard [das sno:bɔɐt]
summit station/top station	die Bergstation [di bɛɐkʃtaˌtsjo:n]
toboggan	der Schlitten [dɐ ʃlɪtn]
tow lift	der Schlepplift [dɐ ʃlɛplɪft]
week('s) pass	der Wochenpass [dɐ vɔxnpas]

Other Sports

athletics	die Leichtathletik [di laɪçtʔatˌle:tɪk]
bowling (ninepin)	das Kegeln [das ke:gln]
bowling (tenpin)	das Bowling [das bo:lɪŋ]
inline skating	das Inlineskating [das ʔɪnlaɪnˌskɛɪtɪŋ]
miniature golf	das Minigolf [das mɪnigɔlf]
motor sport	der Motorsport [dɐ mo:tɔʃpɔɐt]
to go roller-skating	Rollschuh fahren [ʀɔlʃu: fa:rən]
skateboard	das Skateboard [das skɛɪtbɔɐt]
to skateboard	Skateboard fahren [skɛɪtbɔɐt fa:rən]

Sporting Events

Can you tell me what sporting events there are here?
Können Sie mir bitte sagen, welche Sportveranstaltungen es hier gibt? [kœnn zi miɐ 'bɪtə za:gn 'vɛlçə 'ʃpɔɐtfɐˌʔanʃtaltʊŋŋ əs hiɐ gɪpt]

I'd like to see the soccer match.
Ich möchte mir das Fußballspiel ansehen.
[ʔɪç 'mœçtə miɐ das 'fu:sbalʃpi:l ʔanze:n]

When/Where is it?
Wann/Wo findet es statt? [van/vo: fɪndət əs ʃtat]

What's the score?
Wie steht's? [viː ʃteːts]

Two to one.
Zwei zu eins. [tsvaɪ tsʊ ʔaɪns]

A tie, three to three.
Drei-drei. [draɪ draɪ]

Foul!
Foul! [faʊl]

Good shot!
Schöner Schuss! [ˈʃøːne ʃʊs]

Goal!
Tor! [toɐ]

athlete	der Sportler/die Sportlerin [de ˈʃpɔʁtle/di ˈʃpɔʁtlərɪn]
bike racing	das Radrennen [das ˈʁaːtʁɛnn]
championship	die Meisterschaft [di ˈmaɪsteʃaft]
contest	der Wettkampf [de ˈvɛtkamf]
corner kick	der Eckstoß [de ˈʔɛkʃtoːs]
cross	die Flanke [di flaŋkə]
defeat	die Niederlage [di ˈniːdela:gə]
draw	unentschieden [ˈʔʊnɛntʃiːdn]
free kick	der Freistoß [de ˈfʁaɪʃtoːs]
game	das Spiel [ʃpiːl]
kickoff	der Anstoß [de ˈanʃtoːs]
to lose	verlieren [feˈliːʁən]
match	das Spiel [ʃpiːl]
offside	abseits [ˈʔapzaɪts]
pass	der Pass [de pas]
penalty box	der Strafraum [de ˈʃtʁaːfʁaʊm]
penalty kick	der Elfmeter [de ˈʔɛlfˈmeːte]
program	das Programm [das pʁoˈgʁam]
race	das Rennen [das ʁɛnn]
referee	der Schiedsrichter [de ˈʃiːtsʁɪçte]
to score a goal	ein Tor schießen [ˈʔaɪn toɐ ʃiːsn]
sports field	der Sportplatz [de ˈʃpɔʁtplats]
stadium	das Stadion [das ˈʃtaːdjon]
ticket	die Eintrittskarte [di ˈʔaɪntʁɪtsˌkaːtə]
ticket office	die Kasse [di ˈkasə]
umpire	der Schiedsrichter [de ˈʃiːtsʁɪçte]
victory/win	der Sieg [de ziːk]
to win	gewinnen [gəˈvɪnn]

137

Creative Vacations

I'm interested in ...
Ich interessiere mich für ... [ˀɪç ˀɪntrəˈsiːrə mɪç fyɐ ...]

a pottery course.
einen Töpferkurs. [ˀaɪnn ˈtœpfekʊɐs]

a German course.
einen Deutschkurs. [ˀaɪnn ˈdɔɪtʃkʊɐs]

for beginners
für Anfänger [fyɐ ˀanfɛŋɐ]

for advanced learners
für Fortgeschrittene [fyɐ ˈfɔɐtɡəʃrɪtnə]

How many hours per day are we together?
Wie viele Stunden pro Tag arbeiten wir zusammen?
[ˈviː_fiːlə ˈʃtʊndn pro taːk ˀaːbaɪtn viɐ tsuˈzamm]

Is the number of participants limited?
Ist die Teilnehmerzahl begrenzt? [ˀɪst di ˈtaɪlneːmɐtsaːl bəˈɡrɛntst]

When is the registration deadline?
Bis wann muss man sich anmelden?
[bis van mʊs man zɪç ˀanmɛldn]

Are the costs of materials included?
Sind die Materialkosten inklusive?
[zɪnt di materiˈaːlkɔstn ˀɪŋkluˈziːvə]

What should I bring along?
Was soll ich mitbringen? [vas zɔl ɪç ˈmɪtbrɪŋŋ]

carpentry workshop	die Holzwerkstatt [di ˈhɔltsˌvɛɛkʃtat]
to cook	kochen [ˈkɔxn]
course	der Kurs [dɐ kʊɐs]
dance theater	das Tanztheater [das ˈtantsteˌˀaːtɐ]
drama workshop	der Schauspielworkshop [dɐ ˈʃaʊʃpiːlˌwəːkʃɔp]
to draw	zeichnen [ˈtsaɪçnn]
drumming	das Trommeln [das ˈtrɔmln]
meditation	die Meditation [di meditaˈtsjoːn]
oil painting	die Ölmalerei [di ˀøːlmaːləˌraɪ]
to paint	malen [maːln]
silk painting	die Seidenmalerei [di ˈzaɪdnmaːləˌraɪ]
to photograph	fotografieren [ˌfotoɡraˈfiːrən]
workshop	der Workshop [dɐ ˈwəːkʃɔp]
yoga	das Yoga [das ˈjoːɡa]

Entertainment

Theater – Concert – Movies

Could you tell me what's on at the theater tonight, please?
Könnten Sie mir bitte sagen, welches Stück heute Abend im Theater gespielt wird? [kœntn zi miɐ ˈbɪtə zaːgn̩ ˈvɛlçəs ʃtʏk ˈhɔɪtə ˈʔaːbmt ʔɪm teˈʔaːtɐ gəˈʃpiːlt vɪɐt]

What's on at the movies tomorrow night?
Was läuft morgen Abend im Kino?
[vas lɔɪft ˌmɔɐgn̩ ˈʔaːbmt ʔɪm ˈkiːno]

Are there concerts in the cathedral?
Werden im Dom Konzerte veranstaltet?
[veɐdn̩ ʔɪm ˈdoːm kɔnˈtsɛɐtə fɐˈʔanʃtaltət]

Can you recommend a good play?
Können Sie mir ein gutes Theaterstück empfehlen?
[ˈkœnn̩ zi miɐ ʔaɪn ˈguːtəs teˈʔaːtɐʃtʏk ʔɛmpˈfeːln̩]

When does the performance start?
Wann beginnt die Vorstellung? [van bəˈgɪnt di ˈfoɐʃtɛlʊŋ]

Where can I get tickets?
Wo bekommt man Karten? [voː bəˈkɔmt man ˈkaːtn̩]

Two tickets for this evening, please.
Bitte zwei Karten für heute Abend.
[ˈbɪtə tsvaɪ ˈkaːtn̩ fyɐ ˈhɔɪtə ˈʔaːbmt]

Two seats at ..., please.
Bitte zwei Plätze zu ... [ˈbɪtə ˈtsvaɪ ˈplɛtsə tsʊ]

Can I have a program, please?
Kann ich bitte ein Programm haben?
[kan ɪç ˈbɪtə ʔaɪn pʁoˈgʁam ˈhaːbm]

advance sale	. . . .	der Vorverkauf [dɐ ˈfoɐfɐkaʊf]
box office	. . . .	die Kasse [di ˈkasə]
cloakroom	. . . .	die Garderobe [di gaˈdʁoːbə]
festival	. . . .	das Festival [das ˈfɛstɪval]
intermission	. . . .	die Pause [di ˈpaʊzə]

performance	die Vorstellung [di ˈfoɐ̯ʃtɛlʊŋ]
program	das Programmheft [das pʀoˈgʀamhɛft]
ticket	die Eintrittskarte [di ˈʔaɪ̯ntʀɪtskaːtə]

Theatre

1st/2nd balcony	erster/zweiter Rang [ˈeɐ̯stɐ/ˈtsvaɪ̯tɐ ʀaŋ]
act	der Akt [dɐ ʔakt]
actor/actress	Schauspieler/Schauspielerin [ˈʃaʊ̯ʃpiːlɐ/ ˈʃaʊ̯ʃpiːləʀɪn]
ballet	das Ballett [das baˈlɛt]
box	die Loge [di ˈloːʒə]
cabaret	das Kabarett [das kabaˈʀeː]
comedy	die Komödie [di koˈmøːdiə]
dancer	der Tänzer/die Tänzerin [dɐ tɛntsɐ/ di tɛntsəˈʀɪn]
drama	das Drama [das ˈdʀaːma]
encore	die Zugabe [di ˈtsuːgaːbə]
music hall	das Varietee [das vaʀiəˈteː]
musical	das Musical [das ˈmjuːzɪkl]
open-air theater	das Freilufttheater [das ˈfʀaɪ̯lʊftəˌʔaːtɐ]
opera	die Oper [di ˈʔoːpɐ]
operetta	die Operette [di ʔopəˈʀɛtə]
orchestra	das Parkett [das paˈkɛt]
performance	die Aufführung [di ʔaʊ̯fyːʀʊŋ]
play	das Schauspiel [das ˈʃaʊ̯ʃpiːl]
play	das Theaterstück [das teˈʔaːtɐʃtʏk]
premiere	die Premiere [di pʀəmˈjeːʀə]
production	die Inszenierung [di ʔɪntsəˈniːʀʊŋ]
program *(booklet)*	das Programmheft [das pʀoˈgʀamhɛft]
revue	das Kabarett [das kabaˈʀeː]
tragedy	die Tragödie [di tʀaˈgøːdiə]
variety theater	das Varietee [das vaʀiəˈteː]

Concerts

blues	der Blues [dɐ bluːs]
choir	der Chor [dɐ koɐ̯]
classical	die Klassik [di ˈklasɪk]
composer	der Komponist/die Komponistin [dɐ kɔmpoˈnɪst/di kɔmpoˈnɪstɪn]
concert	das Konzert [das kɔnˈtsɛɐ̯t]
chamber music concert	das Kammerkonzert [das ˈkamɐkɔnˌtsɛɐ̯t]
church concert	das Kirchenkonzert [das ˈkɪʀçnkɔnˌtsɛɐ̯t]
symphony concert	das Sinfoniekonzert [das zɪmfoˈniːkɔnˌtsɛɐ̯t]

141

conductor	der Dirigent/die Dirigentin [dɐ diʀi'gɛnt/di diʀi'gɛntɪn]
folk music	der Folk [dɐ fo:k]
jazz	der Jazz [dɐ 'dʒɛs]
orchestra	das Orchester [das ʔɔɐ'kɛstɐ]
piano recital	der Klavierabend [dɐ kla'viɐa:bmt]
pop	der Pop [dɐ pɔp]
reggae	der Reggae [dɐ 'ʀɛge:]
rock	der Rock [dɐ ʀɔk]
singer	der Sänger/die Sängerin [dɐ 'zɛŋɐ/di 'zɛŋəʀɪn]
soloist	der Solist/die Solistin [dɐ zo'lɪst/di zo'lɪstɪn]
traditional music	die Volksmusik [di 'fɔlksmʊˌzi:k]

Movies

cast	die Besetzung [di bə'zɛtsʊŋ]
directed by	die Regie [di ʀə'ʒi:]
dubbed	synchronisiert [zʏŋkroni'ziet]
film	der Film [dɐ fɪlm]
action film	der Actionfilm [dɐ ʔ'ɛktʃnfɪlm]
black-and-white film	der Schwarzweißfilm [dɐ ʃva:ts'vaisfɪlm]
cartoon	der Zeichentrickfilm [dɐ 'tsaiçnˌtʀɪkfɪlm]
classic film	der Klassiker [dɐ 'klasɪkɐ]
comedy	die Komödie [di ko'mø:diə]
documentary	der Dokumentarfilm [dɐ dɔkʊmɛn'ta:fɪlm]
drama	das Drama [das 'dʀa:ma]
science-fiction film	der Sciencefictionfilm [dɐ sains'fɪktʃnfɪlm]
short film	der Kurzfilm [dɐ kʊɐtsfɪlm]
thriller	der Thriller [dɐ 'θʀɪlɐ]
western	der Western [dɐ 'vɛstɐn]
film/movie actor	der Filmschauspieler [dɐ 'fɪlmʃaʊʃpi:lɐ]
film/movie actress	die Filmschauspielerin [di 'fɪlmʃaʊʃpi:lərɪn]
leading role	die Hauptrolle [di 'haʊptʀɔlə]
movie	der Film [dɐ fɪlm]
movie theater	das Kino [das 'ki:no]
art house movie theater . .	das Programmkino [das pʀo'gʀamki:no]
drive-in movie	das Freilichtkino [das 'fʀailɪçtki:no]
original version	die Originalfassung [di ʔɔʀɪgi'na:lfasʊŋ]
screen	die Leinwand [di 'lainvant]

screenplay, script	das Drehbuch [das 'dre:bu:x]
special effects	die Spezialeffekte *m pl*
	[di ʃpe'tsja:leˌfɛktə]
subtitles	der Untertitel [dɐ 'ʔuntetɪtl]
supporting role	die Nebenrolle [di 'ne:bmʀɔlə]

Nightlife

What is there to do here in the evenings?

Was kann man hier abends unternehmen?

[vas kan man hie 'ʔa:bmts ʔuntɐ'ne:mm]

Is there a nice bar here?

Gibt es hier eine gemütliche Kneipe?

[gɪpt əs hie ˌʔaɪnə gə'my:tlɪçə 'knaɪpə]

How long are you open today?

Bis wann haben Sie heute auf? [bɪs van 'ha:bm zi 'hɔɪtə ʔauf]

Where can we go dancing?

Wo kann man hier tanzen gehen? [vo: kan man hie 'tantsn ge:n]

Shall we have another dance?

Wollen wir noch einmal tanzen? [vɔln vie nɔx 'ʔaɪnma:l 'tantsn]

> In bars you don't normally pay for each individual drink. The waiter or barkeeper keeps a record of your orders (sometimes on your beer mat) and presents you with the total when you leave. Closing times vary considerably; ask if in doubt. In larger cities bars are often open until well after midnight.

band	die Band [di bɛ(:)nt]
bar	die Bar [di ba:]
bar	die Kneipe [di 'knaɪpə]
casino	das Spielkasino [das 'ʃpi:lkaˌzi:no]
to dance	tanzen [tantsn]
dance band	die Tanzkapelle [di 'tantskaˌpɛlə]
discotheque	die Diskothek [di dɪsko'te:k]
folklore evening	der Folkloreabend [dɐ fɔlk'lo:ʀəˌʔa:bmt]
gambling	das Glücksspiel [das 'glʏkʃpi:l]
to go out	ausgehen [ʔausge:n]
nightclub	der Nachtklub [dɐ 'naxtklʊp]
show	die Show [di ʃo:]

Festivals and Events

Could you tell me when the music festival takes place, please?
Könnten Sie mir bitte sagen, wann das Musikfestival stattfindet?
[kœntn zi miɐ 'bɪtə zaːgn van das mu'ziːkfɛstɪval 'ʃtatfɪndət]

from June to September
von Juni bis September [fɔn 'juːni bɪs zɛp'tɛmbɐ]
every year in August
jedes Jahr im August ['jeːdəs jaː ʔɪm aʊ'gʊst]
every 2 years
alle zwei Jahre [ʔalə tsvaɪ 'jaːʀə]

Typical Festivals and Events

ball	der Ball [dɐ bal]
barbecue	das Grillfest [das 'gʀɪlfɛst]
brass band	die Blaskapelle [di 'blaːska,pɛlə]
carnival	der Fasching [dɐ 'faʃɪŋ]
Christmas market	der Weihnachtsmarkt [dɐ 'vaɪnaxts,maːkt]
circus	der Zirkus [dɐ 'tsɪʀkʊs]
country fair	die Kirmes [di 'kɪʀməs]
dance (party)	das Tanzfest [das 'tantsfɛst]
event	die Veranstaltung [di fɛ'ʔanʃtaltʊŋ]
fair	der Jahrmarkt [dɐ 'jaːmaːkt]
fireworks display	das Feuerwerk [das 'fɔɪvɛɐk]
flea market	der Flohmarkt [dɐ 'floːmaːkt]
flower show	die Gartenschau [di 'gaːtnʃaʊ]
garden party	das Gartenfest [das 'gaːtnfɛst]
New Year's Eve party	die Silvester-Party [di zɪl'vɛstɐpaːti]
parade	der Umzug [dɐ 'ʔʊmtsuːk]
procession	die Prozession [di pʀɔtsɛs'joːn]
village festival	das Dorffest [das 'dɔɐfɛst]

Audio-Video

LOEWE.
GALERIE

confiserie

Shopping

Spending your money
Shopping is a natural activity, and you'll have no trouble doing it in the German-speaking countries. Restrictions in store hours have been liberalized recently, so you can take advantage of opportunities six days a week and well into the evening. If you're looking for clothes, a great time to shop is during the *Sommerschlussverkauf* (summer clearance sale), from the end of July to the middle of August. This is when stores clear out their summer lines and drop prices often by as much as 30% or 40% to do so.

Questions

I'm looking for ...

Are you being helped?
Werden Sie schon bedient? [veɐdn zi ʃon bəˈdiːnt]

Thank you, I'm just looking around.
Danke, ich sehe mich nur um. [daŋkə ʔɪç zeː mɪç nuɐ ʔʊm]

I'd like ...
Ich hätte gern ... [ʔɪç hɛtə gɛɐn]

Do you have ...?
Haben Sie ...? [ˈhaːbm zi]

Can I get you anything else?
Darf es sonst noch (et)was sein? [daːf əs zɔnst nɔx (ʔɛt)vas zaɪn]

Making Purchases

How much is it?
Wie viel kostet es? [ˈviː_fil ˈkɔstət əs]

That's really expensive!
Das ist aber teuer! [das ɪst ʔabɐ ˈtɔɪɐ]

Good. I'll take it.
Gut, ich nehme es. [guːt ʔɪç ˈneːm əs]

Do you take credit cards?
Nehmen Sie Kreditkarten? [ˈneːmm zi kʀeˈdiːtˌkaːtn]

Stores

Excuse me, where can I find ...?
Entschuldigen Sie bitte, wo finde ich ...?
[ʔɛntˈʃʊldɪgn zi ˈbɪtə voː fɪndə ʔɪç]

Öffnungszeiten – opening hours

offen	open
geschlossen	closed
Betriebsferien	closed for vacation

---

antiques shop	das Antiquitätengeschäft [das ˀantɪkvɪˈtɛːtngəʃɛft]
art dealer	der Kunsthändler [dɐ ˈkʊnst,hɛntlɐ]
bakery	die Bäckerei [di bɛkəˈʀaɪ]
barber shop	der (Herren)Friseur [dɐ(ˈhɛʀən)fʀiˈzøɐ]
book store	die Buchhandlung [di ˈbuːxhantlʊŋ]
boutique	die Boutique [di buˈtiːk]
butcher's	die Metzgerei [di mɛtsgəˈʀaɪ]
candy store	das Süßwarengeschäft [das ˈzyːsvaːʀəngəʃɛft]
delicatessen	das Feinkostgeschäft [das ˈfaɪnkɔstgəʃɛft]
department store	das Kaufhaus [das ˈkaʊfhaʊs]
dressmaker	der Schneider/die Schneiderin [dɐ ˈʃnaɪdɐ/ ˈʃnaɪdəʀɪn]
drugstore . . . . (*shop for toiletries*)	die Drogerie [di dʀogəˈʀiː]
dry cleaner's	die Reinigung [di ˈʀaɪnɪgʊŋ]
fish dealer	das Fischgeschäft [das ˈfɪʃgəʃɛft]
flea market	der Flohmarkt [dɐ ˈfloːmaːkt]
florist's	das Blumengeschäft [das ˈbluːmŋgəʃɛft]
greengrocer's/fruit and . . . vegetable store	der Obst- und Gemüsehändler [dɐ ˀoːpst ˀʊnt gəˈmyːzəhɛntlɐ]
grocery store	das Lebensmittelgeschäft [das ˈleːbmsmɪtlgəʃɛft]
hairdresser's	der Friseur [dɐ fʀiˈzøɐ]
health food store	das Reformhaus [das ʀeˈfɔɐmhaʊs]
jeweler's	der Juwelier [dɐ juveˈliɐ]
launderette	der Waschsalon [dɐ ˈvaʃzaˌlɔŋ]
laundry	die Wäscherei [di vɛʃəˈʀaɪ]
liquor store	das Spirituosengeschäft [das ʃpirituˈoːzngəʃɛft]
market	der Markt [dɐ maːkt]
news dealer	der Zeitungshändler [dɐ ˈtsaɪtʊŋshɛntlɐ]
optician's	der Optiker [dɐ ˀɔptikɐ]
organic food store	der Bioladen [der ˈbiolaːdn]

pastry shop	die Konditorei [di kɔndito'ʀaɪ]
perfume store	die Parfümerie [di pafʏmə'ʀiː]
pharmacy	die Apotheke [di ʔapo'teːkə]
photographic materials	die Fotoartikel *m pl* [di 'foːtoʔaˌtɪkl]
second-hand store	der Trödelladen [dɐ 'tʀøːdllaːdn]
shoe store	das Schuhgeschäft [das 'ʃuːgəʃɛft]
shoemaker	der Schuhmacher [dɐ 'ʃuːmaxɐ]
souvenir store	der Souvenirladen [dɐ zʊvə'niːɐlaːdn]
sporting goods store	das Sportgeschäft [das 'ʃpɔɐtgəʃɛft]
stationery store	das Schreibwarengeschäft
	[das 'ʃʀaɪpvaːʀəngəʃɛft]
supermarket	der Supermarkt [dɐ 'zuːpɐmaːkt]
tailor	der Schneider/die Schneiderin
	[dɐ 'ʃnaɪdɐ/ 'ʃnaɪdərɪn]
tobacco shop	der Tabakladen [dɐ 'tabaklaːdn]
toy store	das Spielwarengeschäft
	[das 'ʃpiːlvaːʀəngəʃɛft]
travel agency	das Reisebüro [das 'ʀaɪzəbyˌʀoː]
watchmaker's	der Uhrmacher [dɐ 'ʔuɐmaxɐ]
wine merchant's	die Weinhandlung [di 'vaɪnhantlʊŋ]

Books, Magazines, and Stationery

I'd like ...
Ich hätte gern ... [ʔɪç hɛtə gɛɐn ...]
  a German newspaper.
  eine deutsche Zeitung. [ʔaɪnə 'dɔɪtʃə 'tsaɪtʊŋ]
  a magazine.
  eine Zeitschrift. [ʔaɪnə 'tsaɪtʃʀɪft]
  a travel guide.
  einen Reiseführer. [ʔaɪnn 'ʀaɪzəfyːʀɐ]
  a hiking map for this area.
  eine Wanderkarte dieser Gegend. [ʔaɪnə 'vandɐkaːtə diːzɐ 'geːgŋt]

Books, Magazines, and Newspapers

city map	der Stadtplan [dɐ 'ʃtatplaːn]
comic book	das Comicheft [das 'kɔmɪkhɛft]
cookbook	das Kochbuch [das 'kɔxbuːx]
daily paper	die Tageszeitung [di 'taːgəstsaɪtʊŋ]
detective novel	der Kriminalroman
	[dɐ kʀimi'naːlʀoˌmaːn]
dictionary	das Wörterbuch [das 'vœɐtɐbuːx]
(glossy) magazine	die Illustrierte [di ɪlʊ'stʀiːɐtə]
map *(of country area)*	die Landkarte [di 'lantkaːtə]

(news) magazine	die Zeitschrift [di 'tsaɪtʃʀɪft]
newspaper	die Zeitung [di 'tsaɪtʊŋ]
novel	der Roman [dɐ ʀo'ma:n]
paperback	das Taschenbuch [das 'taʃnbu:x]
road map	die Straßenkarte [di 'ʃtʀa:snka:tə]
thriller	der Kriminalroman [dɐ kʀimi'na:lʀoma:n]
travel guide	der Reiseführer [dɐ 'ʀaɪzəfy:ʀɐ]
women's magazine	die Frauenzeitschrift [di 'fʀaʊntsaɪtʃʀɪft]

Stationery

ballpoint pen	der Kugelschreiber [dɐ 'ku:glʃʀaɪbɐ], der Kuli [dɐ 'ku:li]
colored pencil	der Farbstift [dɐ 'fa:pʃtɪft]
coloring book	das Malbuch [das 'ma:lbu:x]
envelope	der Briefumschlag [dɐ 'bʀi:fʊmʃla:k]
eraser	der Radiergummi [dɐ ʀa'di:ɐˌgʊmi]
felt-tip pen	der Filzstift [dɐ 'fɪltʃɪft]
floppy disks	die Disketten f pl [di dɪs'kɛtn]
glue	der Klebstoff [dɐ 'kle:pʃtɔf]
notepad	der Notizblock [dɐ no'ti:tsblɔk]
paper	das Papier [das pa'pi:ɐ]
pencil	der Bleistift [dɐ 'blaɪʃtɪft]
picture postcard	die Ansichtskarte [di ʔ'anzɪçtska:tə]
Scotch® tape	der Tesafilm® [dɐ 'te:safɪlm]
writing pad	der Block [dɐ blɔk]
writing paper	das Briefpapier [das 'bʀi:fpaˌpi:ɐ]

CDs and Cassettes

➢ also "Electrical Goods" and "Concert"

Do you have any CDs/cassettes by ...?
Haben Sie CDs/Kassetten von ...? ['ha:bm zi tse'de:s/ka'sɛtn fɔn ...]

I'd like a CD of typical Swiss music.
Ich hätte gern eine CD mit typisch Schweizer Musik.
[ʔɪç hɛtə gɛɐn ʔaɪnə tse'de: mɪt 'ty:pɪʃ ʃvaɪtsɐ mu'zi:k]

Can I listen to a little of this, please?
Kann ich hier bitte kurz reinhören?
[kan ʔɪç hiɐ 'bɪtə kʊɐts 'ʀaɪnhø:ʀən]

cassette	die Kassette [di ka'sɛtə]
CD	die CD [di tse'de:]
CD player	der CD-Spieler [dɐ tse'de:ʃpi:lɐ]
DVD	die DVD [di defaʊ'de:]
headphones	der Kopfhörer [dɐ 'kɔpfhø:ʀɐ]

MP3 player	der MP3-Spieler
	[de 'ɛm-peː-draɪ ʃpiːlɐ]
personal stereo	der Walkman® [de 'wɔːkmɛn]
portable CD player	der tragbare CD-Spieler
	[de 'tʀaːkbaːʀə tseˈdeːʃpiːlɐ]
speaker	der Lautsprecher [de 'laʊtʃpʀɛçɐ]
Walkman®	der Walkman® [de 'wɔːkmɛn]

Electrical Goods

> also "Photographic Materials" and "CDs and Cassettes"

adapter	der Adapter [de ʔa'daptɐ]
alarm clock	der Wecker [de 'vɛkɐ]
battery	die Batterie [di batə'ʀiː]
battery charger	das Ladegerät [das 'laːdəgəʀɛːt]
extension cord	die Verlängerungsschnur
	[di fɛ'lɛŋəʀʊŋʃnuɐ]
flashlight	die Taschenlampe [di 'taʃnlampə]
hair dryer	der Föhn [de føːn]
lightbulb	die Glühbirne [di 'glyːbɪʀnə]
pager	der Piepser [de 'piːpsɐ]
pocket calculator	der Taschenrechner [de 'taʃnʀɛçnɐ]

Fashion

> also Colors

Clothing

Can you please show me ...?
Können Sie mir bitte ... zeigen? ['kœnn zi miɐ 'bɪtə ... 'tsaɪgn]

Can I try it on?
Kann ich es anprobieren? [kan ɪç əs ʔanpʀobiːʀən]

What size do you take?
Welche Größe haben Sie? ['vɛlçə 'gʀøːsə 'haːbm ziː]

It's too ...
Das ist mir zu ... ['das ʔɪst miɐ tsu '...]
  tight/big.
  eng/weit. [ʔɛŋ/vaɪt]
  short/long.
  kurz/lang. [kʊɐts/laŋ]
  small/big.
  klein/groß. [klaɪn/gʀoːs]

It's a good fit. I'll take it.
Das passt gut. Ich nehme es. [das past 'guːt ʔɪç 'neːm əs]

It's not quite what I'm looking for.
Das ist nicht ganz, was ich möchte.
[das ʔɪst nɪçt gants vas ɪç 'mœçtə]

bathing cap	die Bademütze [di 'baːdəmʏtsə]
bathrobe	der Bademantel [dɐ 'baːdəmantl]
bikini	der Bikini [dɐ biˈkiːni]
blazer	der Blazer [dɐ 'bleːzɐ]
blouse	die Bluse [di 'bluːzə]
body stocking/bodysuit	der Body [dɐ 'bɔdi]
bow-tie	die Fliege [di 'fliːgə]
bra	der Büstenhalter [dɐ 'bʏstnhaltɐ]
briefs	der (Herren)Slip [dɐ ('hɛʀən)slɪp]
cap	die Mütze [di 'mʏtsə]
cardigan	die Strickjacke [di 'ʃtʀɪkjakə]
coat	der Mantel [dɐ mantl]
cotton	die Baumwolle [di 'baʊmvɔlə]
dress	das Kleid [das klaɪt]
gloves	die Handschuhe m pl [di 'hantʃuːə]
hat	der Hut [dɐ huːt]
jacket	die Jacke [di 'jakə]
jeans	die Jeans [di 'dʒiːns]
leggings	die Leggings [di 'lɛgɪŋs]
linen	das Leinen [das laɪnn]
muffler	der Schal [dɐ ʃaːl]
panties	der (Damen)Slip [dɐ ('daːmən)slɪp]
pants	die Hose [di 'hoːzə]
pants (*underwear*)	die Unterhose [di 'ʊntɐhoːzə]
panty hose	die Strumpfhose [di 'ʃtʀʊmpfhoːzə]
parka	der Anorak [dɐ ʔanoʀak]
pullover	der Pullover [dɐ pʊ'loːvɐ]
raincoat	der Regenmantel [dɐ 'ʀeːgŋmantl]
scarf	das Halstuch [das 'halstuːx]
shirt	das Hemd [das hɛmt]
shorts	die kurze Hose [di 'kʊɐtsə 'hoːzə]
silk	die Seide [di 'zaɪdə]
silk panty hose	die Seidenstrumpfhose [di 'zaɪdnʃtʀʊmpfhoːze]
silk stockings	die Seidenstrümpfe m pl [di 'zaɪdnʃtʀʏmpfə]
skirt	der Rock [dɐ ʀɔk]
sleeve	der Ärmel [dɐ ʔɛɐml]
socks	die Socken f pl [di 'zɔkn]
stockings	die Strümpfe m pl [di 'ʃtʀʏmpfə]
suit (*for men*)	der Anzug [dɐ ʔantsuːk]
suit (*for women*)	das Kostüm [das kɔs'tyːm]
sun hat	der Sonnenhut [dɐ 'zɔnnhuːt]

sweater	der Pullover [dɐ puˈloːvɐ]
swimming trunks	die Badehose [di ˈbaːdəhoːzə]
swimsuit	der Badeanzug [dɐ ˈbaːdəˌʔantsuːk]
tee-shirt	das T-Shirt [das ˈtiːʃœt]
tie	die Krawatte [di kʀaˈvatə]
tracksuit	der Trainingsanzug
	[dɐ ˈtʀɛːnɪŋsˌʔantsuːk]
trousers	die Hose [di ˈhoːzə]
umbrella	der Schirm [dɐ ʃɪʀm]
underpants	die Unterhose [di ˈʊntɐhoːzə]
undershirt	das Unterhemd [das ˈʊntɐhɛmt]
underwear	die Unterwäsche [di ˈʔʊntɐvɛʃə]
vest	die Weste [di ˈvɛstə]
wool	die Wolle [di ˈvɔlə]

Dry Cleaning

I'd like to have these things cleaned/laundered.
Ich möchte diese Sachen reinigen/ waschen lassen.
[ˈʔɪç ˈmœçtə ˌdiːzə ˈzaxn ˈʀaɪnɪgn/vaʃn lasn]

When will they be ready?
Wann sind sie fertig? [van zɪnt zi ˈfɛɐtɪç]

to dry clean	chemisch reinigen [ˈçeːmɪʃ ˈʀaɪnɪgn]
to iron	bügeln [byːgln]
to press	plätten [plɛtn]

Groceries

What can I do for you?
Was darf es sein? [vas daːf əs ˈzaɪn]

I'd like ..., please.
Geben Sie mir bitte ... [geːbm zi miɐ ˈbɪtə]

  a pound of ...
  ein Pfund ... [ˈʔaɪn pfʊnt]

  ten slices of ...
  10 Scheiben ... [ˈtseːn ʃaɪbm]

  a piece of ...
  ein Stück von ... [ˈʔaɪn ˈʃtʏk fɔn]

  a package of ...
  eine Packung ... [ˈʔaɪnə ˈpakʊŋ]

  a jar of ...
  ein Glas ... [ˈʔaɪn glaːs]

  a can of ...
  eine Dose ... [ˈʔaɪnə ˈdoːzə]

a bottle of ...
eine Flasche ... [ˈʔaɪnə ˈflaʃə]
a bag, please.
eine (Einkaufs)tüte. [ˈʔaɪnə (ˈʔaɪnkaʊfs)ˌtyːtə]

Could I try some of this?
Dürfte ich vielleicht etwas hiervon probieren?
[dʏɛft ɪç fiˌlaɪçt ˌɛtvas ˈhiɐfɔn pʁoˈbiːʁən]

Would a little bit more be okay?
Darf es auch etwas mehr sein? [daːf əs aʊx ˌʔɛtvas ˈmeɐ zaɪn]

No, thank you. That's all.
Danke, das ist alles. [ˈdaŋkə das ɪst ˈʔaləs]

Fruit

Obst

apples	die Äpfel *m pl* [di ˈʔɛpfl]
apricots	die Aprikosen *f pl* [di ʔapʁɪˈkoːzn]
bananas	die Bananen *f pl* [di baˈnaːnn]
black currants	die schwarzen Johannisbeeren *f pl*
	[di ˈʃvaːtsn joˈhanɪsbeːʁən]
blackberries	die Brombeeren *f pl* [di ˈbʁɔmbeːʁən]
blueberries	die Heidelbeeren *f pl* [di ˈhaɪdlbeːʁən]
cherries	die Kirschen *f pl* [di kɪɐʃn]
coconut	die Kokosnuss [di ˈkoːkosnʊs]
cranberries	die Preiselbeeren *f pl* [di ˈpʁaɪzlbeːʁən]
dried	getrocknet [ɡəˈtʁɔknət]
fruit	das Obst [das ˈʔoːpst]
gooseberries	die Stachelbeeren *f pl* [di ˈʃtaxlbeːʁən]
grapefruit	die Grapefruit [di ˈɡreːpfruːt]
grapes	die Weintrauben *f pl* [di ˈvaɪntʁaʊbm]
lemons	die Zitronen *f pl* [di tsɪˈtʁoːnn]
mandarins	die Mandarinen *f pl* [di mandaˈʁiːnn]
melon	die Melone [di meˈloːnə]
oranges	die Apfelsinen *f pl* [di ʔapflˈziːnn]
peaches	die Pfirsiche *m pl* [di ˈpfɪɐzɪçə]
pears	die Birnen *f pl* [di bɪʁnn]
pineapple	die Ananas [ˈʔananas]
plums	die Pflaumen *f pl* [di pflaʊmm]
raspberries	die Himbeeren *f pl* [di ˈhɪmbeːʁən]
red currants	die roten Johannisbeeren *f pl*
	[di ʁoːtn joˈhanɪsbeːʁən]
strawberries	die Erdbeeren *f pl* [di ˈʔeɐtbeːʁən]
tangerines	die Tangerinen *f pl* [di tangəˈʁiːnn]

Vegetables / Gemüse

Vegetables	Gemüse
artichokes	die Artischocken f pl [di ʔaːtɪˈʃɔkn̩]
asparagus	der Spargel [ʃpaːgl̩]
avocado	die Avocado [di ʔavoˈkaːdo]
beans	die Bohnen f pl [di boːnn̩]
green beans	grüne Bohnen [ˌgʀyːnə ˈboːnn̩]
white beans	weiße Bohnen [ˌvaɪsə ˈboːnn̩]
kidney beans	rote Bohnen [ˌʀoːtə ˈboːnn̩]
beet(s)	Rote Bete [ˌʀoːtə ˈbeːtə]
cabbage	der Kohl [dɐ koːl]
carrots	die Karotten f pl [di kaˈʀɔtn̩]
cauliflower	der Blumenkohl [ˈbluːmmkoːl]
celeriac	der Sellerie [dɐ ˈzɛləriː]
celery	der Stangensellerie [dɐ ˈʃtaŋŋˌzɛləriː]
corn	der Mais [dɐ maɪs]
cucumber	die Gurke [di ˈgʊɐkə]
eggplants	die Auberginen f pl [di ʔobɐˈʒiːnn̩]
fennel	der Fenchel [dɐ fɛnçl̩]
garlic	der Knoblauch [dɐ ˈknoːblaʊx]
horseradish	der Meerrettich [dɐ ˈmeːʀɛtɪç]
leek	der Lauch [dɐ laʊx]
lentils	die Linsen f pl [di lɪnzn̩]
lettuce	der Kopfsalat [dɐ ˈkɔpfsaˌlaːt]

> *Salat* means: (1) "salad" as in "potato salad," "green salad," etc., and (2) "lettuce." To clarify, use *Kopfsalat* (lettuce) or *Kartoffelsalat, grüner Salat*, etc.
>
> Don't be surprised if you encounter regional dialect words different from those in this list, especially for sausages, rolls, and cakes.

olives	die Oliven f pl [di ʔoˈliːvn̩]
onions	die Zwiebeln f pl [di tsviːbln]
peas	die Erbsen f pl [di ʔɛɐpsn]
peppers	die Paprikaschoten f pl [di ˈpapʀɪkaˌʃoːtn̩]
potatoes	die Kartoffeln f pl [di kaˈtɔfln]
pumpkin	der Kürbis [dɐ ˈkʏɐbɪs]
spinach	der Spinat [dɐ ʃpɪˈnaːt]
tomatoes	die Tomaten f pl [di toˈmaːtn̩]

Herbs and Spices / Kräuter und Gewürze

Herbs and Spices	Kräuter und Gewürze
basil	das Basilikum [das baˈziːlikʊm]
bay leaves	die Lorbeerblätter n pl [di ˈlɔɐbeɐˌblɛtɐ]
borage	der Borretsch [dɐ ˈbɔʀɛtʃ]

caraway seed(s)	der Kümmel [dɐ kʏml]
chervil	der Kerbel [dɐ kɛɐbl]
chili pepper	der Chili [dɐ 'tsɪli]
chives	der Schnittlauch [dɐ 'ʃnɪtlaʊx]
cinnamon	der Zimt [dɐ tsɪmt]
cloves	die Nelken *f pl* [di nɛlkn̩]
coriander	der Koriander [dɐ koʀi'andɐ]
dill	der Dill [dɐ dɪl]
garlic	der Knoblauch [dɐ 'kno:blaʊx]
ginger	der Ingwer [dɐ ˀɪŋvɐ]
herbs	die Kräuter *n pl* [di 'kʀɔɪtɐ]
hot pepper	die Peperoni [di pɛpə'ro:ni]
lovage	der/das Liebstöckel [dɐ/das 'li:pʃtœkl]
marjoram	der Majoran [dɐ 'ma(:)joʀa:n]
mint	die Minze [di 'mɪntsə]
nutmeg	die Muskatnuss [di mʊs'ka:tnʊs]
oregano	der Oregano [dɐ ˀoʀe'ga:no]
paprika	der Paprika [dɐ 'papʀɪka]
parsley	die Petersilie [di pe:tɐ'zi:ljə]
pepper	der Pfeffer [dɐ 'pfɛfɐ]
rosemary	der Rosmarin [dɐ 'ʀo:smaʀi:n]
saffron	der Safran [dɐ 'zafʀa:n]
sage	der Salbei [dɐ 'zalbaɪ]
savory	das Bohnenkraut [das 'bo:nnkʀaʊt]
tarragon	der Estragon [dɐ ˀɛstʀagɔn]
thyme	der Thymian [dɐ 'ty:mia:n]

Bread, Cakes, and Sweets

Backwaren und Süßwaren

The German-speaking countries undoubtedly set the benchmark for bakery goods. What you'll find in every town and city is worthy of any hungry person's attention and would go far beyond the limits of this book. Follow your nose, go in, and point, saying *Was ist das, bitte?*
Kuchen is something baked that is sweet, often combined with other words, like *Apfelkuchen* (apple pastry). *Torte* is roughly like a pie, that is, something sweet is spread over baked dough. *Gebäck* is a collective term used for small baked items, much like cookies. *Brot* always means literally bread, and comes in countless delicious variations.

bread	das Brot [das bʀo:t]
dark rye bread	das Schwarzbrot [das 'ʃva:tsbʀo:t]
white bread	das Weißbrot [das 'vaɪsbʀo:t]
wholegrain bread	das Vollkornbrot [das 'fɔlkɔɐn̩ˌbʀo:t]

155

cake	der Kuchen [de kuːxn]
candy	die Süßigkeiten f pl [di 'zyːsɪçkaɪtn]
chocolate	die Schokolade [di ʃokoˈlaːdə]
chocolate bar	der Schokoriegel [de ˈʃoːkoriːgl]
chocolates	die Pralinen f pl [di pʁaˈliːnn]
cookies	die Kekse m pl [di keːksə]
ice cream	das Eis [das ʔaɪs]
jam/marmalade	die Marmelade [di maməˈlaːdə]

> *Marmalade* in German means any kind of jam. If you want
> orange marmalade, ask for *Orangenmarmelade.*

muesli	das Müsli [das 'myːsli]
rolls	die Brötchen n pl [di bʁøːtçn]
filled rolls	belegte Brötchen [bəˈleːktə bʁøːtçn]
sweets	die Süßigkeiten f pl [di 'zyːsiçkaɪtn]
toast	der Toast [de toːst]

Eggs and Dairy Products Eier und Milchprodukte

butter	die Butter [di 'bʊte]
buttermilk	die Buttermilch [di 'bʊtemɪlç]
cheese	der Käse [de 'kɛːzə]
cottage cheese	der Hüttenkäse [de 'hʏtnkɛːzə]
cream	die Sahne ['zaːnə]
sour cream	die saure Sahne [di zaʊʁə 'zaːnə]
whipping cream	die Schlagsahne ['ʃlaːkzaːnə]
cream cheese	der Frischkäse [de 'fʁɪʃkɛːzə]
eggs	die Eier n pl [di ʔaɪe]
milk	die Milch [mɪlç]
low-fat milk	fettarme Milch ['fɛtʔaːmə mɪlç]
yogurt	der Joghurt [de 'joːgʊet]

Meat   Fleisch und Wurst

beef	das Rindfleisch ['ʁɪntflaɪʃ]
chicken	das Hähnchen [das hɛːnçn]
chop	das Kotelett ['kɔtlɛt]
cold cuts/lunch meat	der Aufschnitt [de ʔaʊfʃnɪt]
cutlet	das Kotelett [das 'kɔtlɛt]
goulash	das Gulasch [das 'gʊlaʃ]
ground meat	das Hackfleisch [das 'hakflaɪʃ]
ham	der Schinken [de ʃɪŋkn]
cooked ham	gekochter Schinken [gəˈkɔxte ʃɪŋkn]
smoked ham	roher Schinken [ʁoːe ʃɪŋkn]
lamb	das Lammfleisch [das 'lamflaɪʃ]
liver sausage	die Leberwurst [di 'leːbevʊest]
meat	das Fleisch [das flaɪʃ]
pork	das Schweinefleisch ['ʃvaɪnəflaɪʃ]

rabbit	das Kaninchen [kaˈniːnçn̩]
salami	die Salami [di zaˈlaːmi]
sausage	die Wurst [di vʊɐst]
small sausages	die Würstchen *n pl* [di vʁɛstçn̩]
	(e.g., frankfurters)
veal	das Kalbfleisch [ˈkalpflaɪʃ]

Fish and Seafood — Fisch und Meeresfrüchte

bream	die Brasse [di ˈbʁasə]
cod	der Kabeljau [dɐ ˈkaːbljaʊ]
crab	der Krebs [dɐ kreːps]
eel	der Aal [dɐ ʔaːl]
herring	der Hering [dɐ ˈheːʁɪŋ]
lobster	der Hummer [dɐ ˈhʊmə]
mackerel	die Makrele [di maˈkʁeːlə]
mussels	die Muscheln *f pl* [di mʊʃln̩]
oysters	die Austern *f pl* [di ˈʔaʊstɐn]
perch	der Barsch [dɐ baːʃ]
plaice	die Scholle [di ˈʃɔlə]
prawns	die Garnelen *f pl* [di gaˈneːln]
salmon	der Lachs [dɐ laks]
shrimp	die Krabben *f pl* [di kʁabm]
sole	die Seezunge [di ˈzeːtsʊŋə]
squid	der Tintenfisch [dɐ ˈtɪntn̩fɪʃ]
swordfish	der Schwertfisch [dɐ ˈʃveetfɪʃ]
trout	die Forelle [di foˈʁɛlə]
tuna	der Thunfisch [dɐ ˈtuːnfɪʃ]

Miscellaneous — Dies und das

almonds	die Mandeln *f pl* [di ˈmandln]
butter	die Butter [di ˈbʊtə]
flour	das Mehl [das meːl]
honey	der Honig [dɐ ˈhoːnɪç]
margarine	die Margarine [di magaˈʁiːnə]
mayonnaise	die Mayonnaise [di maɪoˈneːzə]
mustard	der Senf [dɐ zɛnf/zɛmf]
noodles	die Nudeln *f pl* [di nuːdln]
nuts	die Nüsse *f pl* [di ˈnʏsə]
oil	das Öl [das ʔøːl]
olive oil	das Olivenöl [das ʔoˈliːvnʔøːl]
pasta	die Nudeln *f pl* [di nuːdln]
rice	der Reis [dɐ ʁaɪs]
salt	das Salz [das zalts]
sugar	der Zucker [dɐ ˈtsʊkə]
vegetable stock cube	der Gemüsebrühwürfel
	[dɐ gəˈmyːzəˌbʁyːvvɛfl]
vinegar	der Essig [dɐ ˈʔɛsɪç]

Drinks   ## Getränke

> Wine and liquor are sold openly in all shops offering food or drink. The only restriction is that the buyer must be of age. Identification is rarely, if ever, demanded. If you are looking for especially good wine, there are specialty shops (*Weinhändler* – wine dealer) in almost every larger town or city.

apple juice . . . . der Apfelsaft [dɐ ˀapflzaft]
beer . . . . das Bier [das biɐ]
champagne . . . . der Champagner [dɐ ʃamˈpanjɐ]
cocoa . . . . der Kakao [dɐ kaˈkaʊ]
coffee . . . . der Kaffee [dɐ ˈkafe:/kaˈfe:]
  decaffeinated coffee . . . . . der koffeeinfreie Kaffee
                                   [dɐ kɔfeˀiːnfraɪə ˈkafe:]
mineral water . . . . das Mineralwasser [das mɪnəˈraːlvasɐ]
  sparkling . . . . mit Kohlensäure [mɪt ˈko:l(ə)nzɔɪRə]
  still . . . . ohne Kohlensäure [ˀoːnə ˈko:l(ə)nzɔɪRə]
orange juice . . . . der Orangensaft [dɐ ˀoˈRaŋznzaft]
soft drink . . . . die Limonade [lɪmoˈnaːdə]
tea . . . . der Tee [dɐ te:]
  black tea . . . . der Schwarztee [dɐ ˈʃvaːtste:]
  camomile tea . . . . der Kamillentee [dɐ kaˈmɪl(ə)nte:]
  fruit tea . . . . der Früchtetee [dɐ ˈfRʏçtəte:]
  green tea . . . . der grüne Tee [dɐ ˈgryːnə te:]
  herbal tea . . . . der Kräutertee [dɐ ˈkRɔɪtɐte:]
  peppermint tea . . . . der Pfefferminztee [dɐ ˈpfɛfɐmɪntste:]
  rosehip tea . . . . der Hagebuttentee [dɐ hagəˈbʊtnte:]
  tea bags . . . . der Teebeutel [dɐ ˈte:bɔɪtl]
wine . . . . der Wein [dɐ vaɪn]
  mulled wine . . . . Glühwein [ˈglyːvaɪn]
  red wine . . . . Rotwein [ˈRoːtvaɪn]
  rosé wine . . . . Rosé(wein) [Roˈzeː(vaɪn)]
  white wine . . . . Weißwein [ˈvaɪsvaɪn]

Shampoo and blow dry, please.
Waschen und föhnen, bitte. [ˈvaʃn ˀʊnt føːnn ˈbɪtə]

Wash and cut, please.
Schneiden mit Waschen, bitte. [ˈʃnaɪdn mɪt ˈvaʃn ˈbɪtə]

Dry cut.
Schneiden ohne Waschen. [ˈʃnaɪdn ˀoːnə ˈvaʃn]

I'd like ...
Ich möchte ... [ˀɪç ˈmœçtə ...]

Just trim the ends.
Nur die Spitzen. [nuɐ di ˈʃpɪtsn]

Not too short, please.
Nicht zu kurz, bitte. [nɪçt tsʊ ˈkʊɐts ˈbɪtə]

A bit shorter.
Etwas kürzer. [ˈʔɛtvas ˈkʏɐtsɐ]

Thank you. That's fine.
Vielen Dank. So ist es gut. [ˌfiln ˈdaŋk ˈzoː ˈʔɪst əs ˈguːt]

bangs	der Pony [dɐ ˈpɔni]
beard	der Bart [dɐ baːt]
blond(e)	blond [blɔnt]
to blow dry	föhnen [føːnn]
to comb	kämmen [kɛmm]
curlers	die Lockenwickler m pl [di ˈlɔkŋvɪklɐ]
curls	die Locken f pl [di lɔkn]
dandruff	die Schuppen f pl [di ʃʊpm]
to do someone's hair	frisieren [frɪˈziɐn]
to dye	färben [fɛɐbm]
hair	das Haar [das haː]
dry hair	trockenes Haar [ˈtrɔknəs haː]
greasy hair	fettiges Haar [ˈfɛtɪgəs haː]
hairstyle	die Frisur [di frɪˈzuɐ]
highlights	die Strähnchen n pl [di ˈʃtrɛːnçn]
layered cut	der Stufenschnitt [dɐ ˈʃtuːfnʃnɪt]
mustache	der Schnurrbart [dɐ ˈʃnʊɐbaːt]
parting	der Scheitel [dɐ ʃaɪtl]
perm	die Dauerwelle [di ˈdaʊɐvɛlə]
to set	legen [ˈleːgŋ]
shampoo	das Shampoo [das ˈʃampu]
sideburns	die Koteletten f pl [di kɔtˈlɛtn]
to tint	tönen [tøːnn]

Household Goods

aluminum foil	die Alufolie [di ˈʔalufoːljə]
bottle opener	der Flaschenöffner [dɐ ˈflaʃnˈʔœfnɐ]
can opener	der Dosenöffner [dɐ ˈdoːznˈʔœfnɐ]
candles	die Kerzen f pl [di kɛɐtsn]
charcoal	die Grillkohle [di ˈgrɪlkoːlə]
charcoal starter fluid	der Grillanzünder [dɐ ˈgrɪlantsʏndɐ]
clothesline	die Wäscheleine [di ˈvɛʃəlaɪnə]
clothespins	die Wäscheklammern f pl
	[di ˈvɛʃəklamɐn]

159

corkscrew	der Korkenzieher [dɐ ˈkɔɐkntsiːɐ]
denatured alcohol	der Brennspiritus [dɐ ˈbʀɛnʃpiʀitʊs]
fork	die Gabel [di ˈgaːbl]
garbage bag	der Abfallbeutel [dɐ ˈ⁷apfalbɔɪtl]
glass	das Glas [das glaːs]
grill	der Grill [dɐ gʀɪl]
ice box	die Kühltasche [di ˈkyːltaʃə]
ice pack	das Kühlelement [das ˈkyːlɛlɐˌmɛnt]
kerosene	das Petroleum [das peˈtʀoːleʊm]
knife	das Messer [das ˈmɛsɐ]
paper napkins	die Papierservietten f pl
	[di paˈpiɐzɐˌvjɛtn]
plastic bag	der Plastikbeutel [dɐ ˈplastɪkbɔɪtl]
plastic cup/mug	der Plastikbecher [dɐ ˈplastɪkbɛçɐ]
plastic wrap	die Frischhaltefolie [di ˈfʀɪʃhaltəˌfoːljə]
pocket knife	das Taschenmesser [das ˈtaʃnmɛsɐ]
spoon	der Löffel [dɐ lœfl]
thermos (flask)	die Thermosflasche® [di ˈtɛɐmɔsflaʃə]
trash can liner	der Abfallbeutel [dɐ ˈ⁷apfalbɔɪtl]

Jewelry Store

bracelet	das Armband [das ˈ⁷aːmbant]
brooch	die Brosche [di ˈbʀɔʃə]
costume jewelry	der Modeschmuck [dɐ ˈmoːdəʃmʊk]
crystal	der Kristall [dɐ kʀɪsˈtal]
earrings	die Ohrringe m pl [di ˈ⁷oːʀɪŋə]
earstud	der Ohrstecker [dɐ ˈ⁷oɐʃtɛkɐ]
gold	das Gold [das ˈgɔlt]
jewelry	der Schmuck [dɐ ʃmʊk]
necklace	die Kette [di ˈkɛtə]
pearl	die Perle [di ˈpɛɐlə]
pendant	der Anhänger [dɐ ˈ⁷anhɛŋɐ]
platinum	das Platin [das ˈplaːtiːn]
ring	der Ring [dɐ ʀɪŋ]
silver	das Silber [das ˈzɪlbɐ]
stud earring	der Ohrstecker [dɐ ˈ⁷oɐʃtɛkɐ]
tiepin	die Krawattennadel [di kʀaˈvatnaːdl]
travel alarm	der Reisewecker [dɐ ˈʀaɪəvɛkɐ]
waterproof watch	die wasserdichte Uhr
	[di ˈvasɐdɪçtə ˈ⁷uɐ]
wristwatch	die Armbanduhr [di ˈ⁷aːmbantˌ⁷uɐ]
ladies'	für Damen [fyɐ ˈdaːmən]
men's	für Herren [fyɐ ˈhɛʀən]

Optician

Could you repair these glasses for me, please.
Würden Sie mir bitte diese Brille reparieren?
['vʏedn zi miɐ 'bɪtə 'diːzə 'bʀɪlə ʀɛpa'ʀiɐn]

I'm short-sighted/near-sighted.
Ich bin kurzsichtig. ['ɪç bɪn 'kʊɐtsɪçtɪç]

I'm long-sighted/far-sighted.
Ich bin weitsichtig. ['ɪç bɪn 'vaɪtsɪçtɪç]

What's your eye prescription?
Wie ist Ihre Sehstärke? ['vi ɪst iʀə 'zeːʃtɛɐkə]

... in the right eye, ... in the left eye.
rechts ..., links ... [ʀɛçts ... lɪŋks ...]

When can I pick up the glasses?
Wann kann ich die Brille abholen? [van kan ɪç di 'bʀɪlə 'ʔaphoːln]

I'd like ...
Ich hätte gern ... ['ɪç 'hɛtə 'gɛɐn ...]

some storage solution
eine Aufbewahrungslösung [,'aɪnə 'ʔaʊfbəvaːʀʊŋs,løːzʊŋ]

some cleaning solution
eine Reinigungslösung [,'aɪnə 'ʀaɪnɪgʊŋs,løːzʊŋ]

for hard/soft contact lenses.
für harte/weiche Kontaktlinsen. [fyɐ 'haːtə/'vaɪçə kɔn'taktlɪnzn]

some sunglasses.
eine Sonnenbrille. ['ʔaɪnə 'zɔnnbʀɪlə]

some binoculars.
ein Fernglas. ['ʔaɪn 'fɛɐnglaːs]

Photographic Materials

➢ also Photos

I'd like ...
Ich hätte gern ... ['ɪç 'hɛtə gɛɐn]

a film for this camera.
einen Film für diesen Fotoapparat.
['ʔaɪnn 'fɪlm fyɐ 'diːzn 'foːtoʔapa,ʀaːt]

a color film (for slides).
einen Farbfilm (für Dias). ['aɪnn 'faːpfɪlm (fyɐ 'diaːs)]

a film with 36/24/12 exposures.
einen Film mit sechsunddreißig/ vierundzwanzig/zwölf
Aufnahmen.
['aɪnn 'fɪlm mɪt 'zɛksʊn,dʀasɪç/ 'fieʊn,tsvantsɪç/tsvœlf 'ʔaʊfnaːmm]

... doesn't work/is broken.
... funktioniert nicht/ist kaputt. [fʊŋktsjoˈniet nɪçt/ɪst kaˈpʊt]

Can you repair/fix it?
Können Sie es reparieren? [ˈkœnn zi əs ʀɛpaˈʀien]

black-and-white film	der Schwarzweiß-Film [de ʃvaːtsˈvaɪsfɪlm]
camcorder	der Camcorder [de ˈkamkɔede]
digital camera	die Digitalkamera [di digiˈtaːlˌkameʀa]
DVD	die DVD [di defaʊˈdeː]
film speed	die Filmempfindlichkeit [di ˈfɪlmɛmpfɪntlɪçkaɪt]
flash	das Blitzgerät [das ˈblɪtsgəʀɛːt]
lens	das Objektiv [das ʔɔbjɛkˈtiːf]
light meter	der Belichtungsmesser [de bəˈlɪçtʊŋsˌmɛse]
Polaroid® camera	die Sofortbildkamera [di zoˈfɔetbɪltˌkameʀa]
self-timer	der Selbstauslöser [de ˈzɛlpstaʊsløːze]
shutter	der Auslöser [de ʔˈaʊsløːze]
telephoto lens	das Teleobjektiv [das ˈteːləʔɔbjɛkˌtiːf]
tripod	das Stativ [das ʃtaˈtiːf]
video camera	die Videokamera [di ˈviːdeoˌkameʀa]
video cassette	die Videokassette [di ˈviːdeokaˌsɛtə]
video film	der Videofilm [de ˈviːdeofɪlm]
video recorder	der Videorekorder [de ˈviːdeoʀeˌkɔede]
viewfinder	der Sucher [de ˈzuːxe]

Shoes and Leather Goods

I'd like a pair of shoes.
Ich hätte gern ein Paar Schuhe. [ʔɪç ˈhɛtə gɛen ʔaɪn paː ˈʃuə]

I take (shoe) size ...
Ich habe Schuhgröße ... [ʔɪç ˈhaːbə ˈʃuːgrøːsə]

They're too tight.
Sie sind zu eng. [zi zɪnt tsʊ ʔˈɛŋ]

They're too big.
Sie sind zu groß. [zi zɪnt tsʊ gʀoːs]

backpack	der Rucksack [de ˈʀʊkzak]
bag	die Tasche [di ˈtaʃə]
beach shoes	die Strandschuhe m pl [di ˈʃtʀantʃuə]
belt	der Gürtel [de gʏetl]
boots	die Stiefel m pl [di ʃtiːfl]

fanny pack	die Gürteltasche [di ɡʏɐtltaʃə]
flip-flops	die Badeschuhe *m pl* [di 'ba:dəʃuə]
gym shoes	die Turnschuhe *m pl* [di 'tʊɐnʃuə]
handbag	die Handtasche [di 'han(t)taʃə]
leather coat	der Ledermantel [dɐ 'le:dɐmantl]
leather jacket	die Lederjacke [di 'le:dɐjakə]
leather trousers	die Lederhose [di 'le:dɐho:zə]
rubber boots	die Gummistiefel *m pl* [di 'ɡʊmiʃti:fl]
sandals	die Sandalen *f pl* [di zan'da:ln]
shoe	der Schuh [dɐ ʃu:]
shoe brush	die Schuhbürste [di 'ʃu:bʏɐstə]
shoe cream	die Schuhcreme [di 'ʃu:kʀɛːm]
shoelaces	die Schnürsenkel *m pl* [di 'ʃnyɐzɛŋkl]
shoulder bag	die Umhängetasche [di ʔʊmhɛŋətaʃə]
shoulder strap	der Schulterriemen [dɐ 'ʃʊltɐʀiːmm]
ski boots	die Skistiefel *m pl* [di 'ʃiːʃtiːfl]
sneakers	die Turnschuhe *m pl* [di 'tʊɐnʃuə]
sole	die Sohle [di 'zo:lə]
suitcase	der Koffer [dɐ 'kɔfɐ]
suitcase/cabin tote on wheels	der Trolleykoffer/die Trolleytasche [dɐ 'tʀɔlɪkɔfɐ/di 'tʀɔlɪtaʃə]
travel bag	die Reisetasche [di ʀaɪzətaʃə]

Souvenirs

I'd like ...
Ich hätte gern ... [ʔɪç 'hɛtə ɡɛɐn]

a nice souvenir.
ein hübsches Andenken. [ʔaɪn 'hʏpʃəs ʔandɛŋkn]

something typical of this area.
etwas Typisches aus dieser Gegend.
[ʔɛtvas 'ty:pɪʃ ʔaʊs diːzɐ 'ge:gɛnt]

How much do you want to spend?
Wie viel wollen Sie ausgeben? ['vi:_fi:l vɔln zi ʔaʊsge:bm]

I'd like something that's not too expensive.
Ich möchte etwas nicht zu Teures.
[ʔɪç 'mœçtə ˌʔɛtvas 'nɪç(t) tsʊ 'tɔɪʀəs]

That's lovely.
Das ist aber hübsch. [das ɪst ʔabɐ hʏpʃ]

Thanks, but I didn't find anything (I liked).
Danke schön, ich habe nichts gefunden(, das mir gefällt).
['daŋkə ʃøːn ʔɪç 'ha:bə nɪçts gə'fʊndn (das miɐ gə'fɛlt)]

ceramics	die Keramik [di ke'ʀaːmɪk]
genuine	echt [ˀɛçt]
handmade	handgemacht ['hantɡəmaxt]
jewelry	der Schmuck [dɐ ʃmʊk]
local specialties	die regionalen Spezialitäten [di ʀegio'naːln ʃpɛtsjali'tɛːtn]
pottery	die Töpferwaren f pl [di 'tœpfeva:ʀən]
souvenir	das Souvenir [das zuvə'niːɐ]
wood-carving	die Schnitzerei [di ʃnɪtsə'ʀaɪ]

Tobacco

A pack of filter-tipped ..., please.
Eine Schachtel ... mit Filter, bitte! [ˀaɪnə ʃaxtl ... mɪt 'fɪltɐ 'bɪtə]

A carton of plain ..., please.
Eine Stange ... ohne Filter, bitte! [ˀaɪnə 'ʃtaŋə ...ˀoːnə 'fɪltɐ 'bɪtə]

Ten cigars/cigarillos, please.
Zehn Zigarren/Zigarillos, bitte. [tseːn tsɪ'gaʀən/tsɪga'ʀɪloːs 'bɪtə]

A packet of cigarette tobacco, please.
Ein Päckchen Zigarettentabak, bitte.
[ˀaɪn pɛkçn 'tsɪgaʀɛtn̩ˌtabak 'bɪtə]

A tin of pipe tobacco, please.
Eine Dose Pfeifentabak, bitte. [ˀaɪnə 'doːzə '(p)faɪfn̩ˌtabak 'bɪtə]

ashtray	der Aschenbecher [dɐ ˀaʃnbɛçɐ]
cigar	die Zigarre [di tsɪ'gaʀə]
cigarette	die Zigarette [di tsɪga'ʀɛtə]
cigarillo	das Zigarillo [das tsɪga'ʀɪlo]
lighter	das Feuerzeug [das 'fɔɪɐtsɔɪk]
matches	die Streichhölzer n pl [di 'ʃtʀaɪçhœltsɐ]
pipe	die Pfeife [di 'pfaɪfə]

Drugstore Items

after-shave lotion	das Rasierwasser [das ʀa'ziːɐvasɐ]
brush	die Bürste [di 'bʏʀstə]
comb	der Kamm [dɐ kam]
condom	das Kondom [kɔn'doːm]
cotton swabs	das Wattestäbchen [das 'vatəʃtɛːpçn]
cotton wool	die Watte [di 'vatə]
cream	die Creme [di kʀɛːm]
dental floss	die Zahnseide [di 'tsaːnzaɪdə]
deodorant	das Deo [das 'deo]
detergent (clothes)	das Waschmittel [das 'vaʃmɪtl]
detergent (dishes)	das Spülmittel [das 'ʃpyːlmɪtl]

Band-Aid	das Pflaster [das 'pflastɐ]
dishcloth	das Spültuch [das 'ʃpy:ltu:x]
dishwashing brush	die Spülbürste [di 'ʃpy:lbʏstə]
hair gel	das Haargel [das 'ha:ge:l]
hairpins	die Haarklammern f pl [di 'ha:klamɐn]
Kleenex®	das Tempo(taschentuch)® [das 'tɛmpo,taʃntu:x]
lip balm	die Lippenpomade [di 'lɪpmpoma:də]
lipstick	der Lippenstift [dɐ 'lɪpmʃtɪft]
mascara	die Wimperntusche [di 'vɪmpɛntʊʃə]
mirror	der Spiegel [dɐ ʃpi:gl]
moisturizing cream	die Feuchtigkeitscreme [di 'fɔɪçtɪçkaɪts,kʀɛ:m]
nail polish	der Nagellack [dɐ 'na:gllak]
nail polish remover	der Nagellackentferner [dɐ 'na:gllakɛnt,fɛenɐ]
nail scissors	die Nagelschere [di 'na:glʃe:ʀə]
night cream	die Nachtcreme [di 'naxtkʀɛ:m]
panty liners	die Slipeinlagen f pl [di 'slɪpaɪnla:gŋ]
paper handkerchiefs	die Papiertaschentücher n pl [di pa'pie,taʃnty:çɐ]
perfume	das Parfüm [das pa'fy:m]
powder	der Puder [dɐ 'pu:dɐ]
razor blade	die Rasierklinge [di ʀa'zieklɪŋə]
sanitary napkins	die Damenbinden f pl [di 'da:mmbɪndn]
scent	das Parfüm [das pa'fy:m]
shampoo	das Schampoo [das 'ʃampo/'ʃampu]
shaver	der Rasierapparat [dɐ ʀa'zie?apa,ʀa:t]
shaving brush	der Rasierpinsel [dɐ ʀa'ziepɪnzl]
shaving foam	der Rasierschaum [dɐ ʀa'zieʃaʊm]
shower gel	das Duschgel [das 'du:ʃge:l]
soap	die Seife [di 'zaɪfə]
sun cream	die Sonnencreme [di 'zɔnnkʀɛ:m]
sun protection factor	der Lichtschutzfaktor [dɐ 'lɪçtʃʊts,faktoɐ]
suntan lotion	die Sonnenmilch [di 'zɔnnmɪlç]
suntan oil	das Sonnenöl [das 'zɔnn?ø:l]
tampons	die Tampons m pl [di 'tampɔŋs]
mini/regular/super/super plus	mini/normal/super/super plus ['mi:ni/nɔɐ'ma:l/'zu:pe/,zu:pe 'plʊs]
tea-tree oil	das Teebaumöl [das 'te:baʊm?ø:l]
toilet paper	das Toilettenpapier [das to'lɛtnpa,pie]
toothbrush	die Zahnbürste [di 'tsa:nbʏstə]
toothpaste	die Zahnpasta [di 'tsa:npasta]
toothpick	das Zahnstocher [dɐ 'tsa:nʃtɔxɐ]
washrag	der Waschlappen [dɐ 'vaʃlapm]
washcloth	der Waschlappen [dɐ 'vaʃlapm]

OL.
HAMOMILL

MENTHOL.
ERIAN.

OL.
AURANT.
FLOR.

Health

In an emergency
If you have any need of medical assistance, you will find first-rate facilities and medical personnel in all the German-speaking countries. As anywhere else, expect standards in large cities to be higher than those in small towns. Particularly noteworthy are the university clinics in most cities. Here you will find highly motivated doctors and assistants who almost always speak good English, should you be worried that your German won't be sufficient.

At the Pharmacy

Can you tell me where the nearest pharmacy (with all-night service) is, please?
Können Sie mir sagen, wo die nächste Apotheke (mit Nachtdienst) ist?
[kœnn zi miɐ za:gn vo: di 'nɛːçstə ʔapo'te:kə (mɪt 'naxtdiːnst) ʔɪst]

Could you give me something for ..., please?
Könnten Sie mir bitte etwas gegen ... geben
[kœntn zi miɐ 'bɪtə 'ʔɛtvas ge:gŋ ... ge:bm]

You need a prescription for this.
Für dieses Mittel brauchen Sie ein Rezept.
[fyɐ 'diːzəs 'mɪtl bʀaʊxn zi ʔaɪn ʀe'tsɛpt]

➢**also At the Doctor's Office**

after-sun lotion	die Sonnenbrandlotion [di 'zɔnnbʀant‚loʊʃən]
aspirin	das Aspirin [das ʔaspi'ʀiːn]
Band-Aid	das Pflaster [das 'pflastɐ]
burn ointment	die Brandsalbe [di 'bʀantzalbə]
cardiac stimulant	das Kreislaufmittel [das 'kʀaɪslaʊf‚mɪtl]
condom	das Kondom [das kɔn'doːm]
cotton wool/cotton	die Watte [di 'vatə]
cough mixture/syrup	der Hustensaft [dɐ 'huːstnzaft]
disinfectant	das Desinfektionsmittel [das dezɪnfɛk'tsjoːnsmɪtl]
drops	die Tropfen m pl [di 'tʀɔpfn]
eardrops	die Ohrentropfen m pl [di 'ʔoːʀəntʀɔpfn]
elastic bandage	die Elastikbinde [di ʔe'lastɪkbɪndə]
eyedrops	die Augentropfen m pl [di 'ʔaʊɡŋtʀɔpfn]

gauze bandage	die Mullbinde [di 'mʊlbɪndə]
glucose	der Traubenzucker [dɐ 'tʀaʊbmtsʊkɐ]
headache tablets	die Kopfschmerztabletten f pl
	[di 'kɔpfʃmɛɐtsta,blɛtn]
insect repellent	das Mittel gegen Insektenstiche
	[das 'mɪtl ge:gn̩ ʔɪn'zɛktnʃtɪçə]
insulin	das Insulin [das ʔɪnzʊ'li:n]
laxative	das Abführmittel [das ʔapfyɐ,mɪtl]
medicine	das Medikament [das medɪka'mɛnt]
ointment	die Salbe [di 'zalbə]
pain-killing tablets	die Schmerztabletten f pl
	[di 'ʃmɛɐtsta,blɛtn]
pill	die Tablette [di ta'blɛtə]
powder	der Puder [dɐ 'pu:dɐ]
prescription	das Rezept [das ʀe'tsɛpt]
remedy	das Mittel [das 'mɪtl]
sedative	das Beruhigungsmittel
	[das bə'ʀʊɪgʊŋsmɪtl]
sleeping pills	die Schlaftabletten f pl [di 'ʃla:fta,blɛtn]
sunburn lotion	die Sonnenbrandlotion
	[di 'zɔnnbʀant,loʊʃən]
suppository	das Zäpfchen [das 'tsɛpfçn]
tablet	die Tablette [di ta'blɛtə]
thermometer	das Fieberthermometer
	[das 'fi:bɐtɛɐmo,me:tɐ]
throat lozenges	die Halstabletten f pl [di 'halsta,blɛtn]
tincture of iodine	die Jodtinktur [di 'jo:tɪŋktuɐ]
tranquilizer	das Beruhigungsmittel
	[das bə'ʀʊɪgʊŋsmɪtl]
vitamin pills	die Vitamintabletten f pl
	[di vɪta'mi:nta,blɛtn]

At the Doctor's Office

> also Traveling with Children

Could you recommend a/an ...?
Könnten Sie mir einen ... empfehlen?
['kœntn zi miɐ ʔaɪnn ... ʔɛmp'fe:ln]

dentist
Zahnarzt ['tsa:n̩ʔa:tst]

dermatologist
Hautarzt ['haʊtʔa:tst]

doctor
Arzt/eine Ärztin [ʔa:tst/ʔaɪnə 'ʔɛɐtstɪn]

169

ear, nose, and throat specialist

Hals-Nasen-Ohren-Arzt [hals↓na:zn↓ʔo:rən↓ʔa:tst]

optometrist

Augenarzt [ʔaʊgn̩ʔa:tst]

general practitioner

praktischen Arzt ['pʀaktɪʃn̩ ʔa:tst]

gynaecologist

Frauenarzt ['fʀaʊən̩ʔa:tst]

pediatrician

Kinderarzt ['kɪndɐʔa:tst]

urologist

Urologen [ʔuʀoˈlo:gn̩]

Beipackzettel	Medicine information / application leaflet
Zusammensetzung	Ingredients
Anwendungsgebiete	Areas of application
Gegenanzeigen	Contraindications
Wechselwirkungen	Interactions
Nebenwirkungen	Side-effects
Dosierungsanleitung:	**Dosage:**
1 x / mehrmals täglich einnehmen	Take once / several times per day
1 Tablette	1 tablet
20 Tropfen	20 drops
1 Messbecher	1 measuring cup
vor dem Essen	before meals
nach dem Essen	after meals
auf nüchternen Magen	on an empty stomach
unzerkaut mit etwas Flüssigkeit einnehmen	Swallow whole with water
in etwas Wasser auflösen	Dissolve in a small amount of water
im Mund zergehen lassen	Dissolve in your mouth
dünn auf die Haut auftragen und einreiben	Apply thin layer to skin and rub in
Erwachsene	adults
Säuglinge	infants
Schulkinder	schoolchildren
Kleinkinder	toddlers
Jugendliche	young adults
Für Kinder unzugänglich aufbewahren!	Keep away from children!

Where's his/her office?
Wo ist seine/ihre Praxis? [vo: ?ɪst ˌzaɪnə/ˌ?i:ʀə 'pʀaksɪs]

I'd like to make an appointment.
Ich möchte einen Termin ausmachen.
[?ɪç 'mœçtə ?aɪnn tɛe'mi:n 'ausmaxn]

Medical Complaints

What's the trouble?
Was für Beschwerden haben Sie? ['vas_fye bə'ʃveedn 'ha:bm zi:]

I'm running a temperature.
Ich habe Fieber. [?ɪç 'ha:bə 'fi:bɐ]

I often feel nauseous.
Mir ist oft schlecht. [mie ?ɪst ?ɔft 'ʃlɛçt]

Sometimes I feel dizzy.
Mir ist manchmal schwindlig. [mie ?ɪst 'mançma:l 'ʃvɪndlɪç]

I fainted.
Ich bin ohnmächtig geworden. [?ɪç bɪn '?o:nmɛçtɪç gə'vɔedn]

I have a bad cold.
Ich bin stark erkältet. [?ɪç bɪn ʃta:k ?e'kɛltət]

I have ...
Ich habe ... [?ɪç 'ha:bə]
  a headache.
  Kopfschmerzen. ['kɔpfʃmɛetsn]
  a sore throat.
  Halsschmerzen. ['halsʃmɛetsn]
  a cough.
  Husten. [hu:stn]

I've been stung.
Ich bin gestochen worden. [?ɪç bɪn gə'ʃtɔxn 'vɔedn]

I've been bitten.
Ich bin gebissen worden. [?ɪç bɪn gə'bɪsn 'vɔedn]

I have an upset stomach.
Ich habe mir den Magen verdorben.
[?ɪç ˌha:bə mie den 'ma:gŋ ve'dɔebm]

I have diarrhea.
Ich habe Durchfall. [?ɪç 'ha:bə 'dʊeçfal]

I'm constipated.
Ich habe Verstopfung. [?ɪç 'ha:bə fe'ʃtɔpfʊŋ]

The food doesn't agree with me.
Ich vertrage das Essen nicht. [?ɪç fe'tʀa:gə das '?ɛsn nɪçt]

I can't stand the heat.
Ich vertrage die Hitze nicht. [ʔɪç fɐˈtʀaːgə di ˈhɪtsə nɪçt]

I've hurt myself.
Ich habe mich verletzt. [ʔɪç ˈhaːbə mɪç fɐˈlɛtst]

I fell down.
Ich bin gestürzt. [ʔɪç bɪn gəˈʃtʏɐtst]

Can you prescribe something for ...?
Können Sie mir bitte etwas gegen ... verschreiben?
[ˈkœnn zi miɐ ˈbɪtə ʔˀɛtvas ˈgeːgn̩ ... fɐˈʃʀaɪbm]

I usually take ...
Normalerweise nehme ich ... [nɔˈmaːlɐvaɪzə ˈneːm ɪç]

I have high/low blood pressure.
Ich habe einen hohen/niedrigen Blutdruck.
[ʔɪç ˌhaːbə ʔˀaɪnn ˈhoːn/ˈniːdʀɪgn ˈbluːtdʀʊk]

I'm a diabetic.
Ich bin Diabetiker/Diabetikerin. [ʔɪç bɪn diaˈbeːtɪkɐ/diaˈbeːtɪkəʀɪn]

I'm pregnant.
Ich bin schwanger. [ʔɪç bɪn ˈʃvaŋɐ]

I had ... recently
Ich hatte vor kurzem ... [ʔɪç ˌhatə foɐ ˈkʊɐtsm]

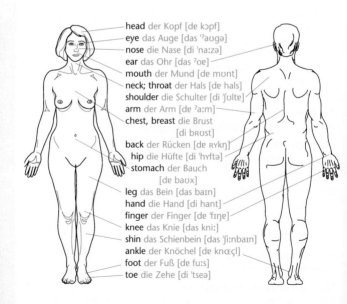

head der Kopf [dɐ kɔpf]
eye das Auge [das ʔˀaʊgə]
nose die Nase [di ˈnaːzə]
ear das Ohr [das ʔoɐ]
mouth der Mund [dɐ mʊnt]
neck; throat der Hals [dɐ hals]
shoulder die Schulter [di ˈʃʊltɐ]
arm der Arm [dɐ ʔaːm]
chest, breast die Brust [di bʀʊst]
back der Rücken [dɐ ʀʏkn̩]
hip die Hüfte [di ˈhʏftə]
stomach der Bauch [dɐ baʊx]
leg das Bein [das baɪn]
hand die Hand [di hant]
finger der Finger [dɐ ˈfɪŋɐ]
knee das Knie [das kniː]
shin das Schienbein [das ˈʃiːnbaɪn]
ankle der Knöchel [dɐ knœçl]
foot der Fuß [dɐ fuːs]
toe die Zehe [di ˈtseə]

What can I do for you?
Was kann ich für Sie tun? [vas kan ıç fyɐ zi 'tuːn]

Where does it hurt?
Wo tut es weh? [voː 'tuːt əs 've:]

I have some pain here.
Ich habe hier Schmerzen. [ʔıç 'haːbə 'hiɐ 'ʃmɛɐtsn]

Uncover your arm, please.
Bitte, machen Sie Ihren Arm frei. ['bɪtə maxn zi ʔiɐn ʔaːm fʀaɪ]

Take off your clothes, please.
Bitte, machen Sie sich frei. ['bɪtə maxn zi zıç 'fʀaɪ]

Take a deep breath.
Tief einatmen. [tiːf ʔaɪnaːtmən]

Hold your breath.
Atem anhalten. [ʔaːtəm ʔanhaltn]

I need to do a blood/urine test.
Ich brauche eine Blutprobe/ Urinprobe.
[ʔıç ˌbʀaʊxə ˌʔaɪnə 'bluːtpʀoːbə/ʔuˈʀiːnpʀoːbə]

You need a few days in bed.
Sie brauchen ein paar Tage Bettruhe.
[zi bʀaʊxn aɪn paː 'taːgə 'bɛtʀuə]

It's nothing serious.
Es ist nichts Ernstes. [ʔəs ɪst nıçts (nɪks) ʔɛɐnstəs]

Do you have a vaccination record?
Haben Sie einen Impfpass? [ha(ː)bm zi ʔaɪnn ʔɪmpfpas]

I've been vaccinated against ...
Ich bin gegen ... geimpft. [ʔıç bın geːgŋ ... gəˈʔɪmpft]

HEALTH

EU nationals are covered free of charge for medical and dental treatment in Germany and Austria on production of an E111 form. Visitors from non-EU countries should take out medical insurance before traveling.

In the Hospital

How long will I have to stay here?
Wie lange muss ich hier bleiben? [vi‿'laŋə mʊs ɪç 'hiɐ blaɪbm]

I can't sleep.
Ich kann nicht einschlafen. [ˀɪç kan nɪçt ˀaɪnʃlaːfn]

Could you give me ..., please.
Geben Sie mir bitte ... ['geːbm zi miɐ ˌbɪtə]

  a glass of water
  ein Glas Wasser [ˀaɪn glaːs 'vasɐ]
  a pain–killing tablet
  eine Schmerztablette [ˌˀaɪnə 'ʃmɛɐtstaˌblɛtə]
  a sleeping pill
  eine Schlaftablette [ˌˀaɪnə 'ʃlaːftaˌblɛtə]
  a hot-water bottle
  eine Wärmflasche [ˀaɪnə 'vɛɐmflaʃə]

When can I get up?
Wann darf ich aufstehen? [van daːf ɪç ˀaʊfʃteːn]

Illnesses and Complaints

abscess	der Abszess [dɐ ˀapsˈɛs]
AIDS	das Aids [das ˀɛɪts]
to be allergic to	allergisch sein gegen ... [ˀalɛˈgɪʃ zaɪn 'geːgn]
allergy	die Allergie [di ˀal(ɛ)ɐˈgiː]
angina	die Angina [di ˀaŋˈgiːna]
appendicitis	die Blinddarmentzündung [di 'blɪntdaːmɛnˌtsʏndʊŋ]
asthma	das Asthma [das ˀastma]
attack	der Anfall [dɐ ˀanfal]
backache	die Rückenschmerzen m pl [di 'ʀʏknʃmɛɐtsn]
bleeding	die Blutung [di 'bluːtʊŋ]
blood poisoning	die Blutvergiftung [di 'bluːtfɐgɪftʊŋ]
broken	gebrochen [gəˈbʀɔxn]
bronchitis	die Bronchitis [di bʀɔnˈçiːtɪs]
bruise (*caused by hitting*)	die Prellung [di 'pʀɛlʊŋ]
bruise (*caused by pinching*)	die Quetschung [di 'kvɛtʃʊŋ]
burn	die Verbrennung [di fɐ'bʀɛnʊŋ]
cancer	der Krebs [dɐ kʀeːps]
cardiac infarction	der Herzinfarkt [dɐ 'hɛɐtsɪnfaːkt]
circulatory disorder	die Kreislaufstörung [di 'kʀaɪslaʊfʃtøˌʀʊŋ]
cold	die Erkältung [di ˀɛ'kɛltʊŋ]
colic	die Kolik [di 'koːlɪk]

174

concussion	die Gehirnerschütterung [di gəˈhɪɐ̯neˌʃtərʊŋ]
constipation	die Verstopfung [di fɐˈʃtɔpfʊŋ]
contagious	ansteckend [ˈʔanʃtɛkn̩t]
cramp	der Krampf [dɐ kʀampf]
cut	die Schnittwunde [di ˈʃnɪtvʊndə]
diabetes	der Diabetes [dɐ diaˈbeːtəs]
diarrhea	der Durchfall [dɐ ˈdʊɐ̯çfal]
difficulty in breathing	die Atembeschwerden f pl [di ˈʔaːtmbəʃveːɐ̯dn̩]
diphtheria	die Diphtherie [di dɪftəˈʀiː]
dizziness	das Schwindelgefühl [das ˈʃvɪndl̩ɡəfyːl]
to faint	in Ohnmacht fallen [ˈʔɪn ˈʔoːnmaxt faln̩]
fever	das Fieber [das ˈfiːbɐ]
fit	der Anfall [dɐ ˈʔanfal]
flu	die Grippe [di ˈɡʀɪpə]
food poisoning	die Lebensmittelvergiftung [di ˈleːbmsmɪtl̩fɐˌɡɪftʊŋ]
fracture	der Knochenbruch [dɐ ˈknɔxnbʀʊx]
growth	die Geschwulst [di ɡəˈʃvʊlst]
hay fever	der Heuschnupfen [dɐ ˈhɔɪʃnʊpfn̩]
headache	die Kopfschmerzen m pl [di ˈkɔpfʃmɛɐ̯tsn̩]
heart attack	der Herzinfarkt [dɐ ˈhɛɐ̯tsɪnfaːkt]
heart defect	der Herzfehler [dɐ ˈhɛɐ̯tsfeːlɐ]
heart trouble	die Herzbeschwerden f pl [ˈhɛɐ̯tsbəʃveːɐ̯dn̩]
heartburn	das Sodbrennen [das ˈzoːtbʀɛnn̩]
hemorrhoids	die Hämorriden f pl [di hɛmoˈʀiːdn̩]
hernia	der Leistenbruch [dɐ ˈlaɪstnbʀʊx]
high blood pressure	der Bluthochdruck [dɐ ˈbluːthoːxdʀʊk]
hoarse	heiser [ˈhaɪzɐ]
to hurt	wehtun [ˈveːtuːn]
to hurt oneself	sich verletzen [zɪç fɐˈlɛtsn̩]
ill	krank [kʀaŋk]
illness	die Krankheit [di ˈkʀaŋkhaɪt]
impaired balance	die Gleichgewichtsstörungen f pl [di ˈɡlaɪçɡəvɪçtsˌʃtøːʀʊŋŋ]
impaired vision	die Sehstörungen f pl [di ˈzeːʃtøːʀʊŋŋ]
indigestion	die Verdauungsstörung [di fɐˈdaʊʊŋʃtøːʀʊŋ]
infection	die Infektion [di ˈʔɪnfɛkˈtsjoːn]
inflammation	die Entzündung [di ˈʔɛnˈtsʏndʊŋ]
inflammation of the middle ear	die Mittelohrentzündung [di ˈmɪtlˈʔoːɐnˌtsʏndʊŋ]
influenza	die Grippe [di ˈɡʀɪpə]
to injure	verletzen [fɐˈlɛtsn̩]

injury	die Verletzung [di fɐˈlɛtsʊŋ]
insect bite	der Insektenstich [dɐ ʔɪnˈzɛktnʃtɪç]
insomnia	die Schlaflosigkeit [di ˈʃlaːfloziçkaɪt]
jaundice	die Gelbsucht [di ˈgɛlpzʊxt]
kidney stone	der Nierenstein [dɐ ˈniːrənʃtaɪn]
lumbago	der Hexenschuss [dɐ ˈhɛksnʃʊs]
migraine	die Migräne [di miˈgrɛːnə]
miscarriage	die Fehlgeburt [di ˈfeːlgəbʊɐt]
nausea	der Brechreiz [dɐ ˈbrɛçraɪts]
nephritis	die Nierenentzündung [di ˈniːrənʔɛnˌtsʏndʊŋ]
nosebleed	das Nasenbluten [das ˈnaːznbluːtn]
pain	die Schmerzen m pl [di ˈʃmɛɐtsn]
painful	schmerzhaft [ˈʃmɛɐtshaft]
paralysis	die Lähmung [di ˈlɛːmʊŋ]
piles	die Hämorriden f pl [di hɛmɔrɪːdn]
pneumonia	die Lungenentzündung [di ˈlʊŋənʔɛnˌtsʏndʊŋ]
poisoning	die Vergiftung [di vɐˈgɪftʊŋ]
polio	die Kinderlähmung [di ˈkɪndɐlɛːmʊŋ]
pulled muscle	die Zerrung [di ˈtsɛrʊŋ]
rash	der Ausschlag [dɐ ʔaʊʃlaːk]
rheumatism	das Rheuma [das ˈrɔɪma]
rupture	der Leistenbruch [dɐ ˈlaɪstnbrʊx]
sciatica	der Ischias [dɐ ʔɪʃias]
shivering fit	der Schüttelfrost [dɐ ˈʃʏtlfrɔst]
sick	krank [kraŋk]
sinusitis	die Stirnhöhlenentzündung [di ˈʃtɪrnhøːlnʔɛnˌtsʏndʊŋ]
sleeplessness	die Schlaflosigkeit [di ˈʃlaːfloziçkaɪt]
smallpox	die Pocken f pl [di pɔkn]
sore throat	die Halsschmerzen m pl [di ˈhalsʃmɛɐtsn]
sprained	verstaucht [fɐˈʃtaʊxt]
stitch	das Seitenstechen [das ˈzaɪtnʃtɛçn]
stomachache	die Magenschmerzen m pl [di ˈmaːgnʃmɛɐtsn]
stroke	der Schlaganfall [dɐ ˈʃlaːkanfal]
sunburn	der Sonnenbrand [dɐ ˈzɔnnbrant]
sunstroke	der Sonnenstich [dɐ ˈzɔnnʃtɪç]
swelling	die Schwellung [di ˈʃvɛlʊŋ]
swollen	geschwollen [gəˈʃvɔln]
tachycardia	das Herzrasen [das ˈhɛɐtsraːzn]
temperature (*fever*)	das Fieber [das ˈfiːbɐ]
tetanus	der Tetanus [dɐ ˈtɛtanʊs]
tonsilitis	die Mandelentzündung [di ˈmandlʔɛnˌtsʏndʊŋ]

torn ligament	der Bänderriss [de 'bɛndeʀɪs]
tumor	die Geschwulst [di gəˈʃvʊlst]
typhoid	der Typhus [de 'ty:fʊs]
ulcer	das Geschwür [das gəˈʃvyɐ]
venereal disease	die Geschlechtskrankheit [di geˈʃlɛçtsˌkʀaŋkhaɪt]
whooping cough	der Keuchhusten [de 'kɔɪçhu:stn]
wind	die Blähungen f pl [di 'blɛːʊŋŋ]
wound	die Wunde [di 'vʊndə]

Body – Doctor – Hospital

abdomen	der Unterleib [de 'ʔʊntelaɪp]
anesthetic	die Narkose [di naˈko:zə]
appendix	der Blinddarm [de 'blɪntda:m]
artificial limb	die Prothese [di pʀoˈteːzə]
bandage	der Verband [de feˈbant]
bladder	die Blase [di 'bla:zə]
to bleed	bluten [blu:tn]
blood	das Blut [das blu:t]
blood group	die Blutgruppe [di 'blu:tgʀʊpə]
blood pressure (high/low)	der Blutdruck (hoher/niedriger) [de 'blutdʀʊk ('ho:ɐ/'ni:dʀɪgɐ)]
bone	der Knochen [de knɔxn]
bowel movement	der Stuhlgang [de 'ʃtu:lgaŋ]
brain	das Gehirn [das gəˈhɪɐn]
to breathe	atmen ['ʔa:tmən]
bronchial tubes	die Bronchien f pl [di 'bʀɔnçɪən]
bypass	der Bypass [de 'baɪpa:s]
certificate	das Attest [das ʔaˈtɛst]
chest	die Brust [di bʀʊst]
collarbone	das Schlüsselbein [das 'ʃlʏslbaɪn]
cough	der Husten [de hu:stn]
diagnosis	die Diagnose [di diaˈgno:zə]
diet	die Diät [di diˈɛːt]
digestion	die Verdauung [di feˈdaʊʊŋ]
to disinfect	desinfizieren [dezɪnfɪˈtsiːʀən]
to dress (a wound)	verbinden [feˈbɪndn]
dressing	der Verband [de feˈbant]
eardrum	das Trommelfell [das 'tʀɔmlfɛl]
esophagus	die Speiseröhre [di 'ʃpaɪzəʀøːʀə]
examination	die Untersuchung [di ʔʊnteˈzu:xʊŋ]
face	das Gesicht [das gəˈzɪçt]
gallbladder	die Gallenblase [di 'galnbla:zə]
health	die Gesundheit [di gəˈzʊnthaɪt]
health resort	der Kurort [de 'kuɐ'ʔɔɐt]
hearing	das Gehör [das gəˈhøɐ]
heart	das Herz [das hɛɐts]

heart specialist	der Herzspezialist [dɐ ˈhɛɛtʃpɛtsjaˌlɪst]
hospital	das Krankenhaus [das ˈkʀaŋknhaʊs]
ill	krank [kʀaŋk]
infusion	die Infusion [di ˀɪnfʊˈzjoːn]
injection	die Spritze [di ˈʃpʀɪtsə]
intestines	der Darm [dɐ daːm]
joint	das Gelenk [das gəˈlɛŋk]
kidney	die Niere [di ˈniːʀə]
lip	die Lippe [di ˈlɪpə]
liver	die Leber [di ˈleːbɐ]
lungs	die Lunge [di ˈlʊŋə]
medical insurance card	die Verischertenkarte [dɪ fɐˈzɪxɐtənkaˌtə]
menstruation	die Menstruation [di mɛnstʀuaˈtsjon]
muscle	der Muskel [dɐ ˈmʊskl]
nerve	der Nerv [dɐ nɛɐf]
nervous	nervös [nɐˈvøːs]
nurse	die Krankenschwester [di ˈkʀaŋkn̩ʃvɛstɐ]
office hours	die Sprechstunde [di ˈʃpʀɛçʃtʊndə]
operation	die Operation [di ˀɔpɐaˈtsjoːn]
pacemaker	der Herzschrittmacher [dɐ ˈhɛɛt(s)ʃʀɪtmaxɐ]
to perspire	schwitzen [ˈʃvɪtsn]
pregnancy	die Schwangerschaft [di ˈʃvaŋɐʃaft]
to prescribe	verschreiben [fɐˈʃʀaɪbm̩]
pulse	der Puls [dɐ pʊls]
pus	der Eiter [dɐ ˀaɪtɐ]
rib	die Rippe [di ˈʀɪpə]
scar	die Narbe [di ˈnaːbə]
sexual organs	die Geschlechtsorgane n pl [di gəˈʃlɛçtsˀɔˌgaːnə]
sick	krank [kʀaŋk]
skin	die Haut [di haʊt]
sonogram	die Ultraschalluntersuchung [di ˀʊltʀaʃalˀʊntɐˌzuːxʊŋ]
specialist	der Facharzt [dɐ ˈfaxaːtst]
spine	die Wirbelsäule [di ˈvɪʀblzɔɪlə]
splint	die Schiene [di ˈʃiːnə]
sting	der Stich [dɐ ʃtɪç]
stitch (stitches)	die Naht [naːt]
to stitch (up)	nähen [nɛːn]
stomach	der Magen [dɐ maːgn̩]
surgeon	der Chirurg/die Chirurgin [dɐ çɪˈʀʊɐk/di çɪˈʀʊɐgin]
to sweat	schwitzen [ˈʃvɪtsn]
throat	die Kehle [di keːlə]
tongue	die Zunge [ˈtsʊŋə]

178

tonsils	die Mandeln *f pl* [di 'mandln]
ultrasound scan	die Ultraschalluntersuchung
	[di ˀʊltraʃalˀʊntɐˌzuːxʊŋ]
unconscious	bewusstlos [bəˈvʊstloːs]
urine	der Urin [dɐ ˀuˈʀiːn]
vaccination	die Impfung [di ˀɪmpfʊŋ]
vaccination record	der Impfpass [dɐ ˀɪmpfpas]
virus	das Virus [das ˈviːʀʊs]
visiting hours	die Besuchszeit [di bəˈzuːxstsaɪt]
to vomit	sich erbrechen [zɪç ˀɛˈbʀɛçn]
waiting room	das Wartezimmer [das ˈvaːtətsɪmɐ]
ward	die Station [di ʃtaˈtsjoːn]
windpipe	die Kehle [di keːlə]
X-ray	die Röntgenaufnahme
	[di ˈʀœnçnˀaʊfnaːmə]
to X-ray	röntgen [ˈʀœnçn]

At the Dentist

I have a (terrible) toothache.
Ich habe (starke) Zahnschmerzen. [ˀɪç ˈhaːbə (ˈʃtaːkə) ˈtsaːnʃmɛɐtsn]

This upper/bottom tooth hurts.
Dieser Zahn oben/unten tut weh. [ˈdiːzɐ tsaːn ˀoːbm/ˀʊntn tuːt veː]

This front/back tooth hurts.
Dieser Zahn vorn/hinten tut weh. [ˈdiːzɐ tsaːn foɐn/ˈhɪntn tuːt veː]

I've lost a filling.
Ich habe eine Füllung verloren. [ˀɪç ˈhaːbə ˀaɪnə ˈfʏlʊŋ fɐˈloɐn]

I've broken a tooth.
Mir ist ein Zahn abgebrochen. [miɐ ˀɪst ˀaɪn ˈtsaːn ˀapgəbʀɔxn]

I'll only do a temporary job.
Ich behandle ihn nur provisorisch.
[ˀɪç bəˈhandlə ˀin nuɐ pʀoviˈzoːʀɪʃ]

I'd like an injection, please.
Geben Sie mir bitte eine Spritze. [ˈgeːbm zi miɐ ˈbɪtə ˌˀaɪnə ˈʃpʀɪtsə]

I don't want an injection.
Geben Sie mir keine Spritze. [ˈgeːbm zi miɐ ˈkaɪnə ˈʃpʀɪtsə]

brace	die Zahnspange [di ˈtsaːnʃpaŋə]
bridge	die Brücke [di ˈbʀʏkə]
cavity	das Loch [das lɔx]
crown	die Krone [di ˈkʀoːnə]
dentures	die Zahnprothese [di ˈtsaːnpʀoˌteːzə]
to extract	ziehen [tsiːn]

filling	die Füllung [di 'fʏlʊŋ], die Plombe [di 'plɔmbə]
gums	das Zahnfleisch [das 'tsaːnflaɪʃ]
incisor	der Schneidezahn [dɐ 'ʃnaɪdətsaːn]
jaw	der Kiefer [dɐ 'kiːfɐ]
molar	der Backenzahn [dɐ 'bakŋtsaːn]
tartar	der Zahnstein [dɐ 'tsaːnʃtaɪn]
tooth	der Zahn [dɐ tsaːn]
tooth decay	die Karies [di 'kaːʀiɛs]
toothache	die Zahnschmerzen *m pl* [di 'tsaːnʃmɛɐtsn]
wisdom tooth	der Weisheitszahn [dɐ 'vaɪshaɪtsaːn]

Essentials from A to Z

Bank

Can you tell me where the nearest bank is, please?
Können Sie mir bitte sagen, wo hier eine Bank ist?
[kænn zi miɐ ˈbɪtə zaːgn voː hiɐ ˀaɪnə ˈbaŋk ˀɪst]

I'd like to change £100 into euros.
Ich möchte einhundert Pfund in Euro wechseln.
[ˀɪç mœçtə ˀaɪnhʊndɛt pfʊnt ˀɪn ˀɔɪʀo ˈvɛksln]

I'd like to change $150 into Swiss francs.
Ich möchte einhundertfünfzig Dollar in Schweizer Franken wechseln.
[ˀɪç mœçtə ˀaɪnhʊndɛtˌfʏnftsɪç ˈdɔlaː ˀɪn ˈʃvaɪtsɐ fʀaŋkŋ vɛksln]

Can you tell me what the exchange rate is today, please?
Können Sie mir bitte sagen, wie heute der Wechselkurs ist?
[kænn zi miɐ ˈbɪtə zaːgn viː hɔɪtə dɐ ˈvɛkslkʊɐs ˀɪst]

I'd like to cash this traveler's check.
Ich möchte diesen Reisescheck einlösen.
[ˀɪç ˈmœçtə diːzn ˈʀaɪzəʃɛk ˀaɪnløːzn]

What's the maximum I can cash on one check?
Auf welchen Betrag kann ich ihn maximal ausstellen?
[ˀaʊf ˈvɛlçn bəˈtʀaːk kan ɪç ˀiːn maksiˈmaːl ˀaʊʃtɛln]

Can I see your check card, please?
Ihre Scheckkarte, bitte. [ˌˀiːʀə ˈʃɛkaːtə ˈbɪtə]

May I see ..., please?
Darf ich bitte ... sehen? [daːf ɪç ˈbɪtə ... zeːn]
 your identity card
 Ihren Ausweis [ˈˀiːʀən ˀaʊsvaɪs]
 your passport
 Ihren Pass [ˈˀiːʀən ˈpas]

Sign here, please.
Unterschreiben Sie bitte hier. [ˀʊntɐˈʃʀaɪbm zi ˈbɪtə ˈhiɐ]

account	das Konto [das ˈkɔnto]
amount	der Betrag [dɐ bəˈtʀaːk]
automated teller machine	der Geldautomat [dɐ ˈgɛltaʊtoˌmaːt]
bank	die Bank [di baŋk]
banknote	der Geldschein [dɐ ˈgɛltʃaɪn]
cash	das Bargeld [das ˈbaːgɛlt]
cashpoint (ATM)	der Geldautomat [dɐ ˈgɛltaʊtoˌmaːt]
cent	der Cent [dɐ sɛnt]
change	das Kleingeld [das ˈklaɪngɛlt]
to change	umtauschen [ˈʔʊmtaʊʃn]
check	der Scheck [dɐ ʃɛk]
check card	die Scheckkarte [di ˈʃɛkaːtə]
chip card	die Chipkarte [di ˈtʃɪpkaːtə]
coin	die Münze [di ˈmʏntsə]
credit card	die Kreditkarte [di kʀeˈdiːtkaːtə]
currency	die Währung [di ˈvɛːʀʊŋ]
euro	der Euro [dɐ ˈʔɔɪʀo]
exchange	der Geldwechsel [dɐ ˈgɛltvɛksl]
exchange rate	der Wechselkurs [dɐ ˈvɛkslkʊɐs]
form	das Formular [das fɔmuˈlaː]
money	das Geld [das gɛlt]
payment	die Zahlung [di ˈtsaːlʊŋ]
to pay out	auszahlen [ˈʔaʊstsaːln]
Personal Identification Number (PIN)	die Geheimzahl [di gəˈhaɪmtsaːl]
receipt	die Quittung [di ˈkvɪtʊŋ]
remittance	die Überweisung [di ˈʔybɐˈvaɪzʊŋ]
service charge	die Bearbeitungsgebühr [di bəˈʔaːbaɪtʊŋsgəˌbyɐ]
signature	die Unterschrift [di ˈʔʊntɐʃʀɪft]
Swiss francs	Schweizer Franken m pl [ˈʃvaɪtsɐ ˈfʀaŋkn]
transfer	die Überweisung [di ˈʔybɐˈvaɪzʊŋ]
traveler's check	der Reisescheck [dɐ ˈʀaɪzəʃɛk]
to write a check	einen Scheck ausstellen [ˈʔaɪnn ʃɛk ˈʔaʊʃtɛln]
wire transfer	die telegrafische Überweisung [di teləˈgʀaːfɪʃə ˈʔyːbɐˈvaɪzʊŋ]

Lost-and-Found Office

> also Police

Could you tell me where the lost-and-found is, please?
Könnten Sie mir bitte sagen, wo das Fundbüro ist?
[kœntn zi miɐ ˈbɪtə zaːgn voː das ˈfʊntbyˌʀoː ˈɪst]

I've lost ...
Ich habe ... verloren. [ˀɪç ˈhaːbə ... fɛˈloɐn]

I left my handbag on the train.
Ich habe meine Handtasche im Zug vergessen.
[ˀɪç ˈhaːbə ˈmaɪnə ˈhantaʃə ˀɪm tsuːk fɛˈgɛsn]

Would you let me know if it turns up, please?
Würden Sie mich bitte benachrichtigen, wenn sie gefunden werden sollte?
[ˌvʏɐdn zi mɪç ˌbɪtə bəˈnaːxrɪçtɪgn vɛn zi gəˈfʊndn veɐdn ˌzɔltə]

Here's the address of my hotel.
Hier ist meine Hotelanschrift. [ˈhiɐ ˀɪst ˈmaɪnə hoˈtɛlanʃrɪft]

Here's my home address.
Hier ist meine Heimatadresse. [ˈhiɐ ˀɪst ˈmaɪnə ˈhaɪmataˌdʀɛsə]

Photos

> also Photographic Materials

Could you take a photo of us?
Könnten Sie ein Foto von uns machen?
[ˈkœntn zi ˀaɪn ˈfoːto fɔn ʊns maxn]

You only have to press this button.
Sie müssen nur auf diesen Knopf drücken.
[zi mʏsn nuɐ ˀaʊf ˈdiːzn ˈknɔpf dʀʏkn]

You set the distance like this.
Die Entfernung stellt man so ein. [di ˀɛntˈfɛɐnʊŋ ʃtɛlt man ˈzoː ˀaɪn]

May I take a photo of you?
Dürfte ich Sie wohl fotografieren? [dʏɐftə ˀɪç zi voːl fotogʀaˈfiːrən]

Smile, please.
Bitte lächeln. [ˈbɪtə ˈlɛçln]

We'll have a lovely reminder of our holiday.
So haben wir eine schöne Erinnerung an unseren Urlaub.
[zo ˈhaːbm viɐ ˀaɪnə ˈʃøːnə ˀeˈˀɪnerʊŋ ˀan ˌˀʊnzen ˈˀuɐlaʊp]

snapshot . . . . der Schnappschuss [deɐ ˈʃnapʃʊs]

Police

Could you tell me where the nearest police station is, please?
Könnten Sie mir bitte sagen, wo das nächste Polizeirevier ist?
[kœntn zi miɐ ˈbɪtə zaːgn voː das ˈnɛːçstə pɔlɪˈtsaɪʀeˌviɐ ˈʔɪst]

I'd like to report ...
Ich möchte ... anzeigen. [ʔɪç ˈmœçtə ... ˈʔantsaɪgn]

a theft
einen Diebstahl [ʔaɪnn ˈdiːpʃtaːl]

a robbery
einen Überfall [ʔaɪnn ˈʔyːbɐfal]

My ... has been stolen.
Mir ist ... gestohlen worden. [miɐ ʔɪst ... gəˈʃtoːln vɔɐdn]

wallet
meine Brieftasche [ˈmaɪnə ˈbʀiːftaʃə]

camera
mein Fotoapparat [maɪn ˈfotoʔapaˌʀaːt]

car
mein Auto [maɪn ˈʔaʊto]

My car has been broken into.
Mein Auto ist aufgebrochen worden.
[maɪn ˈʔaʊto ʔɪst ˈʔaʊfgəbʀɔxn vɔɐdn]

... has been stolen from my car.
Aus meinem Auto ist ... gestohlen worden.
[ʔaʊs ˈmaɪ(nə)m ˈʔaʊto ʔɪst ... gəˈʃtoːln vɔɐdn]

I've lost ...
Ich habe ... verloren. [ʔɪç ˈhaːbə ... feˈloen]

My son/daughter is missing.
Mein Sohn/Meine Tochter ist verschwunden.
[maɪn ˈzoːn/ˌmaɪnə ˈtɔxtɐ ʔɪst feˈʃvʊndn]

This man is harassing me.
Dieser Mann belästigt mich. [ˈdiːzɐ man bəˈlɛstɪçt mɪç]

Can you help me, please?
Können Sie mir bitte helfen? [ˈkœnn zi miɐ ˈbɪtə ˈhɛlfn]

When exactly did this happen?
Wann genau ist das passiert? [van gəˈnaʊ ɪst das paˈsiɐt]

Your name and address, please.
Ihren Namen und Ihre Anschrift, bitte.
[ˈʔiʀən ˈnaːmm ʊnt ˌiʀə ˈʔanʃʀɪft ˈbɪtə]

Please get in touch with your consulate.
Wenden Sie sich bitte an Ihr Konsulat.
[ˈvɛndn zi zɪç an iɐ kɔnzʊˈlaːt]

to arrest	verhaften [fɛ'haftn̩]
to beat up	zusammenschlagen [tsʊ'zammʃla:gn̩]
to break into/open	aufbrechen ['ʔaʊfbʀɛçn̩]
car radio	das Autoradio [das 'ʔaʊto‚ʀa:djo]
car registration documents .	der Kfz-Schein [dɐ ka'ʔef'tsɛtʃaɪn]
check	der Scheck [dɐ ʃɛk]
check card	die Scheckkarte [di 'ʃɛka:tə]
court	das Gericht [das gə'ʀɪçt]
credit card	die Kreditkarte [di 'kʀedi:tka:tə]
crime	das Verbrechen [das fɛ'bʀɛçn̩]
documents	die Papiere n pl [di pa'pi:ʀə]
drugs	das Rauschgift [das 'ʀaʊʃgɪft]
guilt	die Schuld [ʃʊlt]
to harass	belästigen [bə'lɛstɪgn̩]
identity card	der Personalausweis [dɐ pɛzo'na:laʊsvaɪs]
judge	der Richter/die Richterin [dɐ 'ʀɪçtɐ/di 'ʀɪçtəʀɪn]
key	der Schlüssel [dɐ 'ʃlʏsl̩]
lawyer	der Rechtsanwalt [dɐ 'ʀɛçtsanvalt], die Rechtsanwältin [dɪ 'ʀɛçtsanvɛltɪn]
to lose	verlieren [fɛ'li:ʀən]
mugging	der Überfall [dɐ 'ʔy:bɐfal]
papers	die Papiere n pl [di pa'pi:ʀə]
passport	der Reisepass [dɐ 'ʀaɪzəpas]
pickpocket	der Taschendieb [dɐ 'taʃndi:p]
police	die Polizei [di pɔlɪ'tsaɪ]
police car	der Polizeiwagen [dɐ pɔlɪ'tsaɪva:gn̩]
police custody	die Untersuchungshaft [di 'ʔʊntɐ'zu:xʊŋshaft]
policeman/policewoman ...	der Polizist/die Polizistin [dɐ pɔlɪ'tsɪst/di pɔlɪ'tsɪstɪn]
prison	das Gefängnis [das gə'fɛŋnɪs]
purse	die Geldbörse [di 'gɛltbœɐzə]
rape	die Vergewaltigung [di fɐgə'valtɪgʊŋ]
to report	anzeigen ['ʔantsaɪgn̩]
sexual harassment	die sexuelle Belästigung [di sɛksu'ɛlə bə'lɛstɪgʊŋ]
to smuggle	schmuggeln [ʃmʊgln̩]
theft	der Diebstahl [dɐ 'di:pʃta:l]
thief	der Dieb/die Diebin [dɐ di:p/di 'di:bɪn]

Post Office

Can you tell me where ... is, please?
Können Sie mir bitte sagen, wo ... ist?
[kœnn zi miɐ 'bɪtə 'zaːgŋ voː ... ʔɪst]

the nearest post office
das nächste Postamt [das 'nɛːçstə 'pɔstʔamt]
the nearest mailbox
der nächste Briefkasten [dɐ 'nɛːçstə 'bʀiːfkastn̩]

How much does a letter/postcard cost ...
Was kostet ein Brief/eine Postkarte ...
[vas 'kɔstət ʔaɪn 'bʀiːf/ˌʔaɪnə 'pɔstkaːtə nax ...]

to the US?
in die USA? [ʔɪn di ʔuɛsˈʔaː]
to England?
nach England? [nax 'ʔɛŋlant]

I'd like to send this letter ...
Diesen Brief bitte per ... ['diːzn̩ bʀiːf ˌbɪtə pɛɐ]

by airmail.
Luftpost. ['lʊftpɔst]
express.
Express. [ʔɛksˈpʀɛs]

Three ... euro stamps, please.
Drei Briefmarken zu ... Euro, bitte!
[dʀaɪ 'bʀiːfmaːkŋ tsʊ ... 'ʔɔɪʀo 'bɪtə]

Do you have any special-issue stamps?
Haben Sie Sondermarken? [haːbm̩ zi 'zɔndɐmaːkŋ]

➢ also Bank

address	die Adresse [di ʔaˈdʀɛsə]
addressee	der Empfänger [dɐ ʔɛmpˈfɛŋɐ]
by airmail	mit Luftpost [mɪt 'lʊftpɔst]
charge	die Gebühr [di ɡəˈbyɐ]
collection (of mail)	die Leerung [di 'leːʀʊŋ]
customs declaration	die Zollerklärung [di 'tsɔlɐklɛːʀʊŋ]
declaration of value	die Wertangabe [di 'veɐtangaːbə]
dispatch form	die Paketkarte [di paˈkeːtkaːtə]
express letter	der Eilbrief [dɐ ʔaɪlbʀiːf]
fax	das Telefax [das ('teːlə)faks]
fee	die Gebühr [di ɡəˈbyɐ]
to fill in	ausfüllen [ʔaʊsfʏln]
form	das Formular [das fɔmuˈlaː]
to forward	nachsenden ['naːxzɛndn̩]

letter	der Brief [deɐ bʀiːf]
mailbox	der Briefkasten [deɐ 'bʀiːfkastn̩]
main post office	das Hauptpostamt
	[das 'haʊpt͜pɔst͜ʔamt]
parcel	das Paket [das pa'keːt]
post office	das Postamt [das 'pɔstamt]
post office savings book	das Postsparbuch [das 'pɔstʃpaːbuːx]
postage	das Porto [das 'pɔɐto]
postal code, ZIP code	die Postleitzahl [di 'pɔstlaɪtsaːl]
postcard	die Postkarte [di 'pɔstkaːtə]
poste restante	postlagernd ['pɔstlaːgɛnt]
registered letter	der Einschreibebrief
	[deɐ 'ʔaɪnʃʀaɪbəbʀiːf]
sender	der Absender/die Absenderin
	[deɐ 'ʔapzɛndɐ/di 'ʔapzɛndəʀɪn]
small parcel	das Päckchen [das pɛkçn̩]
special-issue stamp	die Sondermarke [di 'zɔndɐmaːkə]
stamp	die Briefmarke [di 'bʀiːfmaːkə]
to stamp	frankieren [fʀaŋ'kiɐn]
stamp machine	der Briefmarkenautomat
	[deɐ 'bʀiːfmaːkŋʔaʊto͜maːt]
telex	das Telex [das 'teːlɛks]
weight	das Gewicht [das gə'vɪçt]
zip code	die Postleitzahl [di 'pɔstlaɪtsaːl]

Telephoning

Can you tell me where the nearest phone booth is, please?
Können Sie mir bitte sagen, wo die nächste Telefonzelle ist?
[kœnn zi miɐ 'bɪtə zaːgŋ 'vo di 'nɛːçstə teləˈfoːntsɛlə 'ʔɪst]

I'd like a phonecard, please.
Ich möchte bitte eine Telefonkarte.
['ʔɪç 'mœçtə bɪtə 'ʔaɪnə teləˈfoːnkaːtə]

What's the area code for ...?
Wie ist bitte die Vorwahl von ...? ['viː 'ʔɪst bɪtə di 'foɐvaːl fɔn]

I'd like to make a call to ...
Bitte ein Ferngespräch nach ... ['bɪtə 'ʔaɪn 'fɛɐngəʃpʀɛːç nax ...]

I'd like to make a collect call.
Ich möchte ein R-Gespräch anmelden.
['ʔɪç 'mœçtə 'ʔaɪn 'ʔɛɐgəʃpʀɛːç 'ʔanmɛldn̩]

Use booth number four.
Gehen Sie in Kabine Nummer vier. ['geːn zi 'ʔɪn ka'biːnə ˌnʊmɐ 'fiɐ]

A Telephone Call

This is ... speaking.
Hier spricht ... ['hie ʃprɪçt ...]

Good morning/afternoon, my name is ...
Guten Tag, mein Name ist ... [guːtn 'taːk maɪn 'naːmə ʔɪst]

Hello, who's speaking, please?
Hallo, mit wem spreche ich, bitte? ['halo: mɪt veːm ʃprɛç ɪç bɪtə]

Can I speak to Mr./Mrs. ..., please?
Kann ich bitte Herrn/Frau ... sprechen?
['kan ɪç 'bɪtə hɛen/frau ... ʃprɛçn]

I'm sorry, he's/she's not here.
Tut mir Leid, er/sie ist nicht da. [tuːt mɪe 'laɪt ɛe/zi ʔɪst nɪçt daː]

Can he call you back?
Kann er Sie zurückrufen? ['kan (e)e zi tsʊ'rykruːfn]

Would you like to leave a message?
Möchten Sie eine Nachricht hinterlassen?
[mœçtn zi ʔaɪnə 'naːxɪçt hɪnteˈlasn]

Would you tell him/her that I called?
Würden Sie ihm/ihr bitte sagen, ich hätte angerufen?
['vvɛdn zi ʔiːm/ʔie 'bɪtə 'zaːgn ʔɪç 'hɛtə ʔangeruːfn]

"The number you have dialed is not in service."
„Kein Anschluss unter dieser Nummer."
[kaɪn ʔanʃlʊs ʔʊnte diːze 'nʊme]

to answer the phone	abnehmen ['ʔapneːmm]
answering machine	der Anrufbeantworter
	[de ʔanfuːfbə,ʔantvɔete]
area code	die Vorwahlnummer [di 'foeva:l,nʊme]
busy	besetzt [bə'zɛtst]
call	der Anruf [de ʔanruːf]
to call	anrufen ['ʔanruːfn]
cellular phone	das Handy [das 'hɛndi]
charge	die Gebühr [di gə'bye]
collect call	das R-Gespräch [das ʔɛegəʃprɛːç]
connection	die Verbindung [di fe'bɪndʊŋ]
conversation	das Gespräch [das gə'ʃprɛːç]
to dial	wählen [vɛːln]
directory assistance	die Auskunft [di 'ʔaʊskʊnft]
engaged	besetzt [bə'zɛtst]
international call	das Auslandsgespräch
	[das ʔaʊslantsgəʃprɛːç]
line	die Verbindung [di fe'bɪndʊŋ]
local call	das Ortsgespräch [das ʔɔetsgəʃprɛːç]

long-distance call	das Ferngespräch [das ˈfɛɐ̯ngəʃpʀɛːç]
mobile (phone)	das Handy [das ˈhɛndi],
	das Mobiltelefon [das moˈbiːltelefoːn]
national code, prefix	die Vorwahlnummer [di ˈfoɐ̯vaːlˌnʊmɐ]
person-to-person call	die Voranmeldung [di ˈfoɐ̯ʔanmɛldʊŋ]
to phone	anrufen [ˈʔanʀuːfn]
phone booth	die Telefonzelle [di teləˈfoːntsɛlə]
phone call	der Anruf [dɐ ˈʔanʀuːf]
phone number	die Telefonnummer [di teləˈfoːnnʊmɐ]
phonecard	die Telefonkarte [di teləˈfoːnkaːtə]
receiver	der Hörer [dɐ ˈhøːʀɐ]
telephone	das Telefon [das ˈteːləfoːn]
telephone directory	das Telefonbuch [das teləˈfoːnbuːx]

Toilet and Bathroom

Where is the toilet, please?
Wo ist bitte die Toilette? [voː ʔɪst ˈbɪtə di toˈlɛtə]

May I use your toilet?
Dürfte ich Ihre Toilette benutzen? [ˈdʏɐ̯ftə ʔɪç ˈʔiːʀə toˈlɛtə bəˈnʊtsn]

Would you give me the key for the toilet, please?
Würden Sie mir bitte den Schlüssel für die Toiletten geben?
[ˈvʏɐ̯dn ziː miɐ̯ ˈbɪtə den ˈʃlʏsl fyɐ̯ di toˈlɛtə geːbm]

clean	sauber [ˈzaʊbɐ]
cubicle	die Kabine [di kaˈbiːnə]
dirty	schmutzig [ˈʃmʊtsɪç]
to flush the toilet	(die Toilette) spülen [(di toˈlɛtə) ʃpyːln]
Gentlemen	Herren [ˈhɛʀən]
Ladies	Damen [daːmm]
Men's Room	die Herrentoilette [di ˈhɛʀəntoˌlɛtə]
sanitary napkins	die Damenbinden *f pl*
	[di ˈdaːmmbɪndn]
soap	die Seife [di ˈzaɪfə]
tampons	die Tampons *m pl* [di ˈtampɔŋs]
toilet paper	das Toilettenpapier [das toˈlɛtnpaˌpiɐ̯]
towel	das Handtuch [das ˈhan(t)tuːx]
washbasin, sink	das Waschbecken [das ˈvaʃbɛkn]
Women's Room	die Damentoilette [di ˈdaːmmtoˌlɛtə]

A Short Guide to German Grammar

Articles

The article indicates the gender of a noun. There are three genders in German: masculine, feminine, and neuter, as well as four cases: nominative, accusative, genitive, and dative.

	definite article				indefinite article			
	m	f	n	pl	m	f	n	pl
nom.	der	die	das	die	ein	eine	ein	*no article*
acc.	den	die	das	die	einen	eine	ein	*used with*
gen.	des	der	des	der	eines	einer	eines	*plural nouns*
dat.	dem	der	dem	den	einem	einer	einem	

Nouns

All German nouns are written with a capital letter.
There are three declensions: strong, weak, and mixed. (These terms classify nouns according to their endings in the genitive case.)
Nouns which end in "*s*," "*sch*," "*ß/ss*," and "*z* " always have an "*-es*" in the genitive case.
Some nouns are declined like adjectives.

1. Strong masculine and neuter nouns

	nom. plural: +e	nom. plural: umlaut+e	nom. plural: +er	nom. plural: umlaut+er
singular				
nom.	der Tag (the day)	der Traum (the dream)	das Kind (the child)	das Dach (the roof)
acc.	den Tag	den Traum	das Kind	das Dach
gen.	des Tag(e)s	des Traum(e)s	des Kind(e)s	des Dach(e)s
dat.	dem Tag(e)	dem Traum(e)	dem Kind(e)	dem Dach(e)
plural				
nom.	die Tage	die Träume	die Kinder	die Dächer
acc.	die Tage	die Träume	die Kinder	die Dächer
gen.	der Tage	der Träume	der Kinder	der Dächer
dat.	den Tagen	den Träumen	den Kindern	den Dächern

	nom. plural: +s	nom. plural: umlaut only	nom. plural: no change	nom. plural: no change
singular				
nom.	das Auto (the car)	der Vogel (the bird)	der Tischler (the carpenter)	der Lappen (the cloth)
acc.	das Auto	den Vogel	den Tischler	den Lappen
gen.	des Autos	des Vogels	des Tischlers	des Lappens
dat.	dem Auto	dem Vogel	dem Tischler	dem Lappen
plural				
nom.	die Autos	die Vögel	die Tischler	die Lappen
acc.	die Autos	die Vögel	die Tischler	die Lappen
gen.	der Autos	der Vögel	der Tischler	der Lappen
dat.	den Autos	den Vögeln	den Tischlern	den Lappen

2. Strong feminine nouns

	nom. plural: umlaut+e	nom. plural: umlaut only	nom. plural: +s
singular			
nom.	die Wand (the wall)	die Mutter (the mother)	die Bar (the bar)
acc.	die Wand	die Mutter	die Bar
gen.	der Wand	der Mutter	der Bar
dat.	der Wand	der Mutter	der Bar
plural			
nom.	die Wände	die Mütter	die Bars
acc.	die Wände	die Mütter	die Bars
gen.	der Wände	der Mütter	der Bars
dat.	den Wänden	den Müttern	den Bars

3. Weak masculine nouns

singular			
nom.	der Bauer	der Bär	der Hase
	(the farmer)	(the bear)	(the hare)
acc.	den Bauern	den Bären	den Hasen
gen.	des Bauern	des Bären	des Hasen
dat.	dem Bauern	dem Bären	dem Hasen
plural			
nom.	die Bauern	die Bären	die Hasen
acc.	die Bauern	die Bären	die Hasen
gen.	der Bauern	der Bären	der Hasen
dat.	den Bauern	den Bären	den Hasen

4. Weak feminine nouns

singular				
nom.	die Uhr	die Feder	die Gabe	die Ärztin
	(the clock)	(the feather)	(the gift)	(the doctor)
acc.	die Uhr	die Feder	die Gabe	die Ärztin
gen.	der Uhr	der Feder	der Gabe	der Ärztin
dat.	der Uhr	der Feder	der Gabe	der Ärztin
plural				
nom.	die Uhren	die Federn	die Gaben	die Ärztinnen
acc.	die Uhren	die Federn	die Gaben	die Ärztinnen
gen.	der Uhren	der Federn	der Gaben	der Ärztinnen
dat.	den Uhren	den Federn	den Gaben	den Ärztinnen

5. Mixed masculine and neuter nouns

These are declined as strong nouns in the singular and weak nouns in the plural.

singular				
nom.	das Auge	das Ohr	der Name	das Herz
	(the eye)	(the ear)	(the name)	(the heart)
acc.	das Auge	das Ohr	den Namen	das Herz
gen.	des Auges	des Ohr(e)s	der Namens	des Herzens
dat.	dem Auge	dem Ohr(e)	dem Namen	dem Herzen
plural				
nom.	die Augen	die Ohren	die Namen	die Herzen
acc.	die Augen	die Ohren	die Namen	die Herzen
gen.	der Augen	der Ohren	der Namen	der Herzen
dat.	den Augen	den Ohren	den Namen	den Herzen

6. Nouns declined as adjectives

masculine singular		
nom.	der Reisende	ein Reisender
	(the traveler)	
acc.	den Reisenden	einen Reisenden
gen.	des Reisenden	eines Reisenden
dat.	dem Reisenden	einem Reisenden

plural		
nom.	die Reisenden	Reisende
acc.	die Reisenden	Reisende
gen.	der Reisenden	Reisender
dat.	den Reisenden	Reisenden

feminine singular		
nom.	die Reisende	eine Reisende
acc.	die Reisende	eine Reisende
gen.	der Reisenden	einer Reisenden
dat.	der Reisenden	einer Reisenden

plural		
nom.	die Reisenden	Reisende
acc.	die Reisenden	Reisende
gen.	der Reisenden	Reisender
dat.	den Reisenden	Reisenden

neuter singular		
nom.	das Neugeborene	ein Neugeborenes
	(the newborn [baby])	
acc.	das Neugeborene	ein Neugeborenes
gen.	des Neugeborenen	eines Neugeborenen
dat.	dem Neugeborenen	einem Neugeborenen

plural		
nom.	die Neugeborenen	Neugeborene
acc.	die Neugeborenen	Neugeborene
gen.	der Neugeborenen	Neugeborener
dat.	den Neugeborenen	Neugeborenen

There are three types of adjective declension: strong, weak, and mixed.

The strong declension

is used when there is no article, pronoun, or other word preceeding the adjective indicating the case (e.g. *manch(e)*, *mehrere* etc.). It is also used with cardinal numbers and expressions like *ein paar* and *ein bisschen.*

	m	f	n
singular			
nom.	guter Wein (good wine)	schöne Frau (beautiful woman)	liebes Kind (well-behaved child)
acc.	guten Wein	schöne Frau	liebes Kind
gen.	guten Wein(e)s	schöner Frau	lieben Kindes
dat.	gutem Wein(e)	schöner Frau	liebem Kind(e)
plural			
nom.	gute Weine	schöne Frauen	liebe Kinder
acc.	gute Weine	schöne Frauen	liebe Kinder
gen.	guter Weine	schöner Frauen	lieber Kinder
dat.	guten Weinen	schönen Frauen	lieben Kindern

The weak declension

is used with adjectives preceded by the definite article or with any other word already clearly showing the case of the noun (e.g. *diese(r,s)*, *folgende(r,s)* etc.).

	m	f	n
singular			
nom.	der gute Wein	die schöne Frau	das liebe Kind
acc.	den guten Wein	die schöne Frau	das liebe Kind
gen.	des guten Wein(e)s	der schönen Frau	des lieben Kindes
dat.	dem guten Wein	der schönen Frau	dem lieben Kind
plural			
nom.	die guten Weine	die schönen Frauen	die lieben Kinder
acc.	die guten Weine	die schönen Frauen	die lieben Kinder
gen.	der guten Weine	der schönen Frauen	der lieben Kinder
dat.	den guten Weinen	den schönen Frauen	den lieben Kindern

The mixed declension

is used with singular masculine and neuter nouns and the indefinite articles *ein* and *kein* and with the possessive pronouns *mein, dein, sein, unser, euer, ihr.*

	m	n
singular		
nom.	ein guter Wein (a good wine)	ein liebes Kind (a well-behaved child)
acc.	einen guten Wein	ein liebes Kind
gen.	eines guten Wein(e)s	eines lieben Kindes
dat.	einem guten Wein(e)	einem lieben Kind

Adverbs

• For the adverbial use of adjectives, the unchanged basic form of the adjective is used.

Verbs

Present Tense

The basic ending of German verbs is "-en" (*machen, sagen, essen* etc.). To form the present tense remove the "-en" and add the corresponding personal endings to the stem of the verb. There is no continuous form in German, e.g. *„Ich gehe um acht Uhr ins Büro."* can be translated as *"I go to the office at eight o'clock."* (routine) or *"I'm going to the office at eight o'clock."* (single event).

		machen (to do)	legen (to put)	sagen (to say)
I	ich	mache	lege	sage
you	du	machst	legst	sagst
he she it	er sie es	macht	legt	sagt
we	wir	machen	legen	sagen
you	ihr	macht	legt	sagt
they	sie	machen	legen	sagen

• The vowel "-a-" in some verbs changes to the umlaut "-ä-."

tragen   ich trage, du trägst, er/sie/es trägt,
              wir tragen, ihr tragt, sie tragen

Auxilary verbs *haben, sein,* and *werden*

Present tense

	sein (to be)	**haben** (to have)	**werden** (to become)
ich	bin	habe	werde
du	bist	hast	wirst
er sie es	ist	hat	wird
wir	sind	haben	werden
ihr	seid	habt	werdet
sie	sind	haben	werden

Past tense and past participle

	sein (to be)	**haben** (to have)	**werden** (to become)
ich	war	hatte	wurde
du	warst	hattest	wurdest
er sie es	war	hatte	wurde
wir	waren	hatten	wurden
ihr	wart	hattet	wurdet
sie	waren	hatten	wurden
past participle	bin gewesen	habe gehabt	bin geworden

Modal auxilaries

Here is a list of the most important ones. Note that most are irregular.

Present tense

	können (be able to)	**dürfen** (be allowed to)	**mögen** (like)	**müssen** (have to)	**sollen** (should)	**wollen** (want to)
ich	kann	darf	mag	muss	soll	will
du	kannst	darfst	magst	musst	sollst	willst
er sie es	kann	darf	mag	muss	soll	will
wir	können	dürfen	mögen	müssen	sollen	wollen
ihr	könnt	dürft	mögt	müsst	sollt	wollt
sie	können	dürfen	mögen	müssen	sollen	wollen

Past Tense

There are two tenses for the past in German, the imperfect and the present perfect. Both describe events which took place in the past. There is no past continuous form.

Gestern war ich krank.	Yesterday I was ill.
Letztes Jahr sind wir in Berlin gewesen.	Last year we were in Berlin.

To form the **imperfect**, the following verb endings are added to the stem of the verb:

	machen (to do)	**begegnen** (to meet)	**wetten** (to bet)
ich	mach**te**	begegne**te**	wett**ete**
du	mach**test**	begegne**test**	wett**etest**
er sie es	mach**te**	begegne**te**	wett**ete**
wir	mach**ten**	begegne**ten**	wett**eten**
ihr	mach**tet**	begegne**tet**	wett**etet**
sie	mach**ten**	begegne**ten**	wett**eten**

The **present perfect** is the most common way of referring to the past and is formed with the present tense of either *haben* (to have) or *sein* (to be) followed by the past participle of the verb. The past participle of regular verbs is formed by adding the prefix "*ge-*" and the ending "*-t*" to the stem.

machen	**ge-mach-t**	fragen	**ge-frag-t**
(to do)	(done)	(to ask)	(asked)

Most verbs take *haben* to form the present perfect:

Er hat es gemacht.	He's done it. / He did it.
Ich habe es gesagt.	I've said it. / I said it.

sein is used with verbs of motion and verbs that indicate a transition from one state to another. Many irregular verbs form the present perfect with the prefix "*ge-*," a vowel change and the ending "*-en.*"

Wir sind gefahren.	We drove.

Future

- The future tense is formed with the auxiliary verb *werden* and the infinitive.

	fahren (to drive)	sein (to be)	haben (to have)	können (to be able to)
ich	werde fahren	werde sein	werde haben	werde können
du	wirst fahren	wirst sein	wirst haben	wirst können
er } sie } es }	wird fahren	wird sein	wird haben	wird können
wir	werden fahren	werden sein	werden haben	werden können
ihr	werdet fahren	werdet sein	werdet haben	werdet können
sie	werden fahren	werden sein	werden haben	werden können

- Often the present tense is also used to express the future.

Questions

Simple questions are formed by changing the order of subject and verb.

Es regnet.	It's raining.
Regnet es?	Is it raining?
Der Laden macht um 9 Uhr auf.	The shop opens at 9 o'clock.
Macht der Laden um 9 Uhr auf?	Does the shop open at 9 o'clock?

Negation

To negate a sentence add **nicht** after the main verb.

Sie wohnt in Berlin.	She lives in Berlin.
Er wohnt **nicht** in Berlin	He doesn't live in Berlin.

Nicht + **ein,eine,einen** etc. becomes **kein, keine, keinen** etc.

Ich habe eine Fahrkarte	I have a ticket.
Ich habe keine Fahrkarte	I don't have a ticket.

Pronouns agree with the gender and case/number of the noun they refer to.

1. Personal pronouns

nominative	accusative	genitive	dative
ich (I)	mich (me)	meiner	mir
du (you)	dich (you)	deiner	dir
er (he)	ihn (him)	seiner	ihm
sie (she)	sie (her)	ihrer	ihr
es (it)	es (it)	seiner	ihm
wir (we)	uns (us)	unser	uns
ihr (you)	euch (you)	euer	euch
sie (they)	sie (them)	ihrer	ihnen
Sie (you)	Sie (you)		

- **du** is the familiar form of address when speaking to family, friends, and children.
- **Sie** is the polite form of address (for both the singular and plural).
- **ihr** is the familiar form of address used when speaking to more than one person.

2. Reflexive pronouns

These are used with reflexive verbs such as *sich freuen, sich waschen, sich bedanken.*

myself	mich	ich freue mich
yourself	dich *(familiar)*	du freust dich
	sich *(polite)*	Sie freuen sich
himself / herself / itself	sich	er/sie/es freut sich
ourselves	uns	wir freuen uns
yourselves	euch *(familiar)*	ihr freut euch
	sich *(polite)*	Sie freuen sich
themselves	sich	sie freuen sich

3. Possessive pronouns

	m	f	n	pl
singular				
nom.	mein	meine	mein	meine
acc.	meinen	meine	mein	meine
gen.	meines	meiner	meines	meiner
dat.	meinem	meiner	meinem	meinen
• *dein* (your), *sein* (his), *ihr* (her), *sein* (its) are declined like *mein* (my).				
1st person plural (our)				
nom.	unser	uns(e)re	unser	uns(e)re
acc.	uns(e)ren / unsern	uns(e)re	unser	unsre
gen.	uns(e)res	uns(e)rer	uns(e)res	uns(e)rer
dat.	uns(e)rem / unserm	uns(e)rer	uns(e)rem / unserm	uns(e)ren
2nd person plural (your)				
nom.	euer	eure	euer	eure
acc.	euren	eure	euer	eure
gen.	eures	eurer	eures	eurer
dat.	eurem	eurer	eurem	euren
3rd person plural (their)				
nom.	ihr	ihre	ihr	ihre
acc.	ihren	ihre	ihr	ihre
gen.	ihres	ihrer	ihres	ihrer
dat.	ihrem	ihrer	ihrem	ihren

A Short Guide to German Pronunciation

Vowels

Vowel sounds in German can be **long** or **short**.

A vowel is usually **long** if it is followed by a _single_ consonant:

Schlaf, schlafen, Kino, groß   (exception: mit)

or if it is followed by a silent **h**:

mehr, mähen, hohlen

or if it is doubled:

Meer, Haar, Boot

The vowel combination **ie** is usually long:

wie viel, Ziel, ziehen

A vowel is usually **short** if it is followed by _two or more_ consonants:

nass, Hund, Tisch, immer, Koch   (exception: hoch)

or if it comes before **ck**:

Hecke, Rucksack, backen, Bäcker, Stücke

NB: if the root form of the word is long (e.g. sagen, groß) but the inflected form is followed by two consonants, the vowel remains long: gesagt, größte

Long and Short "a"

The **long a** sound – which can be written **a, aa,** or **ah** – is like the English **a** in _car, calm, father_:

Glas, Haar, wahr, kam, Kahn

The **short a** sound is somewhere between the vowel sound in _fan_ and _fun,_ pronounced in a short, clipped way:

Land, danke, Stadt, Kamm, kann

Long and Short "e"

The **long e** sound – which can be written **e, ee,** or **eh** – is like the English **a** in _bathe_ or _hay_ (but without sliding away into _ee_ as the English does):

hebt, Meer, mehr, geht

The **short e** sound is like the **e** in _bed, net:_

Bett, Netz, wenn, leckt

Many German words end in a single unstressed **-e** or **-el**. This should be pronounced as in the final syllable of _Tina, sister,_ or _bubble, trouble:_

danke, Stelle, Gabel, Stachel

German words ending in a single unstressed **-er** should be pronounced very similarly but with the addition of a gently rolled **r** at the end; contrast:

bitte – bitter; Fische – Fischer

Long and Short "i"

The **long i** sound is like the English **ee** in *feet* or the **ea** in *beach:*
Kilo, Bibel, wir

The **short i** sound is like the **i** in *bit:*
mit, mich

Long and Short "o"

The **long o** sound – which can be written **o**, **oo** or **oh** – is somewhere between the English **o** sound in *go* or *show* (but with the <u>lips</u> more <u>rounded</u> and the <u>mouth</u> more <u>open</u>) and the **aw** sound in *lawn:*
tot, Hose, Boot, Moos, froh, holen

The **short o** sound is like the **o** in *pot* only <u>shorter</u> and with a more <u>rounded</u> mouth:
Sonne, Gott, hoffen, kochen

Long and Short "u"

The **long u** sound – which can be written **u** or **uh** – is like the English **oo** in *hoot* or *rule* but with more <u>rounded</u> lips:
Fuß, gut, Ruf, Schule, Stuhl, Tuch, Uhr, zu

The **short u** sound is a shorter version of the vowel sound in *put* or *foot:*
Fluss, Hund, Mutter, Suppe, unter, putzen

Long and Short "ä"

The **long ä** sound – which can be written **ä** or **äh** – is somewhere between the vowel sounds in *day* (but without sliding away into *ee* as the English does) and *dare:*
Mädchen, wählen, täglich, spät, Lärm

The **short ä** sound is like the **e** in *get, set:*
Männer, Hände, hätte, lästig

Long and Short "ö"

The **long ö** sound – which can be written **ö** or **öh** – sounds a bit like the vowel sounds in *earth* and *learn* but said with <u>rounded</u> lips:
schön, böse, Flöte, Größe, Söhne, Höhle, hören, mögen

The **short ö** sound is a shorter, more clipped version of the above:
Löffel, Stöcke, Hölle, können, möchte

Long and Short "ü"

These are the hardest sounds in the German alphabet for the English speaker to master.

The **long ü** sound – which can be written **ü** or **üh** – is produced by saying an *ee* sound with <u>very rounded</u> lips.

Try saying *Tier* like this and with a bit of luck it should sound like *Tür*; try *spielen* too - this should come out as *"spülen"*.

früh, für, grün, müde, Schüler, Hügel, über

The **short ü** sound is a shorter, more clipped version of the above:

Stück, dünn, Küsse, hübsch, müssen

Groups of Vowels

ai, ay, ei, ey sound like the **i** in "*mine:*
Mai, Main, Bayern, mein, Rhein, Speyer

au sounds like a shorter more clipped version of the **ow** in *now:*
Frau, braun, auch

äu, eu sound like the **oy** in *boy:*
Fräulein, Gebäude, neu, Freund

ie sounds like the **ee** in *deep* (but with a little more precision than in English):
die, viel, Lied, Bier, ziehen

When **ie** occurs at the end of a word, it can be pronounced in two separate ways: if the final syllable of the word is <u>stressed</u>, it is pronounced as the normal **ie** outlined above:
Biographie, Philosophie, Symphonie

But when it is <u>unstressed</u>, it is pronounced as two separate vowels:
Familie *(fa-mee-leeya)*

Consonants

b and **d** are usually pronounced as they are in English, except at the end of a word or syllable or before **s** or **t**, when the **b** sounds more like a **p** and the **d** sounds more like a **t**:

baden – Bad	Diebe – Dieb(stahl)	Handel – Hand
Hunde – Hund	leider – Leid	lieben – lieb(ster)
rauben – Raub	schreiben – Schreibtisch	wenden – Wand
gibt	siebter	Stadt

ch - has a multiplicity of regional variations but when it follows an **a, o, u,** or **au** it is like the rather harsh guttural **ch** in the Scottish *Loch Ness*:

nach, lachen, Koch, Tochter, Buch, Kuchen, auch, rauchen

Otherwise it sounds a lot softer, rather like the **h** sound at the beginning of *hymn* or *humor*:

> brechen, ich, lächeln, möchte, Bücher, Küche, euch, geräuchert, Milch, welche, manche, Hähnchen, München, durch, Kirche

ch at the beginning of a word indicates a word that has been imported from a foreign language; if this is French then it sounds like **sh**: Chalet, Champagner, Chance, Chef

others sound like **k**:

> Chaos, Charakter, Cholera, Chor, Christ

or like the **ch** in *mich*:

> Chemie, chinesisch, Chirurg

and others are taken directly from languages like English and spoken as closely as possible to the original:

> Champion, Chart, Chat, checken

chs usually sounds like the **x** in *axe*:

> Lachs, sechs, wachsen, Wechsel

(exceptions: machst [harsh "ch"] nächste [soft "ch"])

ck sounds like the English **k** and the vowel preceding it is always short and stressed:

> backen, Gepäck, Glück, lecker, Rock, zurück
> [Try these problem words: glücklich, schrecklich]

g is usually pronounced like the **g** in *gold* when it comes before a vowel:

> Geld, gelb

but at the end of a word or syllable or before **s** or **t**, it sounds more like a strangulated **k**:

> Berge – Berg   bürgen – Burg   fliegen – fliegt
> schlagen – Schlag(sahne)   tagen – Tag

ig at the end of a word, is pronounced just like the German **ich**, i.e. ending in a sound rather like the **h** in *hymn* or *humor*:

> fertig, Honig, hungrig, König, richtig, sonnig, zwanzig

gn, kn - both consonants are pronounced:

> Gnade, Kneipe, Knie, Knopf

h is clearly pronounced at the beginning of a word or second element in a compound noun:

> Haushalt, hier, holen, Buchhandlung

however, when it comes after a vowel, it is not usually sounded and the preceding vowel is lengthened:

> fahren, gehen, Lehrer, stehen

j sounds like the **y** in *yes*:

> ja, Jacke, jetzt, Johannes, Junge, Juni, Major

l sounds a little lighter and flatter than an English **l**, quite close to the sound in *million*:

 alles, Liebe

ng always sounds like the nasal sound in *song, singer, ring,* even in the middle of a word (never like *finger*):

 singen, schwanger, Engel, England, Zunge

q - as in English, **q** is always followed by a **u** but is pronounced **kv**:

 Quittung, quer, Quiz

r has a multiplicity of regional variations but the basic sound when it occurs before a vowel is somewhere between a growl and a gargle made at the back of the throat:

 drei, fahren, Frau, Jahre, Lehrerin, rot, Straße, trocken, warum

At the end of a word however, the **r** is hardly pronounced at all, rather as in the English words: *beer, brother, year*:

 Bier, Bruder, Jahr

s sounds like the **s** in *sister*, except when it comes before a vowel, when it sounds like the **z** in *zoo*:

 das, Glas, Maske, Maus, Pflaster, Reis
 Masern, reisen, See, sie, Vase, Versicherung

sch sounds like the **sh** in *shoe*:

 Geschichte, Schuh, Schule, schwimmen, Tisch, waschen

sp and **st** – when they occur at the <u>beginning</u> of a word or the beginning of the second element in a compound noun, or after unstressed *Ge* or *ge*, sound like **shp** and **sht**:

 (Ball)Spiel, Sport, Sprache, (Haupt)Stadt, Stein, (Haupt)Straße, Gespräch, gesprochen, Gestank, gestohlen

Otherwise, they are pronounced as they would be in English:

 Dienstag, Gast, ist, kosten, Liste, sagst

ss or **ß** is always pronounced like an English **ss**; when the preceding vowel is <u>short</u> it is written **ss**; when it comes after a <u>long</u> vowel or <u>diphthong</u> it is written **ß**:

 besser, dass, muss, müssen, Pass, Schloss, Schlüssel, wissen
 groß, Gruß, Grüße, schließen, Schoß, Spaß, Strauß, süß, weiß

th sounds like an English **t**:

 Apotheke, Theater, Thema

tz is pronounced **ts**:

 Blitz, Dutzend, jetzt, Metzger, Platz, plötzlich, putzen

v, f, ph sound like the English **f** in *before, father, from*:

 bevor, Vater, vier, von, frei, für, Triumph, Typhus

In a few loan words from other languages however, **v** is pronounced as it is in English:

> Klavier, Vase, Verb

w sounds like the English **v** in *very, video*:

> Wasser, wenn, wieder, wir, Witwe, zuwinken
> [Try these problem words:
> Volkswagen, vorwärts, wievielte, wovon]

y – the pronunciation of the German **y** depends on the position of the letter in the word; if it occurs <u>within a word</u> it sounds like an **ü**:

> Physik, Pyramide, Rhythmus, typisch

If **y** occurs at the beginning or end of a word, then it is pronounced in exactly the same way as it is in English:

> Handy, Hobby, Yoga, Yucca,

z sounds like the **ts** in *cats, nuts* - even at the beginning of a word:

> Herz, März, salzig, zehn, Zeit, Zimmer, zu, zwanzig

A

Aal *m* ['a:l] eel
ab ['ap] from
abbestellen ['apbəʃtɛln] *(tickets etc.)* cancel
Abblendlicht *n* ['apblɛntlɪçt] dimmed headlights
abbrechen ['apbʀɛçn] to stop
Abend *m* ['a:bmt] evening, night
Abendessen *n* ['a:bmt'ɛsn] dinner
abends ['a:bms] in the evening
aber ['a:bɐ] but
abfahren (von) ['apfa: (ʀə)n fɔn] start (from), leave
Abfahrt *f* ['apfa:t] departure
Abfall *m* ['apfal] trash, garbage
Abfallbeutel *m* ['apfalbɔɪtl] trash can liner
Abfalleimer *m* ['apfal 'aɪmɐ] trash can
Abflug *m* ['apflu:k] departure, take-off
Abführmittel *n* ['apfyɐ mɪtl] laxative
abgeben ['apge:bm] hand in, leave
abgelegen ['apgəle:gn] isolated
abholen ['apho:ln] call for, pick up; **abholen lassen** ['apho:ln lasn] send for
Abkürzung *f* ['apkʰʏɐtsʊŋ] abbreviation; short-cut
ablehnen ['aple:nn] decline, refuse
abnehmen ['apne:mm]
abreisen (nach) ['apʀaɪzn (nax)] leave (for)
absagen ['apza:gn] *(appointment)* cancel
Abschied nehmen ['apʃi:t ne:mm] say goodbye

abschleppen ['apʃlɛpm] tow (away)
Abschleppseil *n* ['apʃlɛpzaɪl] tow rope
Abschleppwagen *m* ['apʃlɛpva:gn] tow truck
abschließen ['apʃli:sn] to lock
abseits ['apzaɪts] offside
Absender/in *m/f* ['apzɛndɐ/ -dəʀɪn] sender
Abstand *m* ['apʃtant] distance
abstellen ['apʃtɛln] to park
Abszess *m* ['aps'ɛs] abscess
Abtei *f* ['ap'taɪ] abbey
Abteil *n* ['ap'taɪl] compartment
Achtung ['axtʊŋ] attention; **Achtung!** ['axtʊŋ] look out!
Actionfilm *m* ['ɛktʃnfɪlm] action film
Adapter *m* ['a'daptɐ] adapter
Adresse *f* ['a'dʀɛsə] address
adressieren ['adʀɛ'si:ʀən/-'si:ən] to address
Aerobic *n* ['ɛ'ʀɔbɪk] aerobics
Agentur *f* ['agɛn'tʰuɐ] agency
ähnlich ['ɛ:nlɪç] similar
Ahnung *f* ['a:nʊŋ] idea
Akt *m* ['akt] *(play)* act; *(painting)* nude
Alarmanlage *f* ['a'la:manla:gə] alarm system
alkoholfrei ['alko'ho:lfʀaɪ] non-alcoholic
alle ['alə] all
allein ['a'laɪn] alone
Allergie *f* ['al(ɛ)ɐ'gi:] allergy
alles ['aləs] everything
als ['als] when; *(comparison)* than
also ['alzo:] so, thus
alt ['alt] old
Altar *m* ['al'ta:] altar
Alter *n* ['altʰɐ] age
Alufolie *f* ['alufo:ljə] aluminum foil

Amerika [ʔaˈmeːʁɪkʰaː] America
Amerikaner/in *m/f*
[ʔameʁɪˈkaːnɐ/-ˈkaːnəʁɪn]
American
Ampel *f* [ˈampl] traffic light
amputiert [ampuˈtiɐt] amputated
Amt *n* [ˈamt] office, department
amtlich [ˈamtlɪç] official
Ananas *f* [ˈananas] pineapple
anbieten [ˈanbiːtn] to offer
anders [ˈandɐs] different(ly)
anderswo [ˈandɐsvoː] elsewhere
Anfall *m* [ˈanfal] attack, fit
Anfang *m* [ˈanfaŋ] beginning
anfangen [ˈanfaŋŋ] begin
Angabe *f* [ˈangaːbə] statement
Angel *f* [ˈaŋl] fishing rod
Angelegenheit *f*
[ˈangələgŋhaɪt] matter
angeln [ˈaŋln] go fishing
Angelschein *m* [ˈaŋlʃaɪn] fishing
license
angenehm [ˈangəneːm] agreeable, pleasant
Angina *f* [aŋˈgiːna] angina
Angst *f* [ˈaŋst] fear
anhalten [ˈanhaltn] to stop
Anhänger *m* [ˈanhɛŋɐ] pendant
Ankunft *f* [ˈankʊnft] arrival
Ankunftszeit *f* [ˈankʊnf tsaɪt]
time of arrival
Anlage *f* [ˈanlaːgə] *(letter)*
enclosure; park
Anlass *m* [ˈanlas] cause, reason
Anlasser *m* [ˈanlasɐ] starter
(motor)
anlegen in [ˈanleːgŋ ʔɪn] dock
at, land at
anmelden [ˈanmɛldn] announce;
sich anmelden [zɪç ˈanmɛldn]
register
Anmeldung *f* [ˈanmɛldʊŋ] registration
annehmen [ˈaneːmm] accept
Anorak *m* [ˈanoʁak] parka
Anreisetag *m* [ˈanʁaɪzə taːk]
day of arrival
Anruf *m* [ˈanʁuːf] (phone) call

Anrufbeantworter *m*
[ˈanfuːfbə ˈantvɔɐtɐ] answering
machine
anrufen [ˈanʁuːfn] to call, to
phone
anschauen [ˈanʃaʊn] look at
Anschluss *m* [ˈanʃlʊs] connection
Anschrift *f* [ˈanʃʁɪft] address
ansehen [ˈanzeːn] look at
Ansicht *f* [ˈanzɪçt] opinion, view
Ansichtskarte *f* [ˈanzɪçtskaːtə]
picture postcard
anstatt [ʔanˈʃtat] instead of
ansteckend [ˈanʃtɛkŋt]
contagious
anstrengend [ˈanʃtʁɛŋŋt]
strenuous
antik [ʔanˈtiːk] ancient
Antiquitätengeschäft *n*
[ʔantɪkvɪˈtɛːtŋgəʃɛft] antiques
shop
Antwort *f* [ˈantvɔɐt] answer
antworten [ˈantvɔɐtn] to answer,
to reply
anwenden [ˈanvɛndn] to use
Anwendung *f* [ˈanvɛndʊŋ] use
anwesend [ˈanveːznt] present
anzeigen [ˈantsaɪgŋ] to report
anziehen [ˈantsiːn] put on; sich
anziehen [zɪç ˈantsiːn] dress, get
dressed
Anzug *m* [ˈantsuːk] *(for men)* suit
anzünden [ˈantsʏndn] to light
Äpfel *m pl* [ˈɛpfl] apples
Apfelsinen *f pl* [apflˈziːnn]
oranges
Apotheke *f* [apoˈteːkə] pharmacy
Apparat *m* [ʔapʰaˈʁaːt] gadget;
(Foto~) camera; *(Fernseh~)* television set
Appetit *m* [ʔapəˈtɪt] appetite
Aprikosen *f pl* [ʔapʁɪˈkoːzn]
apricots
April [ʔaˈpʁɪl] April
Aquarell *n* [ˈakvaˈʁɛl] watercolor
(picture)
Arbeit *f* [ˈaːbaɪt] work; job
arbeiten [ˈaːbaɪtn] to work

arbeitslos [ˈʔaːbaɪtsloːs] unemployed

Archäologie f [ˈʔaːçeoloˈgiː] archaeology

Architekt/Architektin [ˈʔaːçɪˈtɛkt/ˈʔaːçɪˈtɛkt ɪn] architect

Architektur f [ˈʔaːçitɛkˈtuɐ] architecture

ärgerlich [ˈʔɛɐgelɪç] *(adj)* cross

arm [ˈʔaːm] poor

Armband n [ˈʔaːmbant] bracelet

Armbanduhr f [ˈʔaːmbant ˈʔuɐ] wristwatch

Ärmel m [ˈʔɛɐml] sleeve

Art f [ˈʔaːt] kind, sort

Artischocken f pl [ˈʔaːtɪˈʃɔkn] artichokes

Aschenbecher m [ˈʔaʃnbɛçɐ] ashtray

Aspirin n [ˈʔaspiˈʀiːn] aspirin

Asthma n [ˈʔastma] asthma

Atembeschwerden f pl [ˈʔaːtmbəʃveɐdn] difficulty in breathing

Atlantik m [ˈʔatˈlantʰɪk] Atlantic

atmen [ˈʔaːtmən] breathe

Attest n [ˈʔaˈtɛst] certificate

Auberginen f pl [ˈʔobɐˈʒiːnn] eggplants

auch [ˈʔaʊx] also; too; auch nicht [ˈʔaʊx nɪç(t)] nor, neither

auf [ˈʔaʊf] on

aufbrechen [ˈʔaʊfbʀɛçn] break into/open

Aufenthalt m [ˈʔaʊfntʰalt] stay; *(train)* stop

Aufenthaltsraum m [ˈʔaʊfntalts ʀaʊm] lounge

auffordern [ˈʔaʊfɔdɐn] ask, invite

aufgeben [ˈʔaʊfgeːbm] *(luggage)* check

aufhalten, sich ~ [zɪç ˈʔaʊfhaltn] to stay

aufhören [ˈʔaʊfhøɐn] to stop

aufladen [ˈʔaʊflaːdn] put on, load

aufmachen [ˈʔaʊfmaxn] to open

aufpassen [ˈʔaʊfpasn] pay attention (to)

aufrufen [ˈʔaʊfʀuːfn] call (out)

aufschieben [ˈʔaʊfʃiːbm] postpone, put off

Aufschnitt m [ˈʔaʊfʃnɪt] cold cuts, lunch meat

aufschreiben [ˈʔaʊfʃʀaɪbm] write down

aufstehen [ˈʔaʊfʃteːn] get up

aufwachen [ˈʔaʊfvaxn] wake up

aufwärts [ˈʔaʊfvɛɐts] up(wards)

Aufzug m [ˈʔaʊftsuːk] elevator

Auge n [ˈʔaʊgə] eye

Augentropfen m pl [ˈʔaʊgn̩tʀɔpfn] eyedrops

August [ˈʔaʊˈgʊst] August

aus [ˈʔaʊs] from; out of

Ausbildung f [ˈʔaʊsbɪldʊŋ] education, training

Ausdruck m [ˈʔaʊsdʀʊk] expression

ausdrücklich [ˈʔaʊsdʀʏklɪç] explicit(ly)

Ausflug m [ˈʔaʊsfluːk] excursion, trip

ausfüllen [ˈʔaʊsfʏln] fill in

Ausgang m [ˈʔaʊsgaŋ] exit, way out

ausgeben [ˈʔaʊsgeːbm] spend

ausgehen [ˈʔaʊsgeːn] go out

ausgeschlossen [ˈʔaʊsgə ʃlɔsn] impossible

ausgezeichnet [ˈʔaʊsgə tsaɪçnət] excellent

Ausgrabungen f pl [ˈʔaʊsgʀaːbʊŋŋ] excavations

Auskunft f [ˈʔaʊskʰʊnft] information; *(Telefon~)* telephone operator

Ausland, im/ins ~ [ˈʔɪm /ˈʔɪns ˈʔaʊslant] abroad

Ausländer/in m/f [ˈʔaʊslɛndɐ/ -lɛndəʀɪn] foreigner

ausländisch [ˈʔaʊslɛndɪʃ] foreign

Auslandsflug m [ˈʔaʊslantsfluːk] international flight

Auslandsgespräch n [ˈʔaʊslantsgə ʃpʀɛːç] international call

ausleihen [ˈʔaʊslaɪn] borrow

Auslöser m ['ʔaʊsløːze] *(camera)* shutter release

ausmachen ['ʔaʊsmaxn] *(light)* turn off, *(fire)* put out; agree

Auspuff m ['ʔaʊspʊf] exhaust (pipe)

ausrichten ['ʔaʊsrɪçtn] tell

ausruhen, sich ~ [zɪç 'ʔaʊsruːn] to rest

Aussage f ['ʔaʊszaːgə] statement

aussagen ['ʔaʊszaːgn] to state

Ausschlag m ['ʔaʊʃlaːk] rash

aussehen ['ʔaʊseːn] to look

außen ['ʔaʊsn] outside

außer ['ʔaʊse] except

außerdem ['ʔaʊsedeːm] besides

außergewöhnlich [ʁ'ʔaʊsegə'vøːnlɪç] extraordinary

außerhalb ['ʔaʊsehalp] outside

Aussicht f ['ʔaʊszɪçt] view

Aussichtspunkt m ['ʔaʊszɪçtspʊŋt] vantage point

aussprechen ['ʔaʊ(s)ʃprɛçn] pronounce

Ausstellung f ['ʔaʊʃtɛlʊŋ] exhibition, show

aussuchen ['ʔaʊsuːxn] pick out

Austausch m ['ʔaʊstaʊʃ] exchange

austauschen ['ʔaʊstʰaʊʃn] to exchange

Austern f pl ['ʔaʊstɐn] oysters

ausüben ['ʔaʊsʔyːbm] *(profession)* practice

Ausverkauf m ['ʔaʊsfɛkʰaʊf] (clearance) sale

Auswahl f ['ʔaʊsvaːl] choice

auszahlen ['ʔaʊstsaːln] pay out

Auto n ['ʔaʊtʰoː] car; **Auto fahren** ['ʔaʊtʰoːfaːn] drive a car

Autobahn f ['ʔaʊtobaːn] freeway, expressway

Autobahnausfahrt f ['ʔaʊtobaːn 'ʔaʊsfaːt] (freeway) exit

Autobahngebühren f ['ʔaʊtobaːngə byːʁən] freeway toll

Automat m ['ʔaʊtʰoʼmaːt] vending machine

Automatikgetriebe n ['ʔaʊtoʼmaːtɪkgə tʁiːbə] automatic (transmission)

automatisch ['ʔaʊtʰoʼmaːtʰɪʃ] automatic

Autoradio n ['ʔaʊto ʁaːdjo] car radio

Avocado f ['ʔavoʼkaːdo] avocado

B

Baby n ['beːbiː] baby

Babyfon n ['beːbifoːn] baby monitor

Babylift ['beːbilɪft] bunny lift

Babyschale f ['beːbiʃaːlə] baby seat

Babysitter m ['beːbisɪtɐ] babysitter

Bäckerei f [bɛkəʼʁaɪ] bakery

Badeanzug m ['baːdə ʔantsuːk] swimsuit

Badehose f ['baːdəhoːzə] swimming trunks

Bademantel m ['baːdəmantl] bathrobe

Bademeister/in m/f ['baːdəmaɪstɐ/-tɐrɪn] lifeguard

baden [baːdn] to swim

Badeort m ['baːdəʔɔɐt] seaside resort, beach resort

Badeschuhe m pl ['baːdəʃuə] flip-flops

Badewanne f ['baːdəvanə] bathtub

Badezimmer n ['baːdətsɪmə] bathroom

Badminton n ['bɛtmɪntn] badminton

Bahnhof m ['baːnhoːf] station

bald [balt] soon

Balkon m [balʼkɔn] balcony

Ball m [bal] ball; *(event)* ball, dance

Ballett n [baʼlɛt] ballet

211

Bananen *f pl* [ba'na:nn] bananas

Band *f* [bɛ(:)nt] band

Bänderriss *m* ['bɛndeʀɪs] torn ligament

Bank *f* [baŋk] bank; bench

Bar *f* [ba:] bar

bar zahlen ['ba: tsa:ln] pay (in) cash

Bargeld *n* ['ba:gɛlt] cash

barock [ba'ʀɔk] baroque

Barsch *m* [ba:ʃ] *(fish)* perch

Bart *m* [ba:t] beard

Basilikum *n* [ba'zi:lɪkʊm] basil

Basketball *m* ['ba:skətbal] basketball

Batterie *f* [batə'ʀi:] battery

Bauch *m* [baʊx] stomach

Bauernhof *m* ['baʊenho:f] farm

Baum *m* [baʊm] tree

Baumwolle *f* ['baʊmvɔlə] cotton

beachten [bə'ʔaxtn] pay attention to

beantworten [bə'ʔantvɔetn] to reply, to answer

Bearbeitungsgebühr *f* [bə'ʔa:baɪtʊŋsgə byɐ] service charge

bedauern [bə'daʊen] to regret

bedeutend [bə'dɔɪtnt] important

Bedeutung *f* [bə'dɔɪtʰʊŋ] meaning; importance

bedienen [bə'di:nn] serve

Bedienung *f* [bə'di:nʊŋ] service; waitress

beeilen, sich ~ [zɪç bə'ʔaɪln] to hurry

beeindruckend [bə'ʔaɪndʀʊknt] impressive

befahrbar [bə'fa:ba:] passable

befinden, sich ~ [zɪç bə'fɪndn] be

befreundet sein [bə'fʀɔɪndət zaɪn] be friends

befriedigt [bə'fʀi:dɪçt] satisfied

befürchten [bə'fʏeçtn] to fear, be afraid (of)

begegnen [bə'ge:kn (ə)n] meet

begeistert (von) [bə'gaɪstet fɔn] enthusiastic (about)

Beginn *m* [bə'gɪn] beginning

beginnen [bə'gɪnn] begin

begleiten [bə'glaɪtn] accompany

Begleitperson *f* [bə'glaɪtpɛ(ɐ)e zo:n] accompanying person

begrüßen [bə'gʀy:sn] greet, welcome

behalten [bə'haltn] keep

Behälter *m* [bə'hɛltʰe] container

behandeln [bə'handln] to treat

behaupten [bə'haʊptn] maintain; insist

Behinderte *m/f* [bə'hɪndetə] disabled person

behindertengerecht [bə'hɪndetngə ʀɛçt] suitable for the disabled

Behindertentoilette *f* [bə'hɪndetnto lɛtə] toilet for the disabled

Behinderung *f* [bə'hɪndəʀʊŋ] disability, handicap

Behörde *f* [bə'høedə] authorities

beide ['baɪdə] both

Beifall *m* ['baɪfal] applause

beige [be:ʃ] beige

Bein *n* [baɪn] leg

beinahe ['baɪna:] almost, nearly

Beispiel *n* ['baɪʃpi:l] example; **zum Beispiel** [tsʊm 'baɪʃpi:l] for example

beißen [baɪsn] to bite

bekannt [bə'kʰant] well-known; **bekannt machen** [bə'kʰant maxn] introduce

Bekannte *m/f* [bə'kantə] acquaintance, friend

Bekanntschaft *f* [bə'kʰantʃaft] acquaintance

bekommen [bə'kʰɔmm] get, receive

belästigen [bə'lɛstɪgn] bother, harrass (sexually)

belegte Brötchen [bə'le:ktə bʀø:tçn] filled rolls

beleidigen [bə'laɪdɪgn] to insult

Beleidigung *f* [bə'laɪdɪgn] insult

Belgien ['bɛlgɪən] Belgium

Belichtungsmesser *m* [bə'lɪçtʊŋs mɛsɐ] light meter
Beliebige, jeder ~ [ʁje:dɐ bə'li:bɪgə] any
belohnen [bəlo:nn] to reward
Belohnung *f* [bə'lo:nʊŋ] reward
bemerken [bə'mɛɐkŋ] to notice; *(say)* to remark
bemühen, sich ~ [zɪç bə'my:n] try hard
benachrichtigen [bə'na:xʁɪçtɪgŋ] inform
benötigen [bə'nø:tʰɪgŋ] need
benutzen [bə'nʊtsn] to use; *(means of transportation)* to take
Benzinkanister *m* [bɛn'tsi:nka nɪstɐ] gas can
Benzinpumpe *f* [bɛn'tsi:npʊmpə] gas pump
beobachten [bə'ʔo:baxtn] observe, watch
bequem [bə'kve:m] comfortable
berechnen [bə'ʁɛçn (ə)n] calculate
bereit [bə'ʁaɪt] ready
bereits [bə'ʁaɪts] already
Berg *m* [bɛɐk] mountain
Bergdorf *n* ['bɛɐkdoɐf] mountain village
Bergstation *f* ['bɛɐkʃta tsjo:n] summit station, top station
Bergsteigen *n* ['bɛɐkʃtaɪgŋ] mountaineering/mountain climbing
Beruf *m* [bə'ʁu:f] job, profession
beruhigen, sich ~ [zɪç bə'ʁʊɪgŋ] calm down
Beruhigungsmittel *n* [bə'ʁʊɪgʊŋsmɪtl] sedative, tranquilizer
berühmt [bə'ʁy:mt] famous
berühren [bə'ʁy:ʁən /-'ʁyən] to touch
Berührung *f* [bə'ʁy:ʁʊŋ] contact
beschädigen [bə'ʃɛ:dɪgŋ] to damage
Beschädigung *f* [bə'ʃɛ:dɪgʊŋ] damage

Bescheid wissen [bə'ʃaɪt vɪsn] know
bescheinigen [bə'ʃaɪnɪgŋ] certify
Bescheinigung *f* [bə'ʃaɪnɪgʊŋ] statement
beschließen [bə'ʃli:sn] decide; make up one's mind
beschreiben [bə'ʃʁaɪbm] describe
besetzt [bə'zɛtst] *(seat)* occupied, taken; full; *(telephone)* engaged, busy
besichtigen [bə'zɪçtɪgŋ] to visit
Besichtigung *f* [bə'zɪçtɪgʊŋ] tour
besitzen [bə'zɪtsn] to own
Besitzer/in *m/f* [bə'zɪtsɐ/-'zɪtsəʁɪn] owner
besonders [bə'zɔndɐs] particularly, especially
besorgen [bə'zɔɐgn] get
besser ['bɛsɐ] better
bestätigen [bə'ʃtɛ:tʰɪgŋ] confirm
bestechen [bə'ʃtɛçn] to bribe, to corrupt
bestechlich [bə'ʃtɛçlɪç] corrupt
Besteck *n* [bə'ʃtɛk] cutlery
bestehen auf [bə'ʃte:n ʔaʊf] insist on; **bestehen aus** ['bə'ʃte:n ʔaʊs] consist of
bestellen [bə'ʃtɛln] to order
Bestellung *f* [bə'ʃtɛlʊŋ] order
beste(r, s) ['bɛstə (-tɐ, -təs)] best
bestimmt [bə'ʃtɪmt] certain(ly)
Besuch *m* [bə'zu:x] visit
besuchen, jdn ~ [ʁjemandn bə'zu:xn] visit s. o., call on s. o.
Besuchszeit *f* [bə'zu:xstsaɪt] visiting hours
beten [be:tn] pray
betrachten [bə'tʁaxtn] look at
Betrag *m* [bə'tʁa:k] amount
betragen [bə'tʁa:gn] be, come/amount to
Betreuung *f* [bə'tʁɔɪʊŋ] care
Betrug *m* [bə'tʁu:k] swindle; fraud
betrügerisch [bə'tʁy:gəʁɪʃ] deceitful
betrunken [bə'tʁʊŋkn] drunk

Bett *n* [bɛt] bed; **ins Bett gehen** [ˈʔɪns ˈbɛt geːn] go to bed
Bettdecke *f* [ˈbɛtdɛkə] blanket
Bettwäsche *f* [ˈbɛtvɛʃə] bed linen
beunruhigen, sich ~ [zɪç bəˈʔʊnʀʊɪgn] to worry
bevor [bəˈfoɐ] before
Bewohner/in *m/f* [bəˈvoːnɐ/ -ˈvoːnəʀɪn] inhabitant
bewölkt [bəˈvœlkt] *(weather)* cloudy
bewusst [bəˈvʊst] aware
bewusstlos [bəˈvʊstloːs] unconscious
bezahlen [bəˈtsaːln] to pay
bezaubernd [bəˈtsaʊbɐnt] charming
Biene *f* [ˈbiːnə] bee
Bier *n* [biɐ] beer
bieten [biːtn] to offer
Bikini *m* [biˈkiːni] bikini
Bild *n* [bɪlt] picture; illustration; painting
bilden [bɪldn] to form
Bildhauer/in *m/f* [ˈbɪlthaʊɐ/ˈbɪlthaʊəʀɪn] sculptor
billig [ˈbɪlɪç] cheap
Bioladen *m* [ˈbiolaːdn] organic food store
Birnen *f pl* [bɪɛnn] pears
bis [bɪs] to; *(time)* til(l), until; **bis jetzt** [bɪs ˈjɛtst] til(l) now
Bitte *f* [ˈbɪtʰə] request
bitten, jdn um etw. ~ [ˈkjemandn ʊm ʀˈʔɛtvas ˈbɪtn] ask s.o. for s.th.
bitter [ˈbɪtʰɐ] bitter
Blähungen *f pl* [ˈblɛːʊŋŋ] *(med)* flatulence
Blase *f* [ˈblaːzə] bladder; blister
blau [blaʊ] blue
Blazer *m* [ˈbleːzɐ] blazer
bleiben [blaɪbm] remain, stay
Blick *m* [blɪk] look; view
blind [blɪnt] blind
Blinddarmentzündung *f* [ˈblɪntdaːmɛn tsʏndʊŋ] appendicitis
Blinde *m/f* [ˈblɪndə] blind person

Blindenhund *m* [ˈblɪndnhʊnt] guide dog
Blindenschrift *f* [ˈblɪndnʃʀɪft] Braille
Blinklicht *n* [ˈblɪŋklɪçt] indicator
Blitz *m* [blɪts] lightning
Blitzgerät *n* [ˈblɪtsgəʀɛːt] *(camera)* flash
Block *m* [blɔk] writing pad
blöd(e) [bløːt / ˈbløːdə] silly, stupid
blond [blɔnt] blond(e)
Blues *m* [bluːs] blues
Blume *f* [ˈbluːmə] flower
Blumengeschäft *n* [ˈbluːmmgəʃɛft] florist's shop
Blumenkohl *m* [ˈbluːmmkoːl] cauliflower
Blumenstrauß *m* [ˈbluːmmʃtʀaʊs] bunch of flowers
Bluse *f* [ˈbluːzə] blouse
Blut *n* [bluːt] blood
bluten [bluːtn] bleed
Blutgruppe *f* [ˈbluːtgʀʊpə] blood group
Bluthochdruck *m* [ˈbluːthoːxdrʊk] high blood pressure
Blutung *f* [ˈbluːtʊŋ] bleeding
Blutvergiftung *f* [ˈbluːtfɐgɪftʊŋ] blood poisoning
Bö *f* [bøː] gust of wind
Boden *m* [boːdn] ground; floor
Bogen *m* [ˈboːgn] arch
Bohnen *f pl* [boːnn] beans
Bordkarte *f* [ˈbɔɛtkaːtə] boarding card
böse [ˈbøːzə] evil; naughty; angry
botanischer Garten *m* [boˈtanɪʃə ˈgaːtn] botanical garden
Botschaft *f* [ˈboːtʃaft] embassy
Boutique *f* [buˈtiːk] boutique
Brand *m* [bʀant] fire
Bratensoße *f* [ˈbʀaːtnzoːsə] gravy
brauchen [bʀaʊxn] need, want; *(time)* take
braun [bʀaʊn] brown
Brechreiz *m* [ˈbʀɛçʀaɪts] nausea
breit [bʀaɪt] broad, wide

Breite *f* ['bʀaɪtə] width
Bremse *f* ['bʀɛmzə] brake; horsefly
Bremsflüssigkeit *f* ['bʀɛmsflʏsɪçkaɪt] brake fluid
Bremslichter *f* ['bʀɛmslɪçtə] brake lights
brennen [bʀɛnn] to burn
Brennholz *n* ['bʀɛnhɔlts] firewood
Brennspiritus *m* ['bʀɛn ʃpiʀɪtʊs] denatured alcohol
Brief *m* [bʀiːf] letter
Briefmarke *f* ['bʀiːf maːkə] *(postage)* stamp
Briefmarkenautomat *m* ['bʀiːfmaːkŋʔaʊto maːt] stamp machine
Briefpapier *n* ['bʀiːfpapiə] writing paper, stationery
Brieftasche *f* ['bʀiːftʰaʃə] wallet, billfold
Briefumschlag *m* ['bʀiːfʊmʃlaːk] envelope
bringen [('heɐ)bʀɪŋŋ] bring
Brombeeren *f pl* ['bʀɔmbeːʀən] blackberries
Bronchien *f pl* ['bʀɔnçɪən] bronchial tubes
Bronchitis *f* [bʀɔn'çiːtɪs] bronchitis
Bronze *f* ['bʀɔ̃ːsə] bronze
Brosche *f* ['bʀɔʃə] brooch
Brot *n* [bʀoːt] bread
Brötchen *n pl* [bʀøːtçn] rolls
Brücke *f* ['bʀʏkə] bridge
Bruder *m* ['bruːdə] brother
Brunnen *m* [('bʀʊnn] fountain, well
Brust *f* [bʀʊst] chest
Buch *n* [buːx] book
buchen [buːxn] *(seat)* to reserve
Buchhandlung *f* ['buːxhantlʊn] book store
Büchse *f* ['bʏksə] can
buchstabieren [buxʃta'biːʀən/-'biən] to spell
Bucht *f* [bʊxt] bay
Buchung *f* ['buːxʊŋ] reservation

bügeln [byːgln] to iron
Bummel *m* [bʊml] stroll
Bungalow *m* ['bʊŋgalo:] bungalow
Burg *f* [bʊɐk] *(fortress)* castle
Bürgschaft *f* ['bʏɐkʃaft] security
Büro *n* [by'ʀo:] office
Bürste *f* ['bʏɐstə] brush
Bus *m* [bʊs] bus
Busbahnhof *m* ['bʊs baːnhoːf] bus station
Busch *m* [bʊʃ] bush
Butter *f* ['bʊte] butter
Buttermilch *f* ['bʊtemɪlç] buttermilk
Bypass *m* ['baɪpaːs] bypass

C

Café *n* [kʰa'fe:] café
Camcorder *m* ['kamkhɔɐdə] camcorder
Camping *n* ['kɛmpɪn] camping
Campingführer *m* ['kɛmpɪnfyːʀe] camping guide
Campingplatz *m* ['kɛmpɪnplats] campground
CD *f* [tse'de:] CD
CD-Spieler *m* [tse'de:ʃpiːle] CD player
Champagner *m* [ʃam'panje] champagne
Chauffeur *m* [ʃɔ'føe] chauffeur, driver
Chef/Chefin *m/f* [ʃɛf/ʃɛfɪn] boss, head
chemisch reinigen ['çe:mɪʃ 'ʀaɪnɪgn] dry-clean
Chipkarte *f* ['tʃɪpka:tə] chip card
Chirurg/Chirurgin *m/f* [çɪ'ʀʊek/çɪ'ʀʊegɪn] surgeon
Chor *m* [koɐ] choir
Christentum *n* ['kʀɪstntuːm] Christianity
Clubhaus *n* ['klʊphaʊs] clubhouse
Cousin/e *m/f* [kʰʊ'zɛŋ / kʰʊ'ziːnə] cousin

Creme *f* [kʀɛːm] cream
Curling *n* ['kəːlɪŋ] curling

D

da [daː] *(place)* there; *(time)* then; *(reason)* as, because; **da sein** ['daːzaɪn] be present, be there
Dach *n* [dax] roof
dagegen sein [da'geːgn̩ zaɪn] be against s. th.
daheim [da'haɪm] at home
daher ['daːheɐ] therefore
damals ['daːma(ː)ls] then, at that time
Damen [daːmn̩] Ladies
Damenbinden *f pl* ['daːmmbɪndn̩] sanitary napkins
Damenslip *m* ['daːmənslɪp] panties
danach [da'naːx] afterwards
danken ['daŋkŋ] thank
dann [dan] then
Darm *m* [daːm] intestines
dass [das] that
dasselbe [das'zɛlbə] the same
Datum *n* ['daːtʰʊm] date
dauern ['daʊɐn] to last
Dauerwelle *f* ['daʊɐvɛlə] permanent
Deck *n* [dɛk] deck
Decke *f* ['dɛkə] ceiling
Defekt *m* [de'fɛkt] fault
dein [daɪn] your
denken (an) ['dɛŋkŋ ʔan] think (of)
Denkmal *n* ['dɛŋkmaːl] monument
denn [dɛn] for; because
Deo *n* ['deo] deodorant
derselbe [deɐ'zɛlbə] the same
deshalb ['dɛshalp] therefore
Desinfektionsmittel *n* [dezɪnfɛk'tsjoːnsmɪtl̩] disinfectant
desinfizieren [dezɪnfɪ'tsiːʀən] disinfect

deutlich ['dɔɪtlɪç] distinct(ly), clear(ly)
deutsch [dɔɪtʃ] German
Deutsche *m/f* ['dɔɪtʃə] German
Deutschland ['dɔɪtʃlant] Germany
Dezember [de'tsɛmbɐ] December
Diabetes *m* [dia'beːtəs] diabetes
Diabetiker/in *m/f* [dia'beːtɪkɐ/-kəʀɪn] *(person)* diabetic
diabetisch [dia'beːtɪʃ] diabetic
Diagnose *f* [dia'gnoːzə] diagnosis
Diät *f* [di'ɛːt] diet
dich [dɪç] you
dicht [dɪçt] *(crowd, fog etc.)* thick
dick [dɪk] thick, swollen; *(person)* stout, fat
Dieb/Diebin *m/f* [diːp/'diːbɪn] thief
Diebstahl *m* ['diːpʃtaːl] theft
dienen [diːnn̩] to serve
Dienst *m* [diːnst] service
Dienstag ['diːnstaːk] Tuesday
diese ['diːzə] these, those
diese(r, s) ['diːzɐ/'diːzɐ/'diːzəs] that, this
Digitalkamera *f* [digi'taːl kaməʀa] digital camera
Ding *n* [dɪŋ] thing
Diphtherie *f* [dɪftə'ʀiː] diphtheria
dir [diɐ] to/for you
direkt [di'ʀɛkt] direct
Dirigent/Dirigentin *m/f* [diʀi'gɛnt/diʀi'gɛntɪn] conductor
Diskothek *f* [dɪsko'teːk] discotheque
doch [dɔx] yet, however
Dokumentarfilm *m* [dokumɛn'taːfɪlm] documentary
Donnerstag ['dɔnɐstaːk] Thursday
Doppel *n* [dɔpl̩] doubles
doppelt [dɔplt] *(adj)* double; *(adv)* twice
Dorf *n* [dœɐf] village
dort [dɔɐt] there
dorthin ['dɔɐthɪn] *(location)* there
Dose *f* ['doːzə] can

Dosenöffner m ['do:zn²ŋfnɐ] can opener

Drachenfliegen n ['dʀaxnfli:gŋ] hang-gliding

Drama n ['dʀa:ma] drama

draußen ['dʀausn] outside

Dressing f ['dʀɛsɪŋ] *(food)* dressing

drin [dʀɪn] inside

dringend [dʀɪŋnt] urgent

drinnen [dʀɪnn] indoors

dritte(r, s) ['dʀɪtɐ (-tɐ, -təs)] third

du [du:] you

dumm [dʊm] stupid

dunkel [dʊŋkl] dark

dunkelblau [dʊŋkl'blau] dark blue

dünn [dʏn] thin; slim, slender

durch [dʊʀç] through; *(quer ~)* across; by (means of)

durchaus nicht [dʊʀç²aus nɪç(t)] not at all

Durchfall m ['dʊʀçfal] diarrhea

durchgebraten ['dʊʀçgəbʀa:tn] well-done

Durchreise, auf der ~ ['auf de 'dʊʀçʀaɪzə] passing through

durchschnittlich ['dʊʀçʃnɪtlɪç] average

dürfen [dʏʀfn] be allowed

dürftig ['dʏʀftɪç] *(sparse)* thin

Dusche f ['du:ʃə] shower

Duschgel n ['du:ʃge:l] shower gel

Duschsitz m ['du:ʃzɪts] shower seat

Dynastie f [dʏnas'ti:] dynasty

E

E-Rollstuhl m ['²e: ʀɔlʃtu:l] electric wheelchair

Ebbe f ['²ɛbə] low tide

eben ['²e:bm] flat; smooth; *(time)* just now

Ebene f ['²e:bənə] plain

ebenerdig ['²e:bm²eɐdɪç] at ground level

echt ['²ɛçt] genuine

Ecke f ['²ɛkʰə] corner

Ehefrau f ['²e:əfʀau] wife

Ehemann m ['²e:əman] husband

Ehepaar n ['²e:əpa:] couple

eher ['²eɐ] rather

Eier n pl ['²aɪɐ] eggs

eigen ['²aɪgŋ] own; peculiar, strange, odd, weird

Eigenschaft f ['²aɪgŋʃaft] quality, characteristic

eigentlich ['²aɪgŋtlɪç] actual(ly)

Eigentümer/in m/f ['²aɪgŋty:mɐ/-məʀɪn] owner

eilig ['²aɪlɪç] urgent; es eilig haben ['²əs ²aɪlɪç ha:bm] be in a hurry

einchecken ['²aɪntʃɛkn] check in

ein(e) ['²eɪn /'²eɪnə] a, one

einfach ['²aɪnfax] simple

Einfahrt f ['²aɪnfa:t] entrance

einfarbig ['²aɪnfaʀbɪç] plain

Eingang m ['²aɪngaŋ] entrance

einheimisch ['²aɪnhaɪmɪʃ] native, local

einig sein ['²aɪnɪç zaɪn] agree

einige ['²aɪnɪgə] some

einigen, sich ~ [zɪç ²aɪnɪgŋ] agree

einkaufen ['²aɪnkʰaufn] buy, go shopping

einladen ['²aɪnla:dn] invite

einmal ['²eɪ (n)ma:l] once

einpacken ['²aɪnpʰakŋ] wrap, pack

eins ['²aɪns] one

einsam ['²aɪnza:m] lonely; secluded, isolated

Einschreibebrief m ['²aɪnʃʀaɪbəbʀi:f] registered letter

einsteigen ['²aɪnʃtaɪgŋ] get in/on

eintreffen ['²aɪntʀɛfn] arrive (at)

Eintritt m ['²aɪntʀɪt] entrance, admission

Eintrittskarte f ['²aɪntʀɪts kʰa:tʰə] (admission) ticket

Eintrittspreis *m* [ˈʔaɪntrɪtspraɪs] admission charge

Einwohner/in *m/f* [ˈʔaɪnvoːnɐ/ -nərɪn] inhabitant

Einzel *n* [ˈʔaɪntsəl] singles

einzelne, jeder ~ [ʁjeːdə ˈʔaɪntslnə] each

einzig [ˈʔaɪntsɪç] only

Eis *n* [ˈʔaɪs] ice

Eisbahn *f* [ˈʔaɪsbaːn] ice rink

Eishockey *n* [ˈʔaɪshɔkeː] ice hockey

Eiter *m* [ˈʔaɪtə] pus

Elastikbinde *f* [ʔeˈlastɪkbɪndə] elastic bandage

elektrisch [ʔeˈlɛktrɪʃ] electric

Eltern *pl* [ˈʔɛlthen] parents

empfangen [ʔɛmpˈfaŋŋ] receive; greet, welcome

Empfänger *m* [ʔɛmpˈfɛŋə] addressee

empfehlen [ʔɛmpˈfeːln] recommend

Ende *n* [ˈʔɛndə] end

endgültig [ˈʔɛntɡʏltʰɪç] definite; definitely

endlich [ˈʔɛntlɪç] finally

Endstation *f* [ˈʔɛntʃtatsjoːn] terminus, end of the line

eng [ˈʔɛŋ] narrow; *(clothes)* tight

England [ˈʔɛŋlant] England

Engländer/in *m/f* [ˈʔɛŋlɛndə/ -dərɪn] Englishman/-woman

englisch [ˈʔɛŋlɪʃ] English

entdecken [ʔɛntˈdɛkn] discover

Entfernung *f* [ʔɛntˈfɛɐnʊŋ] distance

entgegengesetzt [ʔɛntˈɡeːɡŋɡə zɛtst] opposite

entscheiden [ʔɛntˈʃaɪdn] decide

entschuldigen [ʔɛntˈʃʊldɪɡn] to excuse; **sich ~** [zɪç ʔɛntˈʃʊldɪɡn] apologize

Entschuldigung *f* [ʔɛntˈʃʊldɪɡʊŋ] apology; excuse; **Entschuldigung!** sorry!; **Ich bitte um Entschuldigung!** [ʔɪç ˈbɪtə ʔʊm ɛntˈʃʊldɪɡʊŋ] I beg your pardon!;

Entschuldigung, ... excuse me, ...

enttäuscht [ʔɛnˈtʰɔɪʃt] disappointed

entweder ... oder [ˈʔɛntveːdə ... ˈʔoːdə] either ... or

entwickeln [ʔɛntˈvɪkln] develop

entzückend [ʔɛnˈtsʏkŋt] charming, delightful

Entzündung *f* [ʔɛnˈtsʏndʊŋ] inflammation

Epilepsie *f* [ʔepilɛpˈsi] epilepsy

Epoche *f* [ʔeˈpɔxə] epoch

er [ˈʔeɐ] he

Erbsen *f pl* [ˈʔɛɐpsn] peas

Erdbeeren *f pl* [ˈʔeɐtbeːrən] strawberries

Erde *f* [ˈʔeɐdə] earth

Erdgeschoss *n* [ˈʔeɐtɡəʃɔs] ground floor, first floor

Ereignis *n* [ʔeˈʔaɪknɪs] event

erfahren [ʔeˈfaː(ʁə)n] learn, hear, experience; *(adj)* experienced

Erfolg *m* [ʔeˈfɔlk] success

erfreut (über) [ʔeˈfrɔɪt (ˈʔyːbə)] pleased (with), glad (of)

erhalten [ʔeˈhaltn] receive, get

erholen, sich ~ [zɪç ʔeˈhoːln] recover

Erholung *f* [ʔeˈhoːlʊŋ] rest

erinnern, sich ~ [zɪç ɐˈʔɪnən] remember

Erkältung *f* [ʔeˈkɛltʊŋ] cold

Ermäßigung *f* [ʔeˈmɛːsɪɡʊŋ] reduction

ernst [ˈʔɛɐnst] serious

erreichen [ʔeˈʁaɪçn] to reach

Ersatz *m* [ʔeˈzats] replacement; compensation

Ersatzreifen *m* [ʔeˈzatsʁaɪfn] spare tire

erschöpft [ʔeˈʃœpft] exhausted

erschrecken [ʔeˈʃʁɛkŋ] frighten, startle; be alarmed

erschrocken [ʔeˈʃʁɔkŋ] afraid, alarmed

ersetzen [ʔeˈzɛtsn] replace

erst [eɐst] first of all; *(not later than)* only

218

erste(r, s) [ˈʔeːɐstə (-tɐ, -təs)] first
ertragen [ˈʔeˈtʀaːgn] to bear, to stand
Erwachsene(r) m/f [ˈʔeˈvaks (ə)nə/ˈʔeˈvaks(ə)nɐ] adult
erwarten [ˈʔeˈvaːtn] expect, wait for
erwidern [ˈʔeˈviːdɐn] to reply
erzählen [ˈʔeˈtsɛːln] tell
Erzeugnis n [ˈʔeˈtsɔɪknɪs] product
Erziehung f [ˈʔeˈtsiʊŋ] education
essbar [ˈʔɛsbaː] edible
essen [ˈʔɛsn] eat
Essen n [ˈʔɛsn] meal; food
Essig m [ˈʔɛsɪç] vinegar
Esszimmer n [ˈʔɛstsɪmɐ] (private) dining room
Etagenbett n [ˈʔeˈtaːʒnbɛt] bunk bed
etwa [ˈʔɛtvaː] about
etwas [ˈʔɛtvas] something; anything; a little
EU-Bürger/in [ˈʔeˈʔuː bʏɐgɐ/-gəʀɪn] EU citizen
euch [ʔɔɪç] you
euer [ˈʔɔɪɐ] your
Euro m [ˈʔɔɪʀo] euro
Europa [ʔɔɪˈʀoːpʰaː] Europe
Europäer/in m/f [ʔɔɪʀoˈpɛːɐ/-pɛːəʀɪn] European
europäisch [ʔɔɪʀoˈpʰɛːɪʃ] European
eventuell [ˈʔevɛntuˈ(ʔ)ɛl] perhaps, possible
Exponat n [ˈʔɛkspoˈnaːt] exhibit
Expressionismus m [ˈʔɛkspʀɛsjoˈnɪsmus] expressionism
extra [ˈʔɛkstʀaː] extra, special

F

Fabrik f [faˈbʀi (ː)k] factory
Facharzt/-ärztin m/f [ˈfaxaːtst/ˈfaxˈʔɛɐtstɪn] specialist
Fähre f [ˈfɛːʀə] ferry
fahren [faː (ʀə)n] go (by train, car etc.); drive

Fahrer/in m/f [ˈfaːʀɐ/ˈfaːʀəʀɪn] driver
Fahrgast m [ˈfaːgast] passenger
Fahrkartenautomat m [ˈfaːkaːtnʔauto maːt] ticket machine
Fahrkartenschalter m [ˈfaːkaːtn ʃaltɐ] ticket office
Fahrplan m [ˈfaːplaːn] timetable
Fahrpreis m [ˈfaːpʀaɪs] fare
Fahrrad n [ˈfaːʀat] bicycle, bike
Fahrradweg m [ˈfaːʀatveːk] bike path
Fahrstuhl m [ˈfaːʃtuːl] elevator
Fahrt f [faːt] journey, trip, voyage; (car) drive
fair [fɛɐ] fair
fallen [faln] to fall
falls [fals] in case, if
Fallschirmspringen n [ˈfalʃɪɐmʃpʀɪŋn] parachuting
falsch [falʃ] wrong; deceitful
Faltrollstuhl m [ˈfalt ʀɔlʃtuːl] folding wheelchair
Familie f [faˈmiːljə] family
fangen [faŋn] to catch
färben [fɛɐbm] to dye
farbig [ˈfaʀbɪç] colored
Farbstift m [ˈfaːpʃtɪft] colored pencil
Fassade f [faˈsaːdə] façade, front
fast [fast] almost, nearly
faul [faʊl] lazy; (fruit) rotten
Februar [ˈfeːbʀuaː] February
Federball m [ˈfeːdəbal] shuttlecock; badminton
fehlen [feːln] be missing
Fehler m [ˈfeːlɐ] mistake; fault
Fehlgeburt f [ˈfeːlgəbʊɐt] miscarriage
fein [faɪn] fine; delicate; distinguished
Feinkostgeschäft n [ˈfaɪnkɔstgə ʃɛft] delicatessen
Feld n [fɛlt] field
Fell n [fɛl] fur, fleece
Fels m [fɛls] rock; cliff
Fenchel m [fɛnçl] fennel
Fenster n [ˈfɛnstɐ] window

Fensterplatz m ['fɛnstɐplats] window seat

Ferien pl ['fe:ʀɪən ('feːɐjən)] vacation

Ferienanlage f ['fe:ʀɪən²anlaːgə] vacation property

Ferienhaus n ['fe:ʀɪənhaʊs] vacation house

Ferngespräch n ['fɛɐngəʃpʀɛːç] long-distance call

Fernlicht n ['fɛɐnlɪçt] full beam, high beam

Fernsehapparat m ['fɛɐnzeː²apaʀaːt] TV set

Fernsehraum m ['fɛɐnzeː ʀaʊm] television lounge

fertig ['fɛɐtʰɪç] ready; finished

fest [fɛst] firm, solid, rigid

Fest n [fɛst] celebration(s), party

Festival n ['fɛstɪval] festival

feststellen ['fɛ(st)ʃtɛln] to state

Festung f ['fɛstʊŋ] fortress

fett [fɛt] fat; greasy

fettarme Milch ['fɛt²aːmə mɪlç] low-fat milk

feucht [fɔɪçt] moist, damp

Feuer n ['fɔɪɐ] fire

feuergefährlich ['fɔɪɐgə feːlɪç] (in)flammable

Feuerlöscher m ['fɔɪɐlœʃɐ] fire extinguisher

Feuermelder m ['fɔɪɐmɛldɐ] fire alarm

Feuerwerk n ['fɔɪɐvɛɐk] fireworks display

Feuerzeug n ['fɔɪɐtsɔɪk] lighter

Fieber n ['fiːbɐ] fever

Fieberthermometer n ['fiːbɐtɛɐmo meːtɐ] thermometer

Film m [fɪlm] film

Filmempfindlichkeit f ['fɪlmɛmpfɪntlɪçkaɪt] film speed

Filmschauspieler/-in m/f ['fɪlmʃaʊʃpiːlɐ/-lərɪn] film/movie actor/actress

finden [fɪndn] to find

Finger m ['fɪŋɐ] finger

finster ['fɪnstɐ] dark

Firma f ['fɪʀmaː] firm, company

Fischerhafen m ['fɪʃɐhaːfn] fishing port

Fischgeschäft n ['fɪʃgəʃɛft] fish dealer

fit [fɪt] fit

Fitnesscenter n ['fɪtnəs tsɛntɐ] fitness center

FKK-Strand m ['²ɛfkaːkaːʃtʀant] nudist beach

flach [flax] flat; level

Fläschchenwärmer m ['flɛʃçənvɛɐmɐ] bottle warmer

Flasche f ['flaʃə] bottle

Flaschenöffner m ['flaʃn²œfnɐ] bottle opener

Fleck m [flɛk] stain

Fleisch n [flaɪʃ] meat

Flickzeug n ['flɪktsɔɪk] repair kit

Fliege f ['fliːgə] fly

fliegen [fliːgn] to fly

Flohmarkt m ['floːmaːkt] flea market

Flug m [fluːk] flight

Flügel m [flyːgl] wing

Fluggesellschaft f ['fluːkgə zɛlʃaft] airline

Flughafen m ['fluːkhaːfn] airport

Flughafenbus m ['fluːkhaːfn bʊs] airport bus

Flughafengebühr f ['fluːkhaːfngə byɐ] airport tax

Flugsteig m ['fluːkʃtaɪg] (airport) gate

Fluss m [flʊs] river

flüssig ['flʏsɪç] liquid

Flut f [fluːt] high tide

Föhn m [føːn] hair dryer

föhnen [føːnn] to blow-dry

fordern ['fɔɐdɐn] ask

Form f [fɔɐm] form, shape

Format n [fɔˈmaːt] (paper) size

Formular n [fɔmʊˈlaː] (paper) form

fort [fɔɐt] away

Foto n ['foto] photo

Fotografie f [fotogʀaˈfiː] photography

fotografieren [ʁfotogʁa'fi:ʁən] to photograph

Frage f ['fʁa:gə] question

fragen [fʁa:gn] ask

frankieren [fʁaŋ'ki:ən] to stamp

französisch [fʁan'tsø:zɪʃ] French

Frau f [fʁaʊ] woman; wife; Madam; Ms. Mrs.

Fräulein n ['fʁɔ (ɪ)laɪn] young lady; Miss

frei [fʁaɪ] free; exempt; im Freien ['ɪm 'fʁaɪn] in the open air, outdoors

Freilichtkino n ['fʁaɪlɪçtki:no] drive-in movie

Freitag ['fʁaɪta:k] Friday

Freizeitpark m ['fʁaɪtsaɪt pa:k] amusement park

fremd [fʁɛmt] strange; foreign; unknown

Fremde m/f ['fʁɛmdə] stranger; foreigner

Fremdenführer/in m/f ['fʁɛmdnfy:ʁe/-fy:ʁəʁɪn] guide

Freude f ['fʁɔɪdə] joy, pleasure

freuen, sich ~ (über) [zɪç 'fʁɔɪn (ʁy:bə)] be pleased (with/about); sich ~ auf [zɪç 'fʁɔɪn ʔaʊf] look forward to

Freund/in m/f [fʁɔɪnt/'fʁɔɪndɪn] friend; boyfriend/girlfriend

freundlich ['fʁɔɪntlɪç] friendly, kind

Friedhof m ['fʁi:to:f] cemetery, graveyard

frieren ['fʁi:ʁən /fʁiən] be cold, freeze

frisch [fʁɪʃ] fresh; (clothing) clean

Frischhaltefolie f ['fʁɪʃhaltə fo:ljə] plastic wrap

Friseur m [fʁi'zøe] hairdresser

Frisur f [fʁi'zuɐ] hairstyle

froh [fʁo:] glad; happy; merry

Frost m [fʁɔst] frost

Frostschutzmittel n ['fʁɔstʃʊtsmɪtl] antifreeze

Frühling m ['fʁy:lɪŋ] (season) spring

Frühstück n ['fʁy:ʃtʏk] breakfast

frühstücken ['fʁy:ʃtʏkŋ] have breakfast

Frühstücksbüfett n ['fʁy:ʃtʏksbʏ fe:] buffet breakfast

Frühstücksraum m ['fʁy:ʃtʏksʁaʊm] breakfast room

fühlen [fy:ln] to feel

Führerschein m ['fy:ʁəʃaɪn] driver's license

Führung f ['fy:ʁʊŋ] guided tour

funktionieren [fʊŋktsjo'ni:ʁən/-'niən] to work, to function

für [fye] for

Furcht f [fʊʁçt] fear

fürchten ['fʏeçtn] to fear; sich ~ (vor) [zɪç 'fʏeçtn foe] be afraid (of)

fürchterlich ['fʏeçtəlɪç] terrible, dreadful, horrible

Fuß m [fu:s] foot

Fußball m ['fu:sbal] soccer

Fußballspiel n ['fu:sbal ʃpi:l] soccer match

Fußgänger/in m/f ['fu:sgɛŋe/-gɛŋəʁɪn] pedestrian

Fußgängerzone f ['fu:sgɛŋe tso:nə] pedestrian zone

G

Gabel f ['ga:bl] fork

Galerie f [galə'ʁi:] gallery

Gallenblase f ['galnbla:zə] gallbladder

Gang m [gaŋ] (meal) course; corridor; (engine) gear

ganz [gants] (adj) whole; entire, complete; (adv) quite

gar [ga:] cooked, done

gar nicht ['ga:ɬnɪç(t)] not at all

Garage f [ga'ʁa:ʒə] garage

Garantie f [gaʁan'tʰi:] guarantee

Garderobe f [ga'dʁo:bə] cloakroom

Garnelen f pl [ga'ne:ln] prawns

Garten m ['ga:tn] garden

Gasflasche f [ˈgaːsflaʃə] gas canister

Gaskartusche f [ˈgaːska tʊʃə] gas cartridge

Gaspedal n [ˈgaːspedaːl] accelerator, gas pedal

Gasse f [ˈgasə] alley, lane

Gast m [gast] guest

Gastfreundschaft f [ˈgastfRɔɪntʃaft] hospitality

Gastgeber/in [ˈgastgeːbɐ / -bəRɪn] host/hostess

gebacken [gəˈbakŋ] baked

Gebäude n [gəˈbɔɪdə] building

geben [geːbm] give

Gebirge n [gəˈbɪRgə] mountains

geboren [gəˈboːRən / gəˈboɐn] born

gebraten [gəˈbRaːtn] roasted

Gebrauch m [gəˈbRaʊx] use

gebrauchen [gəˈbRaʊx] to use

gebräuchlich [gəˈbRɔɪçlɪç] common

gebrochen [gəˈbRɔxn] broken

Gebühren f pl [gəˈbyːRən / -ˈbyɐn] fees

Geburtsdatum n [gəˈbʊɐtsdaːtʊm] date of birth

Geburtsname m [gəˈbʊɐtsnaːmə] maiden name

Geburtsort m [gəˈbʊɐtsʔɔɐt] place of birth

Geburtstag m [gəˈbʊɐtstʰaːk] birthday

gedämpft [gəˈdɛmpft] steamed

Gedenkstätte f [gəˈdɛŋkʃtɛtə] memorial

Geduld f [gəˈdʊlt] patience

gedünstet [gəˈdʏnstət] steamed

Gefahr f [gəˈfaː] danger

gefährlich [gəˈfeːlɪç] dangerous

gefallen [gəˈfaln] to please

Gefallen m [gəˈfaln] favour

Gefängnis n [gəˈfɛŋnɪs] prison

Gefäß n [gəˈfɛːs] container

Gefühl n [gəˈfyːl] feeling

gefüllt [gəˈfʏlt] stuffed

gegen [geːgŋ] against; *(sport)* versus; towards; *(time)* about

Gegend f [ˈgeːgŋt] region, area, district

Gegenstand m [ˈgeːgŋʃtant] object

Gegenteil n [ˈgeːgŋtʰaɪl] opposite, contrary

gegenüber [gegŋˈʔyːbɐ] opposite

Geheimzahl f [gəˈhaɪmtsaːl] Personal Identification Number (PIN)

gehen [geːn] to go; to walk

Gehirn n [gəˈhɪRən] brain

Gehirnerschütterung f [gəˈhɪRnɐ ʃytəRʊŋ] concussion

Gehör n [gəˈhøɐ] hearing

gehören [gəˈhøːRən / -ˈhøɐn] belong to

gehörlos [gəˈhøɐloːs] deaf

Gehörlose m/f [gəˈhøɐloːzə] deaf person

geistig behindert [ˈgaɪstɪç bəˈhɪndɐt] mentally handicapped

gekocht [gəˈkɔxt] boiled, cooked

Gelände n [geˈlɛndə] ground; grounds

gelb [gɛlp] yellow

Geld n [gɛlt] money

Geldautomat m [ˈgɛltaʊto maːt] automated teller machine, cashpoint

Geldbeutel m [ˈgɛltbɔɪtl] purse

Geldbörse f [ˈgɛltbœɐzə] purse

Geldschein m [ˈgɛltʃaɪn] banknote

Geldstrafe f [ˈgɛltʃtRaːfə] *(monetary)* fine

gelegentlich [gələːgŋtlɪç] occasional(ly)

Gelenk n [gəˈlɛŋk] joint

Gemälde n [gəˈmɛːldə] painting

gemeinsam [gəˈmaɪnza(ː)m] common; together

Gemüse n [gəˈmyːzə] vegetables

gemütlich [gəˈmyːtlɪç] comfortable, cosy

genau [gəˈnaʊ] exact(ly)

genauso ... wie [gəˈnaʊzo ... vi] just as ... as

genießen [gə'ni:sn] enjoy
genug [gə'nu:k] enough, sufficient
geöffnet [gə'ʔœfnət] open
Gepäck n [ge'pɛk] baggage, luggage
Gepäckaufbewahrung f [gə'pɛk 'ʔaʊfbəva:rʊŋ] baggage deposit
Gepäckausgabe f [gə'pɛk'aʊsga:bə] baggage claim
Gepäckschalter m [gə'pɛkʃaltɐ] baggage counter
Gepäckwagen m [gə'pɛkva:gŋ] baggage cart
gerade [g (ə)'ʁa:də] straight; *(time)* just
geradeaus [gʁa:də'ʔaʊs] straight on/straight ahead
geräuchert [gə'ʁɔɪçɐt] smoked
Geräusch n [gə'ʁɔɪʃ] noise
gerecht [gə'ʁɛçt] just, fair
Gericht n [gə'ʁɪçt] *(food)* dish; (law) court
gering [gə'ʁɪŋ] little, small
gern [gɛɐn] gladly; nicht gern [nɪç(t) gɛɐn] reluctantly
Geruch m [gə'ʁu (:)x] smell
Geschäft n [gə'ʃɛft] shop, store
Geschenk n [gə'ʃɛŋk] present, gift
Geschichte f [gə'ʃɪçtə] history; story
Geschirr n [gə'ʃɪɐ] crockery
Geschirrspülbecken n [gə'ʃɪɐspy:lbɛkŋ] sink
Geschirrspülmaschine f [gə'ʃɪɐʃpy:lma ʃinə] dishwasher
Geschirrtuch n [gə'ʃɪɐtu:x] tea towel
geschlossen [gə'ʃlɔsn] shut, closed
Geschmack m [gə'ʃmak] taste
geschmort [gə'ʃmoɐt] braised
Geschwindigkeit f [gə'ʃvɪndɪçkʰaɪt] speed
geschwollen [gə'ʃvɔln] swollen
Geschwulst f [gə'ʃvʊlst] tumor, growth
Geschwür n [gə'ʃvyɐ] ulcer

Gesellschaft f [gə'zɛlʃaft] company
Gespräch n [gə'ʃpʁɛ:ç] conversation, talk
gestern ['gɛstɐn] yesterday
gesund [gə'zʊnt] healthy
Getränk n [gə'tʁɛŋk] drink
Getriebe n [gə'tʁi:bə] transmission
Gewicht n [gə'vɪçt] weight
Gewinn m [gə'vɪn] profit
gewinnen [gə'vɪnn] to win
gewiss [gə'vɪs] certain(ly), sure(ly)
gewöhnlich [gə'vø:nlɪç] usual, ordinary
gewohnt [gə'vo:nt] usual
gewöhnt sein [ʁ'ʔɛtvas gə'vø:nt zaɪn] be used to
Gewölbe n [gə'vœlbə] vault(s)
Gewürz n [gə'vʏɐts] spice, seasoning
Giebel m [gi:bl] gable
Gift n [gɪft] poison
giftig ['gɪftɪç] poisonous
glänzend [glɛntsnt] splendid, glorious
Glas n [gla:s] glass
Glasmalerei f ['gla:sma:lə ʁaɪ] glass painting
glauben [glaʊbm] believe
gleich [glaɪç] same; immediately, at once
gleichfalls ['glaɪçfals] also; likewise
gleichzeitig ['glaɪçtsaɪtʰɪç] simultaneous(ly)
Gleis n [glaɪs] platform
Glück n [glʏk] luck; success
glücklich ['glʏklɪç] happy; lucky
Glückwunsch m ['glʏkvʊnʃ] congratulations
Glühbirne f ['gly:bɪɐnə] light bulb
Gold n ['gɔlt] gold
Goldschmiedekunst f ['gɔltʃmi:də kʊnst] gold work
Golf n [gɔlf] golf
Golfclub m ['gɔlfklʊp] *(establishment)* golf club

Golfschläger m
['gɔlfʃlɛːgɐ] *(implement)* golf club

Gotik f ['goːtɪk] Gothic

Gott m [gɔt] God

Grab n [gʀaːp] grave, tomb

Grabmal n ['gʀaːbmaːl] *(tomb)* monument

Grafik f ['gʀaːfɪk] graphic arts

Gramm n [gʀam] gram(s)

Gras n [gʀaːs] grass

Gräte f ['gʀɛːtə] fishbone

gratis ['gʀaːtɪs] free

gratulieren [gʀatʰʊ'liːʀən /-'liɛn] congratulate

grau [gʀaʊ] grey

Grenze f ['gʀɛntsə] border

Grieche/Griechin m/f ['gʀiːçə/'gʀiːçɪn] Greek

griechisch *adj* ['gʀiːçɪʃ] Greek

Grill m [gʀɪl] grill; **vom Grill** [fɔm 'gʀɪl] grilled

Grillkohle f ['gʀɪlkoːlə] charcoal

Grippe f ['gʀɪpə] flu, influenza

groß [gʀoːs] big, large; tall; great

großartig ['gʀoːs(ʔ)aːʀtɪç] great

Größe f ['gʀøːsə] size; height

Großmutter f ['gʀoːsmʊtʰɐ] grandmother

Großvater m ['gʀoːsfaːtʰɐ] grandfather

grün [gʀyːn] green

Grund m [gʀʊnt] reason, cause

grüne Bohnen [ʁgʀyːnə 'boːnn] green beans

grüne Versicherungskarte f ['gʀyːnə fɛ'zɪçəʀʊŋskaːtə] green card

Gruppe f ['gʀʊpʰə] group

grüßen ['gʀyːsn] greet

gültig ['gʏltʰɪç] valid

Gummistiefel m pl ['gʊmiʃtiːfl] rubber boots

Gurke f ['gʊɐkə] cucumber

Gürtel m [gʏʀtl] belt

gut [guːt] *(adj)* good; *(adv)* well

Gutschein m ['guːtʃaɪn] voucher

Gymnastik f [gʏm'nastɪk] gymnastics

H

Haar n [haː] hair

Haargel n ['haːgeːl] hair gel

Haarklammern f pl ['haːklamən] hairpins

haben ['haːbm] have

Hackfleisch n ['hakflaɪʃ] ground meat

Hafen m ['haːfn] port

Hähnchen n ['hɛːnçn] chicken

Haken m ['haːkŋ] hook

halb [halp] *(adj/adv)* half

Hälfte f ['hɛlftə] half

Halle f ['halə] hall

Hals m [hals] neck, throat

Halsschmerzen m pl ['halsʃmɛɐtsn] sore throat

Halstabletten f pl ['halsta blɛtn] throat lozenges

Halstuch n ['halstuːx] *(decorative)* scarf

halt! [halt] halt!, stop!

haltbar ['haltbaː] durable; **~ bis** use by

Haltegriff m ['haltəgʀɪf] handle

halten [haltn] hold; keep; last; stop

Haltestelle f ['haltəʃtɛlə] stop

Hand f [hant] hand

Handball m ['hantbal] handball

Handbike n ['hɛntbaɪk] hand-operated bike

Handbremse f ['hantbʀɛmzə] hand brake

Handgas n ['hantgaːs] hand throttle

handgemacht ['hantgəmaxt] handmade

Handlauf m ['hantlaʊf] handrail

Handschuhe m pl ['hantʃuːə] gloves

Handtasche f ['han(t)taʃə] handbag

Handtuch n ['han(t)tuːx] towel

Handy n ['hɛndi] mobile (phone)

hart [haːt] hard, solid

hässlich ['hɛslɪç] ugly

häufig ['hɔɪfɪç] frequent(ly)
Hauptbahnhof *m*
['haʊptba:nho:f ('haʊpba:nof)]
main train station
Hauptpostamt *n*
['haʊpt pɔst⁊amt] main post
office
Hauptquartier *n* ['haʊptkva tie]
headquarters
Hauptrolle *f* ['haʊptʀɔlə] leading
role
hauptsächlich ['haʊptzɛçlɪç]
especially; mainly
Hauptsaison *f* ['haʊptzɛ zɔŋ]
high season
Hauptspeise *f* ['haʊptʃpaɪzə]
main course
Hauptstadt *f* ['haʊptʃtat] capital
Hauptstraße *f* ['haʊptʃtra:sə]
main street
Haus *n* [haʊs] house; im Haus
['ɪm haʊs] indoors
Hausbesitzer/in *m/f*
['haʊsbəzɪtsɐ/-bəzɪtsəʀɪn] land-
lord/landlady
Hausboot *n* ['haʊsbo:t]
houseboat
hausgemacht ['haʊsɡəmaxt]
homemade
Hausnummer *f* ['haʊsnʊmɐ]
house number
Haustiere *n pl* ['haʊsti:ʀə] pets
Haut *f* [haʊt] skin
heben [e:bm] to lift
heilig ['haɪlɪç] holy
Heiligabend [ʁhaɪlɪç ⁊a:bmt]
Christmas Eve
Heiliger Abend ['haɪlɪɡɐ
⁊a:bmt] Christmas Eve
Heilmittel *n* ['haɪlmɪtl] remedy
Heimat *f* ['haɪma:t] home, native
country
Heimreise *f* ['haɪmʀaɪzə] return
journey, trip home
heiraten ['haɪʀa:tn] marry
heiser ['haɪzɐ] hoarse
heiß [haɪs] hot
heißen [haɪsn] be called
heiter ['haɪtɐ] *(weather)* clear

heizen [haɪtsn] to heat
Heizung *f* ['haɪtsʊŋ] heating
hellblau [hɛl'blaʊ] light blue
Hemd *n* [hɛmt] shirt
herb [hɛɐp] *(wine)* dry
Herbst *m* ['hɛɐpst] autumn, fall
Herd *m* [heɐt] stove
herein! [hɛ'ʀaɪn] come in!
Hering *m* ['he:ʀɪŋ] herring
Herr *m* [hɛɐ] gentleman; Mr
Herrenfriseur *m* ['hɛʀənfʀɪ'zøɐ]
barber, barbershop
Herrenslip *m* ['hɛʀənslɪp] briefs
Herrentoilette *f* ['hɛʀəntɔ lɛtə]
Men's Room
herrlich ['hɛɐlɪç] glorious,
splendid, terrific
herum [hɛ'ʀʊm] around
Herz *n* [hɛɐts] heart
Herzbeschwerden *f pl*
['hɛɐtsbəʃveedn] heart trouble
Herzinfarkt *m* ['hɛɐtsɪnfa:kt]
cardiac infarction, heart attack
herzlich ['hɛɐtslɪç] warm, sincere
Herzschrittmacher *m*
['hɛɐt(s)ʃʀɪtmaxɐ] pacemaker
Heuschnupfen *m* ['hɔɪʃnʊpfn]
hay fever
heute ['hɔɪtə] today; heute
Morgen [hɔɪtɐ 'mɔɐɡn] this
morning; heute Abend [hɔɪtɐ
⁊a:bmt] this evening; heute
Nacht [hɔɪtʰ(ə) 'naxt] tonight
Hexenschuss *m* ['hɛksnʃʊs]
lumbago
hier [hie] here
Hilfe *f* ['hɪlfə] help, aid; erste
Hilfe [ʁ⁊eestə 'hɪlfə] first aid
Himmel *m* [hɪml] sky; heaven
hinausgehen [hɪ'naʊsge:n] go
out, leave
hindern ['hɪndɐn] prevent, hinder
hinlegen ['hɪnle:ɡn] put down;
sich ~ [zɪç 'hɪnle:ɡn] lie down
hinter ['hɪntʰɐ] behind
hinterlassen [hɪntɐ'lasn] to leave
hinterlegen [hɪntʰɐ'le:ɡn] to
deposit
hinzufügen [hɪn'tsu:fy:ɡn] add

Hitze f ['hɪtsə] heat
hoch [ho:x] high
höchstens [hø:çstns / hø:kstns]
at the most, at best
Hochzeit f ['hɔxtsaɪt] wedding
Hof m [ho:f] (court)yard
höflich ['hø:flɪç] polite
Höhe f ['hø:ə] height
Höhepunkt m ['hø:əpʰʊŋkt]
highlight; *(career)* peak, height;
(film, play) climax
Höhle f ['hø:lə] cave
holen [ho:ln] fetch, get
Holz n [hɔlts] wood
Holzschnitt m ['hɔltʃnɪt]
woodcut
Honig m ['ho:nɪç] honey
hören ['hø:ʀən / høːn] hear
Hörer m ['hø:ʀɐ] receiver
Hose f ['ho:zə] trousers, pants
hübsch [hʏpʃ] pretty, cute
Hüfte f ['hʏftə] hip
Hügel m [hy:gl] hill
Hund m [hʊnt] dog
hungrig ['hʊŋʀɪç] hungry
Hupe f ['hu:pə] *(car)* horn
Husten m [hu:stn] cough
Hustensaft m ['hu:stnzaft] cough
mixture/syrup
Hut m [hu:t] hat
Hütte f ['hʏtʰə] hut, cabin

I

ich [ʔɪç] I
Idee f [ʔi'de:] idea
Ihnen [ʔi:nn] *(polite)* to/for you
ihr [ʔiɐ] her, their
Illustrierte f [ɪlʊ'stʀietə] *(glossy)*
magazine
im Stande sein [ʔɪm'ʃtandə zaɪn]
be able to
im Voraus [ʔɪm 'fo:ʀaʊs] in
advance
Imbiss m [ʔɪmbɪs] snack
immer [ʔɪmɐ] always

Impfpass m [ʔɪm(p)fpas]
vaccination record
Impfung f [ʔɪmpfʊŋ] vaccination
Impressionismus m
[ʔɪmpʀɛsjo'nɪsmʊs] impressionism
in [ʔɪn] in
in Ohnmacht fallen [ʔɪn
ʔo:nmaxt faln] to faint
inbegriffen [ʔɪnbəgʀɪfn]
included
Infektion f [ʔɪnfɛk'tsjo:n]
infection
informieren [ʔɪnfɔ'mi:ʀən/-
'miɐn] inform
Infusion f [ʔɪnfʊ'zjo:n] infusion
Inhalt m [ʔɪnhalt] contents
Inlandsflug m [ʔɪnlantsflu:k]
domestic flight
innen [ʔɪnn] inside
Innenhof m [ʔɪnnho:f] inner
courtyard
Innenstadt f [ʔɪnnʃtat] city
center, downtown
Inschrift f [ʔɪnʃʀɪft] inscription
Insekt n [ʔɪn'zɛkt] insect
Insel f [ʔɪnzl] island
Insulin n [ʔɪnzʊ'li:n] insulin
Inszenierung f
[ʔɪntsə'ni:ʀʊŋ] *(stage)* production
interessant [ʔɪntʀə'sant]
interesting
interessieren, sich ~ (für) [zɪç
ʔɪntʀə'si:ʀən /-'siɐn fyɐ] be
interested (in)
irisch [ʔi:ʀɪʃ] Irish
Irland [ʔɪrlant] Ireland, Eire
irren, sich ~ [zɪç ʔɪʀən/ʔɪɐn] be
mistaken
Irrtum m [ʔɪʀtʰu:m] mistake
Ischias m [ʔɪʃias] sciatica

J

Jacke f ['jakə] jacket
Jahr n [ja:] year
Jahreszeit f ['ja:ʀəstsaɪt] season

Jahrhundert *n* [ja'hʊndɐt] century

jährlich ['jɛɐlɪç] annual(ly)

Jahrmarkt *m* ['ja:ma:kt] fair

Jänner ['jɛnɐ] *(Austria)* January

Januar ['janʊa:] January

Jazz *m* ['dʒɛs] jazz

Jazzgymnastik *f* ['dʒɛsgʏm nastɪk] jazz aerobics

Jeans *f* ['dʒi:ns] jeans

jede(r, s) ['je:də(-dɐ, -dəs)] every, each

jedermann ['je:dɐman] everybody

jedoch [je'dɔx] however

jemand ['je:mant] somebody; anybody

jene(r, s) ['je:nə (-nɐ, -nəs)] that, *(pl)* those

jetzt [jɛtst] now

Jodtinktur *f* ['jo:tɪŋktuɐ] tincture of iodine

joggen ['dʒɔgn] to jog

Joghurt *m* ['jo:gʊɐt] yogurt

Jugendstil *m* ['ju:gn̩tsti:l] art nouveau

Juli ['ju:li] July

jung [jʊŋ] young

Junge *m* ['jʊŋə] boy

Junggeselle *m* ['jʊŋgəzɛlə] bachelor

Juni ['ju:ni] June

Juwelier *m* [juve'liɐ] jeweler's

K

Kabarett *n* [kaba'ʀe:] cabaret

Kabine *f* [ka'bi:nə] cabin; cubicle

Kaffee *m* ['kafe:/ka'fe:] coffee

Kaffeemaschine *f* ['kafemaʃi:nə] coffee machine

Kai *m* [kaɪ] quay

Kalbfleisch *n* ['kalpflaɪʃ] veal

kalt [kʰalt] cold

Kamera *f* ['kaməʀa:] camera

Kamillentee *m* [ka'mɪl(ə)nte:] camomile tea

Kamm *m* [kam] comb

kämmen [kɛmm] to comb

Kanal *m* [kʰa'na:l] canal; channel

Kaninchen *n* [ka'ni:nçn] rabbit

Kanu *n* ['ka:nu] canoe

Kapelle *f* [ka'pɛlə] chapel

Kapitän *m* [kapi'tɛ:n] captain

kaputt [kʰa'pʰʊt] broken, out of order

Karfreitag [ka:'fʀaɪta:k] Good Friday

Karotten *f pl* [ka'ʀɔtn] carrots

Karte *f* ['ka:tə] ticket

Kartoffeln *f pl* [ka'tɔfln] potatoes

Käse *m* ['kɛ:zə] cheese

Kasse *f* ['kʰasə] cash-desk; box office, ticket office

Kassette *f* [ka'sɛtə] cassette

Kathedrale *f* [kate'dʀa:lə] cathedral

Katze *f* ['kʰatsə] cat

kaufen [kʰaʊfn] to buy

Kaufhaus *n* ['kaʊfhaʊs] department store

kaum [kʰaʊm] hardly, scarcely, barely

Kaution *f* [kʰaʊ'tsjo:n] security, down payment

Kehle *f* [ke:lə] throat

kein [kʰaɪn] no

keiner ['kʰaɪnɐ] nobody

Kellner/in *m/f* ['kɛlnɐ/'kɛlnəʀɪn] waiter/waitress

kennen [kʰɛnn] to know; **kennen lernen** ['kʰɛnnlɛɐnn] to meet

Keramik *f* [ke'ʀa:mɪk] ceramics

Kerzen *f pl* [kɛɐtsn] candles

Ketschup *n* ['kɛtʃap] ketchup

Kette *f* ['kɛtə] chain; necklace

Keuchhusten *m* ['kɔɪçhu:stn] whooping cough

Kfz-Schein *m* [ka'ʔɛf'tsɛtʃaɪn] car registration documents

Kiefer *m* ['ki:fɐ] jaw; pine

Kilo *n* ['ki:lo] kilogram(s)

Kilometer *m* [ʁkilo'me:tɐ] kilometer

Kind *n* [kʰɪnt] child

Kinder n pl ['kɪndɐ] children

Kinderbecken n ['kɪndɐbɛkn̩] children's pool

Kinderbetreuung f ['kɪndɐbətrɔjʊn] babysitting service

Kinderbett n ['kɪndɐbɛt] crib

Kinderermäßigung f ['kɪndɐʔmɛːsɪgʊn] reduced fee for children

Kinderkleidung f ['kɪndɐklaɪdʊn] children's clothing

Kinderkrankheit f ['kɪndɐ kraŋkhaɪt] children's illness

Kinderlähmung f ['kɪndɐlɛːmʊn] polio

Kindernahrung f ['kɪndɐnaːrʊn] baby food

Kindersitz m ['kɪndɐzɪts] child seat

Kinderspielplatz m ['kɪndɐʃpiːlplats] children's playground

Kinderteller m ['kɪndɐtɛlɐ] children's portion

Kino n ['kiːno] movie theater

Kirche f ['kɪrçə] church

Kirchturm m ['kɪrçtʊɐm] steeple

Kirmes f ['kɪrməs] country fair

Kirschen f pl [kɪrʃn̩] cherries

Kiste f ['khɪstə] box, chest

Klang m [klaŋ] sound

klar [klaː] clear

Klasse f ['klasə] class

Klassik f ['klasɪk] classical

Klassiker m ['klasɪkɐ] classic film

Klassizismus m [klasɪ'tsɪsmʊs] classicism

Kleid f [klaɪt] dress

Kleiderbügel m ['klaɪdɐbyːgl̩] coat hanger

Kleiderhaken m ['klaɪdɐhaːkn̩] clothes hook

Kleidung f ['klaɪdʊn] clothing

klein [klaɪn] little, small

Klima n ['kliːmaː] climate

Klimaanlage f ['kliːmeʔan laːgə] air-conditioning

Klingel f ['klɪŋl̩] bell

Klippe f ['klɪpə] cliff

Kloster n ['kloːstɐ] monastery; convent

klug [kluːk] clever, intelligent

Kneipe f ['knaɪpə] pub

Knie n [kniː] knee

Knoblauch m ['knoːblaʊx] garlic

Knöchel m [knœçl̩] ankle

Knochen m [knɔxn̩] bone

Knochenbruch m ['knɔxnbrʊx] fracture

Koch m [kɔx] cook

Kochbuch n ['kɔxbuːx] cookbook

kochen [khɔxn̩] to cook; (coffee, tea) make; (water) boil

Kocher m ['kɔxɐ] camp stove

Köchin f ['khœxɪn] cook

Kochnische f ['kɔxniːʃə] kitchenette

Koffer m ['khɔfɐ] suitcase

Kofferraum m ['kɔfɐraʊm] trunk

Kohl m [koːl] cabbage

Kokosnuss f ['koːkosnʊs] coconut

Kolik f ['koːlɪk] colic

Kollege/Kollegin m/f [khoˈleːgə /khoˈleːgɪn] colleague

kommen [khɔmn̩] come

Komödie f [koˈmøːdiə] comedy

Kompass m ['khɔmphas] compass

Komponist/in m/f [kɔmpoˈnɪst/ -ɪn] composer

Konditorei f [kɔnditoˈraɪ] pastry shop

Kondom n [kɔnˈdoːm] condom

König m ['køːnɪç] king

Königin f ['køːnɪgɪn] queen

können ['khœnn̩] be able to, can

Konsulat n [khɔnzuˈlaːt] consulate

Kontakt m [khɔnˈthakt] contact

Konto n ['kɔnto] account

Kontrolleur/in m/f [kɔntroˈløɐ/ -ˈløRɪn] inspector

kontrollieren [khɔntroˈliːrən/ -ˈliən] to control; to check

Konzert n [kɔnˈtsɛɐt] concert

Kopf m [kɔpf] head

Kopfhörer m ['kɔpfhøːrɐ] headphones

Kopfkissen n ['kɔpfkɪsn] pillow
Kopfsalat m ['kɔpfsa laːt] lettuce
Kopfschmerzen m pl ['kɔpfʃmɛɛtsn] headache
Kopfschmerztabletten f pl ['kɔpfʃmɛɛtsta blɛtn] headache tablets
Kopie f [ko'piː] copy
Korb m [kɔɛp] basket
Korkenzieher m ['kɔɛkntsiːɐ] corkscrew
Körper m ['kœɛpʰɐ] body
kosten [kʰɔstn] to cost
kostenlos ['kʰɔstnloːs] free (of charge)
kostspielig ['kɔs(t)ʃpiːlɪç] expensive
Kostüm n [kɔs'tyːm] *(women's)* suit
Kotelett n ['kɔtlɛt] chop, cutlet
Krabben f pl [krabm] shrimp
kräftig ['krɛftɪç] strong
Krafttraining n ['kraftrɛːnɪŋ] weight training
Krampf m [krampf] cramp
krank [kraŋk] ill, sick; **krank werden** ['kraŋk veɛdn] be taken ill, get sick
Krankenhaus n ['kraŋknhaʊs] hospital
Krankenkasse f ['kraŋknkasə] health insurance company
Krankenschwester f ['kraŋknʃvɛstɐ] nurse
Krankenwagen m ['kraŋknvaːgn] ambulance
Krankheit f ['kraŋkhaɪt] illness
Kräuter n pl ['krɔɪtɐ] herbs
Krawatte f [kra'vatə] tie
kreativ [krea'tiːf] creative
Krebs m [kreːps] cancer; crab
Kreditkarte f [kredi:tka:tə] credit card
Kreislaufmittel n ['kraɪslaʊf mɪtl] cardiac stimulant
Kreislaufstörung f ['kraɪslaʊf ʃtøːrʊŋ] circulatory disorder
Kreuz n [krɔɪts] cross

Kreuzgang m ['krɔɪtsgaŋ] cloister
Kreuzung f ['krɔɪtsʊŋ] intersection, junction
kriegen [kriːgn] catch, get
Kriminalroman m [krɪmi'naːlroma:n] thriller
Kristall m [krɪs'tal] crystal
Krone f ['kroːnə] crown
Krücke f ['krʏkə] crutch
Küche f ['kʰʏçə] kitchen
Kuchen m [kuːxn] cake
Kugelschreiber m ['kuːglʃraɪbɐ] ballpoint pen
kühl [kʰyːl] cool
Kühlelement n ['kyːlɛlə mɛnt] ice pack
Kühler m ['kyːlɐ] *(car)* radiator
Kühlschrank m ['kyːlʃraŋk] fridge, refrigerator
Kühlwasser n ['kyːlvasɐ] cooling water
Kuli m ['kuːli] ballpoint pen
Kultur f [kʰʊl'tʰuɐ] culture
Kümmel m [kʏml] caraway seed(s)
Kunde/Kundin m/f ['kʰʊndə /'kʰʊndɪn] customer
Kunst f [kʊnst] art
Kunstgewerbe n ['kʊnstgəveɛbə] arts and crafts
Kunsthändler/in m/f ['kʊnst hɛntlɐ/- hɛntlərɪn] art dealer
Kuppel f [kʊpl] dome
Kupplung f ['kʊplʊŋ] *(car)* clutch
Kürbis m ['kʏrbɪs] pumpkin
Kurs m [kʊɐs] course
Kurve f ['kʊɐvə] bend, curve
kurz [kʰʊɐts] short
kurze Hose f ['kʊɐtsə 'hoːzə] shorts
Kurzfilm m [kʊɐtsfɪlm] short film
kurzfristig ['kʰʊɐtsfrɪstɪç] at short notice
kürzlich ['kʏrtslɪç] recently
Kurzschluss m ['kʊɐtʃlʊs] short-circuit
Kuss m [kʰʊs] kiss

küssen [kʰʏsn] to kiss
Küste f ['kʰʏstə] coast

L

lachen [laxn] to laugh
lächerlich ['lɛçɐlɪç] ridiculous
Ladegerät n ['la:dəgəʀɛ:t] battery charger
Laden m ['la:dn] shop, store
Lage f ['la:gə] situation; position, location
Lähmung f ['lɛ:mʊn] paralysis
Lammfleisch n ['lamflaɪʃ] (meat) lamb
Lampe f ['lampə] lamp
Land n [lant] country; land
Landgut n ['lantgu:t] estate
Landkarte f ['lantkʰa:tʰə] map
Landschaft f ['lantʃaft] scenery
Landsmann m ['lantsman] fellow countryman
Landstraße f ['lantʃtʀa:sə] country road
Landung f ['landʊn] landing
lang [lan] long
langsam ['lanza:m] slow(ly)
langweilig ['lanvaɪlɪç] boring
Lärm m [lɛɐm] noise
lassen [lasn] to let; to leave
lästig ['lɛstɪç] annoying
laufen ['laʊfn] to run; to go; to walk
laut [laʊt] loud; noisy
Lautsprecher m ['laʊtʃpʀɛçɐ] speaker
leben [le:bm] to live
Leben n [le:bm] life
Lebensmittel n ['le:bmsmɪtl] food
Lebensmittelgeschäft n ['le:bmsmɪtlgə ʃɛft] food store, grocery store
Lebensmittelvergiftung f ['le:bmsmɪtlfɐ gɪftʊn] food poisoning
Leber f ['le:bɐ] liver

lebhaft ['le:phaft] lively
lecker ['lɛkɐ] tasty
Lederjacke f ['le:dɐjakə] leather jacket
ledig ['le:dɪç] single
leer [leɐ] empty
Leerlauf m ['leɐlaʊf] (gear) neutral
Leerung f ['le:ʀʊn] collection (of mail)
legen [le:gn] put
Leggings f ['lɛgɪns] leggings
lehren ['le:ʀən / leɐn] teach
leicht [laɪçt] easy; slight; (weight) light
Leichtathletik f ['laɪçtʔat le:tɪk] track and field
leider ['laɪdɐ] unfortunately
leihen [laɪn] lend; borrow
Leinen n [laɪnn] linen
leise ['laɪzə] quiet(ly)
Leistenbruch m ['laɪstnbʀʊx] hernia, rupture
Leiter/in m/f ['laɪtɐ/'laɪtəʀɪn] head, manager, boss
Leitung f ['laɪtʊn] (telephone) line
lernen [lɛɐn] learn
lesen [le:zn] read
letzte(r, s) ['lɛtstʰə (-tʰɐ, -tʰəs)] last
Leute pl ['lɔɪtʰə] people
Licht n [lɪçt] light
Lichtmaschine f ['lɪçtmaʃi:nə] generator
Lichtschutzfaktor m ['lɪçtʃʊts faktoɐ] sun protection factor
lieb [li:p] nice; **jdn lieb haben** [ʁjemandn 'li:p ha:bm] be fond of s.o.; **Liebe(r)** ['li:bə/'li:bɐ] Dear
Liebe f ['li:bə] love
lieben [li:bm] to love
liebenswürdig ['li:bmsvʏɐdɪç] kind
lieber ['li:bɐ] (adv) rather
Liebling m ['li:plɪn] darling; favorite
Lied n [li:t] song
liegen [li:gn] to lie

Liegewiese f ['li:gəvi:zə] sun-bathing area

Lift m [lɪft] elevator, lift

lila ['li:la] purple

Limonade f [lɪmo'na:də] soft drink

Linie f ['li:njə] line

linke(r, s) ['lɪŋkʰə (-kʰe, -kʰəs)] left(-hand)

links [lɪŋks] on the left, to the left

Linsen f pl [lɪnzn] lentils

Lippe f ['lɪpə] lip

Lippenstift m ['lɪpmʃtɪft] lipstick

Liter m ['li:te] litre

Loch n [lɔx] hole, puncture

Locken f pl [lɔkn] curls

Lockenwickler m pl ['lɔknvɪklɐ] curlers

Löffel m [lœfl] spoon

Loge f ['lo:ʒə] box

Lorbeerblätter n pl ['lɔebee blɛtɐ] bay leaves

Luft f [lʊft] air

lüften ['lʏftn] to air

Luftkissenboot n ['lʊftkɪsnbo:t] hovercraft

Luftpumpe f ['lʊftpʊmpə] pump

Lüge f ['ly:gə] lie

lügen [ly:gn] to (tell a) lie

Lunge f ['lʊŋə] lungs

Lungenentzündung f ['lʊŋən²ɛn tsʏndʊŋ] pneumonia

Lust f [lʊst] pleasure, joy; desire; lust

lustig ['lʊstɪç] merry, in a good mood; funny

luxuriös [lʊksʊʀi'ø:s] luxurious

M

machen ['maxn] do; make

Mädchen n ['mɛ:tçn] girl

Magen m [ma:gn] stomach

Magenschmerzen m pl ['ma:gnʃmɛɐtsn] stomachache

mager ['ma:gɐ] lean, thin

Mahlzeit f ['ma:ltsaɪt] meal

Mai [maɪ] May

Makrele f [ma'kʀe:lə] mackerel

Mal n [ma:l] time

Malbuch n ['ma:lbu:x] coloring book

malen [ma:ln] to paint

Maler/in m/f ['ma:lɐ/'ma:ləʀɪn] painter

Malerei f [ma:lə'ʀaɪ] *(type of art)* painting

manchmal ['mançma:l] sometimes

Mandarinen f pl [manda'ʀi:nn] mandarins

Mandelentzündung f ['mandl²ɛn tsʏndʊŋ] tonsilitis

Mandeln f pl ['mandln] almonds; tonsils

Mangel m [maŋl] defect, fault; lack, shortage

Mann m [man] man; husband

Männer f [m] men

Mannschaft f ['manʃaft] team; crew

Mantel m [mantl] coat

Margarine f [maga'ʀi:nə] margarine

Marke f ['ma:kə] *(postage)* stamp

Markt m [ma:kt] market

Marmelade f [mamə'la:də] jam, marmalade

März [mɛɐts] March

Maschine f [ma'ʃi:nə] machine

Masern f pl ['ma:zen] measles

Massage f [ma'sa:ʒə] massage

Material n [matʰ (ə)ʀi'a:l] material

Matratze f [ma'tʀatsə] mattress

Mauer f ['maʊɐ] *(external)* wall

Medikament n [medɪka'mɛnt] medicine

Meer n [mee] sea

Mehl n [me:l] flour

mehr [mee] more; **mehr als** ['mee ²als] more than

mein [maɪn] my

meinen [maɪnn] to mean; think

meinetwegen ['maɪnət ve:gn̩]
I don't mind

Meinung f ['maɪnʊŋ] opinion,
view

melden [mɛldn̩] announce; inform

Melone f [me'lo:nə] melon

Mensch m [mɛnʃ] person,
man/woman; man

Menstruation f [mɛnstʀua'tsjon]
menstruation

Menü n [me'ny:] set meal

merken [mɛɐkn̩] be aware of;
sich etw. ~ [zɪç ᵊɛtvas 'mɛɐkn̩]
remember s. th.

Messe f ['mɛsə] *(rel.)* mass; fair,
exhibition

Messer n ['mɛsɐ] knife

Meter m ['me:tɐ] meter

Metzgerei f [mɛtsgə'ʀaɪ]
butcher's

mich [mɪç] me

Miete f ['mi:tə] rent

mieten ['mi:tn̩] to rent

Migräne f [mi'gʀɛ:nə] migraine

Mikrowelle f ['mi:kʀovɛlə]
microwave

Milch f [mɪlç] milk

mild [mɪlt] mild

Millimeter m ['mɪli me:tɐ] millimeter

mindestens ['mɪndəstns] at least

Minigolf n ['mɪnigɔlf] miniature
golf

Minute f [mi'nu:tʰə] minute

mir [miɐ] (to) me

Missverständnis n
['mɪsfɛʃtɛntnɪs] misunderstanding

mit [mɪt] with

mitbringen ['mɪtbʀɪŋŋ] bring

Mittag m ['mɪtʰa:k] noon, midday

Mittagessen n ['mɪtak ᵊɛsn]
lunch

Mitte f ['mɪtʰə] middle

mitteilen ['mɪtaɪln] inform

Mitteilung f ['mɪtʰaɪlʊŋ] announcement; memo

Mittel n ['mɪtl] means; remedy

Mittelalter n ['mɪtlᵊaltɐ] Middle
Ages

Mittelohrentzündung f
['mɪtlᵊoɐᵊɛn tsʏndʊŋ]
inflammation of the middle ear

Mittwoch ['mɪtvɔx] Wednesday

Möbel n [mø:bl] furniture

Mobiltelefon n [mo'bi:ltelə fo:n]
mobile phone

Mode f ['mo:də] fashion

Modell n [mo'dɛl] model

modern [mo'dɛen] modern, up to
date

Modeschmuck m ['mo:dəʃmʊk]
costume jewelry

mögen ['mø:gn̩] to like; to want

möglich ['mø:klɪç] possible

Monat m ['mo:na:t] month

monatlich ['mo:natlɪç] monthly

Mond m [mo:nt] moon

Montag ['mo:nta:k] Monday

Morgen m [mɔɐgn̩] morning

morgen früh/morgen Abend
[mɔɐgn̩ ˈfʀy:/mɔɐgn̩ ᵊ a:bmt]
tomorrow morning/tomorrow
evening

morgens ['mɔɐgn̩s] in the
morning

Mosaik n [moza'ᵊi:k] mosaic

Motel n [mo'tɛl] motel

Motor m ['mo:toɐ] engine, motor

Motorboot n ['mo:tɔbo:t]
motorboat

Motorhaube f ['mo:tɔ haʊbə]
hood

Mountainbike n ['maʊntnbaɪk]
mountain bike

Möwe f ['mø:və] seagull

Mücke f ['mʏkʰə] gnat, mosquito

müde ['my:də] tired

Müll m [mʏl] trash, garbage

Mullbinde f ['mʊlbɪndə] gauze
bandage

Mülltonne f ['mʏltʰɔnə] garbage
can, trash can

Mumps m [mʊmps] mumps

Mund m [mʊnt] mouth

Mündung f ['mʏndʊŋ] *(river)*
mouth

Münze f ['mʏntsə] coin

Muscheln *f pl* [muʃln] mussels
Museum *n* [mu'ze:ʊm] museum
Musical *n* ['mju:zɪkl] musical
Musik *f* [mu'zi:k] music; **Musik hören** [mu'zi:k 'hø:rən] listen to music
musizieren [muzɪ'tsi:rən] make music
Muskatnuss *f* [mus'ka:tnʊs] nutmeg
Muskel *m* ['muskl] muscle
Müsli *n* ['my:sli] muesli
müssen [mysn] have to, must
Mutter *f* [muthɐ] mother
Mütze *f* ['mytsə] cap

N

nach [na:x] after; to
nach oben [nax 'ʔo:bm] up
nachher ['na:x(h)eɐ] afterwards
Nachmittag *m* ['na:xmɪtha:k] afternoon
nachmittags ['naxmɪta:ks] in the afternoon
nachprüfen ['na:xpry:fn] to check
Nachricht *f* ['na:xrɪçt] message; news
Nachsaison *f* ['na:xze zɔŋ] low season, off-season
nachsehen ['na:xze:n] to check
nachsenden ['na:xzɛndn] send on
nächste(r, s) ['nɛ:çstə/'nɛ:kstə (-stɐ, -stəs)] next
Nacht *f* [naxt] night
Nachtisch *m* ['na:xtɪʃ] dessert
Nachtklub *m* ['naxtklʊp] night club
nachts [naxts] at night
Nachttisch *m* ['naxttɪʃ] bedside table
nackt [nakt] naked, nude
Nagellack *m* ['na:gllak] nail polish

Nagellackentferner *m* ['na:gllakɛnt fɛɐnɐ] nail polish remover
Nagelschere *f* ['na:glʃe:rə] nail scissors
nahe ['na: (ə)] near, close; **nahe bei** [na: baɪ] close to
Nähe, in der ~ von ['ʔɪn dɐ 'nɛə fɔn] near
nähen [nɛ:n] sew, stitch (up)
nähere Angaben ['nɛərə 'ʔanga:bm] particulars
Nahrung *f* ['na:rʊŋ] food
Nahverkehrszug *m* ['na:fɐ keɐstsu:k] local train
Name *m* [na:mə] name
Narbe *f* ['na:bə] scar
Nase *f* ['na:zə] nose
Nasenbluten *n* ['na:znblu:tn] nosebleed
nass [nas] wet
Nationalitätskennzeichen *n* [natsjonalɪ'tɛ:tskɛntsaɪçn] international car index mark
Nationalpark *m* [natsjo'na:lpa:k] national park
Natur *f* [na'thuɐ] nature
natürlich [na'thyɐlɪç] natural(ly); of course
Naturschutzgebiet *n* [na'tuɐʃʊtsgəbi:t] nature reserve
Nebel *m* ['ne:bl] fog
neben ['ne:bm] next to, beside
Nebenkosten *f* ['ne:bmkɔstn] additional costs
nehmen [ne:mm] to take
nein [naɪn] no
Nelken *f pl* [nɛlkn] cloves
nennen [nɛnn] to name, to call
Neoprenanzug *m* [neo'pre:n ʔantsu:k] wetsuit
Nerv *m* [nɛɐf] nerve
nervös [nɐ'vø:s] nervous
nett [nɛt] nice
neu [nɔɪ] new
neugierig ['nɔɪgi:rɪç] curious
Neujahr [nɔɐja:] New Year's Day
nicht [nɪçt] not; **noch nicht** [nɔx 'nɪç(t)] not yet

Nichtraucherabteil *n*
['nɪçtʀaʊxəˀap taɪl] no-smoking
compartment
nichts [nɪçts / ʀɪks] nothing
nie [niː] never
niemand ['niːmant] nobody
Niere *f* ['niːʀə] kidney
Nierenstein *m* ['niːʀənʃtaɪn]
kidney stone
nirgends ['nɪʀgŋ (t)s] nowhere
noch [nɔx] still
Norden *m* [nɔɐdn] north
Nordirland [nɔɐt'ˀiːʀlant]
Northern Ireland
Nordsee *f* [di 'nɔɐtzeː] North Sea
normal [nɔ'maːl] normal; standard
normalerweise [nɔ'maːlɐvaɪzə]
normally, usually
Notausgang *m* ['noːtˀaʊsgaŋ]
emergency exit
Notfall ['noːtfal] emergency
nötig ['nøːtɪç] necessary
Notizblock *m* [no'tiːtsblɔk]
notepad
Notrufsäule *f* ['noːtʀufzɔɪlə]
emergency telephone
notwendig ['noːtvɛndɪç]
necessary
November [no'vɛmbɐ] November
nüchtern ['nʏçtɐn] sober
Nudeln *f pl* [nuːdln] noodles,
pasta
Nummer *f* ['nʊmɐ] number
nummerieren [nʊmə'ʀiːʀən/-
'ʀiːən] to number
Nummernschild *n* ['nʊmɐnʃɪlt]
license plate
nun [nuːn] now; well
nur [nuɐ] only
Nüsse *f pl* ['nʏsə] nuts

O

ob [ɔp] whether
oben ['oːbm] up
Objektiv *n* ['ɔbjɛk'tiːf] lens

Obst *n* [ˀoːpst] fruit
Obst- und Gemüsehändler *m*
[ˀoːpst ˀʊnt gə'myːzəhɛntlɐ] fruit
and vegetable store, greengrocer's
obwohl [ɔp'voːl] although
oder ['oːdɐ] or
offen [ˀɔfn] open
öffentlich ['ˀœfntlɪç] public
offiziell [ˀɔfɪ'tsjɛl] official
öffnen [ˀœfn (ə)n] to open
Öffnungszeiten *f pl*
[ˀœfnʊŋstsaɪtn] opening hours,
hours of business
oft [ˀɔft] often
ohne [ˀoːnə] without
ohne Kohlensäure [ˀoːnə
'koːl(ə)nzɔɪʀə] still, uncarbonated
Ohr *n* [ˀoɐ] ear
Ohrentropfen *m pl*
[ˀoːʀəntʀɔpfn] eardrops
Ohrringe *m pl* [ˀoːʀɪŋə] earrings
Oktober [ˀɔk'toːbɐ] October
Öl *n* [ˀøːl] oil
Ölgemälde *n*
['ˀøːlgə mɛːldə] *(picture)* oil
painting
Oliven *f pl* [ˀo'liːvn] olives
Olivenöl *n* [ˀo'liːvnˀøːl] olive oil
Ölmalerei *f*
['ˀøːlmaːlə ʀaɪ] *(activity)* oil
painting
Ölquelle *f* ['ˀøːl'kvɛlə] oil well
Ölwechsel *m* ['ˀøːlvɛksl] oil
change
Oper *f* ['oːpɐ] opera
Operation *f* ['ˀɔpəʀa'tsjoːn]
operation; surgery
Operette *f* [ˀɔpə'ʀɛtə] operetta
Optiker *m* ['ˀɔptɪkɐ] optician's
Orangensaft *m* [ˀo'ʀanʒnzaft]
orange juice
Orchester *n* [ˀɔɐ'kɛstɐ] orchestra
Orden *m* [ˀɔɐdn] *(rel.)* order
ordinär [ˀɔdi'nɛːɐ] vulgar
Ordnung *f* ['ˀɔɐtnʊŋ] order
Original *n* ['ˀɔʀɪgi'naːl] original
Originalfassung *f*
['ˀɔʀɪgi'naːlfasʊŋ] original version

Ort *m* [ˈʔɔet] place; spot
Ortschaft *f* [ˈʔɔetʃaft] village, town
Ortsgespräch *n* [ˈʔɔetsɡəʃpʀɛːç] local call
Osten *m* [ˈʔɔstn] east
Ostermontag [ʁˈoːstəˈmoːntaːk] Easter Monday
Österreich [ˈʔøːstəʀaɪç] Austria
Österreicher/in *m/f* [ˈʔøːstəʀaɪçɐ/-ʀaɪçəʀɪn] Austrian

P

Paar [ˈpʰaː] pair; couple
paar, ein ~ [(ˈʔaɪ)n ˈpʰaː] a few
Päckchen *n* [ˈpɛkçn] small packet
packen [ˈpakn] to pack
Packung *f* [ˈpakʊŋ] box, pack
Paket *n* [paˈkeːt] parcel
Palast *m* [paˈlast] palace
Panne *f* [ˈpanə] breakdown, flat tire
Pannendienst *m* [ˈpanndiːnst] emergency road service
Papier *n* [paˈpiɐ] paper; **Papiere** *n pl* [paˈpiːʀə] documents, papers
Papierservietten *f pl* [paˈpiɐzə vjɛtn] paper napkins
Papiertaschentücher *n pl* [paˈpiɐ taʃntyːçɐ] paper handkerchiefs
Paprika *m* [ˈpapʀɪka] paprika
Paprikaschoten *f pl* [ˈpapʀɪka ʃoːtn] peppers
Parfüm *n* [paˈfyːm] perfume, scent
Parfümerie *f* [pafʏməˈʀiː] perfumery
Park *m* [ˈpʰaːk] park
parken [ˈpʰaːkn] to park
Parkett *n* [paˈkɛt] stalls
Pass *m* [pas] *(mountain)* pass
Passagier *m* [pasaˈʒiɐ] passenger
passen [ˈpʰasn] to fit; to suit
Pauschalpreis *m* [paʊˈʃaːlpʀaɪs] flat rate

Pelz *m* [pɛlts] fur
Perle *f* [ˈpɛələ] pearl
Person *f* [pʰɛˈzoːn] person
Personalausweis *m* [p(ɛ)ezoˈnaːl ˈʔaʊsvaɪs] identity card
Personalien *pl* [pʰezoˈnaːljən] particulars, personal data
persönlich [pʰɛˈzøːnlɪç] personal
Petersilie *f* [peˈteˈziːljə] parsley
Petroleum *n* [peˈtʀoːleʊm] kerosene
Pfad *m* [(p)faːt] path
Pfand *n* [(p)fant] deposit; security
Pfeffer *m* [ˈpfɛfə] pepper
Pfeiler *m* [ˈpfaɪlə] pillar
Pferd *n* [pfeɐt] horse
Pfirsiche *m pl* [ˈpfiɐzɪçə] peaches
Pflanze *f* [ˈ (p)flantsə] plant
Pflaster *n* [ˈpflastə] plaster
pflegebedürftig [ˈpfleːɡəbədʏftɪç] in need of care
Pfund *n* [(p)fʊnt] pound(s)
Pilot *m* [piˈloːt] pilot
Pilz *m* [pɪlts] mushroom; fungal infection
Pkw *m* [ˈpeːkaveː] car
Plakat *n* [plaˈkʰaːt] poster
Planschbecken *n* [ˈplanʃbɛkn] wading pool
Plastikbeutel *m* [ˈplastɪkbɔɪtl] plastic bag
Platz *m* [plats] place; seat
Platzreservierung *f* [ˈplatsʀeze viːʀʊŋ] seat reservation
Plombe *f* [ˈplɔmbə] *(tooth)* filling
plötzlich [ˈplœtslɪç] suddenly
Polizei *f* [poliˈtsaɪ] police
Polizeiwagen *m* [poliˈtsaɪvaːɡn] police car
Polizist/Polizistin *m/f* [poliˈtsɪst/poliˈtsɪstɪn] policeman/policewoman
Pony *m* [ˈpɔni] bangs
Portal *n* [pɔ(e)ˈtaːl] portal
Portier *m* [pɔeˈtjeː] porter
Portion *f* [pɔˈtsjoːn] portion

Porto n ['pɔɐto] postage
Porträt n [pɔ(ɐ)'trɛː] portrait
Porzellan n [pɔ(ɐ)tsə'laːn] porcelain, china
Postamt n ['pɔstamt] post office
Postkarte f ['pɔstkaːtə] postcard
postlagernd ['pɔstlaːgɛnt] poste restante
Postleitzahl f ['pɔstlaɪtsaːl] postal code, ZIP code
Postsparbuch n ['pɔstʃpaːbuːx] post office savings book
praktisch ['pRaktʰɪʃ] practical(ly)
Preis m [pRaɪs] price; prize
Prellung f ['pRɛlʊŋ] bruise
Premiere f [pRəm'jeːRə] premiere
Priester m [pRiːstɐ] priest
prima ['pRiːmaː] great
privat [pRɪ'vaːt] private
Probe f ['pRoːbə] experiment, test, trial
Problem n [pRo'bleːm] problem
Produkt n [pRo'dʊkt] product
Programmheft n [pRo'gRamhɛft] (booklet) program
Promillegrenze f [pRo'mɪlə gRɛntsə] legal blood alcohol limit
Prospekt m [pRos'pɛkt] prospectus, leaflet, brochure
Prothese f [pRo'teːzə] artificial limb
provisorisch [pRovi'zoːRɪʃ] provisional, temporary
Prozent n [pRo'tsɛnt] percent
Prozession f [pRotsɛs'joːn] procession
Prüfung f ['pRyːfʊŋ] examination, test
Publikum n ['pʰʊblɪkʰʊm] public; audience
Puder m ['puːdɐ] powder
Pullover m [pʊ'loːvɐ] pullover, sweater
Puls m [pʊls] pulse
pünktlich ['pʰʏŋktlɪç] punctual(ly); on time
putzen ['pʰʊtsn̩] to clean

Qualität f [kvalɪ'tʰɛːt] quality
Quelle f ['kvɛlə] source; spring
quer durch [kveɐ dʊɐç] straight across/through
Quetschung f ['kvɛtʃʊŋ] bruise
Quittung f ['kvɪtʰʊŋ] receipt

R-Gespräch n ['ʔɛɐgə ʃpRɛːç] collect call
Rabatt m [Ra'bat] discount
Rad n [Raːt] wheel
Rad fahren ['Raːt 'faːRən] to ride a bike
Radarkontrolle f [Ra'daːkɔn tRɔlə] radar check
Radierung f [Ra'diːRʊŋ] etching
Radio n ['Raːdjoː] radio
Radsport m ['Raːtʃpɔɐt] cycling
Radtour f ['Raːttuɐ] bike tour
Rampe f ['Rampə] ramp
rasch [Raʃ] quick
Rasen m [Raːzn̩] lawn, grass
Rasierapparat m [Ra'ziɐʔapa Raːt] shaver
Rasierklinge f [Ra'ziɐklɪŋə] razor blade
Rasierpinsel m [Ra'ziɐpɪnzl] shaving brush
Rasierschaum m [Ra'ziɐʃaʊm] shaving foam
Rasierwasser n [Ra'ziɐvasə] after-shave lotion
Rathaus n ['Raːthaʊs] town hall
Rauch m [Raʊx] smoke
rauchen [Raʊxn̩] to smoke
Raucher/in m/f ['Raʊxɐ/'RaʊxəRɪn] smoker
Raucherabteil n ['Raʊxɐʔap taɪl] smoking compartment
Raum m [Raʊm] space; room
rechnen ['Rɛçn(ə)n] calculate
Rechnung f ['Rɛçnʊŋ] bill, invoice

Recht *n* [rɛçt] right

rechte(r, s) ['rɛçtə (-tɐ, -təs)] right(-hand)

rechts [rɛçts] on the right, to the right

Rechtsanwalt/-anwältin *m/f* ['rɛçtsanvalt/-anvɛltɪn] lawyer

rechtzeitig ['rɛçtsaɪtʰɪç] in time

reden [re:dn] to talk

Reformhaus *n* [re'fɔrmhaʊs] health food store

regelmäßig ['re:glmɛ:sɪç] regular(ly)

Regen *m* ['re:gn] rain

Regenmantel *m* ['re:gnmantl] raincoat

Regenschauer *m* ['re:gnʃaʊɐ] shower

Regie *f* [rəˈʒi:] *(film)* direction; directed by

Regierung *f* [re'gi:rʊŋ] government

regnerisch ['re:knərɪʃ] rainy

reich [raɪç] rich

reichen [raɪçn] be sufficient; hand over, pass

reif [raɪf] ripe

Reifen *m* ['raɪfn] tire

Reifenpanne ['raɪfn panə] flat tire

reinigen ['raɪnɪgn] to clean

Reinigung *f* ['raɪnɪgʊŋ] drycleaner's

Reis *m* [raɪs] rice

Reise *f* ['raɪzə] journey, trip

Reisebüro *n* ['raɪzəby ro:] travel agency

Reiseführer *m* ['raɪzə fy:rɐ] guidebook

Reiseführer/in *m/f* ['raɪzə fy:rɐ/- fy:rərɪn] guide, courier

Reisegesellschaft *f* ['raɪzəgə zɛlʃaft] party of tourists

reisen [raɪzn] to travel

Reisende *m/f* ['raɪzndə] tourist

Reisepass *m* ['raɪzəpas] passport

Reisescheck *m* ['raɪzəʃɛk] traveler's check

Reisetasche *f* ['raɪzətaʃə] travel bag

reißen [raɪsn] to tear; to pull

reiten ['raɪtn] to ride

Reitschule *f* ['raɪtʃu:lə] riding school

Religion *f* [relɪ'gjo:n] religion

Renaissance *f* [rənɛ'sa):s] Renaissance

rennen [rɛnn] to run

Rennrad *n* ['rɛnra:t] racing bike

Reparatur *f* [rɛpara'tuɐ] repair

reparieren [rɛpʰa'ri:rən /-'riən] to repair

reservieren [rezɛ'vi:rən /-'viən] to reserve

Reservierung *f* [rezɛ'vi:rʊŋ] reservation

Rest *m* [rɛst] *(remainder)* rest

Rettungsboot *n* ['rɛtʊŋsbo:t] lifeboat

Rettungsring *m* ['rɛtʊŋsrɪŋ] life belt, life preserver

Revue *f* [rə'vy:] show

Rezept *n* [re'tsɛpt] prescription

Rezeption *f* [retsɛp'tsjo:n] reception

Rheuma *n* ['rɔɪma] rheumatism

Richter/in *m/f* ['rɪçtɐ/'rɪçtərɪn] judge

richtig ['rɪçtɪç] right; proper

Richtung *f* ['rɪçtʊŋ] direction

riechen [ri:çn] to smell

Rindfleisch *n* ['rɪntflaɪʃ] beef

Rock *m* [rɔk] skirt

roh [ro:] raw; **roher Schinken** [ro:ɐ ʃɪŋkn] smoked ham

Rollschuhe *m pl* ['rɔlʃu:ə] roller skates

Rollstuhl *m* ['rɔlʃtu:l] wheelchair

Rollstuhlfahrer/in *m/f* ['rɔlʃtu:l fa:rɐ/- fa:rərɪn] wheelchair user

Rollstuhlkabine *f* ['rɔlʃtu:lka bi:nə] wheelchair cabin

Roman *m* [ro'ma:n] novel

röntgen ['rœnçn] to X-ray

Röntgenaufnahme f
['ʀœnçnʔaʊfnaːmə] X-ray
rosa ['ʀoːza] pink
Rosmarin m ['ʀoːsmaʀiːn]
rosemary
rot [ʀoːt] red
Röteln f pl [ʀøːtln] German
measles
Rotwein ['ʀoːtvaɪn] red wine
Route f ['ʀuːtʰə] route
Rücken m [ʀʏkŋ] back
Rückenschmerzen m pl
['ʀʏkŋʃmɛɐtsn] backache
Rückfahrkarte f ['ʀʏkfaː kaːtə]
round-trip ticket
Rückfahrt f ['ʀʏkfaːt] return
journey, trip back
Rückholservice m
['ʀʏkhoːlœsœɐvɪs] pick-up service
Rückkehr f ['ʀʏkʰeɐ] return
Rücklicht n ['ʀʏklɪçt] rear light,
tail light
Rucksack m ['ʀʊkzak] rucksack,
backpack
Rückspiegel m ['ʀʏkʃpiːgl] rear-
view mirror
rückwärts ['ʀʏkvɛɐts] backwards
Rückwärtsgang m
['ʀʏkvɛɐtsgaŋ] reverse gear
Ruderboot n ['ʀuːdɐboːt]
rowboat
rudern ['ʀuːdɐn] to row
rufen [ʀuːfn] to call
Ruhe f [ʀuə] rest; calm; silence
ruhen [ʀuːn] to rest
ruhig [ʀʊɪç] silent, quiet, calm
Ruine f [ʀuʔiːnə] ruin
rund [ʀʊnt] (adj) round
Runde f ['ʀʊndə] round
Rundfahrt f ['ʀʊntfaːt] round
trip, tour

S

Saal m [zaːl] room; hall
Sache f ['zaxə] thing; matter, affair
Sack m [zak] sack; bag

Safaripark m [zaˈfaːʀipaːk] safari
park
Safe m [sɛɪf/seːf] safe
Safran m ['zafʀaːn] saffron
saftig ['zaftɪç] juicy
sagen [zaːgn] say; tell
Sahne f ['zaːnə] cream
Saison f [zɛˈzɔŋ] season
Salami f [zaˈlaːmi] salami
Salat m [zaˈlaːt] salad
Salatbüfett n [zaˈlaːtbʏˈfeː] salad
bar
Salbe f ['zalbə] ointment
Salbei m ['zalbaɪ] sage
Salz n [zalts] salt
sammeln [zamln] collect
Samstag ['zamstaːk] Saturday
Sandalen f pl [zanˈdaːln] sandals
Sandburg f ['zantbuɐk] sand
castle
Sandkasten m ['zantkastn] sand
box
Sänger/in m/f ['zɛŋɐ/'zɛŋəʀɪn]
singer
Satz m [zats] sentence
sauber ['zaʊbɐ] clean
sauer ['zaʊɐ] sour
Sauger m ['zaʊgɐ] nipple
Saugflasche f ['zaʊkflaʃə] baby
bottle
Säule f ['zɔɪlə] column, pillar
Sauna f ['zaʊna] sauna
saure Sahne f [zaʊʀə 'zaːnə] sour
cream
Schachtel f [ʃaxtl] box
schade, wie ~! [vi 'ʃaːdə] what a
pity/shame!
Schaden m [ʃaːdn] damage
Schadenersatz m ['ʃaːdnʔɐ zats]
compensation
schaffen [ʃafn] make, create;
manage; work
Schafsfell n ['ʃaːfsfɛl] fleece
Schal m [ʃaːl] scarf
Schalter m ['ʃaltɐ] switch
Schampoo n ['ʃampo/'ʃampu]
shampoo
scharf [ʃaːf] (spicy) hot
Schatten m [ʃatn] shade, shadow

schätzen [ˈʃɛtsn̩] *(person)* to like; to estimate *(amount etc.)*

schauen [ˈʃaʊn] to look

Schaufenster *n* [ˈʃaʊfɛnstɐ] shop window

Schauspiel *n* [ˈʃaʊʃpiːl] play

Schauspieler/in [ˈʃaʊʃpiːlɐ/-ˈʃpiːlərɪn] actor/actress

Scheck *m* [ʃɛk] check

Scheibe *f* [ˈʃaɪbə] slice

Scheibenwischer *m* [ˈʃaɪbm̩vɪʃɐ] windshield wiper

Scheinwerfer *m* [ˈʃaɪnvɛɐfɐ] headlight

Scheitel *m* [ˈʃaɪtl̩] part

schenken [ˈʃɛŋkn̩] give (as a present)

Scherz *m* [ʃɛɐts] joke

schicken [ˈʃɪkn̩] send

Schiebedach *n* [ˈʃiːbədax] sunroof

Schienbein *n* [ˈʃiːnbaɪn] shin

Schiene *f* [ˈʃiːnə] splint

Schild *n* [ʃɪlt] sign

Schinken *m* [ˈʃɪŋkn̩] ham

Schirm *m* [ʃɪɐm] umbrella

Schlaf *m* [ʃlaːf] sleep

Schlafcouch *f* [ˈʃlaːfkaʊtʃ] studio couch

schlafen [ˈʃlaːfn̩] to sleep

Schlaflosigkeit *f* [ˈʃlaːflozɪçkaɪt] insomnia, sleeplessness

Schlaftabletten *f pl* [ˈʃlaːfta blɛtn̩] sleeping pills

Schlafzimmer *n* [ˈʃlaːftsɪmɐ] bedroom

Schlaganfall *m* [ˈʃlaːkanfal] stroke

Schläger *m* [ˈʃlɛːgɐ] racquet

Schlagsahne *f* [ˈʃlaːkzaːnə] whipping cream

Schlange *f* [ˈʃlaŋə] snake

schlank [ʃlaŋk] slim, slender

schlau [ʃlaʊ] clever

Schlauchboot *n* [ˈʃlaʊxboːt] rubber boat

schlecht [ʃlɛçt] bad; badly

schließen [ˈʃliːsn̩] to shut, to close

schlimm [ʃlɪm] bad

Schlitten *m* [ʃlɪtn̩] sled, toboggan

Schlittschuh laufen [ˈʃlɪtʃuː laʊfn̩] go ice skating

Schlittschuhe *m pl* [ˈʃlɪtʃuːə] ice skates

Schloss *n* [ʃlɔs] castle; *(door)* lock

Schlucht *f* [ʃluxt] ravine

Schluss *m* [ʃlʊs] end

Schlüssel *m* [ˈʃlʏsl̩] key

Schlüsselbein *n* [ˈʃlʏsl̩baɪn] collarbone

schmal [ʃmaːl] narrow; slim, thin

schmerzen [ˈʃmɛɐtsn̩] to hurt

schmerzhaft [ˈʃmɛɐtshaft] painful

Schmerztabletten *f pl* [ˈʃmɛɐtsta blɛtn̩] pain-killing tablets

Schmuck *m* [ʃmʊk] jewelry

Schmuggel *m* [ʃmʊgl̩] smuggle

schmuggeln [ʃmʊgl̩n] to smuggle

schmutzig [ˈʃmʊtsɪç] dirty

Schnappschuss *m* [ˈʃnapʃʊs] snapshot

schnarchen [ˈʃnaɐçn̩] to snore

Schnee *m* [ʃneː] snow

schneiden [ˈʃnaɪdn̩] to cut

Schneider/in *m/f* [ˈʃnaɪdɐ/ˈʃnaɪdərɪn] dressmaker, tailor

schnell [ʃnɛl] quick(ly), fast

Schnittwunde *f* [ˈʃnɪtvʊndə] cut

Schnitzerei *f* [ʃnɪtsəˈraɪ] wood-carving

Schnorchel *m* [ˈʃnɔɐçl̩] snorkel

schnorcheln [ˈʃnɔɐçl̩n] go snorkeling

Schnuller *m* [ˈʃnʊlɐ] *(baby's)* pacifier

Schnupfen *m* [ˈʃnʊpfn̩] cold

Schnurrbart *m* [ˈʃnʊɐbaːt] mustache

Schokolade *f* [ʃokoˈlaːdə] chocolate

Schokoriegel *m* [ˈʃoːkoriːgl̩] chocolate bar

schon [ʃoːn] already

schön [ʃøːn] beautiful(ly)

Schonkost *f* [ˈʃoːnkɔst] diet

Schonzeit *f* [ˈʃoːntsaɪt] off-season

schottisch [ˈʃɔtʰɪʃ] Scottish

Schottland [ˈʃɔtlant] Scotland

Schraube f [ˈʃʀaʊbə] screw

schrecklich [ˈʃʀɛklɪç] terrible, terribly, awful(ly), dreadful(ly)

schreiben [ʃʀaɪbm] write

Schreibtelefon n [ˈʃʀaɪpteləfoːn] keyboard telephone

Schreibwarengeschäft n [ˈʃʀaɪpvaːʀəngə ʃɛft] stationery store

schreien [ˈʃʀaɪn] to shout; to scream

schriftlich [ˈʃʀɪftlɪç] in writing

schüchtern [ˈʃʏçtɐn] shy

Schuh m [ʃuː] shoe

Schuhbürste f [ˈʃuːbʏɐstə] shoe brush

Schuhcreme f [ˈʃuːkʀɛːm] shoe cream

Schuhgeschäft n [ˈʃuːgəʃɛft] shoe shop

Schuhmacher m [ˈʃuːmaxɐ] shoe-maker's

Schuld f [ʃʊlt] guilt

Schule f [ˈʃuːlə] school

Schulter f [ˈʃʊltɐ] shoulder

Schuppen f pl [ʃʊpm] dandruff

Schüssel f [ˈʃʏsl] bowl

Schutz m [ʃʊts] security

schwach [ʃvax] weak, feeble

Schwager m [ˈʃvaːgɐ] brother-in-law

Schwägerin f [ˈʃvɛːgəʀɪn] sister-in-law

Schwangerschaft f [ˈʃvaŋɐʃaft] pregnancy

schwarz [ʃvaːts] black

Schwarzbrot n [ˈʃvaːtsbʀoːt] dark rye bread

Schwarzweiß-Film m [ʃvaːtsˈvaɪsfɪlm] black-and-white film

schweigen [ʃvaɪgŋ] be silent, keep quiet

Schweinefleisch n [ˈʃvaɪnəflaɪʃ] pork

Schweiz f [ʃvaɪts] Switzerland

Schweizer Franken m pl [ʁʃvaɪtsə ˈfʀaŋkn̩] Swiss francs

Schweizer/in m/f [ˈʃvaɪtsə/ˈʃvaɪtsəʀɪn] Swiss (man/woman)

Schwellung f [ˈʃvɛlʊŋ] swelling

schwer [ʃveɐ] heavy; (illness) serious; difficult

Schwerbehinderte m/f [ˈʃveɐbəhɪndetə] severely handicapped person

schwerhörig [ˈʃveɐhøːʀɪç] hard of hearing

Schwertfisch m [ˈʃveɐtfɪʃ] swordfish

Schwester f [ˈʃvɛstɐ] sister

schwierig [ˈʃviːʀɪç] difficult

Schwimmbad n [ˈʃvɪmbaːt] swimming pool

schwimmen [ʃvɪmm] to swim

Schwimmer/in m/f [ˈʃvɪmɐ/ˈʃvɪməʀɪn] swimmer

Schwimmflügel m pl [ˈʃvɪmflyːgl] water wings

Schwimmkurs m [ˈʃvɪmkuɐs] swimming lessons

Schwimmring m [ˈʃvɪmʀɪŋ] rubber ring

Schwimmweste f [ˈʃvɪmvɛstə] life jacket

Schwindelgefühl n [ˈʃvɪndlgəfyːl] dizziness

schwitzen [ˈʃvɪtsn̩] perspire, sweat

schwül [ʃvyːl] humid

See f [di zeː] sea

Seefahrt f [ˈzeːfaːt] voyage

seekrank [ˈzeːkʀaŋk] seasick

Seereise f [ˈzeːʀaɪzə] voyage

Seezunge f [ˈzeːtsʊŋə] (fish) sole

Segelboot n [ˈzeːglboːt] sailboat

Segelfliegen n [ˈzeːglfliːgŋ] gliding

segeln [ˈzeːgln] to sail

Segeltörn m [ˈzeːgltœɐn] sailing cruise

sehbehindert [ˈseːbəhɪndet] partially sighted

sehen [ˈzeːn] see

Sehenswürdigkeiten *f pl*
['ze:nsvʏɐdɪçkaɪtn] sights

sehr [zeɐ] very; very much

Seide *f* ['zaɪdə] silk

Seidenmalerei *f*
['zaɪdnma:lə ʀaɪ] silk painting

Seife *f* ['zaɪfə] soap

Seil *n* [zaɪl] rope

Seilbahn *f* ['zaɪlba:n] cable
railway, funicular

sein [zaɪn] *(vb)* to be

sein [zaɪn] *(poss. pron.)* his; its

seit [zaɪt] since; for

Seite *f* ['zaɪtʰə] side; page

Sekunde *f* [ze'kʰʊndə] second

Selbstauslöser *m*
['zɛlpstausløːze] self-timer

Selbstbedienung *f*
['zɛlps (t)bədi:nʊŋ] self-service

selbstverständlich
[zɛlp(st)fɛ'ʃtɛntlɪç] of course

Sellerie *m* ['zɛləʀi:] celeriac

selten [zɛltn] rare; seldom

senden ['zɛndn] send

Senf *m* [zɛnf (zɛmf)] mustard

September [zɛp'tɛmbɐ]
September

servieren [zɛ'vi:ʀən /-'vien] serve

Serviette *f* [zɛ'vjɛtə] napkin

setzen [zɛtsn] put

sexuelle Belästigung *f* [sɛksu'ɛlə
bə'lɛstɪgʊŋ] sexual harassment

Show *f* [ʃo:] show

sicher ['zɪçɐ] safe; sure, certain(ly)

Sicherheit *f* ['zɪçɐhaɪt] safety;
security

Sicherheitsgebühr *f*
['zɪçɐhaɪtsgə byɐ] security charge

Sicherheitsgurt *m*
['zɪçɐhaɪtsgʊɐt] seat belt

Sicherheitskontrolle *f*
['zɪçɐhaɪtskɔn tʀɔlə] security
control

Sicherung *f* ['zɪçəʀʊŋ] fuse

Sicht *f* [zɪçt] visibility; view

sie [zi:] she, her; they, them

Sie [zi:] you

Silber *n* ['zɪlbɐ] silver

Silvester [sɪl'vɛstɐ] New Year's
Eve

Sinfoniekonzert *n*
[zɪmfo'ni:kɔn tsɛɐt] symphony
concert

singen [zɪŋŋ] sing

Sitz *m* [zɪts] seat; (place of)
residence; headquarters

sitzen [zɪtsn] sit

Sitzplatz *m* ['zɪtsplats] seat

Skateboard *n* ['skɛɪtbɔɐt] skateboard; Skateboard fahren
['skɛɪtbɔɐt 'fa:ʀən] to skateboard

Ski *m* [ʃi:] ski

Skibindungen *f pl* ['ʃi:bɪndʊŋŋ]
ski bindings

Skibrille *f* ['ʃi:bʀɪlə] ski goggles

Skikurs *m* ['ʃi:kʊɐs] skiing course

Skilehrer/in *m/f* ['ʃi:le:ʀe/-
le:ʀəʀɪn] ski instructor

Skistiefel *m pl* ['ʃi:ʃti:fl] ski boots

Skistöcke *m pl* ['ʃi:ʃtœkə] ski
poles

Skulptur *f* [skʊlp'tuɐ] sculpture

Slipeinlagen *f pl* ['slɪpaɪnla:gn]
panty liners

so [zo:] so, thus

Socken *f pl* ['zɔkn] socks

Sodbrennen *n* ['zo:tbʀɛnn] heartburn

sofort [zo'fɔɐt] at once

Sofortbildkamera *f*
[zo'fɔɐtbɪlt kaməʀa] Polaroid®
camera

Sohle *f* ['zo:lə] *(shoe)* sole

Sohn *m* [zo:n] son

Solarium *n* [zo'la:ʀɪʊm] solarium

Solist/Solistin *m/f*
[zo'lɪst/zo'lɪstɪn] soloist

sollen [zɔln] shall, should

Sommer *m* ['zɔmɐ] summer

Sondermarke *f* ['zɔndema:kə]
special-issue stamp

sondern ['zɔndɐn] but

Sonnabend ['zɔna:bmt] Saturday

Sonne *f* ['zɔnə] sun

Sonnenbrand *m* ['zɔnnbʀant]
sunburn

Sonnencreme f ['zɔnnkʁɛːm] sun cream

Sonnenhut m ['zɔnnhuːt] sun hat

Sonnenmilch f ['zɔnnmɪlç] suntan lotion

Sonnenöl n ['zɔnnˀøːl] suntan oil

Sonnenstich m ['zɔnnʃtɪç] sunstroke

sonnig ['zɔnɪç] sunny

Sonntag m ['zɔntaːk] Sunday

Sorge f ['zɔʁɡə] worry

sorgen, sich ~ um [zɪç 'zɔʁɡn ˀʊm] be worried about

sorgfältig ['zɔʁkfɛltɪç] careful

Sorte f ['zɔʁtə] kind, sort

Soße f ['zoːsə] gravy, sauce

Souvenir n [zʊvəˈniɐ̯] souvenir

Souvenirladen m [zʊvəˈniɐ̯laːdn] souvenir shop

Spargel m [ʃpaˈɡl] asparagus

spärlich ['ʃpɛːɐ̯lɪç] *(sparse)* thin

Spaß m [ʃpaːs] joke; fun

spät [ʃpɛːt] late

spazieren gehen [ʃpaˈtsiːʁəngeːn /-ˈtsiɐ̯ɡeːn] go for a walk

Spaziergang m [ʃpaˈtsiːɐ̯ɡaŋ] walk, stroll; **einen Spaziergang machen** [(ˀaɪn)n ʃpaˈtsiːɐ̯ɡaŋ maxn] go for a walk

Speisekarte f ['ʃpaɪzəkaːtə] menu

Speiseröhre f ['ʃpaɪzəʁøːʁə] esophagus

Speisesaal m ['ʃpaɪzəzaːl] dining room

Speisewagen m ['ʃpaɪzəvaːɡn] restaurant car

Spezialität f [ʃpetsjaliˈtɛːt] specialty

speziell [ʃpɛˈtsjɛl] special

Spiegel m [ʃpiˈɡl] mirror

Spiel n [ʃpiːl] game, match

spielen [ʃpiːln] to play

Spielkamerad/in m/f ['ʃpiːlkaməˈʁaːt/-kaməˈʁaːdɪn] playmate

Spielkasino n ['ʃpiːlka ziːno] gambling casino

Spielsachen f pl ['ʃpiːl zaxn] toys

Spielwarengeschäft n ['ʃpiːlvaːʁəngəˈʃɛft] toy store

Spinat m [ʃpiˈnaːt] spinach

Spirituosengeschäft n [ʃpiʁitu'oːzngəʃɛft] liquor store

Sport m [ʃpɔʁt] sport

Sportgeschäft n ['ʃpɔʁtgəʃɛft] sporting goods store

Sportler/in m/f ['ʃpɔʁtlɐ/'ʃpɔʁtləʁɪn] athlete

Sportplatz m ['ʃpɔʁtplats] sports field, athletics field

Sprache f ['ʃpʁaːxə] language

sprechen [ʃpʁɛçn] speak

Sprechstunde f ['ʃpʁɛçʃtʊndə] *(physician)* office hours

Springbrunnen m ['ʃpʁɪŋbʁʊnn] fountain

Spritze f ['ʃpʁɪtsə] injection

Spülbürste f ['ʃpyːlbʏʁstə] dishwashing brush

Spülmittel n ['ʃpyːlmɪtl] dishwashing detergent

Spültuch n ['ʃpyːltuːx] dishcloth

Staat m [ʃtaːt] state, country

Staatsangehörigkeit f ['ʃtaːts ˀangehøːʁɪçkaɪt] nationality

Stadion n ['ʃtaːdjon] stadium

Stadt f [ʃtat] town, city

Stadtmauern f pl ['ʃtatmaʊɐn] town/city walls

Stadtplan m ['ʃtatplaːn] town plan, city map

Stadtrundfahrt f ['ʃtatʁʊntfaːt] sightseeing tour of the town/city

Stadtteil m ['ʃtatʰaɪl] district

Stadtzentrum n ['ʃtattsɛntʁʊm] city center

stammen aus [ʃtamm] come from

Standlicht n ['ʃtantlɪçt] sidelights

stark [ʃtaːk] strong; *(pain)* severe

Starthilfekabel n ['ʃtaːtʰɪlfəkaːbl] jumper cables

Station f [ʃtaˈtsjoːn] station, stop; ward

Stativ n [ʃtaˈtiːf] tripod

statt [ʃtat] instead of

stattfinden ['ʃtatfɪndn] take place

Statue f ['ʃta:tuə] statue

Stau m [ʃtaʊ] traffic jam

Staub m [ʃtaʊp] dust

stechen [ʃtɛçn] to sting, to bite

Steckdose f ['ʃtɛkdo:zə] power point, socket

Stecker m ['ʃtɛkɐ] plug

stehen [ʃte:n] to stand

stehen bleiben ['ʃte:nblaɪbm] to stop, stand still

stehlen [ʃte:ln] to steal

steil [ʃtaɪl] steep

Stein m [ʃtaɪn] stone

steinig ['ʃtaɪnɪç] stony

Stelle f ['ʃtɛlə] spot, place; job

stellen [ʃtɛln] put

Stellung f ['ʃtɛlʊŋ] job, position

Stempel m [ʃtɛmpl] stamp

Stern m [ʃtɛɐn] star

Sternwarte f ['ʃtɛɐnva:tə] observatory

stets [ʃte:ts] always

Steward/Stewardess m/f ['stjua:t/'stjuadɛs] flight attendant, steward/stewardess

Stich m [ʃtɪç] sting, bite

Stiefel m pl [ʃti:fl] boots

Stil m [sti:l (ʃti:l)] style

still [ʃtɪl] quiet, silent; still, calm

Stillleben n ['ʃtɪlle:bm] still life

Stimme f ['ʃtɪmə] voice; vote

stinken [ʃtɪŋkn] to smell, to stink

Stirnhöhlenentzündung f ['ʃtɪɐnhø:ln?ɛn tsʏndʊŋ] sinusitis

Stock m [ʃtɔk] stick

Stockwerk n ['ʃtɔkvɛɐk] floor, story

Stoff m [ʃtɔf] material

stören [ʃtøɐn] disturb, bother

stornieren [ʃtɔ'nien] cancel

Stoßstange f ['ʃto:ʃtaŋə] bumper

Strafe f ['ʃtra:fə] punishment; fine

Strafraum m ['ʃtra:fraʊm] penalty box

Strähnchen n pl ['ʃtrɛ:nçn] highlights

Strand m [ʃtrant] beach

Strandschuhe m pl ['ʃtrantʃuə] flip-flops

Straße f ['ʃtra:sə] street; road

Straßenbahn f ['ʃtra:snba:n] streetcar

Straßenkarte f ['ʃtra:snka:tə] road map

Strecke f ['ʃtrɛkʰə] distance; *(railway)* line; road, route

Streichhölzer n pl ['ʃtraɪçhœltsə] matches

streng [ʃtrɛŋ] severe; strict

Strickjacke f ['ʃtrɪkjakə] cardigan

Strohhalm m ['ʃtro:halm] straw

Strom m [ʃtro:m] (large) river; *(electricity)* current

Strompauschale f ['ʃtro:mpaʊ ʃa:lə] flat rate for electricity

Stromspannung f ['ʃtro:m ʃpanʊŋ] voltage

Strömung f ['ʃtrø:mʊŋ] *(water)* current

Strümpfe m pl ['ʃtrʏmpfə] stockings

Strumpfhose f ['ʃtrʊmpfho:zə] panty hose

Stück n [ʃtʏk] piece; play

studieren [ʃtʊ'di:rən /-'dien] to study

Stufe f ['ʃtu:fə] step

Stufenschnitt m ['ʃtu:fnʃnɪt] layered cut

Stuhl m [ʃtu:l] chair

Stuhlgang m ['ʃtu:lgaŋ] bowel movement

stumm [ʃtʊm] mute

Stunde f ['ʃtʊndə] hour; lesson; eine halbe Stunde [(ʁ?aɪ)nə ʁhalbə 'ʃtʊndə] half an hour

stündlich ['ʃtʏntlɪç] every hour, hourly

Sturm m [ʃtʊɐm] gale, storm

Sturz m [ʃtʊɐts] fall

stürzen [ʃtʏɐtsn] to fall

Sturzhelm m ['ʃtʊɐtshɛlm] crash helmet

suchen [zu:xn] look for

Sucher m ['zuːxɐ] viewfinder
Süden m [zyːdn] south
südlich von ['zyːtlɪç fɔn] south of
Summe f ['zʊmə] sum; amount
Supermarkt m ['zuːpɐmaːkt] supermarket
Suppe f ['zʊpə] soup
Suppenteller m ['zʊpmtɛlɐ] soup plate
Surfbrett n ['sœːfbʀɛt] surfboard
surfen ['sœːfn] to surf
süß [zyːs] sweet
Süßigkeiten f pl ['zyːsɪçkaɪtn] candy
Süßstoff m ['zyːʃtɔf] sweetener
Süßwarengeschäft n ['zyːsvaːʀəngə ʃɛft] candy store
Swimmingpool m ['svɪmɪŋpuːl] (private) swimming pool
sympathisch [sʏm'pʰaːtʰɪʃ] nice, pleasant

T

Tabak m ['tʰabak] tobacco
Tabakladen m ['tabaklaːdn] tobacco store
Tablette f [ta'blɛtə] pill, tablet
Tacho(meter) m [ʁtaxo('meːtɐ)] speedometer
Tag m [tʰaːk] day; **jeden ~** [jeːdn taːk] every day
Tagesausflug m ['taːgəs ʔaʊsfluːk] day trip
Tagesgericht n ['taːgəsgəʀɪçt] dish of the day
Tageskarte f ['taːgəskaːtə] day ticket
Tagesmenü n ['taːgəsme nyː] special (of the day)
Tagespass m ['taːgəspas] day pass
täglich [tɛːklɪç] daily
tagsüber ['taːksʔyːbɐ] during the day
Tal n [taːl] valley

Tampons m pl ['tampɔŋs] tampons
Tank m [taŋk] gas tank
tanken [tʰaŋkn] fill up
Tanz m [tʰants] dance
tanzen [tantsn] to dance
Tänzer/in m/f [tɛntsɐ/tɛntsəˈʀɪn] dancer
Tanzkapelle f ['tantska pɛlə] dance band
Tanztheater n ['tantste ʔaːtɐ] dance theater
Tasche f ['tʰaʃə] pocket; bag
Taschenbuch n ['taʃnbuːx] paperback
Taschendieb/in m/f ['taʃndiːp/ - diːbɪn] pickpocket
Taschenmesser n ['taʃnmɛsɐ] pocket knife
Taschenrechner m ['taʃnʀɛçnɐ] pocket calculator
Tasse f ['tʰasə] cup
Taststock m ['tastʃtɔk] cane
Tätigkeit f ['tɛːtɪçkaɪt] (job) work
taubstumm ['taʊpʃtʊm] deaf-mute
tauchen [taʊxn] to dive
Taucherausrüstung f ['taʊxɐʔaʊsʀʏstʊŋ] diving equipment
Taucherbrille f ['taʊxɐbʀɪlə] diving goggles
tauschen [tʰaʊʃn] to exchange, to swap; (money) to change
täuschen, sich ~ [zɪç 'tʰɔɪʃn] be mistaken, be wrong
Taxifahrer/in m/f ['taksifaːʀɐ/ -faːʀəʀɪn] taxi driver
Taxistand m ['taksi ʃtant] taxi stand
Tee m [teː] tea
Teebeutel m ['teːbɔɪtl] tea bag
Teelöffel m ['teːlœfl] teaspoon
Teil m [tʰaɪl] part
teilnehmen (an) ['tʰaɪlneːmm (ʔan)] take part (in)
Telefon n ['teːləfoːn] telephone
Telefonbuch n [teləˈfoːnbuːx] telephone directory

telefonieren [tʰeləfoˈniːʀən/ -ˈniːən] make a phone call, to phone
Telefonkarte f [teləˈfoːnkaːtə] phonecard
Telefonnummer f [teləˈfoːnnʊmɐ] phone number
Telefonzelle f [teləˈfoːntsɛlə] phone booth
telegrafische Überweisung f [teləˈgʀaːfɪʃə ˀyːbəˈvaɪzʊŋ] wire transfer
Teleobjektiv n [ˈteːləˀɔbjɛk tiːf] telephoto lens
Telex n [ˈteːlɛks] telex
Teller m [ˈtɛlə] plate
Tempel m [tɛmpl] temple
Temperatur f [ʁtɛmpəʀaˈtuɐ] temperature
Tennis n [ˈtɛnɪs] tennis
Tennisschläger m [ˈtɛnɪʃlɛːgə] tennis racquet
Termin m [tʰɛˈmiːn] appointment; deadline
Terminal n [ˈtɛːmɪnəl] terminal
Terrakotta f [tɛʀaˈkɔta] terracotta
Terrasse f [teˈʀasə] terrace
Tetanus m [ˈtɛtanʊs] tetanus
teuer [ˈtʰɔɪɐ] expensive
Theater n [teˈˀaːtə] theater
Theaterkasse f [teˈˀaːtə kasə] box-office
Thriller m [ˈθʀɪlɐ] thriller
Thunfisch m [ˈtuːnfɪʃ] tuna
Thymian m [ˈtyːmiaːn] thyme
tief [tʰiːf] deep; low
Tier n [tʰiɐ] animal
Tintenfisch m [ˈtɪntnfɪʃ] squid
Tipp m [tʰɪp] (information) tip
Tisch m [tʰɪʃ] table
Tischtennis n [ˈtɪʃtɛnɪs] table tennis, Ping-Pong
Tischtuch n [ˈtɪʃtuːx] tablecloth
Toast m [toːst] toast
Toaster m [ˈtoːstə] toaster
Tochter f [ˈtʰɔxtʰə] daughter
Toilette f [toˈlɛtə] lavatory, toilet
Toilettenpapier n [toˈlɛtnpa piɐ] toilet paper

toll [tɔl] wonderful
Tomaten f pl [toˈmaːtn] tomatoes
Ton m [toːn] sound, tone; (color) shade
tönen [tøːnn] to tint
Töpferei f [tœpfəˈʀaɪ] (place) pottery
Töpfern [ˈtœpfen] (activity) pottery
Töpferwaren f pl [ˈtœpfevaːʀən] (product) pottery
Tor n [toɐ] gate; (sport) goal
Torwart/in m/f [ˈtoɐvaːt/ˈtoɐvaːtin] goalkeeper
Tour f [tʰuɐ] tour, excursion, trip
Tourist/in m/f [tuˈʀɪst/tuˈʀɪstɪn] tourist
tragen [tʀaːgŋ] carry; wear
Tragödie f [tʀaˈgøːdiə] tragedy
trampen [tʀɛmpm] hitchhike
Traum m [tʀaʊm] dream
träumen [tʀɔɪmm] to dream
traurig [ˈtʀaʊʀɪç] sad
treffen [tʀɛfn] meet
Trekkingrad n [ˈtʀɛkɪŋʀaːt] trekking bike
Treppe f [ˈtʀɛpʰə] stairs, staircase; steps
trinken [tʀɪŋkŋ] to drink
Trinkflasche f [ˈtʀɪŋkflaʃə] baby bottle
Trinkgeld n [ˈtʀɪŋkgɛlt] (gratuity) tip
Trinkwasser n [ˈtʀɪŋkvasɐ] drinking water
trocken [ˈtʀɔkŋ] dry
Trödelladen m [ˈtʀøːdllaːdn] second-hand store
Trommelfell n [ˈtʀɔmlfɛl] eardrum
tropfen [tʀɔpfn] to drip; (nose) to run
Tropfen m pl [ˈtʀɔpfn] drops
Tropfsteinhöhle f [ˈtʀɔpfʃtaɪn høːlə] dripstone cave
trotzdem [ˈtʀɔtsdeːm] nevertheless
trüb [tʀyːp] (liquid) cloudy; (weather) overcast, cloudy
Tuch n [tʰuːx] cloth

tun [tʰuːn] do
Tunnel m [tʰʊnl] tunnel
Tür f [tyɐ] door
Türbreite f ['tyɐbʁaɪtə] door width
Türcode m ['tyɐkoːt] door code
türkisfarben [tʏɐ'kiːsfaːbm] turquoise
Turm m [tʊɐm] tower
Türöffner m ['tyɐʔœfnɐ] door opener
Türschwelle f ['tyɐʃvɛlə] doorstep
Tüte f [tʰyːtʰə] bag; *(ice cream)* cone
Typhus m ['tyːfʊs] typhoid
typisch ['tʰyːpʰɪʃ] typical

U

U-Bahn f [ʔuːbaːn] subway
üben [ʔyːbm] practice
über [ʔyːbɐ] over
überall [ʔybɐ'ʔal] everywhere
überbacken [ʔybɐ'bakŋ] au gratin
Überfall m [ʔyːbɐfal] mugging
Übergang m [ʔyːbɐgaŋ] crossing; transition
überholen [ʔybɐ'hoːln] overtake, pass
übermorgen [ʔyːbɐmɔʁgŋ] the day after tomorrow
übernachten [ʔybɐ'naxtn] stay (overnight), spend the night
überqueren [ʔybɐ'kveːʁən/ -'kveen] to cross
Überreste m pl [ʔyːbɐʁɛstə] remains
überschreiten [ʔybɐ'ʃʁaɪtn] to cross
übersetzen [ʔybɐ'zɛtsn] translate
Überweisung f [ʔybɐ'vaɪzʊŋ] remittance, transfer
üblich [ʔyːplɪç] usual
Ufer n [ʔuːfɐ] *(river)* bank; shore
Uhrmacher m [ʔuemaxɐ] watchmaker('s)
um [ʔʊm] around; *(time)* at, about

umbuchen [ʔʊmbuːxn] change the reservation
Umgebung [ʔʊm'geːbʊŋ] surroundings
umgekehrt [ʔʊmgəkʰeɐt] reverse
Umhängetasche f [ʔʊmhɛŋə taʃə] shoulder bag
umkehren [ʔʊmkʰeːʁən/-kʰeen] turn back
umsonst [ʔʊm'zɔnst] free (of charge); in vain
umsteigen [ʔʊmʃtaɪgŋ] to change *(trains etc.)*
umtauschen [ʔʊmtʰaʊʃn] to change, to exchange
Umweg m [ʔʊmveːk] detour
Umwelt f [ʔʊmvɛlt] environment
umziehen, sich ~ [zɪç ʔʊmtsiːn] to change (clothes)
unangenehm [ʔʊnangəneːm] unpleasant
unbedingt [ʔʊnbədɪŋt] really
und [ʔʊnt] and
unentschieden [ʔʊnɛnt ʃiːdn] *(sport)* tie
unerfreulich [ʔʊnefʁɔɪlɪç] unpleasant
unerträglich [ʔʊnɐ tʁɛːklɪç] intolerable, unbearable
Unfall m [ʔʊnfal] accident
ungeeignet [ʔʊngəʔaɪknət] unfit, unsuited
ungefähr [ʔʊngə feɐ] about
ungern [ʔʊngɛɐn] reluctantly
ungewöhnlich [ʔʊngəvøːnlɪç] unusual
unglaublich [ʔʊn'glaʊplɪç] incredible
Unglück n [ʔʊnglʏkʰ] accident; misfortune
unglücklicherweise [ʁʔʊnglʏklɪçə'vaɪzə] unfortunately
Universität f [ʔʊniveɐzi'tʰɛːt] university
unmöglich [ʔʊn møːglɪç] impossible
Unrecht haben [ʔʊnʁɛçt haːbm] be wrong
uns [ʔʊns] us

unser(e) [ˈʔʊnzɐ (-ʀə)] our
unten [ˈʔʊntn̩] below
unter [ˈʔʊntʰɐ] under; among
unterbrechen [ˈʔʊntʰɐˈbʀɛçn̩] interrupt
Unterführung f [ˈʔʊntʰɐˈfyːʀʊŋ] underpass
unterhalb [ˈʔʊntʰɐhalp] below
unterhalten [ˈʔʊntɐˈhaltn̩] *(feed)* keep, maintain, support; entertain; sich ~ [zɪç ˈʔʊntʰɐˈhaltn̩] to talk; to amuse oneself
Unterhaltung f [ˈʔʊntʰɐˈhaltʰʊŋ] conversation; entertainment
Unterhemd n [ˈʔʊntehɛmt] vest
Unterhose f [ˈʔʊntehoːzə] pants
Unterkunft f [ˈʔʊntʰekʰʊnft] accommodations
Unternehmen n [ˈʔʊntɐˈneːmm̩] firm
unterrichten [ˈʔʊntʰɐˈʀɪçtn̩] inform; teach
Unterrichtsstunde f [ˈʔʊntɐʀɪçt ʃtʊndə] lesson
unterschreiben [ˈʔʊntʰɐˈʃʀaɪbm̩] to sign
Unterschrift f [ˈʔʊntʰɐʃʀɪft] signature
Untersuchung f [ˈʔʊntɐˈzuːxʊŋ] examination
Untersuchungshaft f [ˈʔʊntɐˈzuːxʊŋshaft] police custody
Untertasse f [ˈʔʊntetasə] saucer
Untertitel m [ˈʔʊntetɪtl̩] subtitles
Unterwäsche f [ˈʔʊntevɛʃə] underwear
unverschämt [ˈʔʊnfeʃɛːmt] impertinent, cheeky, rude
unwahrscheinlich [ˈʔʊnvaʃaɪnlɪç] unlikely, improbable
unwichtig [ˈʔʊnvɪçtɪç] unimportant
Urin m [ʔuˈʀiːn] urine
Urlaub m [ˈʔuɐlaʊp] vacation
Ursache f [ˈʔuɐzaxə] cause, reason
Urteil n [ˈʔuɐtaɪl] judgement; opinion

V

Varietee n [vaʀiəˈteː] music hall, variety theater
Vase f [ˈvaːzə] vase
Vater m [ˈfaːtʰɐ] father
Vaterland n [ˈfaːtelant] native country
Vegetarier/in [vegəˈtaːʀɪɐ/vegəˈtaːʀɪəʀɪn] *(person)* vegetarian
vegetarisch [vegəˈtaːʀɪʃ] vegetarian
Ventilator m [vɛntiˈlaːtoɐ] fan
Verabredung f [fɐˈʔapʀeːdʊŋ] appointment; date
verabschieden, sich ~ [zɪç fɐˈʔapʃiːdn̩] say goodbye
verändern [fɐˈʔɛndɐn] to change, alter
Veränderung f [fɐˈʔɛndəʀʊŋ] change
Veranstaltung f [fɐˈʔanʃtaltʰʊŋ] event
verantwortlich [fɐˈʔantvɔɐtlɪç] responsible
Verband m [fɐˈbant] bandage, dressing
verbinden [fɐˈbɪndn̩] join, connect; *(med.)* to dress
Verbindung f [fɐˈbɪndʊŋ] connection
verboten [fɐˈboːtn̩] forbidden, prohibited
Verbrechen n [fɐˈbʀɛçn̩] crime
verbrennen [fɐˈbʀɛnn̩] to burn
Verbrennung f [fɐˈbʀɛnʊŋ] burn
verbringen [fɐˈbʀɪŋŋ] spend *(time)*
Verdauung f [fɐˈdaʊʊŋ] digestion
Verdauungsstörung f [fɐˈdaʊʊŋʃtøːʀʊŋ] indigestion
verdorben [fɐˈdɔɐbm̩] spoiled; rotten; corrupt
Verein m [fɐˈʔaɪn] association, club

vereinbaren [fɛ'ʔaɪnbaː(ʀə)n] agree on

verfehlen [fɛ'feːln] *(not attain)* to miss

Vergangenheit *f* [fɛ'gaŋŋhaɪt] past

vergehen [fɛ'geːn] *(time)* to pass

vergessen [fɛ'gɛsn] forget

Vergewaltigung *f* [fɛgə'valtɪgʊŋ] rape

Vergiftung *f* [vɛ'gɪftʊŋ] poisoning

Vergnügen *n* [fɛ'gnyːgn] pleasure

verhaften [fɛ'haftn] to arrest

Verhandlung *f* [fɛ'handlʊŋ] *(court)* trial

verheiratet [fɛ'haɪʀaːtət] married

verhindern [fɛ'hɪndɐn] prevent

verirren, sich ~ [zɪç fɛ'ʔɪʀən/-ʔɪɐn] lose one's way, get lost

Verkauf *m* [fɛ'kʰaʊf] sale

verkaufen [fɛ'kʰaʊfn] to sell

Verkehr *m* [fɛ'kʰeɐ] traffic

verkehren [fɛ'keːʀən/-'keɐn] *(bus etc.)* to run

Verkehrsbüro *n* [fɛ'keɐsbyʀoː] tourist information office

verlängern [fɛ'lɛŋən] extend

Verlängerungsschnur *f* [fɛ'lɛŋəʀʊŋ ʃnuɐ] extension cord

verlassen [fɛ'lasn] to leave

verletzen [fɛ'lɛtsn] injure

Verletzte *m/f* [fɛ'lɛtstə] injured person

Verletzung *f* [fɛ'lɛtsʊŋ] injury

verlieren [fɛ'liːʀən /-'liɐn] lose

Verlobte *m/f* [fɛ'loːptə] fiancé/fiancée

vermieten [fɛ'miːtn] rent (out)

verpacken [fɛ'pakŋ] pack, wrap

Verpackung *f* [fɛ'pʰakʰʊŋ] packing, wrapping

verpassen [fɛ'pʰasn] to miss *(bus, opportunity)*

Verpflegung *f* [fɛ'(p)fleːgʊŋ] food; board

verrechnen, sich ~ [zɪç fɛ'ʀɛçn(ə)n] miscalculate, make a mistake

verreisen [fɛ'ʀaɪzn] go on a journey

verrückt [fɛ'ʀʏkt] mad, crazy

verschieben [fɛ'ʃiːbm] put off, postpone

verschieden [fɛ'ʃiːdn] different(ly)

verschließen [fɛ'ʃliːsn] to lock

Verschluss *m* [fɛ'ʃlʊs] *(door)* lock

verschreiben [fɛ'ʃʀaɪbm] prescribe

Versicherung *f* [fɛ'zɪçəʀʊŋ] insurance

Verspätung *f* [fɛ'ʃpɛːtʊŋ] delay

Verstand *m* [fɛ'ʃtant] *(mind)* reason

verstaucht [fɛ'ʃtaʊxt] sprained

verstehen [fɛ'ʃteːn] understand

Verstopfung *f* [fɛ'ʃtɔpfʊŋ] constipation

Versuch *m* [fɛ'zuːx] attempt, try; experiment, test

versuchen [fɛ'zuːxn] to try; to taste

vertauschen [fɛ'taʊʃn] mistake for

Vertrag *m* [fɛ'tʀaːk] contract

Vertrauen *n* [fɛ'tʀaʊn] confidence

verunglücken [fɛ'ʔʊnglʏkn] have an accident

verursachen [fɛ'ʔuɐzaxn] to cause

Verwaltung *f* [fɛ'valtʰʊŋ] administration

verwandt [fɛ'vant] related

verwechseln [fɛ'vɛksln] confuse, mix up

verwenden [fɛ'vɛndn] to employ, to use

Verwendung *f* [fɛ'vɛndʊŋ] use

verwitwet [fɛ'vɪtvət] widowed

verzögern [fɛ'tsøːgen] to delay

Videofilm *m* ['viːdeofɪlm] video film

Videokamera *f* ['viːdeo kaməʀa] video camera

Videokassette f ['vi:deoka sɛtə]
video cassette

Videorekorder m
['vi:deoʀe kɔɐdɐ] video recorder

viel [fi:l] a lot of; much

vielleicht [fɪ'laɪçt] perhaps, maybe

vielmehr ['fi:lmeɐ] rather

Viertelstunde f [fɪʀtl'ʃtʊndə]
quarter of an hour

Virus n ['vi:ʀʊs] virus

Visum n ['vi:zʊm] visa

Vogel m [fo:gl] bird

Vogelschutzgebiet n
['fo:glʃʊtsgəbi:t] bird reserve

Volk n [fɔlk] people

voll [fɔl] full; crowded

vollenden [fɔl'ʔɛndn] to complete

Volleyball m ['vɔlɪbal] volleyball

völlig ['fœlɪç] complete(ly)

Vollkasko f ['fɔlkasko] fully
comprehensive insurance

von [fɔn] from; of; by

vor [foɐ] in front of; before

Voranmeldung f
['foɐ'ʔanmɛldʊn] reservation

vorbei [fɔ'baɪ] over, past

vorbeigehen [fɔ'baɪge:n] go
by/past; pass

vorbereiten ['foɐbəʀaɪtn] prepare

vorbestellen ['foɐbəʃtɛln] to book

Vorfall m ['foɐfal] incident

vorgestern ['fɔagɛstɐn] the day
before yesterday

vorher ['foɐheɐ] before

vorläufig ['foɐlɔɪfɪç] temporary

Vormittag m ['foɐmɪtʰa:k]
morning

vormittags ['fɔɐmɪta:ks]
in/during the morning

vorn [fɔɐn] in front

Vorname m ['foɐna:mə] Christian
name, first name

vornehm ['foɐne:m]
distinguished, posh, noble

Vorort ['foɐ'ʔɔɐt, 'foɐʃtat] suburb

Vorrat m ['fo:ʀa:t] stock, store,
provisions

Vorsaison f ['foɐze zɔn] low
season, off-season

Vorschlag m ['foɐʃla:k] suggestion

Vorschrift f ['foɐʃʀɪft] rule

Vorsicht f ['foɐzɪçt] caution

vorsichtig ['foɐzɪçtɪç] careful,
cautious

Vorspeise f ['foɐʃpaɪzə] hors
d'oeuvre, appetizer

Vorstadt f ['foɐʃtat] suburb

vorstellen ['foɐʃtɛln] introduce

Vorstellung f ['foɐʃtɛlʊn]
introduction; notion, idea; *(theatre)*
performance

Vorteil m ['fɔɐtʰaɪl] advantage

vorüber [fo'ʀy:bɐ] past, over;
gone

vorübergehen [fo'ʀy:bɐge:n]
(time) to pass

vorübergehend [fo'ʀy:bɐge:nt]
temporary

Vorverkauf m ['foɐfɐkaʊf]
advance sale

Vorwahlnummer f
['foɐva:l nʊmɐ] area code

vorwärts ['fɔɐvɛɐts] forward(s)

vorzeigen ['foɐtsaɪgn] to show

Vorzug m ['foɐtsu:k] advantage

W

wach [vax] awake

wagen [va:gn] to dare

Wagenheber m ['va:gnhe:bɐ]
jack

Wagennummer f ['va:gnnʊmɐ]
(train) coach number

Wahl f [va:l] choice

wählen ['vɛ:ln] to choose; to vote;
(telephone) to dial

wahr [va:] true

während ['vɛ:ʀənt (veɐnt)]
during; while

wahrscheinlich [va'ʃaɪnlɪç] probable; probably

Währung f ['vɛ:ʀʊn] currency

Wahrzeichen n ['va:tsaɪçn]
emblem, symbol; landmark

Wald *m* [valt] forest, woods

Wales [wɛɪls (vɛɪls)] Wales

Waliser/in *m/f*
[va'li:ze/va'li:zərɪn]
Welshman/Welshwoman

walisisch [va'li:zɪʃ] Welsh

Wallfahrtsort *m* ['valfa:ts ʔɔɐ̯t]
place of pilgrimage

Wand *f* [vant] wall

Wanderkarte *f* ['vandeka:tə]
hiking map

wandern ['vanden] to hike, to
ramble

Wanderung ['vandəʀʊŋ] hike

Ware *f* ['va:ʀə] product

warm [va:m] warm; **warmes
Wasser** ['kaltəs 'vasɐ] hot water

Wärme *f* ['vɛɐ̯mə] heat

wärmen ['vɛɐ̯mm] to heat, to
warm

Warnblinkanlage *f*
['va:nblɪŋkʔanla:gə] hazard
warning lights

Warndreieck *n* ['va:ndʀaɪɛk]
warning triangle

warten (auf) [va:tn (ʔaʊf)] wait
(for)

Wartesaal *m* ['va:təza:l] waiting
room

Wartezimmer *n* ['va:tətsɪmɐ]
waiting room

was [vas] what

Waschbecken *n* ['vaʃbɛkn]
washbasin

Wäscheklammern *f pl*
['vɛʃəklamen] clothespins

Wäscheleine *f* ['vɛʃəlaɪnə]
clothesline

waschen [vaʃn] to wash

Wäscherei *f* [vɛʃə'ʀaɪ] laundry

Waschlappen *m* ['vaʃlapm]
washcloth

Waschmittel *n* ['vaʃmɪtl]
(clothes) detergent

Waschraum *m* ['vaʃʀaʊm] washroom

Waschsalon *m* ['vaʃza lɔŋ]
launderette

Wasser *n* ['vasɐ] water

Wasserfall *m* ['vasɐfal] waterfall

Wasserglas *n* ['vasɐgla:s] tumbler

Wasserhahn *m*
['vasɐha:n] *(water)* tap, faucet

Wasserkanister *m*
['vasɐkan ɪstɐ] water canister

Wasserski fahren ['vasɐʃi:
'fa:ʀən] go water-skiing

Wasserverbrauch *m*
['vasɐfɐbʀaʊx] water consumption

Watte *f* ['vatə] cotton wool

Wattestäbchen *n* ['vatəʃtɛ:pçn]
cotton-tipped swab

Wechsel *m* [vɛksl] change;
exchange

Wechselgeld *n* ['vɛkslgɛlt]
(money) change

wechselhaft ['vɛkslhaft] changeable

Wechselkurs *m* ['vɛkslkʊɐ̯s]
exchange rate

wechseln [(gɛlt) vɛksln] to
change *(money)*

wecken [vɛkn] wake

Wecker *m* ['vɛke] alarm clock

weg [vɛk] away; gone

Weg *m* [ve:k] way; path; road

wegen [ve:gn] because of

weggehen ['vɛkge:n] go away,
leave

Wegweiser *m* ['ve:kvaɪze]
(directions) sign

wehtun ['ve:tu:n] to hurt

weich [vaɪç] soft

weigern, sich ~ [zɪç 'vaɪgen] to
refuse

Weihnachten ['vaɪnaxtn]
Christmas

weil [vaɪl] because, since

Wein *m* [vaɪn] wine

Weinberg *m* ['vaɪnbɛek] vineyard

weinen [vaɪnn] to cry

Weinglas *n* ['vaɪngla:s] wineglass

Weinhandlung *f* ['vaɪnhantlʊŋ]
wine dealer

Weintrauben *f pl* ['vaɪntʀaʊbm]
grapes

Weise *f* ['vaɪzə] way

Weisheitszahn m ['vaɪshaɪtsa:n] wisdom tooth

weiß [vaɪs] white

Weißbrot n ['vaɪsbʀo:t] white bread

Weißwein ['vaɪsvaɪn] white wine

weit [vaɪt] wide; *(distance)* long; far

Welt f [vɛlt] world

wenig ['ve:nɪç] little, few

wenigstens ['ve (:)nɪkstns] at least

wenn [vɛn] if; when

werden [veɐdn] become

Werkstatt f ['vɛɐkʃtat] *(repairs)* garage

werktags ['vɛɐktʰa:ks] on weekdays

Werkzeug n ['vɛɐktsɔɪk] tools

Wertangabe f ['veɐtanga:bə] declaration of value

wertlos ['veɐtlo:s] worthless

Wertsachen f pl ['veɐtzaxn] valuables

Wespe f ['vɛspə] wasp

Weste f ['vɛstə] vest

Westen m [vɛstn] west

Western m ['vɛsten] *(film)* western

Wettervorhersage f ['vɛtɐfo heɐza:gə] weather forecast

Wettkampf m ['vɛtkamf] competition, contest

wichtig ['vɪçtɪç] important

Wickeltisch m ['vɪkltɪʃ] baby's changing table

wie [vi:] how; *(comparison)* like; wie schade! [vi 'ʃa:də] what a pity/shame!

wieder ['vi:dɐ] again

wiedergeben ['vi:dɐge:bm] give back, return

wiederholen [vidɐ'ho:ln] to repeat

wiederkommen ['vi:dɐkʰɔmm] come back, return

Wiedersehen, auf ~ [ʔaʊf 'vi(:)deze:n] goodbye

Wiese f ['vi:zə] meadow

wild [vɪlt] wild(ly)

Willkommen n [vɪl'kʰɔmm] welcome

willkommen [vɪl'kʰɔmm] *(adj)* welcome; willkommen heißen [vɪl'kʰɔmm haɪsn] to welcome

Wimperntusche f ['vɪmpɛntʊʃə] mascara

Wind m [vɪnt] wind

Windeln f pl [vɪndln] diapers

Windpocken f pl ['vɪntpɔkŋ] chicken pox

Windschutzscheibe f ['vɪntʃʊtʃaɪbə] windshield

Windstärke f ['vɪntʃtɛɛkə] wind-force

Windsurfen n ['vɪntsœɐfn] windsurfing

Winkel m ['vɪŋkl] corner

Winter m ['vɪntɐ] winter

Winterreifen m ['vɪntɐʀaɪfn] winter tires

wir [viɐ / vɐ] we

Wirbelsäule f ['vɪɐblzɔɪlə] spine

wirklich ['vɪɐklɪç] real; true; really, truly

wissen [vɪsn] know

Witz m [vɪts] joke

Woche f ['vɔxə] week

Wochenende n ['vɔxnʔɛndə] weekend

Wochenendpauschale f ['vɔxnʔɛntpaʊʃa:lə] weekend rate

wochentags ['vɔxntʰa:ks] on weekdays

wöchentlich ['vœçntlɪç] weekly; once a week

wohl [vo:l] *(comfortable)* well

wohlwollend ['vo:lvɔlnt] kind

wohnen [vo:nn] to live, to stay

Wohnort m ['vo:nʔɐt] place of residence

Wohnung f ['vo:nʊŋ] apartment

Wohnzimmer n ['vo:ntsɪmɐ] living room

Wolke f ['vɔlkə] cloud

Wolle f ['vɔlə] wool

wollen [vɔln] to want, to wish

Wort n [vɔɐt] word

Wunde f ['vʊndə] wound
wunderbar ['vʊndɐbaː] wonderful, marvelous
wundern, sich ~ (über) [zɪç 'vʊndɐn (ˈʁ²ybɐ)] be surprised (at/about)
Wunsch m [vʊnʃ] request
wünschen [vʏnʃn] to want; to wish for
Wurm m [vʊɐm] worm
Wurst f [vʊɐst] sausage
würzen [vvɛtsn] to season
wütend [vyːtnt] furious

Y

Yoga n ['joːga] yoga

Z

zäh [tsɛː] tough
Zahl f [tsaːl] number, figure
zahlen ['tsaːln] to pay
zählen [tsɛːln] to count
Zahlung f ['tsaːlʊŋ] payment
Zahn m [tsaːn] tooth
Zahnbürste f ['tsaːnbʏɐstə] toothbrush
Zahnfleisch n ['tsaːnflaɪʃ] gums
Zahnpasta f ['tsaːnpasta] toothpaste
Zahnschmerzen m pl ['tsaːnʃmɛɐtsn] toothache
Zahnstocher m ['tsaːnʃtɔxɐ] toothpick
Zäpfchen n ['tsɛpfçn] suppository
zart [tsaːt] *(soft)* tender
zärtlich ['tsɛɐtlɪç] tender, gentle
Zehe f ['tseːə] toe
Zeichen n ['tsaɪçn] sign
Zeichensprache f ['tsaɪçnʃpʁaːxə] sign language
Zeichentrickfilm m ['tsaɪçn tʁɪkfɪlm] cartoon
zeichnen ['tsaɪçn (ə)n] to draw

Zeichnung f ['tsaɪçnʊŋ] drawing
zeigen ['tsaɪgn] to show
Zeit f [tsaɪt] time
Zeitschrift f ['tsaɪtʃʁɪft] *(news)* magazine
Zeitung f ['tsaɪtʰʊŋ] newspaper
Zeitungshändler m ['tsaɪtʊŋshɛntlɐ] news dealer
Zelt n [tsɛlt] tent
zelten ['tsɛltn] to camp
Zentimeter m [ʁtsɛntiˈmeːtɐ] centimeter
zentral [tsɛnˈtʁaːl] central
Zerrung f ['tsɛʁʊŋ] pulled muscle
ziehen [tsiːn] to pull
Ziel n [tsiːl] aim; target; goal; destination
ziemlich ['tsiːmlɪç] fairly, rather, pretty, quite
Zigarette f [tsɪgaˈʁɛtə] cigarette
Zigarillo n [tsɪgaˈʁɪlo] cigarillo
Zigarre f [tsɪˈgaʁə] cigar
Zimmer n ['tsɪmɐ] room
Zimmermädchen n ['tsɪmɐmɛːtçn] maid
Zimmertelefon n ['tsɪmɐteləˌfoːn] in-room telephone
Zirkus m ['tsɪʁkʊs] circus
Zitronen f pl [tsɪˈtʁoːnn] lemons
Zoll m ['tsɔl] customs
Zollerklärung f ['tsɔlɛklɛːʁʊŋ] customs declaration
zollfrei ['tsɔlfʁaɪ] duty-free
Zollgebühren f pl ['tsɔlgəbyːʁən] customs duty
zollpflichtig ['tsɔl(p)flɪçtɪç] subject to duty
Zoo m [tsoː] zoo
zornig ['tsɔɐnɪç] angry
zu [tsu (ː)] to; shut, closed; too; **zu viel** [tsʊˈfiːl] too much
zubereiten ['tsuːbəʁaɪtn] prepare, cook; mix *(drinks)*
Zucker m ['tsʊkɐ] sugar
zuerst [tsʊˈʔeɐst] (at) first
zufällig ['tsuːfɛlɪç] by chance
zufrieden [tsʊˈfʁiːdn] satisfied
Zug m [tsuːk] train

Zugang *m* ['tsu:gaŋ] access, entrance

zugänglich ['tsu:gɛŋlɪç] accessible

Zukunft *f* ['tsu:kʰʊnft] future

zukünftig ['tsu:kʰʏnftɪç] *(adj)* future

zulassen ['tsu:lasn] to register *(car)*

zulässig ['tsu:lɛsɪç] permitted, allowed

zuletzt [tsʊ'lɛtst] finally; last

zumachen ['tsu:maxn] to close, to shut

zunächst [tsʊ'nɛ:çst/-'nɛ:kst] first (of all)

Zündkerze *f* ['tsʏntkɛɐtsə] spark plug

Zündschlüssel *m* ['tsʏntʃlʏsl] ignition key

Zündung *f* ['tsʏndʊŋ] ignition

Zunge *f* ['tsʊŋə] tongue

zurück [tsʊ'ʀʏk] back

zurückbringen [tsʊ'ʀʏkbʀɪŋŋ] bring back

zurückfahren [tsʊ'ʀʏkfa: (ʀə)n] drive back, return

zurückgeben [tsʊ'ʀʏkge:bm] give back

zurückkehren [tsʊ'ʀʏkʰe:ʀən/ -kʰeen] come back, return

zurückweisen [tsʊ'ʀʏkvaɪzn] to refuse

zurzeit [tsʊɐ'tsaɪt] at the moment

zusagen ['tsu:za:gn] accept *(invitation)*

zusammen [tsʊ'zamm] together

zusammenschlagen [tsʊ'zammʃla:gn] beat up

Zusammenstoß *m* [tsʊ'zammʃto:s] collision, crash

zusätzlich ['tsu:zɛtslɪç] additional; in addition

zuschauen ['tsu:ʃaʊn] to watch

Zuschauer/in *m/f* ['tsu:ʃaʊɐ/'tsu:ʃaʊəʀɪn] viewer, spectator

Zustand *m* ['tsu:ʃtant] state, condition

zuständig ['tsu:ʃtɛndɪç] responsible

zweimal ['tsvaɪma:l] twice

zweitens ['tsvaɪtns] second(ly)

zweite(r, s) ['tsvaɪtə (-tɐ/-təs)] second

Zwiebeln *f pl* ['tsvi:bln] onions

zwischen ['tsvɪʃn] between; among

Zwischenfall *m* ['tsvɪʃnfal] incident

Zwischenlandung *f* ['tsvɪʃn landʊŋ] stopover

Zwischenstecker *m* ['tsvɪʃnʃtɛkɐ] adapter

A

abbey die Abtei [di ʔap'taɪ]
abbreviation die Abkürzung [di ʔapkʏɐtsʊn]
able, be ~ to im Stande sein [ʔɪm'ʃtandə zaɪn], können [kœnn]
about ungefähr [ʔʊngəˈfeɐ], etwa [ˈʔɛtvaː]; (time) gegen [geːgn]
about noon gegen Mittag [ˈgeːgn ˈmɪtaːk]
abroad im/ins Ausland [ʔɪm/ʔɪns ʔaʊslant]
abscess der Abszess [dɐ ʔapsˈɛs]
accelerator das Gaspedal [das ˈgaːspedaːl]
accept annehmen [ˈʔaneːmm]; (invitation) zusagen [ˈtsuːzaːgn]
access der Zugang [dɐ ˈtsuːgan]
accessible zugänglich [ˈtsuːgɛnlɪç]
accident der Unfall [dɐ ˈʔʊnfal]; have an accident verunglücken [fɐʔʊnglʏkn]
accommodation die Unterkunft [di ˈʔʊntɐkʊnft]
accompany begleiten [bəˈglaɪtn]
accompanying person die Begleitperson [di bəˈglaɪtpɛɐzoːn]
account das Konto [das ˈkɔnto]
acquaintance die Bekanntschaft [di bəˈkantʃaft]; (person) der/die Bekannte [dɐ/di bəˈkantə]
across quer durch [kveɐ dʊɐç]
act der Akt [dɐ ʔakt]
action film der Actionfilm [dɐ ˈʔɛkʃnfɪlm]
actor/actress der Schauspieler/die Schauspielerin [dɐ ˈʃaʊʃpiːlɐ/di ˈʃaʊʃpiːlərɪn]
actual(ly) eigentlich [ˈʔaɪgntlɪç]

adapter der Adapter [dɐ ʔaˈdaptɐ], der Zwischenstecker [dɐ ˈtsvɪʃnʃtɛkɐ]
add hinzufügen [hɪnˈtsuːfyːgn]; in addition zusätzlich [ˈtsuːzɛtslɪç]; additional zusätzlich [ˈtsuːzɛtslɪç]
additional costs die Nebenkosten [di ˈneːbmkɔstn]
address die Anschrift [di ˈʔanʃrɪft], die Adresse [di ʔaˈdrɛsə]; (vb) adressieren [ʔadrɛˈsiːrən/-ˈsiːn]
addressee der Empfänger [dɐ ʔɛmpˈfɛnɐ]
administration die Verwaltung [di fɐˈvaltʊn]
admission charge der Eintrittspreis [dɐ ˈʔaɪntrɪtspraɪs]
admission ticket die Eintrittskarte [di ˈʔaɪntrɪts kaːtə]
adult der/die Erwachsene [dɐ/di ʔeˈvaks(ə)nə]
advance, in ~ im Voraus [ʔɪm ˈfoːraʊs]
advance sale der Vorverkauf [dɐ ˈfoɐfekaʊf]
advantage der Vorzug [dɐ ˈfoɐtsuːk]; der Vorteil [dɐ ˈfɔetaɪl]
aerobics das Aerobic [das ˈʔɛˈrɔbɪk]
afraid erschrocken [ʔeˈʃrɔkn]; be afraid (of) sich fürchten (vor) [zɪç ˈfʏrçtn foɐ]; befürchten [bəˈfʏrçtn]
after nach [naːx]
after-shave lotion das Rasierwasser [das raˈziːevasə]
afternoon der Nachmittag [dɐ ˈnaːxmɪtaːk]; in the afternoon nachmittags [ˈnaxmɪtaːks]
afterwards nachher [ˈnaːx(h)eɐ], danach [daˈnaːx]
again wieder [ˈviːdɐ]

against gegen [ge:gn]; be against it dagegen sein [da'ge:gn zaɪn]

age das Alter [das ˀaltɐ]

agency die Agentur [di ˀagɛn'tuɐ]

agree sich einigen [zɪç ˀaɪnɪgn]; einig sein [ˀaɪnɪç zaɪn]; *(on a date, time etc.)* ausmachen [ˀaʊsmaxn]; agree on vereinbaren [fɐˀaɪnba:(ʀə)n]

agreeable angenehm [ˀangəne:m]

aid die Hilfe [di 'hɪlfə]; first aid erste Hilfe [ʀˀeestə 'hɪlfə]

aim das Ziel [das tsi:l]

air die Luft [di lʊft]; lüften ['lʏftn]

air-conditioning die Klimaanlage [di 'kli:meˀan la:gə]

airline die Fluggesellschaft [di 'flu:kgə zɛlʃaft]

airport der Flughafen [dɐ 'flu:kha:fn]

airport bus der Flughafenbus [dɐ 'flu:kha:fn bʊs]

airport tax die Flughafengebühr [di 'flu:kha:fngə bye]

alarm clock der Wecker [dɐ 'vɛkɐ]

alarm system die Alarmanlage [di ˀa'la:manla:gə]

alarmed erschrocken [ˀe'ʃʀɔkn]

all alle [ˀalə]; ganz [gants]

allergy die Allergie [di ˀal(ɛ)ɐ'gi:]

alley die Gasse [di 'gasə]

allowed zulässig ['tsu:lɛsɪç]; be allowed dürfen [dʏɐfn]

almonds die Mandeln *f pl* [di 'mandln]

almost fast [fast], beinahe ['baɪna:]

alone allein [ˀa'laɪn]

already bereits [bə'ʀaɪts], schon [ʃo:n]

also auch [ˀaʊx], gleichfalls ['glaɪçfals]

altar der Altar [dɐ ˀal'ta:]

although obwohl [ˀɔp'vo:l]

aluminum foil die Alufolie [di ˀalufo:ljə]

always immer [ˀɪmɐ], stets [ʃte:ts]

ambulance der Krankenwagen [dɐ 'kraŋkŋva:gn]

America Amerika [ˀa'me:ʀika:]

American der Amerikaner/die Amerikanerin [dɐ ˀameʀɪ'ka:nɐ/di ˀameʀɪ'ka:nəʀɪn]

among zwischen ['tsvɪʃn]

amount der Betrag [dɐ bə'tʀa:k]

amputated amputiert [ampu'tiet]

amusement park der Freizeitpark [dɐ 'fʀaɪtsaɪt pa:k]

ancient antik [ˀan'ti:k]

and und [ˀʊnt]

angina die Angina [di ˀaŋ'gi:na]

angry zornig ['tsɔɛnɪç]; böse ['bø:zə]

animal das Tier [das tie]

ankle der Knöchel [dɐ knœçl]

announce melden [mɛldn], anmelden [ˀanmɛldn]

announcement die Mitteilung [di 'mɪtaɪlʊŋ]

annoying lästig ['lɛstɪç]

annual(ly) jährlich ['jɛəlɪç]

answer die Antwort [di ˀantvɔet]; *(vb)* antworten [ˀantvɔetn], beantworten [bəˀantvɔetn]

answering machine der Anrufbeantworter [dɐ ˀanʀu:fbɐ ˀantvɔetɐ]

antifreeze das Frostschutzmittel [das 'fʀɔstʃʊtsmɪtl]

antique shop das Antiquitäten-geschäft [das ˀantɪkvɪ'tɛ:tngəʃɛft]

any jeder Beliebige [ʀje:dɐ bə'li:bɪgə]; *(in questions)* einige ['ˀaɪnɪgə]

anybody *(in questions)* jemand ['je:mant]

anything *(in questions)* etwas ['ˀɛtvas]

apartment die Wohnung [di 'vo:nʊŋ]

apologize sich entschuldigen [zɪç ˀɛnt'ʃʊldɪgn]

appendicitis die Blinddarmentzündung [di 'blɪntda:mɛn tsʏndʊŋ]

appetite der Appetit [dɐ ʔapəˈtɪt]
applause der Beifall [dɐ ˈbaɪfal]
apples die Äpfel *m pl* [di ˈɛpfl]
appointment der Termin [dɐ teˈmiːn]; *(meeting)* die Verabredung [di fɐˈʔapʀeːdʊŋ]
apricots die Aprikosen *f pl* [di ʔapʀɪˈkoːzn]
April April [ˈaˈpʀɪl]
arch der Bogen [dɐ ˈboːgn]
archaeology die Archäologie [di ʔaˈçeoloˈgiː]
architect Architekt/Architektin [ˈaˈçɪˈtɛkt/ˈaˈçɪˈtɛkt ɪn]
architecture die Architektur [di ʔaˈçitɛkˈtuɐ]
area die Gegend [di ˈgeːgn̩t]
area code die Vorwahlnummer [di ˈfoːevaːl nʊmɐ]
arm der Arm [dɐ ʔaːm]
around herum [hɐˈʀʊm]
arrest verhaften [fɐˈhaftn̩]
arrival die Ankunft [di ʔankʊnft]
arrive (at) eintreffen [ʔaɪntʀɛfn̩]
art die Kunst [di kʊnst]
art dealer der Kunsthändler [dɐ ˈkʊnst hɛntlɐ]
art nouveau der Jugendstil [dɐ ˈjuːgn̩tstiːl]
artichokes die Artischocken *f pl* [di ʔaˈtɪʃɔkn̩]
artificial limb die Prothese [di pʀoˈteːzə]
arts and crafts das Kunstgewerbe [das ˈkʊnstgəveebə]
as *(reason)* da [daː]
ashtray der Aschenbecher [dɐ ʔaʃnbɛçɐ]
ask fragen [fʀaːgn̩], fordern [ˈfɔɐdɐn], auffordern [ʔaufɔɐdɐn]; ask s.o. for s.th. jdn um etw. bitten [ʁjemandn ʊm ʁʔɛtvas ˈbɪtn̩]
asparagus der Spargel [ʃpaːgl]
aspirin das Aspirin [das ʔaspiˈʀiːn]
association der Verein [dɐ fɐˈʔaɪn]
asthma das Asthma [das ˈʔastma]
at *(time)* um [ʔʊm]

athlete der Sportler/die Sportlerin [dɐ ˈʃpɔetlɐ/di ˈʃpɔetlɐʀɪn]
athletics die Leichtathletik [di ˈlaɪçtʔat leːtɪk]
Atlantic der Atlantik [dɐ ʔatˈlantɪk]
attack der Anfall [dɐ ˈʔanfal]
attention die Achtung [di ˈʔaxtʊŋ]; pay attention (to) aufpassen [ʔaufpasn̩], beachten [bəˈʔaxtn̩]
au gratin überbacken [ˈyːbɐˈbakn̩]
August August [ʔauˈgʊst]
Austria Österreich [das ˈʔøːstəʀaɪç]
Austrian der Österreicher/die Österreicherin [dɐ ˈʔøːstəʀaɪçɐ/di ˈʔøːstəʀaɪçɐʀɪn]
authorities die Behörde [di bəˈhøedə]
automated teller machine der Geldautomat [dɐ ˈgɛltauto maːt]
automatic automatisch [ʔautoˈmaːtɪʃ]
automatic (transmission) das Automatikgetriebe [das ʔautoˈmaːtɪkgə tʀiːbə]
autumn der Herbst [dɐ ˈhɛɐpst]
average durchschnittlich [ˈdʊɐçʃnɪtlɪç]
avocado die Avocado [di ʔavoˈkaːdo]
awake wach [vax]
aware bewusst [bəˈvʊst]; be aware of merken [mɛɐkn̩]
away weg [vɛk], fort [fɔet]
awful schrecklich [ˈʃʀɛklɪç]

B

baby das Baby [das ˈbeːbiː]
baby bottle die Saugflasche [di ˈzaukflaʃə]
baby food die Kindernahrung [di ˈkɪndɐnaːʀʊŋ]

baby monitor das Babyfon [das 'be:bifo:n]
baby seat die Babyschale [di 'be:bifa:lə]
baby's changing table der Wickeltisch [dɐ 'vɪkltɪʃ]
babysitter der Babysitter [dɐ 'be:bɪsɪtɐ]
babysitting service die Kinderbetreuung [di 'kɪndɐbətʀɔjʊŋ]
bachelor der Junggeselle [dɐ 'jʊŋɡəzɛlə]
back der Rücken [dɐ ʀʏkŋ]; *(adv)* zurück [tsʊ'ʀʏk]
backache die Rückenschmerzen *m pl* [di 'ʀʏkŋʃmɛɐtsn]
backpack der Rucksack [dɐ 'ʀʊkzak]
backwards rückwärts ['ʀʏkvɛɐts]
bad schlimm [ʃlɪm], schlecht [ʃlɛçt]
badly schlecht [ʃlɛçt]
badminton das Badminton [das 'bɛtmɪntn]
bag der Sack [dɐ zak], die Tüte [di 'ty:tə], die Handtasche [di 'han(t)taʃə]
baggage das Gepäck [das ɡe'pɛk]
baggage car der Gepäckwagen [dɐ ɡə'pɛkva:ɡn]
baggage claim die Gepäckausgabe [di ɡə'pɛk'ʔaʊsɡa:bə]
baggage deposit die Gepäckaufbewahrung [di ɡə'pɛk 'ʔaʊfbəva:ʀʊŋ]
baggage room die Gepäckaufbewahrung [di ɡə'pɛk 'ʔaʊfbəva:ʀʊŋ]
baked gebacken [ɡə'bakŋ]
baker's die Bäckerei [di bɛkə'ʀaɪ]
balcony der Balkon [dɐ bal'kɔn]
ball der Ball [dɐ bal]; *(festivity)* der Ball [dɐ bal]
ballet das Ballett [das ba'lɛt]
ballpoint pen der Kugelschreiber [dɐ 'ku:ɡlʃʀaɪbɐ]
bananas die Bananen *f pl* [di ba'na:nn]

band die Band [di bɛ(:)nt]
Band-Aid das Pflaster [das 'pflastɐ]
bandage der Verband [dɐ fɛ'bant]
bangs *(hair)* der Pony [dɐ 'pɔni]
bank die Bank [di baŋk]; *(river)* das Ufer [das 'ʔu:fɐ]
banknote der Geldschein [dɐ 'ɡɛltʃaɪn]
bar die Bar [di ba:]
barber der (Herren)Friseur [dɐ('hɛʀən)fʀɪ'zøɐ]
baroque barock [ba'ʀɔk]
basil das Basilikum [das ba'zi:lɪkʊm]
basket der Korb [dɐ kɔɐp]
basketball der Basketball [dɐ 'ba:skɛtbal]
bathrobe der Bademantel [dɐ 'ba:dəmantl]
bathroom das Badezimmer [das 'ba:dətsɪmɐ]
bathtub die Badewanne [di 'ba:dəvanə]
battery die Batterie [di batə'ʀi:]
battery charger das Ladegerät [das 'la:dəɡəʀɛ:t]
bay die Bucht [di bʊxt]
bay leaves die Lorbeerblätter *n pl* [di 'lɔɐbeɐ blɛtɐ]
be sein [zaɪn], sich befinden [zɪç bə'fɪndn]
beach der Strand [dɐ ʃtʀant]
beach shoes die Strandschuhe *m pl* [di 'ʃtʀantʃuə]
beans die Bohnen *f pl* [di bo:nn]
beard der Bart [dɐ ba:t]
beat up zusammenschlagen [tsʊ'zammʃla:ɡŋ]
beautiful schön [ʃø:n]
because weil [vaɪl]; da [da:]; because of wegen [ve:ɡn]
become werden [veɐdn]
bed das Bett [das bɛt]; go to bed ins Bett gehen ['ʔɪns 'bɛt ɡe:n]
bed linen die Bettwäsche [di 'bɛtvɛʃə]

bedroom das Schlafzimmer [das 'ʃlaːftsɪmɐ]
bedside table der Nachttisch [dɐ 'naxttɪʃ]
bee die Biene [di 'biːnə]
beef das Rindfleisch ['ʀɪntflaɪʃ]
beer das Bier [das biɐ]
before vor [foɐ]; *(conj)* bevor [bə'foɐ]; *(previously)* vorher ['foɐheɐ]
begin anfangen ['ʔanfaŋŋ], beginnen [bə'gɪnn]
beginning der Anfang [dɐ 'ʔanfaŋ], der Beginn [dɐ bə'gɪn]
behind hinter ['hɪntɐ]
beige beige [beːʃ]
Belgian der Belgier/die Belgierin [dɐ 'bɛlgɪɐ/di 'bɛlgɪəʀɪn]
Belgium Belgien ['bɛlgɪən]
believe glauben [glaʊbm]
bell die Klingel [di klɪŋl]
belong to gehören [gə'høːʀən/-'høɐn]
below unterhalb ['ʔʊntɐhalp], unten ['ʔʊntn]
belt der Gürtel [dɐ gʏɐtl]
bench die (Sitz)Bank [di ('zɪts)baŋk]
bend die Kurve [di 'kʊɐvə]
beside neben ['neːbm]
besides außerdem ['ʔaʊsɐdeːm]
best beste(r, s) ['bɛstə (-tɐ, -təs)]; at best höchstens ['høːçstns/'høːkstns]
better besser ['bɛsɐ]
between zwischen ['tsvɪʃn]
bicycle das Fahrrad [das 'faːrat]
big groß [gʀoːs]
bike das Fahrrad [das 'faːrat]
bike tour die Radtour [di 'ʀattuɐ]
bikini der Bikini [dɐ bi'kiːni]
bill die Rechnung [di 'ʀɛçnʊŋ]
bird der Vogel [dɐ foːgl]
bird reserve das Vogelschutzgebiet [das 'foːglʃʊtsgəbiːt]
birthday der Geburtstag [dɐ gə'bʊɐtstaːk]
bite *(vb)* beißen [baɪsn]
bitter bitter ['bɪtɐ]

black schwarz [ʃvaːts]
black-and-white film der Schwarzweiß-Film [dɐ ʃvaːts'vaɪsfɪlm]
blackberries die Brombeeren *f pl* [di 'bʀɔmbeːʀən]
bladder die Blase [di 'blaːzə]
blanket die Bettdecke [di 'bɛtdɛkə]
blazer der Blazer [dɐ 'bleːzɐ]
bleed bluten [bluːtn]
bleeding die Blutung [di 'bluːtʊŋ]
blind blind [blɪnt]
blind person der/die Blinde [dɐ/di 'blɪndə]
blond(e) blond [blɔnt]
blood das Blut [das bluːt]
blood group die Blutgruppe [di 'bluːtgʀʊpə]
blood poisoning die Blutvergiftung [di 'bluːtfɛɐgɪftʊŋ]
blouse die Bluse [di 'bluːzə]
blow dry föhnen [føːnn]
blue blau [blaʊ]
blues der Blues [dɐ bluːs]
boarding card die Bordkarte [di 'bɔɐtkaːtə]
body der Körper [dɐ 'kœɐpɐ]
boil kochen [kɔxn]
boiled gekocht [gə'kɔxt]
bone der Knochen [dɐ knɔxn]
book das Buch [das buːx]; *(vb)* buchen [buːxn], vorbestellen ['foɐbəʃtɛln]
book store die Buchhandlung [di 'buːxhantlʊŋ]
boots die Stiefel *m pl* [di ʃtiːfl]
border die Grenze [di 'gʀɛntsə]
boring langweilig ['laŋvaɪlɪç]
born geboren [gə'boːʀən (gə'boɐn)]
borrow (aus)leihen [('ʔaʊs)laɪn]
boss der Leiter/die Leiterin [dɐ 'laɪtɐ/di 'laɪtəʀɪn], der Chef/die Chefin [dɐ ʃɛf/di ʃɛfɪn]
botanical gardens der botanische Garten [dɐ bo'tanɪʃə 'gaːtn]
both beide ['baɪdə]

bother belästigen [bə'lɛstɪgn̩], stören [ʃtøɐn]
bottle die Flasche [di 'flaʃə]
bottle opener der Flaschenöffner [dɐ 'flaʃn̩ʔœfnɐ]
bottle warmer der Fläschchen- wärmer [dɐ 'flɛʃçənvɛemɐ]
boutique die Boutique [di bu'ti:k]
bowel movement der Stuhlgang [dɐ 'ʃtu:lgaŋ]
bowl die Schüssel [di ʃʏsl̩]
box die Kiste [di 'kɪstə], die Schachtel [di ʃaxtl̩], die Packung [di 'pakʊŋ]; *(theater)* die Loge [di 'lo:ʒə]
box office die (Theater)Kasse [di (te'ʔa:tɐ) kasə]
boy der Junge [dɐ 'jʊŋə]
bracelet das Armband [das 'ʔa:mbant]
Braille die Blindenschrift [di 'blɪndn̩ʃrɪft]
brain das Gehirn [das gə'hɪɐn]
braised geschmort [gə'ʃmoɐt]
brake die Bremse [di 'brɛmzə]
brake fluid die Bremsflüssigkeit [di 'brɛmsflʏsɪçkaɪt]
brake lights die Bremslichter [di 'brɛmslɪçtɐ]
bread das Brot [das bro:t]
break into/open aufbrechen ['ʔaʊfbrɛçn̩]
breakdown die Panne [di 'panə]
breakfast das Frühstück [das 'fry:ʃtʏk; **have breakfast** frühstücken ['fry:ʃtʏkn̩]
breakfast room der Frühstücks- raum [dɐ 'fry:ʃtʏksraʊm]
breathe atmen ['ʔa:tmən]
bridge die Brücke [di 'brʏkə]
briefs der (Herren)Slip [dɐ ('hɛrən)slɪp]
bring mitbringen ['mɪtbrɪŋn̩]; *(her-)* bringen [('hee)brɪŋn̩]; **bring back** zurückbringen [tsʊ'rʏkbrɪŋn̩]
broad breit [braɪt]
brochure der Prospekt [dɐ pros'pɛkt]

broken kaputt [ka'pʊt]; *(bone)* gebrochen [gə'brɔxn̩]
bronchial tubes die Bronchien *f pl* [di 'brɔnçiən]
bronchitis die Bronchitis [di brɔn'çi:tɪs]
bronze die Bronze [di 'brɔŋsə]
brooch die Brosche [di 'brɔʃə]
brother der Bruder [dɐ 'bru:dɐ]
brother-in-law der Schwager [dɐ 'ʃva:gɐ]
brown braun [braʊn]
bruise *(caused by hitting)* die Prellung [di 'prɛlʊŋ]; *(caused by pinching)* die Quetschung [di 'kvɛtʃʊŋ]
brush die Bürste [di 'bʏɐstə]
buffet breakfast das Frühstücksbüfett [das 'fry:ʃtʏksbʏ fe:]
building das Gebäude [das gə'bɔɪdə]
bumper die Stoßstange [di 'ʃto:ʃtaŋə]
bunch of flowers der Blumenstrauß [dɐ 'blu:mm̩ʃtraʊs]
bungalow der Bungalow [dɐ 'bʊŋgalo:]
bunk bed das Etagenbett [das 'ʔe'ta:ʒn̩bɛt]
bunny lift Babylift ['be:bilɪft]
burn die Verbrennung [di fɐ'brɛnʊŋ]; *(vb)* brennen [brɛnn̩]; verbrennen [fɐ'brɛnn̩]
bus der Bus [dɐ bʊs]
bus station der Busbahnhof [dɐ 'bʊs ba:nho:f]
bush der Busch [dɐ bʊʃ]
but aber ['ʔa:bɐ]; sondern ['zɔndɐn]
butcher shop die Metzgerei [di mɛtsgə'raɪ]
butter die Butter [di 'bʊtɐ]
buttermilk die Buttermilch [di 'bʊtɐmɪlç]
buy kaufen [kaʊfn̩], einkaufen ['ʔaɪnkaʊfn̩]
by von [fɔn]; **by (means of)** durch [dʊɐç]

bypass der Bypass [de 'baɪpaːs]

C

cabaret das Kabarett [das kaba'ʀeː]
cabbage der Kohl [de koːl]
cabin die Kabine [di ka'biːnə]
cable railway die (Stand)Seilbahn [di (ʃtant) zaɪlbaːn]
café das Café [das ka'feː]
cake der Kuchen [de kuːxn]
calculate rechnen ['ʀɛçn(ə)n], berechnen [bə'ʀɛçn(ə)n]
call der Anruf [de ʔanʀuːf]; *(vb, phone)* anrufen ['ʔanʀuːfn]; *(shout)* rufen [ʀuːfn]; *(call out)* aufrufen ['ʔaʊfʀuːfn]; *(name)* nennen [nɛnn]; be called heißen [haɪsn]; call for *(pick up)* abholen ['ʔaphoːln]; call on s.o. jdn besuchen [ʁjemandn bə'zuːxn]; be called heißen [haɪsn]
calm die Ruhe [di 'ʀuə]; *(adj)* ruhig [ʀuːɪç], still [ʃtɪl]; calm down sich beruhigen [zɪç bə'ʀuːɪgn]
camcorder der Camcorder [de 'kamkhɔede]
camera die Kamera [di 'kaməʀaː]
camomile tea der Kamillentee [de ka'mɪl(ə)nteː]
camp *(vb)* zelten ['tsɛltn]
campground der Campingplatz [de 'kɛmpɪŋplats]
camping das Camping [das 'kɛmpɪŋ]
camping guide der Campingführer [de 'kɛmpɪŋfyːʀe]
can die Büchse [di 'bʏksə], die Dose [di 'doːzə]
can opener der Dosenöffner [de 'doːzn̩ʔœfne]

canal der Kanal [de ka'naːl]
cancel *(tickets etc.)* abbestellen ['ʔapbəʃtɛln]; *(appointment)* absagen ['ʔapzaːgn]; *(flight)* stornieren [ʃtɔ'niːen]
cancer der Krebs [de kʀeːps]
candles die Kerzen *f pl* [di kɛetsn]
candy store das Süßwarengeschäft [das 'zyːsvaːʀəngə ʃɛft]
cane der Taststock [de 'tastʃtɔk]
canoe das Kanu [das 'kaːnu]
cap die Mütze [di 'mʏtsə]
capital die Hauptstadt [di 'haʊptʃtat]
captain der Kapitän [de kapi'tɛːn]
car das Auto [das ʔaʊtoː], der Wagen [de 'vaːgn], der Pkw [de 'peːkaveː]
car number (train) die Wagennummer [di 'vaːgn̩nʊme]
car radio das Autoradio [das ʔaʊto ʀaːdjo]
car registration documents der Kfz-Schein [de kaʔefʦɛtʃaɪn]
caraway seed(s) der Kümmel [de kʏml]
cardiac infarction der Herzinfarkt [de 'hɛetsɪnfaːkt]
cardiac stimulant das Kreislaufmittel [das 'kʀaɪslaʊf mɪtl]
cardigan die Strickjacke [di 'ʃtʀɪkjakə]
care die Betreuung [di bə'tʀɔɪʊŋ]; in need of care pflegebedürftig ['pfleːgəbədʏeftɪç]
careful vorsichtig ['foeʀzɪçtɪç], sorgfältig ['zɔekfɛltɪç]
carrots die Karotten *f pl* [di ka'ʀɔtn]
carry tragen [tʀaːgn]
cartoon der Zeichentrickfilm [de 'tsaɪçn tʀɪkfɪlm]
cash das Bargeld [das 'baːgɛlt]
cash: to pay (in) ~ bar zahlen ['baː tsaːln]

cashpoint der Geldautomat [de 'gɛltaʊto maːt]

casino das Spielkasino [das 'ʃpiːlka ziːno]

cassette die Kassette [di ka'sɛtə]

castle *(fortress)* die Burg [di bʊɐk]; *(palace)* das Schloss [das ʃlɔs]

cat die Katze [di 'katsə]

catch fangen [faŋŋ]; *(train)* kriegen [kriːgŋ]

cathedral die Kathedrale [di kate'draːlə]

cauliflower der Blumenkohl ['bluːmenkoːl]

cause die Ursache [di 'ʔuɐzaxə], der Anlass [de 'ʔanlas], der Grund [de grʊnt]; *(vb)* verursachen [fe'ʔuɐzaxn]

caution die Vorsicht [di 'foɐzɪçt]

cautious vorsichtig ['foɐzɪçtɪç]

cave die Höhle [di 'høːlə]

CD die CD [di tseː'deː]

CD player der CD-Spieler [de tseː'deːʃpiːlɐ]

ceiling die Decke [di 'dɛkə]

celebration(s) das Fest [das fɛst]

celeriac der Sellerie [de 'zɛləriː]

cemetery der Friedhof [de 'friːtoːf]

centimeter der Zentimeter [de ʦɛnti'meːtɐ]

central zentral [ʦɛn'traːl]

century das Jahrhundert [das ja'hʊndɐt]

ceramics die Keramik [di ke'raːmɪk]

certain *(adj)* gewiss [gə'vɪs], bestimmt [bə'ʃtɪmt], sicher ['zɪçɐ]; certainly *(adv)* gewiss [gə'vɪs], unbedingt ['ʔʊnbə'dɪŋt]

certificate das Attest [das ʔa'tɛst]

certify bescheinigen [bə'ʃaɪnɪgŋ]

chair der Stuhl [de ʃtuːl]

champagne der Champagner [de ʃam'panjɐ]

chance, by ~ zufällig ['tsuːfɛlɪç]

change der Wechsel [de vɛksl], die Veränderung [di fe'ʔɛndərʊŋ]; *(money)* das Wechselgeld [das 'vɛkslgɛlt]; *(vb)* verändern [fe'ʔɛndɐn]; *(money)* wechseln [(gɛlt) vɛksln], umtauschen ['ʔʊmtaʊʃn]; *(trains)* umsteigen ['ʔʊmʃtaɪgŋ]; *(clothes)* sich umziehen [zɪç 'ʔʊmtsiːn]; change the reservation umbuchen ['ʔʊmbuːxn]

changeable wechselhaft ['vɛkslhaft]

channel der Kanal [de ka'naːl]

chapel die Kapelle [di ka'pɛlə]

charcoal die Grillkohle [di 'grɪlkoːlə]

charming entzückend [ʔɛn'tsʏknt], bezaubernd [bə'tsaɪçnʊŋ]

cheap billig ['bɪlɪç]

check der Scheck [de ʃɛk]; *(vb)* kontrollieren [kɔntro'liːrən/-'liːen], nachprüfen ['naːxpryːfn], nachsehen ['naːxzeːn]; check in einchecken ['ʔaɪntʃɛkn]

cheeky unverschämt ['ʔʊnfeʃɛːmt]

cheese der Käse [de 'kɛːzə]

cherries die Kirschen *f pl* [di kɪrʃn]

chest die Brust [di brʊst]; *(box)* die Kiste [di 'kɪstə]

chicken das Hähnchen [das hɛːnçn]

chicken pox die Windpocken *f pl* [di 'vɪntpɔkn]

child das Kind [das kɪnt]; children *(pl)* die Kinder *n pl* [di 'kɪndɐ]

child seat der Kindersitz [de 'kɪndɐzɪts]

childhood disease die Kinderkrankheit [di 'kɪndɐ kraŋkhaɪt]

children's clothing die Kinderkleidung [di 'kɪndɐklaɪdʊŋ]

children's playground der Kinderspielplatz [de 'kɪndɐʃpiːlplats]

children's pool das Kinderbecken [das 'kɪndebɛkn]
children's portion der Kinderteller [de 'kɪndetɛle]
china das Porzellan [das pɔetsə'la:n]
chip card die Chipkarte [di 'tʃɪpka:tə]
chocolate die Schokolade [di ʃoko'la:də]
chocolate bar der Schokoriegel [de 'ʃo:koRi:gl]
choice die Auswahl [di '7ausva:l], die Wahl [di va:l]
choir der Chor [de koe]
choose wählen ['vɛ:ln]
chop das Kotelett ['kɔtlɛt]
Christian name der Vorname [de 'foena:mə]
Christianity das Christentum [das 'kRɪstntu:m]
Christmas Weihnachten ['vaɪnaxtn]
Christmas Eve Heiliger Abend ['haɪlɪgɐ '7a:bmt], Heiligabend [ʁhaɪlɪç '7a:bmt]
church die Kirche [di 'kɪɐçə]
cigar die Zigarre [di tsɪ'gaRə]
cigarette die Zigarette [di tsɪga'Rɛtə]
cigarillo das Zigarillo [das tsɪga'Rɪlo]
cinema das Kino [das 'ki:no]
circulatory disorder die Kreislaufstörung [di 'kRaɪslaʊf ʃtøːRʊŋ]
circus der Zirkus [de 'tsɪɐkʊs]
city center das Stadtzentrum [das 'ʃtattsɛntRʊm]
city map der Stadtplan [de 'ʃtatpla:n]
class die Klasse [di 'klasə]
classic film der Klassiker [de 'klasɪkɐ]
classical die Klassik [di 'klasɪk]
classicism der Klassizismus [de klasɪ'tsɪsmʊs]

clean sauber ['zaʊbɐ]; *(washing)* frisch [fRɪʃ]; *(vb)* putzen [pʊtsn], reinigen ['Raɪnɪgn]
clear klar [kla:]; *(weather)* heiter ['haɪtɐ]
clearance sale der Ausverkauf [de '7ausfɐkaʊf]
clever klug [klu:k], schlau [ʃlaʊ]
cliff die Klippe [di 'klɪpə]
climate das Klima [das 'kli:ma:]
cloakroom die Garderobe [di ga'dRo:bə]
cloister der Kreuzgang [de 'kRɔɪtsgaŋ]
close *(vb)* schließen [ʃliːsn], zu-machen ['tsu:maxn]
closed geschlossen [gə'ʃlɔsn]
close (to) *(adj)* nahe (bei) ['na:(ə) baɪ]
cloth das Tuch [das tu:x]
clothes hook der Kleiderhaken [de 'klaɪdɐha:kn]
clothesline die Wäscheleine [di 'vɛʃəlaɪnə]
clothespins die Wäscheklammern *f pl* [di 'vɛʃəklamɐn]
clothing die Kleidung [di 'klaɪdʊŋ]
cloud die Wolke [di 'vɔlkə]
cloudy *(liquid)* trüb [tRy:p]; *(weather)* bewölkt [bə'vœlkt]
cloves die Nelken *f pl* [di nɛlkn]
club der Verein [de fɐ'7aɪn]
clubhouse das Clubhaus [das 'klʊphaʊs]
clutch die Kupplung [di 'kʊplʊŋ]
coast die Küste [di 'kʏstə]
coat der Mantel [de mantl]
coat hanger der Kleiderbügel [de 'klaɪdɐby:gl]
cobbler der Schuhmacher [de 'ʃu:maxɐ]
coconut die Kokosnuss [di 'ko:kosnʊs]
coffee der Kaffee [de 'kafe:/ka'fe:]
coffee machine die Kaffeemaschine [di 'kafemaʃi:nə]
coin die Münze [di 'mʏntsə]

cold die Erkältung [di ˀeˈkɛltʊŋ] , der Schnupfen [de ʃnʊpfn]; *(adj)* kalt [kalt]; be cold frieren [ˈfʀiːʀən/fʀien]

cold cuts der Aufschnitt [de ˀˀaʊfʃnɪt]

cold water kaltes Wasser [ˈvaːməs ˈvasɐ]

colic die Kolik [di ˈkoːlɪk]

collarbone das Schlüsselbein [das ˈʃlʏslbaɪn]

colleague der Kollege/die Kollegin [de koˈleːgə/di koˈleːgɪn]

collect sammeln [zamln]

collect call das R-Gespräch [das ˀˀɛɐgə ʃpʀɛːç]

collection (of mail) die Leerung [di ˈleːʀʊŋ]

collision der Zusammenstoß [de tsʊˈzammʃtoːs]

colored farbig [ˈfaʀbɪç]

colored pencil der Farbstift [de ˈfaːpʃtɪft]

coloring book das Malbuch [das ˈmaːlbuːx]

column die Säule [di ˈzɔɪlə]

comb der Kamm [de kam]; *(vb)* kämmen [kɛmm]

come kommen [kɔmm]; come back zurückkehren [tsʊˈʀʏkeːʀən/ -keen], wiederkommen [ˈviːdekɔmm]; come from stammen aus [ʃtamm ˀaʊs]; come in! herein! [heˈʀaɪn]

comedy die Komödie [di koˈmøːdiə]

comfortable bequem [bəˈkveːm], gemütlich [gəˈmyːtlɪç]

common *(adj)* gemeinsam [gəˈmaɪnza(ː)m]; gebräuchlich [gəˈbʀɔɪçlɪç], gewöhnlich [gəˈvøːnlɪç]

company die Firma [di ˈfɪʀmaː]; *(people)* die Gesellschaft [di gəˈzɛlʃaft]

compartment das Abteil [das ˀapˈtaɪl]

compass der Kompass [de ˈkɔmpas]

compensation der Ersatz [de ˀeˈzats]; der Schadenersatz [de ˈʃaːdnˀe zats]

complete ganz [gants]; *(vb)* vollenden [fɔlˈˀɛndn]

composer der Komponist/ die Komponistin [de kɔmpoˈnɪst/ di kɔmpoˈnɪstɪn]

concert das Konzert [das kɔnˈtsɛɐt]

concussion die Gehirnerschütterung [di gəˈhɪʀnɐ ʃʏtəʀʊŋ]

condom das Kondom [das kɔnˈdoːm]

conductor der Dirigent/die Dirigentin [de diʀiˈgɛnt/di diʀiˈgɛntɪn]

confidence das Vertrauen [das feˈtʀaʊn]

confirm bestätigen [bəˈʃtɛːtɪgn]

congratulate gratulieren [gʀatʊˈliːʀən/-ˈlien]

congratulations der Glückwunsch [de ˈglʏkvʊnʃ]

connection der Anschluss [de ˀˀanʃlʊs], die Verbindung [di feˈbɪndʊŋ]

consist of bestehen aus [ˈbəˈʃteːn ˀaʊs]

constipation die Verstopfung [di feˈʃtɔpfʊŋ]

consulate das Konsulat [das kɔnzʊˈlaːt]

contact der Kontakt [de kɔnˈtakt], die Berührung [di bəˈʀyːʀʊŋ]

contagious ansteckend [ˀˀanʃtɛknt]

container der Behälter [de bəˈhɛltə], das Gefäß [das gəˈfɛːs]

contents der Inhalt [de ˀˀɪnhalt]

contest der Wettkampf [de ˈvɛtkamf]

contract der Vertrag [de feˈtʀaːk]

contrary das Gegenteil [das ˈgeːgntaɪl]

control *(vb)* kontrollieren [kɔntʀoˈliːʀən/-ˈlien]

convent das (Nonnen)Kloster [das ('nɔnn) klo:stɐ]

conversation das Gespräch [das gə'ʃprɛːç], die Unterhaltung [di ʔʊntɐ'haltʊŋ]

cook der Koch/die Köchin [de kɔx/di 'khœxɪn]; (vb) kochen [kɔxn]; zubereiten ['tsu:bəraɪtn]

cookbook das Kochbuch [das 'kɔxbu:x]

cooked gar [ga:]

cooked ham gekochter Schinken [gə'kɔxtɐ ʃɪŋkn]

cooker der Herd [de heet]; der Kocher [de 'kɔxɐ]

cool frisch [frɪʃ], kühl [ky:l]

cooling water das Kühlwasser [das 'ky:lvasɐ]

copy die Kopie [di ko'pi:]

corkscrew der Korkenzieher [de 'kɔɐkn̩tsi:ɐ]

corner die Ecke [di ʔ'ɛkɐ], der Winkel [de 'vɪŋkl]

corridor der Gang [de gaŋ]

corrupt verdorben [fɐ'dɔɐbm], bestechlich [bə'ʃtɛçlɪç]

cost die Kosten pl [di kɔstn]; (vb) kosten [kɔstn]

costume jewelry der Modeschmuck [de 'mo:dəʃmʊk]

cottage die Hütte [di 'hʏtə]

cotton die Baumwolle [di 'baʊmvɔlə]

cotton swabs das Wattestäbchen [das 'vatəʃtɛ:pçn]

cotton wool die Watte [di 'vatə]

cough der Husten [de hu:stn]

cough mixture/syrup der Hustensaft [de 'hu:stnzaft]

count (vb) zählen [tsɛ:ln]

country das Land [das lant]; native country das Vaterland [das 'fa:tɐlant]; fellow countryman der Landsmann [de 'lantsman]

country road die Landstraße [di 'lantʃtra:sə]

couple das Paar [das pa:]; (married) das Ehepaar [das ʔ'e:əpa:]

course der Kurs [de kʊɐs]; (meal) der Gang [de gaŋ]; of course selbstverständlich [zɛlp(st)fɐ'ʃtɛntlɪç]; natürlich [na'tyɐlɪç]

cousin der Cousin/die Cousine [de kʊ'zɛŋ/di kʊ'zi:nə]

cozy gemütlich [gə'my:tlɪç]

crab der Krebs [de kre:ps]

cramp der Krampf [de krampf]

crash der Zusammenstoß [de tsu'zammʃto:s]

crash helmet der Sturzhelm [de 'ʃtʊɐtshɛlm]

crazy verrückt [fɐ'rʏkt]

cream die Creme [di krɛːm]; (cook) die Sahne [di 'za:nə]

creative kreativ [krea'ti:f]

credit card die Kreditkarte [di kredi:tka:tə]

crew die Mannschaft [di 'manʃaft]

crib das Kinderbett [das 'kɪndɐbɛt]

crime das Verbrechen [das fɐ'brɛçn]

crockery das Geschirr [das gə'ʃɪɐ]

cross das Kreuz [das krɔɪts]; (adj) ärgerlich [ʔ'ɛɐgɐlɪç]; (vb) überqueren [ʔ'y:bɐ'kve:rən/-'kveɐn], überschreiten [ʔ'y:bɐ'ʃraɪtn]

crossing der Übergang [de ʔ'y:bɐgaŋ]

crowded voll [fɔl]

crown die Krone [di 'kro:nə]

crutch die Krücke [di 'krʏkə]

cry (vb) weinen [vaɪnn]

crystal der Kristall [de krɪs'tal]

cubicle die Kabine [di ka'bi:nə]

cucumber die Gurke [di 'gʊɐkə]

culture die Kultur [di kʊl'tuɐ]

cup die Tasse [di 'tasə]

curious neugierig ['nɔɪgi:rɪç]

curlers die Lockenwickler m pl [di 'lɔknvɪklɐ]

curling das Curling [das 'kə:lɪŋ]

curls die Locken f pl [di lɔkn]

currency die Währung [di 'vɛ:rʊŋ]

current *(electricity)* der Strom [de ʃtro:m]; *(water)* die Strömung [di 'ʃtrø:mʊn]
curve die Kurve [di 'kʊevə]
customer der Kunde/die Kundin [de 'kʊndə/di 'kʊndɪn]
customs der Zoll [de tsɔl]
customs declaration die Zoll-erklärung [di 'tsɔlɛklɛ:ʀʊn]
cut die Schnittwunde [di 'ʃnɪtvʊndə]; *(vb)* schneiden [ʃnaɪdn]
cutlery das Besteck [das bə'ʃtɛk]
cutlet das Kotelett [das 'kɔtlɛt]
cycle path der Fahrradweg [de 'fa:ʀatve:k]
cycling der Radsport [de 'ʀa:tʃpɔet]

D

daily täglich [tɛ:klɪç]
damage die Beschädigung [di bə'ʃɛ:dɪgʊn], der Schaden [de ʃa:dn]; *(vb)* beschädigen [bə'ʃɛ:dɪgn], schaden [ʃa:dn]
damp feucht [fɔɪçt]
dance der Tanz [de tants]; *(vb)* tanzen [tantsn]
dance band die Tanzkapelle [di 'tantska pɛlə]
dance theater das Tanztheater [das 'tantste ʔa:te]
dancer der Tänzer/die Tänzerin [de tɛntsɐ/di tɛntsə'ʀɪn]
dandruff die Schuppen *f pl* [di ʃʊpm]
danger die Gefahr [di gə'fa:]
dangerous gefährlich [gə'feːlɪç]
dark dunkel [dʊnkl], finster ['fɪnste]
dark blue dunkelblau [dʊnkl'blaʊ]
dark (rye) bread das Schwarzbrot [das 'ʃva:tsbʀo:t]
darling der Liebling [de 'li:plɪn]

date das Datum [das 'da:tʊm]; *(meeting)* die Verabredung [di fe'ʔapʀe:dʊn]; **up to date** modern [mo'dɛen]
date of birth das Geburtsdatum [das gə'bʊetsda:tʊm]
daughter die Tochter [di 'tɔxte]
day der Tag [de ta:k]
day of arrival der Anreisetag [de 'ʔanʀaɪzə ta:k]
day pass der Tagespass [de 'ta:gəspas]
day ticket die Tageskarte [di 'ta:gəska:tə]
day trip der Tagesausflug [de 'ta:gəs ʔaʊsflu:k]
deadline der Termin [de tɛ'mi:n]
deaf gehörlos [gə'høelo:s], taub [taʊp]
deaf-mute *(adj)* taubstumm ['taʊpʃtʊm]
deaf person der/die Gehörlose [de/di gə'høelo:zə]
debt die Schuld [di ʃʊlt]
deceitful betrügerisch [bə'tʀy:gəʀɪʃ]
December Dezember [de'tsɛmbe]
decide entscheiden [ʔɛnt'ʃaɪdn], beschließen [bə'ʃli:sn]
deck das Deck [das dɛk]
declaration of value die Wert-angabe [di 'veetanga:bə]
decline *(vb)* ablehnen [ʔaple:nn]
deep tief [ti:f]
definite(ly) endgültig [ʔɛntgʏltɪç]
delay die Verspätung [di fe'ʃpɛ:tʊn]; *(vb)* verzögern [fe'tsø:gen]
delicatessen das Feinkostgeschäft [das 'faɪnkɔstgə ʃɛft]
delightful entzückend [ʔɛn'tsʏkn̩t]
denatured alcohol der Brenn-spiritus [de 'bʀɛn ʃpiʀɪtʊs]
deodorant das Deo [das 'deo]
department store das Kaufhaus [das 'kaʊfhaʊs]

departure die Abfahrt [di
ˈ⁷apfaːt], *(flight)* der Abflug [dɐ
ˈ⁷apfluːk]
deposit die Kaution [di
kaʊˈtsjoːn], *(on bottle)* das Pfand
[das (p)fant]; *(vb)* (Geld)
hinterlegen [(gɛlt) hɪntɐˈleːgn̩]
describe beschreiben [bəˈʃraɪbm̩]
dessert der Nachtisch [dɐ ˈnaːxtɪʃ]
destination das (Reise)Ziel [das
(ˈraɪzə-)tsiːl]
detergent *(clothes)* das
Waschmittel [das ˈvaʃmɪtl̩];
(dishes) das Spülmittel [das
ˈʃpyːlmɪtl̩]
detour der Umweg [dɐ ˈ⁷ʊmveːk]
develop entwickeln [ˀɛntˈvɪkln̩]
diabetes der Diabetes
[dɐ diaˈbeːtəs]
diabetic *(person)* der
Diabetiker/die Diabetikerin
[dɐ diaˈbeːtɪkɐ/di diaˈbeːtɪkərɪn];
(adj) diabetisch [diaˈbeːtɪʃ]
diagnosis die Diagnose
[di diaˈgnoːzə]
dial *(vb)* wählen [ˈvɛːln̩]
diapers die Windeln *f pl*
[di vɪndln̩]
diarrhea der Durchfall
[dɐ ˈdʊɐçfal]
diet die Diät [di diˈɛːt], *(food)* die
Schonkost [di ˈʃoːnkɔst]
different(ly) verschieden
[fɐˈʃiːdn̩], anders [ˈ⁷andɐs]
difficult schwierig [ˈʃviːrɪç],
schwer [ʃveːɐ]
difficulty in breathing die
Atembeschwerden *f pl* [di
ˈ⁷aːtmbəʃveːɐdn̩]
digestion die Verdauung
[di fɐˈdaʊʊŋ]
digital camera die Digitalkamera
[di digiˈtaːl kaməra]
dimmed headlights das
Abblendlicht [das ˈ⁷apblɛntlɪçt]
dining room *(hotel)* der
Speisesaal [dɐ ˈʃpaɪzəzaːl]; *(private)*
das Esszimmer [das ˈ⁷ɛstsɪmɐ]

dinner das Abendessen [das
ˈ⁷aːbmtˀɛsn̩]
diphtheria die Diphtherie
[di dɪftəˈriː]
direct direkt [diˈrɛkt]
directed by die Regie [di raˈʒiː]
direction *(way)* die Richtung
[di ˈrɪçtʊŋ]
dirty schmutzig [ˈʃmʊtsɪç]
disability die Behinderung
[di bəˈhɪndərʊŋ]
disabled person der/die
Behinderte [dɐ/di bəˈhɪndɐtə]
disappointed enttäuscht
[ˀɛnˈtɔɪʃt]
discotheque die Diskothek
[di dɪskoˈteːk]
discount der Rabatt [dɐ raˈbat]
discover entdecken [ˀɛntˈdɛkn̩]
dish *(meal)* das Gericht [das
gəˈrɪçt]
dish of the day das Tagesgericht
[das ˈtaːgəsgərɪçt]
dishcloth das Spültuch [das
ˈʃpyːltuːx]
dishwasher die Geschirrspülmaschine [di gəˈʃɪrʃpyːlma ʃinə]
dishwashing brush die
Spülbürste [di ˈʃpyːlbʏrstə]
disinfect desinfizieren
[dezɪnfɪˈtsiːrən]
disinfectant das Desinfektionsmittel [das dezɪnfɛkˈtsjoːnsmɪtl̩]
distance der Abstand [dɐ
ˈ⁷apʃtant], die Entfernung
[di ˀɛntˈfɛɐnʊŋ], die Strecke [di
ˈʃtrɛkə]
distinct deutlich [ˈdɔɪtlɪç]
distinguished fein [faɪn],
vornehm [ˈfoɐneːm]
district die Gegend [di ˈgeːgnt],
der Stadtteil [dɐ ˈʃtataɪl]
disturb stören [ˈʃtøɐn]
dive tauchen [taʊxn̩]
diving equipment die
Taucherausrüstung [di
ˈtaʊxɐˀaʊsrʏstʊŋ]
diving goggles die Taucherbrille
[di ˈtaʊxɐbrɪlə]

dizziness das Schwindelgefühl [das ˈʃvɪndlgəfyːl]
do tun [tuːn], machen [ˈmaxn]
dock at anlegen in [ˈʔanleːgn ˈʔɪn]
documentary der Dokumentarfilm [de dɔkʊmɛnˈtaːfɪlm]
documents die Papiere n pl [di paˈpiːrə]
dog der Hund [de hʊnt]
dome die Kuppel [di kʊpl]
domestic flight der Inlandsflug [de ˈʔɪnlantsfluːk]
done (cooked) gar [gaː]
door die Tür [di tyɐ]
door code der Türcode [de ˈtyɐkoːt]
door opener der Türöffner [de ˈtyɐˀœfnɐ]
door width die Türbreite [di ˈtyɐbraɪtə]
doorstep die Türschwelle [di ˈtyɐʃvɛlə]
double doppelt [dɔplt]
doubles das Doppel [das dɔpl]
drama das Drama [das ˈdʀaːma]
draw zeichnen [ˈtsaɪçnn]; (sport) unentschieden spielen [ˈʔʊnɛnt ʃiːdn ʃpiːln]
drawing die Zeichnung [di ˈtsaɪçnʊŋ]
dreadful schrecklich [ˈʃʀɛklɪç], fürchterlich [ˈfʏrçtəlɪç]
dream der Traum [de tʀaʊm]; (vb) träumen [tʀɔɪmm]
dress das Kleid [das klaɪt]; (vb) sich anziehen [zɪç ˈʔantsiːn]; (med.) verbinden [fɛˈbɪndn]
dressing (med) der Verband [de fɛˈbant]; (cook) das Dressing [das ˈdʀɛsɪŋ]
dressmaker der Schneider/die Schneiderin [de ˈʃnaɪdɐ/di ˈʃnaɪdərɪn]
drink das Getränk [das gəˈtʀɛŋk]; (vb) trinken [tʀɪŋkn]
drinking water das Trinkwasser [das ˈtʀɪŋkvasɐ]

dripstone cave die Tropfsteinhöhle [di ˈtʀɔpfʃtaɪn høːlə]
drive die Fahrt [di faːt]; (vb) fahren [faː(ʀə)n]; **drive a car** Auto fahren [ˈʔaʊtoˈfaːn]; **drive back** zurückfahren [tsʊˈʀʏkfaː(ʀə)n]
drive-in movie das Freilichtkino [das ˈfʀaɪlɪçtkiːno]
driver der Chauffeur [de ʃɔˈføø], der Fahrer/die Fahrerin [de ˈfaːʀə/di ˈfaːʀərɪn]
driver's license der Führerschein [de ˈfyːʀəʃaɪn]
drops die Tropfen m pl [di ˈtʀɔpfn]
drunk betrunken [bəˈtʀʊŋkn]
dry trocken [ˈtʀɔkŋ]; (wine) herb [hɛɐp], trocken [ˈtʀɔkŋ]
dry-clean chemisch reinigen [ˈçeːmɪʃ ˈʀaɪnɪgn]
drycleaner's die Reinigung [di ˈʀaɪnɪgʊŋ]
durable haltbar [ˈhaltbaː]
during während [ˈveːʀənt]
during the day tagsüber [ˈtaːksˀyːbɐ]
during the morning vormittags [ˈfoɐmɪtaːks]
dust der Staub [de ʃtaʊp]
duty die Zollgebühren f pl [di ˈtsɔlgəbyːʀən]
duty-free zollfrei [ˈtsɔlfʀaɪ]
duty-free shop zollfreier Laden [ˈtsɔlfʀaɪɐ laːdn]
dye (vb) färben [fɛɐbm]
dynamo die Lichtmaschine [di ˈlɪçtmaʃiːnə]
dynasty die Dynastie [di dʏnasˈtiː]

E

each jede(r, s) [ˈjeːdə(-de, -dəs)]
ear das Ohr [das ˀoɐ]
eardrops die Ohrentropfen m pl [di ˈʔoːʀəntʀɔpfn]

eardrum das Trommelfell [das 'tʀɔmlfɛl]

earrings die Ohrringe *m pl* [di ʔoːʀɪŋə]

earth die Erde [di ʔeɐdə]

east der Osten [dɐ ʔɔstn]

Easter Monday Ostermontag [ʁʔoːstɐ'moːntaːk]

easy leicht [laɪçt]

eat essen [ʔɛsn]

edible essbar [ʔɛsbaː]

education die Erziehung [di ʔeˈtsiːʊŋ], die Ausbildung [di ʔaʊsbɪldʊŋ]

eel der Aal [dɐ ʔaːl]

eggplants die Auberginen *f pl* [di ʔobeˈʒiːnn]

eggs die Eier *n pl* [di ʔaɪɐ]

Eire Irland [ʔɪʀlant]

either ... or entweder ... oder [ʔɛntveːdɐ ... ʔoːdɐ]

elastic bandage die Elastikbinde [di ʔeˈlastɪkbɪndə]

electric elektrisch [ʔeˈlɛktʀɪʃ]

electric wheelchair der E-Rollstuhl [dɐ ʔeː ʀɔlʃtuːl]

elevator der Fahrstuhl [dɐ ˈfaːʃtuːl], der Aufzug [dɐ ʔaʊftsuːk], der Lift [dɐ lɪft]

elsewhere anderswo [ʔandɛsvoː]

embassy die Botschaft [di ˈboːtʃaft]

emblem das Wahrzeichen [das ˈvaːtsaɪçn]

emergency der Notfall [dɐ ˈnoːtfal]

emergency brake die Handbremse [di ˈhantbʀɛmzə]

emergency exit der Notausgang [dɐ ˈnoːtʔaʊsɡaŋ]

emergency road service der Pannendienst [dɐ ˈpanndiːnst]

emergency telephone die Notrufsäule [di ˈnoːtʀufzɔɪlə]

empty leer [leɐ]

enclosure *(letter)* die Anlage [di ʔanlaːɡə]

end das Ende [das ʔɛndə], der Schluss [dɐ ʃlʊs]

engaged *(telephone)* besetzt [bəˈzɛtst]

engine der Motor [dɐ ˈmoːtoɐ]

England England [ʔɛŋlant]

English englisch [ʔɛŋlɪʃ]; Englishman/-woman der Engländer/die Engländerin [dɐ ʔɛŋlɛndɐ/di ʔɛŋlɛndəʀɪn]

enjoy genießen [ɡəˈniːsn]

enough genug [ɡəˈnuːk]

entertainment die Unterhaltung [di ʔʊntɐˈhaltʊŋ]

enthusiastic (about) begeistert (von) [bəˈɡaɪstɐt fɔn]

entire ganz [ɡants]

entrance die Einfahrt [di ʔaɪnfaːt], der Eingang [dɐ ʔaɪŋaŋ]; der Zugang [dɐ ˈtsuːɡaŋ], *(fee)* der Eintritt [dɐ ʔaɪntʀɪt]

envelope der Briefumschlag [dɐ ˈbʀiːfʊmʃlaːk]

environment die Umwelt [di ʔʊmvɛlt]

epilepsy die Epilepsie [di epilɛpsi]

epoch die Epoche [di ʔeˈpɔxə]

esophagus die Speiseröhre [di ˈʃpaɪzəʀøːʀə]

especially hauptsächlich [ˈhaʊptzɛçlɪç], besonders [bəˈzɔndɐs]

estate das Landgut [das ˈlantɡuːt]

etching die Radierung [di ʀaˈdiːʀʊŋ]

EU citizen EU-Bürger/EU-Bürgerin [ʔeʔuː bʏɐɡe/ʔeʔuː bʏɐɡəʀɪn]

euro der Euro [dɐ ʔɔɪʀo]

Europe Europa [ʔɔɪʀoːpaː]

European der Europäer/die Europäerin [dɐ ʔɔɪʀoˈpɛːɐ/di ʔɔɪʀoˈpɛːəʀɪn]; europäisch [ʔɔɪʀoˈpɛːɪʃ]

evening der Abend [dɐ ʔaːbmt]; in the evening abends [ʔaːbms]

event das Ereignis [das ʔeʔaɪknɪs], die Veranstaltung [di fɐʔanʃtaltʊŋ]

every jede(r, s) [ˈjeːdə(-dɐ, -dəs)]

every day jeden Tag [jeːdn taːk]

every hour stündlich ['ʃtʏntlɪç]
everybody jedermann ['je:dəman]
everything alles ['ʔaləs]
everywhere überall ['ʔybɐ'ʔal]
evil böse ['bø:zə]
exact(ly) genau [gə'naʊ]
examination die Untersuchung
[di ʔʊntɐ'zu:xʊŋ]
example das Beispiel [das
'baɪʃpi:l]; **for example** zum
Beispiel [tsʊm 'baɪʃpi:l]
excavations die Ausgrabungen *f*
pl [di 'ʔaʊsgʀa:bʊŋŋ]
excellent ausgezeichnet
['ʔaʊsgə'tsaɪçnət]
except außer ['ʔaʊsə]
exchange der Austausch
[dɐ 'ʔaʊstaʊʃ], der Wechsel [dɐ
vɛksl]; *(vb)* tauschen [taʊʃn],
austauschen ['ʔaʊstaʊʃn]
exchange rate der Wechselkurs
[dɐ 'vɛkslkʊɐs]
excursion der Ausflug
[dɐ 'ʔaʊsflu:k], die Tour [di tuɐ]
excuse die Entschuldigung
[di ʔɛnt'ʃʊldɪgʊŋ]; *(vb)*
entschuldigen ['ʔɛnt'ʃʊldɪgŋ]
exhaust der Auspuff [dɐ 'ʔaʊspʊf]
exhausted erschöpft ['ʔe'ʃœpft]
exhibit das Exponat [das
ʔɛkspo'na:t]
exhibition die Ausstellung
[di 'ʔaʊʃtɛlʊŋ]
exit der Ausgang [dɐ 'ʔaʊsgaŋ];
(freeway) die (Autobahn)Ausfahrt
[di ('ʔaʊtoba:n-) ʁ'aʊsfa:t]
expect erwarten ['ʔe'va:tn]
expensive kostspielig
['kɔs(t)ʃpi:lɪç], teuer ['tɔɪə]
experienced erfahren
['ʔe'fa:(ʀə)n]
explicit(ly) ausdrücklich
['ʔaʊsdʀʏklɪç]
expression der Ausdruck
[dɐ 'ʔaʊsdʀʊk]
expressionism der
Expressionismus [dɐ
ʔɛkspʀɛsjo'nɪsmʊs]

expressway die Autobahn
[di 'ʔaʊtoba:n]
extend verlängern [fɐ'lɛŋɐn]
extension cord die
Verlängerungsschnur [di
fɐ'lɛŋɐʀʊŋ ʃnuɐ]
extra extra ['ʔɛkstʀa:]
extraordinary außergewöhnlich
[ʁ'aʊsɐgə'vø:nlɪç]
eye das Auge [das 'ʔaʊgə]
eyedrops die Augentropfen *m pl*
[di 'ʔaʊgŋtʀɔpfn]

façade die Fassade [di fa'sa:də]
factory die Fabrik [di fa'bʀi(:)k]
faint *(vb)* in Ohnmacht fallen ['ʔɪn
'ʔo:nmaxt faln]
fair *(fête)* die Kirmes [di 'kɪɐməs];
(exhibition) die Messe [di 'mɛsə];
(adj) gerecht [gə'ʀɛçt], fair [fɛɐ];
(weather) schön [ʃø:n]
fair der Jahrmarkt [dɐ 'ja:ma:kt]
fairly ziemlich ['tsi:mlɪç]
fall der Sturz [dɐ ʃtʊɐts]; der
Herbst [dɐ 'hɛɐpst]; *(vb)* stürzen
[ʃtʏɐtsn], fallen [faln]
family die Familie [di fa'mi:ljə]
famous berühmt [bə'ʀy:mt]
fan der Ventilator [dɐ vɛnti'la:toɐ]
far weit [vaɪt]
fare der Fahrpreis [dɐ 'fa:pʀaɪs]
farm der Bauernhof [dɐ
'baʊɐnho:f]
fashion die Mode [di 'mo:də]
fast schnell [ʃnɛl]
fat fett [fɛt]; *(person)* dick [dɪk]
father der Vater [dɐ 'fa:tɐ]
fault der Fehler [dɐ 'fe:lɐ], der
Mangel [dɐ maŋl], der Defekt
[dɐ de'fɛkt]
fear die Angst [di 'ʔaŋst], die
Furcht [di fʊɐçt]; *(vb)* fürchten
[fʏɐçtn], befürchten [bə'fʏɐçtn]
February Februar ['fe:bʀʊa:]
feeble schwach [ʃvax]

ENGLISH – GERMAN DICTIONARY

269

feel fühlen [fy:ln]
feeling das Gefühl [das gə'fy:l]
fees die Gebühren *f pl* [di gə'by:rən/ -'byɐn]
fennel der Fenchel [dɐ fɛnçl]
ferry die Fähre [di 'fɛ:rə]
festival das Festival [das 'fɛstɪval]
fever das Fieber [das 'fi:bɐ]
few wenig ['ve:nɪç]; **a few** ein paar [(ʔaɪ)n 'pa:]
fiancé/fiancée der/die Verlobte [dɐ/di fɛ'lo:ptə]
field das Feld [das fɛlt]
figure die Nummer [di 'nʊmɐ], die Zahl [di tsa:l]
fill in ausfüllen ['ʔaʊsfvln]
fill up tanken [taŋkn]
filled rolls belegte Brötchen [bə'le:ktə brø:tçn]
filling *(med.)* die Plombe [di 'plɔmbə]
film der Film [dɐ fɪlm]
film actor/actress der Filmschauspieler/die Filmschauspielerin [dɐ 'fɪlmʃaʊʃpi:lɐ/di 'fɪlmʃaʊʃpi:lərɪn]
film speed die Filmempfindlichkeit [di 'fɪlmɛmpfɪntlɪçkaɪt]
finally zuletzt [tsʊ'lɛtst], endlich ['ʔɛntlɪç]
find finden [fɪndn]
fine *(punishment)* die Strafe [di 'ʃtra:fə], die Geldstrafe [di 'gɛltʃtra:fə]; *(thin)* fein [faɪn]
finger der Finger [dɐ 'fɪŋɐ]
fire das Feuer [das 'fɔɪɐ], der Brand [dɐ brant]
fire alarm der Feuermelder [dɐ 'fɔɪɐmɛldɐ]
fire extinguisher der Feuerlöscher [dɐ 'fɔɪɐ lø ʃɐ]
firewood das Brennholz [das 'brɛnhɔlts]
fireworks display das Feuerwerk [das 'fɔɪɐvɛɐk]
firm die Firma [di 'fɪrma:], das Unternehmen [das 'ʔʊntɐ'ne:mm]; *(adj)* fest [fɛst]

first erste(r, -s) ['ʔeɐstə (-tɐ, -təs)]; **first (of all)** zunächst [tsʊ'nɛ:çst/ -'nɛ:kst]; **(at) first** zuerst [tsʊ'ʔeɐst]
first name der Vorname [dɐ 'foɐna:mə]
fish dealer's das Fischgeschäft [das 'fɪʃgəʃɛft]
fishbone die Gräte [di 'grɛ:tə]
fishing license der Angelschein [dɐ 'ʔaŋlʃaɪn]
fishing port der Fischerhafen [dɐ 'fɪʃeha:fn]
fishing rod die Angel [di 'ʔaŋl]
fit der Anfall [dɐ 'ʔanfal]; *(adj)* fit [fɪt]; *(vb)* passen [pasn]
fitness center das Fitnesscenter [das 'fɪtnəs tsɛntɐ]
flash das Blitzgerät [das 'blɪtsgərɛ:t]
flat *(flat tire)* (Reifen)Panne [('raɪfn) panə]; *(adj)* eben [ʔe:bm]
flat rate der Pauschalpreis [dɐ paʊ'ʃa:lpraɪs]
flat rate for electricity die Strompauschale [di 'ʃtro:mpaʊ ʃa:lə]
flea market der Flohmarkt [dɐ 'flo:ma:kt]
fleece das (Schafs)Fell [das ('ʃa:fs-)fɛl]
flight der Flug [dɐ flu:k]
flight attendant der Steward/die Stewardess [dɐ 'stjua:t/di: 'stjuadɛs]
flip-flops die Badeschuhe *m pl* [di 'ba:dəʃuə]
floor der Boden [dɐ bo:dn]; *(story)* das Stockwerk [das 'ʃtɔkvɛɐk]
florist's das Blumengeschäft [das 'blu:mmgəʃɛft]
flour das Mehl [das me:l]
flower die Blume [di 'blu:mə]
flu die Grippe [di 'grɪpə]
fly die Fliege [di 'fli:gə]; *(vb)* fliegen [fli:gn]
fog der Nebel [dɐ 'ne:bl]

folding wheelchair der
Faltrollstuhl [dɐ 'falt ʀɔlʃtuːl]
fond, be ~ of s.o. jdn lieb haben
[ʁjemandn 'liːp haːbm]
food das Essen [das ᵊ'ɛsn], das
Lebensmittel [das 'leːbmsmɪtl]
food poisoning die
Lebensmittelvergiftung [di
'leːbmsmɪtlfɐ gɪftʊŋ]
food store das
Lebensmittelgeschäft [das
'leːbmsmɪtlgə ʃɛft]
foot der Fuß [dɐ fuːs]
for für [fyɐ]; *(time)* seit [zaɪt];
(reason) denn [dɛn]
foreign fremd [fʀɛmt],
ausländisch [ᵊ'aʊslɛndɪʃ]
foreigner der Ausländer/
die Ausländerin [dɐ ᵊ'aʊslɛndɐ/
di ᵊ'aʊslɛndəʀɪn]; der/die Fremde
[dɐ/di 'fʀɛmdə]
forest der Wald [dɐ valt]
forget vergessen [fɐ'gɛsn]
fork die Gabel [di 'gaːbl]
form die Form [di fɔɐm]; *(paper)*
das Formular [das fɔmʊ'laː]; *(vb)*
bilden [bɪldn]
fortress die Festung [di 'fɛstʊŋ]
forward(s) vorwärts [ˈfɔɐvɛɐts];
look forward to sich freuen auf
[zɪç 'fʀɔɪn ᵊaʊf]
fountain der (Spring)Brunnen
[dɐ (ˈʃpʀɪŋ)bʀʊnn]
fracture der Knochenbruch
[dɐ 'knɔxnbʀʊx]
fraud der Betrug [dɐ bə'tʀuːk]
free gratis ['gʀaːtɪs], frei [fʀaɪ],
kostenlos ['kɔstnloːs], umsonst
[ᵊʊm'zɔnst]
freeway die Autobahn
[di ᵊ'aʊtobaːn]
freeway toll die Autobahngebühren [di ᵊ'aʊtobaːngə byːʀən]
freeze *(vb)* frieren ['fʀiːʀən/fʀiɐn]
French französisch [fʀan'tsøːzɪʃ]
frequently häufig ['hɔɪfɪç]
fresh frisch [fʀɪʃ]
Friday Freitag ['fʀaɪtaːk]

fridge der Kühlschrank
[dɐ 'kyːlʃʀaŋk]
friend der Freund/die Freundin
[dɐ fʀɔɪnt/'di fʀɔɪndɪn], der/die
Bekannte [dɐ/di bə'kantə]; be
friends befreundet sein
[bə'fʀɔɪndət zaɪn]
friendly freundlich ['fʀɔɪntlɪç]
frighten erschrecken [ᵊɐ'ʃʀɛkn]
from ab [ᵊap]; von [fɔn], aus
[ᵊaʊs]
front, in ~ vorn [fɔɐn]; in front
of vor [foɐ]
frost der Frost [dɐ fʀɔst]
fruit das Obst [das ᵊoːpst]
fruit and vegetable store der
Obst- und Gemüsehändler
[dɐ ᵊoːpst ᵊʊnt gə'myːzəhɛntlɐ]
full voll [fɔl]
**fully comprehensive
insurance** die Vollkasko [di
'fɔlkasko]
fun der Spaß [dɐ ʃpaːs]
fungal infection der Pilz
[dɐ pɪlts]
funicular die (Stand)Seilbahn
[di (ʃtant) zaɪlbaːn]
funny lustig ['lʊstɪç]
fur das Fell [das fɛl], der Pelz
[dɐ pɛlts]
furious wütend [vyːtnt]
furniture die Möbel *n pl*
[di møːbl]
fuse *(electricity)* die Sicherung
[di 'zɪçəʀʊŋ]
future die Zukunft [di 'tsuːkʊnft];
(adj) zukünftig ['tsuːkʏnftɪç]

G

gable der Giebel [dɐ giːbl]
gadget der Apparat [dɐ ᵊapa'ʀaːt]
gale der Sturm [dɐ ʃtʊɐm]
gallbladder die Gallenblase
[di 'galnblaːzə]
gallery die Galerie [di galə'ʀiː]
game das Spiel [das ʃpiːl]

garage die Garage [di ga'ʀa:ʒə]; *(for repairs)* die Werkstatt [di 'vɛɛkʃtat]

garbage der Müll [de mʏl]

garbage can die Mülltonne [di 'mʏltɔnə]

garden der Garten [de ga:tn]

garlic der Knoblauch [de 'kno:blaʊx]

gas can der Benzinkanister [de bɛn'tsi:nka nɪste]

gas canister die Gasflasche [di ga:sflaʃə]

gas cartridge die Gaskartusche [di 'ga:ska tʊʃə]

gas pedal das Gaspedal [das 'ga:speda:l]

gas pump die Benzinpumpe [di bɛn'tsi:npʊmpə]

gas tank der Tank [de taŋk]

gate das Tor [das toe]; *(airport)* der Flugsteig [de 'flu:kʃtaɪg]

gauze bandage die Mullbinde [di 'mʊlbɪndə]

gear der Gang [de gaŋ]

generator die Lichtmaschine [di 'lɪçtmaʃi:nə]

gentleman der Herr [de hɛe]

Gentlemen Herren ['hɛʀən]

genuine echt [ʔɛçt]

German der/die Deutsche [de/di 'dɔɪtʃə]; *(adj)* deutsch [dɔɪtʃ]

German measles die Röteln *f pl* [di ʀø:tln]

Germany Deutschland ['dɔɪtʃlant]

get *(receive)* bekommen [bə'kɔmm], kriegen [kʀi:gn]; *(obtain)* besorgen [bə'zɔɛgn]; *(fetch)* holen [ho:ln]; get in/on einsteigen ['ʔaɪnʃtaɪgn]; get up aufstehen ['ʔaʊfʃte:n]

gift das Geschenk [das gə'ʃɛŋk]

girl das Mädchen [das 'mɛ:tçn]

give geben [ge:bm]; give back wiedergeben ['vi:dege:bm], zurückgeben [tsʊ'ʀʏkge:bm]

glad froh [fʀo:]; glad (of) erfreut (über) [ʔeˈfʀɔɪt (ʔy:be)]

gladly gern [gɛɐn]

glass das Glas [das gla:s]

glass painting die Glasmalerei [di 'gla:smaːlə ʀaɪ]

gliding das Segelfliegen [das 'ze:glfli:gn]

glorious herrlich ['hɛɐlɪç]

gloves die Handschuhe *m pl* [di 'hantʃu:ə]

gnat die Mücke [di 'mʏkə]

go gehen [ge:n], fahren [fa:(ʀə)n], reisen [ʀaɪzn]; go away weggehen ['vɛk(g)e:n]; go out hinausgehen [hɪ'naʊsge:n]; *(in the evening)* ausgehen ['ʔaʊsge:n]

go fishing angeln ['ʔaŋln]

go ice skating Schlittschuh laufen ['ʃlɪtʃu: laʊfn]

goal das Tor [das toe]

goalkeeper der Torwart [de 'toɛva:t]

God der Gott [de gɔt]

gold das Gold [das 'gɔlt]

gold work die Goldschmiedekunst [di 'gɔltʃmi:də kʊnst]

golf das Golf [das gɔlf]

golf club *(implement)* der Golfschläger [de 'gɔlfʃlɛ:ge]; *(establishment)* der Golfclub ['gɔlfklʊp]

good gut [gu:t]

Good Friday Karfreitag [ka:'fʀaɪta:k]

goodbye auf Wiedersehen [ʔaʊf 'vi(:)deze:n]; say goodbye Abschied nehmen ['ʔapʃi:t ne:mm], sich verabschieden [zɪç fe'ʔapʃi:dn]

Gothic die Gotik [di 'go:tik]

government die Regierung [di ʀe'gi:ʀʊŋ]

gram(s) das Gramm [das gʀam]

grandfather der Großvater [de 'gʀo:sfa:te]

grandmother die Großmutter [di 'gʀo:smʊte]

grapes die Weintrauben *f pl* [di 'vaɪntʀaʊbm]

272

graphic arts die Grafik
[di 'ɡʀa:fɪk]

grass das Gras [das ɡʀa:s]; *(lawn)*
der Rasen [dɐ ʀa:zn]

grave das Grab [das ɡʀa:p]

graveyard der Friedhof
[dɐ 'fʀi:to:f]

gravy die (Braten)Soße [di
('bʀa:tn)zo:sə]

great großartig ['ɡʀo:s(ʔ)a:tɪç],
prima ['pʀi:ma:]; *(important)* groß
[ɡʀo:s]

Greek der Grieche/die Griechin
['ɡʀi:çə/'ɡʀi:çɪn]; *(adj)* griechisch
['ɡʀi:çɪʃ]

green grün [ɡʀy:n]

green beans grüne Bohnen
[ʁɡʀy:nə 'bo:nn]

green card die grüne
Versicherungskarte [di 'ɡry:nə
fɛ'zɪçəʀʊŋska:tə]

greengrocer's der Obst- und
Gemüsehändler [dɐ ʔo:pst ʔʊnt
ɡə'my:zəhɛntlɐ]

greet begrüßen [bə'ɡʀy:sn],
grüßen ['ɡʀy:sn]

grey grau [ɡʀaʊ]

grill der Grill [dɐ ɡʀɪl]

grilled vom Grill [fɔm 'ɡʀɪl]

grocery store das Lebensmittelgeschäft [das 'le:bmsmɪtlɡə ʃɛft]

ground der Boden [dɐ bo:dn],
das Gelände [das ɡe'lɛndə]

ground floor das Erdgeschoss
[das 'ʔeedɡəʃɔs]

ground meat das Hackfleisch
[das 'hakflaɪʃ]

group die Gruppe [di 'ɡʀʊpə]

growth die Geschwulst
[di ɡə'ʃvʊlst]

guarantee die Garantie
[di ɡaʀan'ti:]

guest der Gast [dɐ ɡast]

guide der Fremdenführer/die
Fremdenführerin [dɐ
'fʀɛmdnfy:ʀɐ/di 'fʀɛmdnfy:ʀəʀɪn],
(book) der Reiseführer [dɐ
'ʀaɪzə fy:ʀɐ]

guide dog der Blindenhund
[dɐ 'blɪndnhʊnt]

guided tour die Führung
[di 'fy:ʀʊŋ]

guilt die Schuld [di ʃʊlt]

gums das Zahnfleisch [das
'tsa:nflaɪʃ]

gust of wind die Bö [di bø:]

gymnastics die Gymnastik
[di ɡʏm'nastɪk]

H

hair das Haar [das ha:]

hair dryer der Föhn [dɐ fø:n]

hair gel das Haargel [das 'ha:ge:l]

hairdresser's der Friseur
[dɐ fʀɪ'zøɐ]

hairpins die Haarklammern *f pl*
[di 'ha:klamɐn]

hairstyle die Frisur [di fʀɪ'zuɐ]

half die Hälfte [di 'hɛlftə]; *(adj)*
halb [halp]

hall die Halle [di 'halə]; der Saal
[dɐ za:l]

ham der Schinken [dɐ ʃɪŋkn]

hand die Hand [di hant]; *(vb)*
reichen [ʀaɪçn]; **hand in** abgeben
[ʔapge:bm]

hand brake die Handbremse
[di 'hantbʀɛmzə]

hand-operated bike das
Handbike [das 'hɛntbaɪk]

hand throttle *(car)* das Handgas
[das 'hantga:s]

handbag die Handtasche
[di 'han(t)taʃə]

handball der Handball ['hantbal]

handicap die Behinderung
[di bə'hɪndəʀʊŋ]

handle der Haltegriff
[dɐ 'haltəɡʀɪf]

handmade handgemacht
['hantɡəmaxt]

handrail der Handlauf
[dɐ 'hantlaʊf]

hang-gliding das Drachenfliegen
[das 'dʀaxnfli:ɡn]

happy froh [fʀoː], glücklich ['glʏklɪç]

hard hart [haːt]

hard of hearing schwerhörig ['ʃveːɐhøːʀɪç]

hardly kaum [kaʊm]

hat der Hut [dɐ huːt]

have haben ['haːbm]; **have to** müssen [mʏsn]

hay fever der Heuschnupfen [dɐ 'hɔɪʃnʊpfn]

hazard warning lights die Warnblinkanlage [di 'vaːnblɪŋkʔanlaːgə]

he er [ʔeɐ]

head der Kopf [dɐ kɔpf]; *(boss)* der Leiter/die Leiterin [dɐ 'laɪtɐ/di 'laɪtəʀɪn], der Chef/die Chefin [dɐ ʃɛf/di ʃɛfɪn]

headache die Kopfschmerzen *m pl* [di 'kɔpfʃmɛɐtsn]

headache tablets die Kopfschmerztabletten *f pl* [di 'kɔpfʃmɛɐtsta blɛtn]

headlight der Scheinwerfer [dɐ 'ʃaɪnvɛɐfɐ]

headphones der Kopfhörer [dɐ 'kɔpfhøːʀɐ]

headquarters der Sitz [dɐ zɪts], das Hauptquartier [das 'haʊptkva tiɐ]

health food store das Reformhaus [das ʀeˈfɔɐmhaʊs]

healthy gesund [gəˈzʊnt]

hear hören ['høːʀən/høɐn]

hearing das Gehör [das gəˈhøɐ]

heart das Herz [das hɛɐts]

heart attack der Herzinfarkt [dɐ 'hɛɐtsɪnfaːkt]

heart trouble die Herzbeschwerden *f pl* ['hɛɐtsbəʃveɐdn]

heartburn das Sodbrennen [das 'zoːtbʀɛnn]

heat die Wärme [di 'vɛɐmə], die Hitze [di 'hɪtsə]; *(vb)* wärmen [vɛɐmm], heizen [haɪtsn]

heating die Heizung [di 'haɪtsʊŋ]

heaven *(rel)* der Himmel [dɐ hɪml]

heavy schwer [ʃveɐ]

height die Größe [di 'gʀøːsə], die Höhe [di 'høə]; *(of career)* der Höhepunkt [dɐ 'høəpʊŋkt]

help die Hilfe [di 'hɪlfə]

her *(pronoun)* sie [ziː], ihr [ʔiɐ]; *(possessive pronoun)* ihr [ʔiɐ]

herbs die Kräuter *n pl* [di 'kʀɔɪtɐ]

here hier [hiɐ]

hernia der Leistenbruch [dɐ 'laɪstnbʀʊx]

herring der Hering [dɐ 'heːʀɪŋ]

high hoch [hoːx]

high beam das Fernlicht [das 'fɛɐnlɪçt]

high blood pressure der Bluthochdruck [dɐ 'bluːthoːxdʀʊk]

high season die Hauptsaison [di 'haʊptzɛ zɔŋ]

high tide die Flut [di fluːt]

highlight der Höhepunkt [dɐ 'høəpʊŋkt]

highlights die Strähnchen *n pl* [di 'ʃtʀɛːnçn]

hike die Wanderung [di 'vandəʀʊŋ]; *(vb)* wandern ['vandɐn]

hiking map die Wanderkarte [di 'vandɐkaːtə]

hill der Hügel [dɐ hyːgl]

hinder hindern ['hɪndɐn]

hip die Hüfte [di 'hʏftə]

his sein [zaɪn]

history die Geschichte [di gəˈʃɪçtə]

hitchhike trampen [tʀɛmpm]

hoarse heiser ['haɪzɐ]

hole das Loch [das lɔx]

holy heilig ['haɪlɪç]

home das Heim [das haɪm], das Haus [das haʊs]; *(country)* die Heimat [di 'haɪmaːt]; **at home** daheim [daˈhaɪm]

homemade hausgemacht ['haʊsgəmaxt]

honey der Honig [dɐ 'hoːnɪç]

hood die Motorhaube [di 'mo:tɔ haʊbə]
hook der Haken [dɐ ha:kn̩]
horn die Hupe [di 'hu:pə]
hors d'oeuvre die Vorspeise [di 'foɐʃpaɪzə]
horse das Pferd [das pfeɐt]
hospital das Krankenhaus [das 'kʀaŋkn̩haʊs]
hospitality die Gastfreundschaft [di 'gastfʀɔɪntʃaft]
host/hostess der Gastgeber/ die Gastgeberin [dɐ 'gastge:bɐ/ di 'gastge:bəʀɪn]
hot *(temperature)* heiß [haɪs]; *(spicy)* scharf [ʃaːf]
hot water warmes Wasser ['kaltəs 'vasə]
hour die Stunde [di 'ʃtʊndə]; a quarter of an hour eine Viertelstunde [(ʁˀaɪ)nə fʀɛtl̩'ʃtʊndə]; half an hour eine halbe Stunde [(ʁˀaɪ)nə ʁhalbə 'ʃtʊndə]; ; hours of business die Öffnungszeiten *f pl* [di 'ˀœfnʊŋstsaɪtn̩]
hourly stündlich ['ʃtʏntlɪç]
house das Haus [das haʊs]
house number die Hausnummer [di 'haʊsnʊmə]
houseboat das Hausboot [das 'haʊsbo:t]
hovercraft das Luftkissenboot [das 'lʊftkɪsnbo:t]
how wie [vi:]; how many wie viele [vi: fi:lə]; how much wie viel [vi: fi:l]
however jedoch [je'dɔx], doch [dɔx]
humid schwül [ʃvy:l]
hungry hungrig ['hʊŋʀɪç]
hurry sich beeilen [zɪç bəˀaɪln]; be in a hurry es eilig haben [ˀəs ˀaɪlɪç ha:bm̩]
hurt schmerzen [ʃmɛɐtsn̩], wehtun ['ve:tu:n]
husband der Ehemann [dɐ ˀe:əman]
hut die Hütte [di 'hʏtə]

I ich [ˀɪç]
ice das Eis [das ˀaɪs]
ice hockey das Eishockey [das 'ˀaɪshɔke:]
ice pack das Kühlelement [das 'ky:lɛlə mɛnt]
ice rink die Eisbahn [di 'ˀaɪsba:n]
ice skates die Schlittschuhe *m pl* [di 'ʃlɪtʃu:ə]
idea die Idee [di 'ˀi'de:]; no idea! keine Ahnung! ['kaɪnə 'ˀa:nʊŋ]
identity card der Personalausweis [dɐ pɐ(ɛ)ezoˈna:l 'ˀaʊsvaɪs]
if wenn [vɛn], falls [fals]
ignition die Zündung [di 'tsʏndʊŋ]
ignition key der Zündschlüssel [dɐ 'tsʏntʃlʏsl̩]
ill krank [kʀaŋk]; be taken ill krank werden ['kʀaŋk veɐdn̩]
illness die Krankheit [di 'kʀaŋkhaɪt]
illustration das Bild [das bɪlt]
impertinent unverschämt ['ˀʊnfɐ ʃɛ:mt]
important bedeutend [bə'dɔɪtnt], wichtig ['vɪçtɪç]
impossible ausgeschlossen ['ˀaʊsgə ʃlɔsn], unmöglich ['ˀʊn mø:glɪç]
impressionism der Impressionismus [dɐ ˀɪmpʀɛsjo'nɪsmʊs]
impressive beeindruckend [bə'ˀaɪndʀʊkn̩t]
improbable unwahrscheinlich ['ˀʊnvaʃaɪnlɪç]
in in [ˀɪn]
in case falls [fals]
in-room telephone das Zimmertelefon [das 'tsɪmətelə fo:n]
in writing schriftlich ['ʃʀɪftlɪç]
incident der Vorfall [dɐ 'foɐfal], der Zwischenfall [dɐ 'tsvɪʃnfal]
included inbegriffen ['ˀɪnbəgʀɪfn]

incredible unglaublich
[ˈʊnˈglaʊplɪç]

indicator *(car)* das Blinklicht [das
ˈblɪŋklɪçt]

indigestion die
Verdauungsstörung [di
fɛˈdaʊʊnʃtøːʀʊŋ]

indoors drinnen [dʀɪnn], im Haus
[ˈɪm haʊs]

infection die Infektion
[di ˈɪnfɛkˈtsjoːn]

inflammable feuergefährlich
[ˈfɔɪɛɡəfeːlɪç]

inflammation die Entzündung
[di ˈɛnˈtsʏndʊŋ]

inflammation of the middle
ear die Mittelohrentzündung
[di ˈmɪtlˈʔoɛˈʔɛn tsʏndʊŋ]

influenza die Grippe [di ˈɡʀɪpə]

inform benachrichtigen
[bəˈnaːxʀɪçtɪɡn], informieren
[ˈɪnfɔˈmiːʀən/-ˈmiɛn], mitteilen
[ˈmɪtaɪln]

information die Auskunft
[di ˈʔaʊskʊnft]

infusion die Infusion
[di ˈɪnfuˈzjoːn]

inhabitant der Bewohner/
die Bewohnerin [dɛ bəˈvoːnɛ/
di bəˈvoːnəʀɪn], der Einwohner/
die Einwohnerin [dɛ ˈʔaɪnvoːnɛ/
di ˈʔaɪnvoːnəʀɪn]

injection die Spritze [di ˈʃpʀɪtsə]

injure verletzen [fɛˈlɛtsn]

injured person der/die Verletzte
[dɛ/di fɛˈlɛtstə]

injury die Verletzung [di fɛˈlɛtsʊŋ]

inner courtyard der Innenhof
[dɛ ˈʔɪnnhoːf]

inscription die Inschrift
[di ˈʔɪnʃʀɪft]

insect das Insekt [das ˈɪnˈzɛkt]

inside innen [ˈʔɪnn], drin [dʀɪn]

insist behaupten [bəˈhaʊptn];
insist on bestehen auf [bəˈʃteːn
ˈʔaʊf]

insomnia die Schlaflosigkeit
[di ˈʃlaːfloːzɪçkaɪt]

inspector der Kontrolleur/
die Kontrolleurin [dɛ kɔntʀoˈløɐ/
di kɔntʀoˈløʀɪn]

instead of statt [ʃtat], anstatt
[ˈʔanˈʃtat]

insulin das Insulin [das ˈɪnzʊˈliːn]

insult die Beleidigung
[di bəˈlaɪdɪɡn]; *(vb)* beleidigen
[bəˈlaɪdɪɡn]

insurance die Versicherung
[di fɛˈzɪçəʀʊŋ]

intelligent klug [kluːk]

interested, be ~ (in) sich
interessieren (für) [zɪç
ˈʔɪntʀəˈsiːʀən/-ˈsiɛn (fyɐ)]

interesting interessant
[ˈʔɪntʀəˈsant]

international call
Auslandsgespräch [das
ˈʔaʊslantsɡə ʃpʀɛːç]

international car index mark
das Nationalitätskennzeichen [das
natsjonalɪˈtɛːtskɛntsaɪçn]

international flight der
Auslandsflug [dɛ ˈʔaʊslantsfluːk]

interrupt unterbrechen
[ˈʔʊntɛˈbʀɛçn]

intersection die Kreuzung
[di ˈkʀɔɪtsʊŋ]

intestines der Darm [dɛ daːm]

intolerable unerträglich
[ˈʔʊnɛ tʀɛːklɪç]

introduce vorstellen [ˈfoɐʃtɛln],
bekannt machen [bəˈkant maxn]

introduction die Vorstellung
[di ˈfoɐʃtɛlʊŋ]

invite einladen [ˈʔaɪnlaːdn]

Ireland Irland [ˈʔɪʀlant]; Northern
Ireland Nordirland [nɔatˈʔɪʀlant]

Irish irisch [ˈʔiːʀɪʃ]

iron *(metal)* das Eisen [das ˈʔaɪzn];
(implement) das Bügeleisen [das
ˈbyːɡlˈʔaɪzn]; *(vb)* bügeln [byːgln]

island die Insel [di ˈʔɪnzl]

isolated abgelegen [ˈʔapɡəleːɡn];
einsam [ˈʔaɪnzaːm]

its sein [zaɪn]

J

jack der Wagenheber [dɐ
  'va:gŋhe:bɐ]
jacket die Jacke [di 'jakə]
jam die Marmelade [di
  mamə'la:də]
January Januar ['janʊaː], *(Austria)*
  Jänner ['jɛnɐ]
jaw der Kiefer [dɐ 'ki:fɐ]
jazz der Jazz [dɐ 'dʒɛs]
jazz aerobics die Jazzgymnastik
  [di 'dʒɛsgʏm nastɪk]
jeans die Jeans [di 'dʒi:ns]
jeweler's der Juwelier [dɐ juve'liɐ]
jewelry der Schmuck [dɐ ʃmʊk]
job die Arbeit [di 'ʔa:baɪt];
  (position) die Stellung [di 'ʃtɛlʊŋ]
jog *(vb)* joggen ['dʒɔgŋ]
joint das Gelenk [das gə'lɛŋk]
joke der Spaß [dɐ ʃpa:s], der
  Scherz [dɐ ʃɛɐts], der Witz [dɐ
  vɪts]
journey die Fahrt [di fa:t], die
  Reise [di 'ʀaɪzə]; **go on a journey**
  verreisen [fɐ'ʀaɪzn]; **return
  journey** die Rückfahrt [di 'ʀʏkfa:t];
  journey home die Heimreise
  [di 'haɪmʀaɪzə]
judge der Richter/die Richterin
  [dɐ 'ʀɪçtɐ/di 'ʀɪçtɐʀɪn]
juicy saftig ['zaftɪç]
July Juli ['ju:li]
jumper cables das Starthilfekabel
  [das 'ʃta:thɪlfəka:bl]
junction die Kreuzung
  [di 'kʀɔɪtsʊŋ]
June Juni ['ju:ni]
just *(time)* gerade [g(ə)'ʀa:də];
  just as ... as genauso ... wie
  [gə'naʊzo ... vi]

K

keep behalten [bə'haltn]; halten
  [haltn]

ketchup

ketchup das Ketschup [das
  'kɛtʃap]
key der Schlüssel [dɐ 'ʃlʏsl]
keyboard telephone das
  Schreibtelefon [das 'ʃʀaɪpteləfo:n]
kidney die Niere [di 'ni:ʀə]
kidney stone der Nierenstein
  [dɐ 'ni:ʀənʃtaɪn]
kilogram(s) das Kilo [das 'ki:lo]
kilometer der Kilometer
  [dɐ ʁkilo'me:tɐ]
kind die Art [di ʔa:t], die Sorte [di
  'zɔʁtə]; *(adj)* freundlich ['fʀɔɪntlɪç]
king der König [dɐ 'kø:niç]
kiss der Kuss [dɐ kʊs]; *(vb)* küssen
  [kʏsn]
kitchen die Küche [di 'kʏçə]
kitchenette die Kochnische
  [di 'kɔxni:ʃə]
knee das Knie [das kni:]
knife das Messer [das 'mɛsɐ]
know kennen [kɛnn], wissen
  [vɪsn];

L

Ladies Damen [da:mm]
lady die Dame [di 'da:mə]
lake der See [dɐ ze:]
lamb das Lamm [das lam]; *(meat)*
  das Lammfleisch [das 'lamflaɪʃ]
lamp die Lampe [di 'lampə]
land das Land [das lant]; *(vb)*
  landen ['landn]; **land at** *(ship)*
  anlegen in ['ʔanle:gŋ 'ʔɪn]
landing die Landung [di 'landʊŋ]
landlord/landlady der Haus-
  besitzer/die Hausbesitzerin [dɐ
  'haʊsbəzɪtsɐ/di 'haʊsbəzɪtsəʀɪn]
lane die Gasse [di 'gasə]
language die Sprache [di
  'ʃpʀa:xə]
large groß [gʀo:s]
last *(adj)* letzte(r, -s) ['lɛtstə (-tɐ,
  -təs)]; *(adv)* zuletzt [tsʊ'lɛtst]; *(vb)*
  halten [haltn], dauern ['daʊɐn]
late spät [ʃpɛ:t]

laugh *(vb)* lachen [laxn]
launderette der Waschsalon [dɐ ˈvaʃza lɔŋ]
laundry die Wäscherei [di vɛʃəˈʀaɪ]
lavatory die Toilette [di toˈlɛtə]
lawn der Rasen [dɐ ʀa:zn]
lawyer der Rechtsanwalt/die Rechtsanwältin [dɐ ˈʀɛçtsanvalt/ di ˈʀɛçtsanvɛltɪn]
laxative das Abführmittel [das ˈ²apfyɐ mɪtl]
layered cut der Stufenschnitt [dɐ ˈʃtu:fnʃnɪt]
lazy faul [faʊl]
leading role die Hauptrolle [di ˈhaʊptʀɔlə]
leaflet der Prospekt [dɐ pʀɔsˈpɛkt]
lean mager [ˈma:gɐ]
learn lernen [lɛʀnn]
least, at ~ mindestens [ˈmɪndəstns], wenigstens [ˈve(:)nɪkstns]
leather jacket die Lederjacke [di ˈle:dejakə]
leave abfahren (von) [ˈ²apfa:(ʀə)n fɔn], verlassen [fɛˈlasn], weggehen [ˈvɛkge:n]; *(room)* hinausgehen [hɪˈnaʊsge:n]; *(behind)* hinterlassen [hɪntɐˈlasn]; **leave (for)** abreisen (nach) [ˈ²apʀaɪzn (nax)]
left(-hand) linke(r, -s) [ˈlɪŋkə (-kɐ, -kəs)]; **on the left, to the left** links [lɪŋks]
leg das Bein [das baɪn]
legal blood alcohol limit die Promillegrenze [di pʀoˈmɪlə gʀɛntsə]
leggings die Leggings *pl* [di ˈlɛgɪŋs]
lemons die Zitronen *f pl* [di tsɪˈtʀo:nn]
lend leihen [laɪn]
lens das Objektiv [das ²ɔbjɛkˈti:f]
lentils die Linsen *f pl* [di lɪnzn]
lesson die Unterrichtsstunde [di ²ʊntɐʀɪçt ʃtʊndə]
let *(permit)* lassen [lasn]

letter der Brief [dɐ bʀi:f]
lettuce der Kopfsalat [dɐ ˈkɔpfsa la:t]
level *(adj)* flach [flax]
license plate das Nummernschild [das ˈnʊmɐnʃɪlt]
license plate das Nummernschild [das ˈnʊmɐnʃɪlt]
lie die Lüge [di ˈly:gə]; *(vb)* lügen [ly:gn]; *(in horizontal position)* liegen [li:gn]; **lie down** sich hinlegen [zɪç ˈhɪnle:gn]
life das Leben [das le:bm]
life belt/life preserver der Rettungsring [dɐ ˈʀɛtʊŋsʀɪŋ]
life jacket die Schwimmweste [di ˈʃvɪmvɛstə]
lifeboat das Rettungsboot [das ˈʀɛtʊŋsbo:t]
lifeguard der Bademeister/die Bademeisterin [dɐ ˈba:dəmaɪstɐ/ di ˈba:dəmaɪstəʀɪn]
lift *(ski-)* der Lift [dɐ lɪft]; *(vb)* heben [e:bm]
light das Licht [das lɪçt]; *(adj weight)* leicht [laɪçt]; *(vb)* anzünden [ˈ²antsʏndn]
light blue hellblau [hɛlˈblaʊ]
lightbulb die Glühbirne [di ˈgly:bɪʀnə]
light meter der Belichtungsmesser [dɐ bəˈlɪçtʊŋs mɛsɐ]
lighter das Feuerzeug [das ˈfɔɪɐtsɔɪk]
lightning der Blitz [dɐ blɪts]
like *(comparison)* wie [vi:]; *(vb)* mögen [ˈmø:gn]
line die Linie [di ˈli:njə]; *(railway)* die Strecke [di ˈʃtʀɛkə]; *(telephone)* die Leitung [di ˈlaɪtʊŋ]
linen das Leinen [das laɪnn]
lip die Lippe [di ˈlɪpə]
lipstick der Lippenstift [dɐ ˈlɪpmʃtɪft]
liquid flüssig [ˈflʏsɪç]
liquor store das Spirituosengeschäft [das ʃpiʀituˈo:zngəʃɛft]

listen to music Musik hören [mʊ'ziːk 'høːʀən]
liter der Liter [dɐ 'liːtɐ]
little klein [klaɪn]; *(not much)* wenig ['veːnɪç]
live *(vb)* leben [leːbm], wohnen [voːnn]
lively lebhaft ['leːphaft]
liver die Leber [di 'leːbɐ]
living room das Wohnzimmer [das 'voːntsɪmɐ]
local einheimisch ['ʔaɪnhaɪmɪʃ]
local call das Ortsgespräch [das 'ʔɔʁtsgəʃpʀɛːç]
local train der Nahverkehrszug [dɐ 'naːfɐ keːɐtsuːk]
lock das Schloss [das ʃlɔs]; *(vb)* verschließen [fɐ'ʃliːsn], abschließen ['ʔapʃliːsn]
lonely einsam ['ʔaɪnzaːm]
long lang [laŋ]; *(far)* weit [vaɪt]
long-distance call das Ferngespräch [das 'fɛɐngəʃpʀɛːç]
look der Blick [dɐ blɪk]; *(vb)* sehen [seːn], schauen ['ʃaʊn]; **look at** anschauen ['ʔanʃaʊn], ansehen ['ʔanzeːn]; **look for** suchen ['zuːxn]; **look like** aussehen ['ʔaʊseːn]; **look out!** Achtung! ['ʔaxtʊŋ]
lose verlieren [fɐ'liːʀən/-liɐn]; **lose one's way** sich verirren [zɪç fɐ'ʔɪʀən]
lost, get ~ sich verirren [zɪç fɐ'ʔɪʀen]
loud laut [laʊt]
lounge *(hotel)* der Aufenthaltsraum [dɐ 'ʔaʊfntalts ʀaʊm]
love die Liebe [di 'liːbə]; *(vb)* lieben [liːbm]
low tief [tiːf]
low-fat milk fettarme Milch ['fɛtʔaːmə mɪlç]
low season die Vorsaison [di 'foɐzɛ zɔŋ]; die Nachsaison [di 'naːxzɛ zɔŋ]
low tide die Ebbe [di ʔɛbə]

luck das Glück [das glʏk]
lucky glücklich ['glʏklɪç]
luggage das Gepäck [das ge'pɛk]
luggage claim die Gepäckausgabe [di gə'pɛkʔaʊsgaːbə]
luggage counter der Gepäckschalter [dɐ gə'pɛkʃaltɐ]
lumbago der Hexenschuss [dɐ 'hɛksnʃʊs]
lunch das Mittagessen [das 'mɪtak ʔɛsn]
lunch meat der Aufschnitt [dɐ 'ʔaʊfʃnɪt]
lungs die Lunge [di 'lʊŋə]
luxurious luxuriös [lʊksʊʀi'øːs]

M

machine die Maschine [di ma'ʃiːnə]
mackerel die Makrele [di ma'kʀeːlə]
mad verrückt [fɐ'ʀʏkt]
Madam Frau [fʀaʊ]
magazine *(glossy)* die Illustrierte [di ɪlʊ'stʀiɐtə]; *(news)* die Zeitschrift [di 'tsaɪtʃʀɪft]
maid das Zimmermädchen [das 'tsɪmɛmɛːtçn]
maiden name der Geburtsname [dɐ gə'bʊɐtsnaːmə]
main course die Hauptspeise [di 'haʊptʃpaɪzə]
main post office das Hauptpostamt [das 'haʊpt pɔstʔamt]
main street die Hauptstraße [di 'haʊptʃtʀaːsə]
main train station der Hauptbahnhof [dɐ 'haʊptbaːnhoːf ('haʊpbaːnof)]
maintain behaupten [bə'haʊptn]
make *(produce)* machen ['maxn], schaffen [ʃafn]; *(coffee, tea)* kochen [kɔxn]; **make good** *(damage)* ersetzen [ʔe'zɛtsn]

man der Mann [dɐ man];
(mankind) der Mensch [dɐ mɛnʃ]
mandarins die Mandarinen *f pl*
[di manda'ʀiːnn]
map die Landkarte [di 'lantkaːtə]
March März [mɛɐts]
margarine die Margarine
[di maga'ʀiːnə]
market der Markt [dɐ maːkt]
marmalade die Marmelade
[di mamə'laːdə]
married verheiratet [fɐ'haɪʀaːtət]
marry heiraten ['haɪʀaːtn]
marvelous wunderbar
['vʊndɐbaː]
mascara die Wimperntusche
[di 'vɪmpɐntʊʃə]
mass *(rel)* die Messe [di 'mɛsə]
massage die Massage [ma'saːʒə]
match das Spiel [ʃpiːl]
matches die Streichhölzer *n pl*
[di 'ʃtʀaɪçhœltsɐ]
material das Material [das
mat(ə)ʀi'aːl], der Stoff [dɐ ʃtɔf]
matter die Angelegenheit
[di ˀangəle:gŋhaɪt], die Sache
[di 'zaxə]
mattress die Matratze
[di ma'tʀatsə]
May Mai [maɪ]
maybe vielleicht [fɪ'laɪçt]
mayonnaise die Mayonnaise
[di maɪo'neːzə]
me mich [mɪç], mir [miɐ]
meadow die Wiese [di 'viːzə]
meal das Essen [das ˀɛsn], die
Mahlzeit [di 'maːltsaɪt]
meaning die Bedeutung
[di bə'dɔɪtʊŋ]
means das Mittel [das 'mɪtl]
measles die Masern *f pl* ['maːzɐn]
meat das Fleisch [das flaɪʃ]
medicine das Medikament [das
medɪka'mɛnt]
meet treffen [tʀɛfn], begegnen
[bə'geːkn(ə)n]; kennen lernen
['kɛnnlɛɐnn]

melon die Melone [di me'loːnə]
memorial die Gedenkstätte
[di gə'dɛŋkʃtɛtə]
men die Männer [di m]
men's für Herren [fyɐ 'hɛʀən]
Men's Room die Herrentoilette
[di 'hɛʀənto lɛtə]
menstruation die Menstruation
[di mɛnstʀua'tsjon]
mentally handicapped geistig
behindert ['gaɪstɪç bə'hɪndɐt]
menu die Speisekarte [di
'ʃpaɪzəkaːtə]
merry lustig ['lʊstɪç], froh [fʀoː]
message die Nachricht
[di 'naːxʀɪçt]
meter der Meter [dɐ 'meːtɐ]
microwave die Mikrowelle
[di 'miːkʀovɛlə]
middle die Mitte [di 'mɪtə]
Middle Ages das Mittelalter [das
'mɪtlˀaltɐ]
midge die Mücke [di 'mʏkə]
migraine die Migräne
[di mi'gʀɛːnə]
mild mild [mɪlt]
milk die Milch [mɪlç]
millimeter der Millimeter
[dɐ 'mɪli meːtɐ]
mind, I don't ~ meinetwegen
['maɪnət veːgŋ]
miniature golf das Minigolf [das
'mɪnigɔlf]
minute die Minute [di mi'nuːtə]
mirror der Spiegel [dɐ ʃpiːgl]
miscalculate sich verrechnen [zɪç
fɐ'ʀɛçn(ə)n]
miscarriage die Fehlgeburt
[di 'feːlgəbʊɐt]
misfortune das Unglück [das
ˀʊnglʏk]
Miss das Fräulein [das 'fʀɔ(ɪ)laɪn]
miss *(vb)* verfehlen [fɐ'feːln];
verpassen [fɐ'pasn]; be missing
fehlen [feːln]

mistake Fehler ['fe:lɐ], der Irrtum [dɐ 'ʔɪɐtu:m]; **mistake for** vertauschen [fɐ'taʊʃn], verwechseln [fɐ'vɛksln]; **make a mistake** einen Fehler machen [(ʔaɪn)n 'fe:lɐ maxn], sich verrechnen [zɪç fɐ'ʀɛçn(ə)n]; **be mistaken** sich täuschen [zɪç 'tɔɪʃn], sich irren [zɪç 'ʔɪʀən/'ʔɪɐn]

misunderstanding das Miss-verständnis [das 'mɪsfɛɐʃtɛntnɪs]

mobile (phone) das Handy [das 'hɛndi], das Mobiltelefon [das mo'bi:ltelə fo:n]

model das Modell [das mo'dɛl]

modern modern [mo'dɛɐn]

moist nass [nas], feucht [fɔɪçt]

monastery das (Mönchs)Kloster [das ('mœnçs) klo:stɐ]

Monday Montag ['mo:nta:k]

money das Geld [das gɛlt]

month der Monat [dɐ 'mo:na:t]

monthly monatlich ['mo:natlɪç]

monument *(memorial edifice)* das Denkmal [das 'dɛnkma:l]; *(tomb)* das Grabmal ['gʀa:bma:l]

moon der Mond [dɐ mo:nt]

more mehr [meɐ]; **more than** mehr als ['meɐ ʔals]

morning der Morgen [dɐ mɔɐgŋ], der Vormittag [dɐ 'foɐmɪta:k]; **in the morning** morgens ['mɔɐgŋs]

mosaic das Mosaik [das moza'ʔi:k]

most, at the ~ höchstens [hø:çstns/hø:kstns]

motel das Motel [das mo'tɛl]

mother die Mutter [di mʊtɐ]

motive der Grund [dɐ gʀʊnt]

motor der Motor [dɐ 'mo:toɐ]

motorboat das Motorboot [das 'mo:tɔbo:t]

mountain der Berg [dɐ bɛɐk]

mountain bike das Mountainbike [das 'maʊntnbaɪk]

mountain village das Bergdorf [das 'bɛɐkdoɐf]

mountaineering/mountain climbing das Bergsteigen [das 'bɛɐkʃtaɪgŋ]

mountains das Gebirge [das gə'bɪɐgə]

mouth der Mund [dɐ mʊnt]; *(river)* die Mündung [di 'mʏndʊŋ]

movie actor/actress der Filmschauspieler/ die Filmschauspielerin [dɐ 'fɪlmʃaʊʃpi:lɐ/di 'fɪlmʃaʊʃpi:lərɪn]

movie theater das Kino [das 'ki:no]

Mr. Herr [hɛɐ]

Mrs. Frau [fʀaʊ]

much viel [fi:l]

muesli das Müsli [das 'my:sli]

mugging der Überfall [dɐ 'ʔy:bɐfal]

mumps der Mumps [dɐ mʊmps]

muscle der Muskel [dɐ 'mʊskl]

museum das Museum [das mu'ze:ʊm]

music die Musik [di mu'zi:k]

music hall das Varietee [das vaʀiə'te:]

musical das Musical [das 'mju:zɪkl]

mussels die Muscheln *f pl* [di mʊʃln]

mustache der Schnurrbart [dɐ 'ʃnʊɐba:t]

mustard der Senf [dɐ zɛnf (zɛmf)]

mute stumm [ʃtʊm]

my mein [maɪn];

myself mich [mɪç], mir [miɐ]; **I did it myself** ich habe es selbst gemacht ['ʔɪç ha:bə (ʔə)s 'zɛlpst gə maxt]

N

nail polish der Nagellack [dɐ 'na:gllak]

nail polish remover der Nagellackentferner [dɐ 'na:gllakɛnt fɛɐnɐ]

nail scissors die Nagelschere [di 'na:glʃe:Rə]

naked nackt [nakt]

name der Name [de na:mə]; *(vb)* nennen [nɛnn]

napkin die Serviette [di zɛ'vjɛtə]

narrow schmal [ʃma:l], eng ['ɛŋ]

national park der Nationalpark [de natsjo'na:lpa:k]

nationality die Staatsangehörigkeit [di 'ʃta:ts ʔangəhø:RIçkaɪt]

native einheimisch ['ʔaɪnhaɪmɪʃ]

natural natürlich [na'tyelIç]

nature die Natur [di na'tuɐ]

nature reserve das Naturschutzgebiet [das na'tuɐʃʊtsgəbi:t]

naughty böse ['bø:zə]

nausea der Brechreiz [de 'bRɛçRaɪts]

near nahe ['na:(ə)], in der Nähe von ['ɪn de 'nɛə fɔn], bei [baɪ]

nearly beinahe ['baɪna:], fast [fast]

necessary nötig ['nø:tIç], notwendig ['no:tvɛndɪç]

neck der Hals [de hals]

necklace die Kette [di 'kɛtə]

need brauchen [bRaʊxn], benötigen [bə'nø:tɪgn]

neither auch nicht [ʔaʊx nɪç(t)]

nerve der Nerv [de nɛɐf]

nervous nervös [nɛ'vø:s]

neutral der Leerlauf [de 'leɐlaʊf]

never nie [ni:]

nevertheless trotzdem ['tRɔtsde:m]

new neu [nɔɪ], frisch [fRIʃ]

New Year's Day Neujahr [nɔɪ'ja:]

New Year's Eve Silvester [sɪl'vɛstɐ]

news dealer der Zeitungshändler [de 'tsaɪtʊŋshɛntle]

newspaper die Zeitung [di 'tsaɪtʊŋ]

next nächste(r, s) ['nɛ:çstɐ/'nɛ:kstə (-stɐ, -stəs)]; next to neben ['ne:bm]

nice nett [nɛt], lieb [li:p], sympathisch [sʏm'pa:tɪʃ]

night die Nacht [di naxt]; der Abend [de 'ʔa:bmt]; at night nachts [naxts]

nightclub der Nachtklub [de 'naxtklʊp]

no nein [naɪn]; *(not any)* kein [kaɪn]

no-smoking compartment das Nichtraucherabteil [das 'nɪçtRaʊxɐʔap taɪl]

nobody keine(r, s) ['kaɪnə (-nɐ, -nəs)], niemand ['ni:mant]

noise das Geräusch [das gə'Rɔɪʃ], der Lärm [de lɛɐm]

noisy laut [laʊt]

non-alcoholic alkoholfrei [ʔalko'ho:lfRaɪ]

noon der Mittag [de 'mɪta:k]

nor auch nicht [ʔaʊx nɪçt]

normal normal [nɔ'ma:l]

normally normalerweise [nɔ'ma:levaɪzə]

north der Norden [de nɔɐdn]

North Sea die Nordsee [di 'nɔɐtze:]

nose die Nase [di 'na:zə]

nose bleed das Nasenbluten [das 'na:znblu:tn]

not nicht [nɪçt]; not at all gar nicht ['ga: nɪç(t)], durchaus nicht [dʊɐç'ʔaʊs nɪç(t)]; not yet noch nicht [nɔx 'nɪç(t)]

notepad der Notizblock [de no'ti:tsblɔk]

nothing nichts [nɪçts/nɪks]

notice das Schild [das ʃɪlt]; *(vb)* bemerken [bə'mɛɐkn]

notion die Vorstellung [di 'foɐʃtɛlʊŋ]

novel der Roman [de Ro'ma:n]

November November [no'vɛmbɐ]

now nun [nu:n], jetzt [jɛtst]; till now bis jetzt [bɪs 'jɛtst]

nowhere nirgends ['nɪRegŋ(t)s]

nude *(adj)* nackt [nakt]; *(painting)* der Akt [de ʔakt]

nudist beach der FKK-Strand
[de ˀɛfka'ka:ʃtrant]
number die Nummer [di 'numɐ];
(vb) nummerieren [numɐ'ʀi:ʀən/
-'ʀiːɐn]
nurse die Krankenschwester
[di 'kʀaŋkn̩ʃvɛstɐ]
nutmeg die Muskatnuss
[di mʊs'ka:tnʊs]
nuts die Nüsse *f pl* [di 'nʏsə]

O

object der Gegenstand
[de 'ge:gnʃtant]
observatory die Sternwarte
[di 'ʃtɛɐnva:tə]
occasionally gelegentlich
[gəle:gn̩tlɪç]
occupied *(seat)* besetzt [bə'zɛtst]
October Oktober [ɔk'to:bɐ]
of von [fɔn]; *(material)* aus [ˀaʊs]
off season die Schonzeit
[di 'ʃo:ntsaɪt]
off-season die Vorsaison
[di 'foːɐze zɔŋ]; die Nachsaison
[di 'na:xze zɔŋ]
offer *(vb)* anbieten [ˀanbi:tn̩],
bieten [bi:tn̩]
office das Büro [das by'ʀo:];
(position) das Amt [das ˀamt]
official *(adj)* amtlich [ˀamtlɪç],
offiziell [ˀɔfi'tsjɛl]
offside abseits [ˀapzaɪts]
often oft [ˀɔft]
oil das Öl [das ˀøːl]
oil change der Ölwechsel
[de ˀøːlvɛksl]
oil painting die Ölmalerei
[di ˀøːlma:lə ʀaɪ]
ointment die Salbe [di 'zalbə]
old alt [ˀalt]
olive oil das Olivenöl [das
ˀo'li:vn̩ˀøːl]
olives die Oliven *f pl* [di ˀo'li:vn̩]
on *(switch)* an [ˀan]; *(position)* auf
[ˀaʊf]

on the weekend am
Wochenende [ˀam 'vɔxn̩ˀɛndə]
on weekdays wochentags
['vɔxnta:ks], werktags ['vɛɐkta:ks];
once einmal [ˀaɪ(n)ma:l]; at once
sofort [zo'fɔɐt], gleich [glaɪç]
one *(adj)* ein(e) [ˀaɪn/ˀaɪnə],
(numeral) eins [ˀaɪns]
onions die Zwiebeln *f pl*
[di tsvi:bln̩]
only nur [nuɐ], *(not before)* erst
[eɐst]; *(adj)* einzig [ˀaɪntsɪç]
open offen [ˀɔfn̩], geöffnet
[gə'ˀœfnət]; *(vb)* öffnen
[ˀœfn(ə)n], aufmachen
[ˀaʊfmaxn]; in the open air im
Freien [ˀɪm 'fʀaɪn]
opening hours die Öffnungszeiten *f pl* [di ˀœfnʊŋstsaɪtn]
opera die Oper [di ˀo:pɐ]
operation die Operation
[di ˀɔpəʀa'tsjo:n]
operetta die Operette
[di ˀɔpə'ʀɛtə]
opinion die Meinung [di
'maɪnʊŋ]
opposite das Gegenteil [das
'ge:gn̩taɪl]; *(adj)* entgegengesetzt
[ˀɛnt'ge:gn̩gəzɛtst]; *(prep)* gegenüber [gegn̩ˀy:bɐ]
optician's der Optiker
[de ˀɔptɪkɐ]
or oder [ˀo:dɐ]
orange juice der Orangensaft
[de ˀo'ʀaŋ ʒnzaft]
oranges die Apfelsinen *f pl*
[di ˀapfl'zi:nn̩]
orchestra das Orchester [das
ˀɔɐ'kɛstɐ]
order *(tidiness)* die Ordnung
[di ˀɔɐtnʊŋ]; *(rel)* der Orden [de
ˀɔɐdn̩]; *(restaurant)* die Bestellung
[di bə'ʃtɛlʊŋ]; *(vb)* bestellen
[bə'ʃtɛln]; out of order kaputt
[ka'pʊt]
ordinary gewöhnlich [gə'vøːnlɪç]
organic food store der Bioladen
[de 'biola:dn̩]

original das Original [das
ˈʔɔʀɪgiˈnaːl], **original version**
die Originalfassung
[di ʔɔʀɪgiˈnaːlfasʊn]
ought to sollen [zɔln]
our unser(e) [ˈʔʊnzɐ (-ʀə)]
outside außen [ˈʔaʊsn], außerhalb
[ˈʔaʊsəhalp], draußen [ˈdʀaʊsn]
over *(prep)* über [ˈʔyːbɐ]; *(adv at
an end)* vorüber [foˈʀyːbɐ], vorbei
[fɔˈbaɪ]
overtake überholen [ʔyːbɐˈhoːln]
own eigen [ˈʔaɪgn]; *(vb)* besitzen
[bəˈzɪtsn]
owner der Besitzer/die Besitzerin
[dɐ bəˈzɪtsɐ/di bəˈzɪtsəʀɪn], der
Eigentümer/die Eigentümerin
[dɐ ˈʔaɪgnˌtyːmɐ/di ˈʔaɪgnˌtyːməʀɪn
oysters die Austern *f pl* [di
ˈʔaʊstɐn]

P

pacemaker der
Herzschrittmacher [dɐ
ˈhɛɐ(t)sˌʃʀɪtmaxɐ]
pacifier der Schnuller [dɐ ˈʃnʊlɐ]
pack die Packung [di ˈpakʊŋ]; *(vb)*
packen [pakn], einpacken
[ˈʔaɪnpakn], verpacken [fɛˈpakn]
packing die Verpackung
[di fɛˈpakʊŋ]
page die Seite [di ˈzaɪtə]
pain die Schmerzen *m pl*
[di ˈʃmɛɐtsn]
pain-killing tablets die
Schmerztabletten *f pl* [di
ˈʃmɛɐtstaˌblɛtn]
painful schmerzhaft [ˈʃmɛɐtshaft]
paint die Farbe [di ˈfaːbə]; *(vb)*
malen [maːln]
painter der Maler/die Malerin
[dɐ ˈmaːlɐ/di ˈmaːləʀɪn]
painting *(picture)* das Gemälde
[das gəˈmɛːldə]; *(type of art)* die
Malerei [di maːləˈʀaɪ]
pair das Paar [das paː]

palace der Palast [dɐ paˈlast]
panties der (Damen)Slip
[dɐ (ˈdaːmən)slɪp]
pants *(underwear)* die Unterhose
[di ˈʊntɐhoːzə]; die Hose
[di ˈhoːzə]
panty hose die Strumpfhose [di
ˈʃtʀʊmpfhoːzə]
panty liners die Slipeinlagen *f pl*
[di ˈslɪpaɪnlaːgn]
paper das Papier [das paˈpiɐ]
paper handkerchiefs die
Papiertaschentücher *n pl* [di
paˈpiɐ taʃntyːçɐ]
paper napkins die
Papierservietten *f pl*
[di paˈpiɐzɛ vjɛtn]
paperback das Taschenbuch [das
ˈtaʃnbuːx]
papers die Papiere *n pl*
[di paˈpiːʀə]
paprika der Paprika [dɐ ˈpapʀɪka]
parachuting das
Fallschirmspringen [das
ˈfalʃɪɐmʃpʀɪŋŋ]
paraffin das Petroleum [das
peˈtʀoːleʊm]
paralysis die Lähmung [di
ˈlɛːmʊŋ]
parcel das Paket [das paˈkeːt]
pardon, I beg your ~! Ich bitte
um Entschuldigung [ʔɪç ˈbɪtə ʔʊm
ɛntˈʃʊldɪgʊŋ]
parents die Eltern *n pl* [di ˈʔɛltɐn]
park die Anlage [di ˈʔanlaːgə]; der
Park [dɐ paːk]; *(vb)* abstellen
[ˈʔapʃtɛln], parken [ˈpaːkn]
parka der Anorak [dɐ ˈʔanoʀak]
parsley die Petersilie
[di peːtɛˈziːljə]
part der Teil [dɐ taɪl]
partially sighted sehbehindert
[ˈseːbəhɪndɐt]
particularly besonders
[bəˈzɔndɐs]
particulars die Personalien *f pl*
[di pɛzoˈnaːljən], nähere Angaben
[ˈnɛəʀə ˈʔanga:bm]
parting der Scheitel [dɐ ʃaɪtl]

party das Fest [das fɛst]
pass *(mountain)* der Pass [dɐ pas]; *(vb)* reichen [ʀaɪçn]; *(time)* vergehen [fɐˈgeːn], vorübergehen [foˈʀyːbɐgeːn], vorbeigehen [fɔˈbaɪgeːn]; *(overtake)* überholen [ˈʔyːbɐhoːln]
passable befahrbar [bəˈfaːbaː]
passenger der Fahrgast [dɐ ˈfaːgast], der Passagier [dɐ pasaˈʒiɐ]
passing through auf der Durchreise [ˈʔaʊf dɐ ˈdʊɐçʀaɪzə]
passport der Reisepass [dɐ ˈʀaɪzəpas]
past die Vergangenheit [di fɐˈgaŋhaɪt]; *(adj adv)* vorüber [foˈʀyːbɐ], vorbei [fɔˈbaɪ]
pasta die Nudeln *f pl* [di nuːdln]
pastry shop die Konditorei [di kɔndɪtoˈʀaɪ]
path der Weg [dɐ veːk], der Pfad [dɐ (p)faːt]
patience die Geduld [di gəˈdʊlt]
pay zahlen [ˈtsaːln], bezahlen [bəˈtsaːln]; pay out auszahlen [ˈʔaʊstsaːln]
payment die Zahlung [di ˈtsaːlʊŋ]
peaches die Pfirsiche *m pl* [di ˈpfɪʀzɪçə]
pearl die Perle [di ˈpɛɐlə]
pears die Birnen *f pl* [di bɪʀnən]
peas die Erbsen *f pl* [di ˈʔɛɐpsn]
pedestrian der Fußgänger/die Fußgängerin [dɐ ˈfuːsgɛŋɐ/di ˈfuːsgɛŋəʀɪn]
pedestrian zone die Fußgängerzone [di ˈfuːsgɛŋə tsoːnə]
penalty box der Strafraum [dɐ ˈʃtʀaːfʀaʊm]
pendant der Anhänger [dɐ ˈʔanhɛŋɐ]
people das Volk [das fɔlk], Leute *pl* [ˈlɔɪtə]
pepper der Pfeffer [dɐ ˈpfɛfɐ]
peppers die Paprikaschoten *f pl* [di ˈpapʀɪka ʃoːtn]

percent das Prozent [das pʀoˈtsɛnt]
perch der Barsch [dɐ baːʃ]
performance *(theatre)* die Vorstellung [di ˈfoɐʃtɛlʊŋ]
perfume das Parfüm [das paˈfyːm]
perfume store die Parfümerie [di pafyməˈʀiː]
perhaps vielleicht [fɪˈlaɪçt]; eventuell [ˈʔevɛntuˈ(ʔ)ɛl]
perm die Dauerwelle [di ˈdaʊɐvɛlə]
permitted zulässig [ˈtsuːlɛsɪç]
person die Person [di pɐˈzoːn]; der Mensch [dɐ mɛnʃ]
personal persönlich [pɐˈzøːnlɪç]
Personal Identification Number (PIN) die Geheimzahl [di gəˈhaɪmtsaːl]
perspire schwitzen [ˈʃvɪtsn]
pets die Haustiere *n pl* [di ˈhaʊstiːʀə]
pharmacy die Apotheke [di ʔapoˈteːkə]
phone das Telefon [das ˈteːləfoːn]; *(vb)* telefonieren [teləfoˈniːʀən/-ˈniɛn], anrufen [ˈʔanʀuːfn]
phone booth die Telefonzelle [di teləˈfoːntsɛlə]
phone call der Anruf [dɐ ˈʔanʀuːf]; make a phone call telefonieren [teləfoˈniːʀən/-ˈniɛn]
phone number die Telefonnummer [di teləˈfoːnnʊmɐ]
phonecard die Telefonkarte [di teləˈfoːnkaːtə]
photograph das Foto [das ˈfoto]; *(vb)* fotografieren [ʁfotogʀaˈfiːʀən]
photography die Fotografie [di fotogʀaˈfiː]
pick out aussuchen [ˈʔaʊsuːxn]
pick-up service der Rückholservice [dɐ ˈʀʏkhoːlœsœɐvɪs]
pickpocket der Taschendieb/die Taschendiebin [dɐ ˈtaʃndiːp/di ˈtaʃn diːbɪn]
picture das Bild [das bɪlt]
picture postcard die Ansichtskarte [di ˈʔanzɪçtskaːtə]

piece das Stück [das ʃtʏk]

pier der Pier [dɐ piɐ]

pill die Tablette [di taˈblɛtə]

pillar die Säule [di ˈzɔɪlə], der Pfeiler [dɐ ˈpfaɪlɐ]

pillow das Kopfkissen [das ˈkɔpfkɪsn]

pilot der Pilot/die Pilotin [dɐ piˈloːt/di piˈloːtɪn]

pineapple die Ananas [ˈʔananas]

pink rosa [ˈʀoːza]

pity, what a ~! wie schade! [vi ˈʃaːdə]

place die Stelle [di ˈʃtɛlə], der Platz [dɐ plats], der Ort [dɐ ʔɔɐt]

place of birth der Geburtsort [dɐ ɡəˈbuɐtsʔɔɐt]

place of pilgrimage der Wallfahrtsort [dɐ ˈvalfaːts ʔɔɐt]

place of residence der Wohnort [dɐ ˈvoːnʔɔɐt]

plain die Ebene [di ʔeːbənə]; *(adj)* einfarbig [ʔaɪnfaʀbɪç]

plant die Pflanze [di ˈ(p)flantsə]

plastic bag der Plastikbeutel [dɐ ˈplastɪkbɔɪtl]

plastic wrap die Frischhaltefolie [di ˈfʀɪʃhaltə foːljə]

plate der Teller [dɐ ˈtɛlɐ]

platform das Gleis [das glaɪs]

play das Schauspiel [das ˈʃaʊʃpiːl]; *(vb)* spielen [ʃpiːln]

playmate der Spielkamerad/die Spielkameradin [dɐ ˈʃpiːlkamɐ ʀaːt/ di ˈʃpiːlkamɐ ʀaːdɪn]

pleasant sympathisch [sʏmˈpaːtɪʃ], angenehm [ʔanɡəneːm]

please bitte [ˈbɪtə]; *(vb)* gefallen [ɡəˈfaln]; be pleased (with/about) sich freuen (über) [zɪç ˈfʀɔɪn (ʁʔyːbɐ)]

pleasure die Freude [di ˈfʀɔɪdə], das Vergnügen [das fɐˈɡnyːɡn]

plug der Stecker [dɐ ˈʃtɛkɐ]

pneumonia die Lungenentzündung [di ˈlʊŋənʔɛn tsʏndʊŋ]

pocket die Tasche [di ˈtaʃə]

pocket calculator der Taschenrechner [dɐ ˈtaʃnʀɛçnɐ]

pocket knife das Taschenmesser [das ˈtaʃnmɛsɐ]

poison das Gift [das ɡɪft]

poisoning die Vergiftung [di vɐˈɡɪftʊŋ]

poisonous giftig [ˈɡɪftɪç]

Polaroid® camera die Sofortbildkamera [di zoˈfɔɐtbɪlt kamɐʀa]

police die Polizei [di pɔliˈtsaɪ]

police car der Polizeiwagen [dɐ pɔliˈtsaɪvaːɡn]

police custody die Untersuchungshaft [di ˈʔuntɐˈzuːxʊŋshaft]

policeman/policewoman der Polizist/die Polizistin [dɐ pɔliˈtsɪst/ di pɔliˈtsɪstɪn]

polio die Kinderlähmung [di ˈkɪndɐlɛːmʊŋ]

polite höflich [ˈhøːflɪç]

poor arm [ˈʔaːm]

porcelain das Porzellan [das pɔ(ɐ)tsəˈlaːn]

pork das Schweinefleisch [ˈʃvaɪnəflaɪʃ]

port der Hafen [dɐ ˈhaːfn]; *(wine)* der Portwein [der ˈpɔ(ɐ)tvaɪn]

portal das Portal [das pɔ(ɐ)ˈtaːl]

porter der Portier [dɐ pɔɐˈtjeː]

portion die Portion [di pɔˈtsjoːn]

portrait das Porträt [das pɔ(ɐ)ˈtʀɛː]

posh vornehm [ˈfoɐneːm]

position *(location)* die Lage [di ˈlaːɡə]; *(profession)* die Stellung [di ˈʃtɛlʊŋ]

possible möglich [ˈmøːklɪç]; eventuell [ʔevɛntʊˈ(ʔ)ɛl]

post code die Postleitzahl [di ˈpɔstlaɪtsaːl]

post office das Postamt [das ˈpɔstamt]

post office savings book das Postsparbuch [das ˈpɔstʃpaːbuːx]

postage das Porto [das ˈpɔɐto]

postcard die Postkarte [di ˈpɔstkaːtə]

poste restante postlagernd ['pɔstla:gɛnt]

poster das Plakat [das pla'ka:t]

postpone verschieben [fɛ'ʃi:bm], aufschieben ['ʔaʊfʃi:bm]

potatoes die Kartoffeln *f pl* [di ka'tɔfln]

pottery *(workshop)* die Töpferei [di tœpfə'RaI]; *(products)* die Töpferwaren *f pl* [di 'tœpfɛva:Rən]; *(activity)* Töpfern ['tœpfɛn]

pound(s) das Pfund [das (p)fʊnt]

powder der Puder [de 'pu:dɛ]

power point die Steckdose [di 'ʃtɛkdo:zə]

practical praktisch ['pRaktıʃ]

practice *(vb)* üben ['ʔy:bm]; *(profession)* ausüben ['ʔaʊs'ʔy:bm]

prawns die Garnelen *f pl* [di ga'ne:ln]

pray beten [be:tn]

pregnancy die Schwangerschaft [di 'ʃvaŋɛʃaft]

premiere die Premiere [di pRəm'je:Rə]

prepare vorbereiten ['foɛbəRaItn], zubereiten ['tsu:bəRaItn]

prescribe verschreiben [fɛ'ʃRaIbm]

prescription das Rezept [das Re'tsɛpt]

present das Geschenk [das gə'ʃɛŋk]; *(adj)* anwesend ['ʔanve:znt]; be present da sein ['da:zaIn]

pretty *(adj)* hübsch [hʏpʃ]; *(adv)* ziemlich ['tsi:mlıç]

prevent verhindern [fɛ'hɪndɛn], hindern ['hɪndɛn]

price der Preis [de pRaIs]

priest der Priester [de pRi:stɛ]

prison das Gefängnis [das gə'fɛŋnIs]

private privat [pRI'va:t]

prize der Preis [de pRaIs]

probable wahrscheinlich [va'ʃaInlıç]

probably wahrscheinlich [va'ʃaInlıç]

problem das Problem [das pRo'ble:m]

procession die Prozession [di pRotsɛs'jo:n]

product das Erzeugnis [das 'ʔe'tsɔIknIs], das Produkt [das pRo'dʊkt], die Ware [di 'va:Rə]

production *(theater)* die Inszenierung [di 'ʔIntsə'ni:Rʊŋ]

profession der Beruf [de bə'Ru:f]

profit der Gewinn [de gə'vIn]

program *(booklet)* das Programmheft [das pRo'gRamhɛft]

prohibited verboten [fɛ'bo:tn]

pronounce aussprechen ['ʔaʊ(s)ʃpRɛçn]

proper richtig ['RIçtIç]

prospectus der Prospekt [de pRos'pɛkt]

provisional provisorisch [pRovI'zo:RIʃ]

provisions der Vorrat [de 'fo:Ra:t]

pub die Kneipe [di 'knaIpə]

public das Publikum [das 'pʊblIkʊm]; *(adj)* öffentlich ['ʔœfntlıç]

pull ziehen [tsi:n]

pulled muscle die Zerrung [di 'tsɛRʊŋ]

pullover der Pullover [de pʊ'lo:ve]

pulse der Puls [de pʊls]

pump die Luftpumpe [di 'lʊftpʊmpə]

pumpkin der Kürbis [de 'kʏebIs]

punctual pünktlich ['pʏŋktlıç]

puncture das Loch [das lɔx]; *(flat tire)* die Panne [di 'panə]

punishment die Strafe [di 'ʃtRa:fə]

purple lila ['li:la]

purse der Geldbeutel [de 'gɛltbɔItl], die Geldbörse [di 'gɛltbœezə]; *(handbag)* die Handtasche [di 'han(t)taʃə]

pus der Eiter [de 'ʔaItɛ]

put legen [le:gṇ], stellen [ʃtɛln], setzen [zɛtsn]; **put down** hinlegen ['hɪnle:gṇ]; **put off** verschieben [fɛ'ʃi:bm], aufschieben ['ʔaʊfʃi:bm]; **put on** *(dress)* anziehen ['ʔantsi:n]

Q

quality die Qualität [di kvalɪ'tɛ:t], die Eigenschaft [di 'ʔaɪgṇʃaft]
quay der Kai [dɐ kaɪ]
queen die Königin [di 'kø:nɪgɪn]
question die Frage [di 'fʁa:gə]
quick schnell [ʃnɛl]; rasch [ʁaʃ]
quiet leise ['laɪzə], ruhig [ʁʊɪç]
quite *(entirely)* ganz [gants]; *(somewhat)* ziemlich

R

rabbit das Kaninchen [ka'ni:nçn]
race das Rennen [das ʁɛnn]
racing bike das Rennrad [das 'ʁɛnʁa:t]
racquet der Schläger [dɐ 'ʃlɛ:gɐ]
radar check die Radarkontrolle [di ʁa'da:kɔn tʁɔlə]
radiator der Kühler [dɐ 'ky:lɐ]
radio das Radio [das 'ʁa:djo]
rain der Regen [dɐ 'ʁe:gṇ]
raincoat der Regenmantel [dɐ 'ʁe:gṇmantl]
rainy regnerisch ['ʁe:knərɪʃ]
ramble wandern ['vandɐn]
ramp die Rampe [di 'ʁampə]
rape die Vergewaltigung [di fɐgə'valtɪgʊŋ]; *(vb)* vergewaltigen [fɐgə'valtɪgṇ]
rare selten [zɛltn]
rash der Ausschlag [dɐ 'ʔaʊʃla:k]
rather lieber ['li:bɐ], vielmehr ['fi:lmeːɐ], eher ['ʔeːɐ]; *(somewhat)* ziemlich ['tsi:mlɪç]
ravine die Schlucht [di 'ʃlʊxt]

raw roh [ʁoː]
razor blade die Rasierklinge [di ʁa'ziɐklɪŋə]
reach erreichen ['ʔɐ'ʁaɪçn]
read lesen [le:zn]
ready fertig ['fɛɐtɪç], bereit [bə'ʁaɪt]
real wirklich ['vɪʁklɪç]
really unbedingt ['ʔʊnbədɪŋt]; wirklich ['vɪʁklɪç]
rear light das Rücklicht [das 'ʁʏklɪçt]
rearview mirror der Rückspiegel [dɐ 'ʁʏkʃpi:gl]
reason der Anlass [dɐ 'ʔanlas], der Grund [dɐ gʁʊnt]
receipt die Quittung [di 'kvɪtʊŋ]
receive erhalten ['ʔɐ'haltn], empfangen ['ɛmp'faŋŋ]
receiver der Hörer [dɐ 'hø:ʁɐ]
recently kürzlich ['kʏɐtslɪç]
reception die Rezeption [di ʁetsɛp'tsjo:n]
recommend empfehlen ['ɛmp'fe:ln]
recover sich erholen [zɪç ʔɐ'ho:ln]
red rot [ʁoːt]
red wine Rotwein ['ʁo:tvaɪn]
reduced fee for children die Kinderermäßigung [di 'kɪndɐʔɐ'mɛ:sɪgʊŋ]
reduction die Ermäßigung [di ɐ'mɛ:sɪgʊŋ]
refrigerator der Kühlschrank [dɐ 'ky:lʃʁaŋk]
refuse zurückweisen [tsʊ'ʁʏkvaɪzn], sich weigern [zɪç 'vaɪgɐn], ablehnen ['ʔaple:nn]
region die Gegend [di 'ge:gṇt]
register sich anmelden [zɪç 'ʔanmɛldn]; *(luggage)* aufgeben ['ʔaʊfge:bm]; *(car)* zulassen ['tsu:lasn]
registered letter der Einschreibebrief [dɐ 'ʔaɪnʃʁaɪbəbʁi:f]
registration die Anmeldung [di 'ʔanmɛldʊŋ]

regret das Bedauern [das bə'daʊen]; *(vb)* bedauern [bə'daʊen]

regular regelmäßig ['ʀe:glmɛ:sɪç]

related verwandt [fɐ'vant]

religion die Religion [di ʀelɪ'gjo:n]

reluctantly ungern ['ʔʊngɐen], nicht gern [nɪç(t) gɛen]

remain bleiben [blaɪbm]

remains die Überreste *m pl* [di ʔ'y:bɐʀɛstə]

remark *(vb)* bemerken [bə'mɛɐkn]

remedy das Heilmittel [das 'haɪlmɪtl]

remember sich erinnern [zɪç ɐ'ʔɪnɐn]; remember s. th. sich etw. merken [zɪç ʔ'ɛtvas 'mɛɐkn]

remittance die Überweisung [di ʔ'y:bɐvaɪzʊn]

Renaissance die Renaissance [di ʀənɛ'sa):s]

rent die Miete [di 'mi:tə]; *(vb)* mieten ['mi:tn], vermieten [fɐ'mi:tn]

repair die Reparatur [di ʀɛpaʀa'tuɐ]; *(vb)* reparieren [ʀɛpa'ʀi:ʀən/-'ʀien]

repair kit das Flickzeug [das 'flɪktsɔɪk]

repeat *(vb)* wiederholen [vidɐ'ho:ln]

replace ersetzen [ʔɐ'zɛtsn]

replacement der Ersatz [dɐ ʔɐ'zats]

reply die Antwort [di ʔ'antvɔɐt]; *(vb)* antworten [ʔ'antvɔɐtn], beantworten [bə'ʔantvɔɐtn], erwidern [ʔɐ'vi:den]

report der Bericht; *(vb, a crime)* anzeigen [ʔ'antsaɪɡn]

request die Bitte [di 'bɪtə]

reservation die Reservierung [di ʀɛzɐ'vi:ʀʊn]; die Buchung [di 'bu:xʊn], die Voranmeldung [di 'foɐʔanmɛldʊn]

reserve reservieren [ʀɛzɐ'vi:ʀən/ -'vien]

responsible zuständig ['tsu:ʃtɛndɪç], verantwortlich [fɐ'ʔantvɔɐtlɪç]

rest die Ruhe [di 'ʀuə], die Erholung [di ʔɐ'ho:lʊn]; *(remainder)* der Rest [dɐ ʀɛst]; *(vb)* ruhen [ʀu:n], sich ausruhen [zɪç ʔ'aʊsʀu:n]

restaurant car der Speisewagen [dɐ 'ʃpaɪzəva:ɡn]

return die Rückkehr [di 'ʀʏkeɐ]; *(vb)* wiederkommen ['vi:dɐkɔmm], zurückkehren [tsʊ'ʀʏke:ʀən/ -keɐn]; *(give back)* wiedergeben ['vi:dɐge:bm]

return ticket die Rückfahrkarte [di 'ʀʏkfa: ka:tə]

reverse umgekehrt ['ʔʊmɡəkeɐt]

reverse gear der Rückwärtsgang [dɐ 'ʀʏkvɛɐtsɡan]

reward die Belohnung [di bə'lo:nʊn]; *(vb)* belohnen [bəlo:nn]

rheumatism das Rheuma [das 'ʀɔɪma]

rice der Reis [dɐ ʀaɪs]

rich reich [ʀaɪç]

ride *(vb)* reiten ['ʀaɪtn]

ride a bike *(vb)* Rad fahren ['ʀa:t 'fa:ʀən]

ridiculous lächerlich ['lɛçɐlɪç]

riding school die Reitschule ['ʀaɪtʃu:lə]

right das Recht [das ʀɛçt]; *(adj)* richtig ['ʀɪçtɪç]; on the right, to the right rechts [ʀɛçts]

right-hand rechte(r, s) ['ʀɛçtə (-tɐ, -təs)]

rigid fest [fɛst]

ring (up) telefonieren [teləfo'ni:ʀən/-'nien]

ripe reif [ʀaɪf]

river der Fluss [dɐ flʊs]

road die Straße [di 'ʃtʀa:sə]

road map die Straßenkarte [di 'ʃtʀa:snka:tə]

roasted gebraten [ɡə'bʀa:tn]

rock der Fels [dɐ fɛls]

roller skates die Rollschuhe *m pl* [di 'ʀɔlʃuːə]

rolls die Brötchen *n pl* [di bʀøːtçn]

roof das Dach [das dax]

room das Zimmer [das 'tsɪmɐ], der Saal [dɐ zaːl]; *(space)* der Raum [dɐ ʀaʊm]

rope das Seil [das zaɪl]

rosemary der Rosmarin [dɐ 'ʀoːsmaʀiːn]

rotten faul [faʊl], verdorben [fɐ'dɔɐbm]

round *(drinks, sport)* die Runde [di 'ʀʊndə]; *(adj)* rund [ʀʊnt]

round-trip die Rundfahrt [di 'ʀʊntfaːt]

route die Route [di 'ʀuːtə]; *(road)* die Strecke [di 'ʃtʀɛkə]

row *(vb)* rudern ['ʀuːdɐn]

rowboat das Ruderboot [das 'ʀuːdɐboːt]

rubber boat das Schlauchboot [das 'ʃlaʊxboːt]

rubber boots die Gummistiefel *m pl* [di 'gʊmiʃtiːfl]

rubber ring der Schwimmring [dɐ 'ʃvɪmʀɪŋ]

rubbish der Müll [dɐ mʏl], der Abfall [dɐ 'ʔapfal]

ruin die Ruine [di ʀu'ʔiːnə]

rule die Vorschrift [di 'foɐʃʀɪft]

run rennen [ʀɛnn], laufen [laʊfn]; *(nose)* tropfen [tʀɔpfn]; *(bus etc.)* verkehren [fɐ'keːʀən/-'keɐn]

rupture der Leistenbruch [dɐ 'laɪstnbʀʊx]

S

sad traurig ['tʀaʊʀɪç]

safari park der Safaripark [dɐ za'faːʀipaːk]

safe der Safe [dɐ sɛɪf/seːf]; *(adj)* sicher ['zɪçɐ]

saffron der Safran [dɐ 'zafraːn]

sage der Salbei [dɐ 'zalbaɪ]

sail dasSegel [das 'zeːgl]; *(vb)* segeln ['zeːgln]

sailboat das Segelboot [das 'zeːglboːt]

sailing cruise der Segeltörn [dɐ 'zeːgltœɐn]

salad der Salat [dɐ za'laːt]

salad bar das Salatbüfett [das za'laːtbʏfeː]

salami die Salami [di za'laːmi]

sale der Verkauf [dɐ fɐ'kaʊf]; (clearance) sale der Ausverkauf [dɐ 'ʔaʊsfɐkaʊf]

salt das Salz [das zalts]

same gleich [glaɪç]; the same derselbe [dɐ'zɛlbə], dieselbe [di'zɛlbə], dasselbe [das'zɛlbə]

sand box der Sandkasten [dɐ 'zantkastn]

sand castle die Sandburg [di 'zantbuɐk]

sandals die Sandalen *f pl* [di zan'daːln]

sanitary napkins die Damen-binden *f pl* [di 'daːmmbɪndn]

satisfied befriedigt [bə'fʀiːdɪçt], zufrieden [tsʊ'fʀiːdn]

Saturday *(southern Germany)* Samstag ['zamstaːk], *(northern Germany)*

sauce die Soße [di 'zoːsə]

saucer die Untertasse [di 'ʔʊntɐtasə]

sauna die Sauna [di 'zaʊna]

sausage die Wurst [di vʊɐst], das Würstchen [das 'vʊɐstxən]

say sagen [zaːgn]

scar die Narbe [di 'naːbə]

scarcely kaum [kaʊm]

scarf *(decorative)* das Halstuch [das 'halstuːx]; *(for warmth)* der Schal [dɐ ʃaːl]

scenery die Landschaft [di 'lantʃaft]

scent das Parfüm [das pa'fyːm]

chool die Schule [di 'ʃu:lə]
ciatica der Ischias [de 'ʔɪʃias]
cotland Schottland ['ʃɔtlant]
cottish schottisch ['ʃɔtɪʃ]
cream *(vb)* schreien ['ʃʀaɪn]
crew die Schraube [di 'ʃʀaʊbə]
culptor der Bildhauer/die Bildhauerin [de 'bɪlthaʊɐ/di 'bɪlthaʊəʀɪn]
culpture die Skulptur [di skʊlp'tuɐ]
ea die See [di 'ze:], das Meer [das meɐ]
eagull die Möwe [di 'møːvə]
easick seekrank ['ze:kʀaŋk]
easide resort der Badeort [de 'ba:dəʔɔɐt]
eason die Saison [di zɛ'zɔŋ], die Jahreszeit [di 'ja:ʀəstsaɪt]; *(vb)* würzen [vʀɛtsn]
easoning das Gewürz [das gə'vʀɛts]
eat der Sitz [de zɪts], der Sitzplatz [de 'zɪtsplats]
eat belt der Sicherheitsgurt [de 'zɪçɐhaɪtsgʊɐt]
eat reservation die Platzreservierung [di 'platsʀɛzɐ viːʀʊŋ]
ecluded einsam [ʔaɪnza:m]
econd die Sekunde [di zeˈkʊndə]; *(adj)* zweite(r, s) ['tsvaɪtɐ (-tɐ/-təs)]; **second(ly)** zweitens [tsvaɪtns]
econd-hand store der Trödelladen [de 'tʀøːdlla:dn]
ecurity *(safety)* die Sicherheit [di 'zɪçɐhaɪt]; *(guarantee)* die Kaution [di kaʊ'tsjoːn], die Bürgschaft [di 'bʏɐkʃaft]
ecurity charge die Sicherheitsgebühr [di 'zɪçɐhaɪtsgə byɐ]
ecurity control die Sicherheitskontrolle [di 'zɪçɐhaɪtskɔn tʀɔlə]
edative das Beruhigungsmittel [das bə'ʀʊɪgʊŋsmɪtl]
ee sehen ['ze:n]
eldom selten [zɛltn]

self-service die Selbstbedienung [di 'zɛlps(t)bədi:nʊŋ]
self-timer der Selbstauslöser [de 'zɛlpstaʊslø:zɐ]
sell verkaufen [fɐ'kaʊfn]
send senden ['zɛndn], schicken [ʃɪkn]; **send for** abholen lassen ['ʔapho:ln lasn]; **send on** nachsenden ['na:xzɛndn]
sender der Absender/die Absenderin [de 'ʔapzɛndɐ/di 'ʔapzɛndəʀɪn]
sentence der Satz [de zats]
September September [zɛp'tɛmbɐ]
serious ernst [ʔɛɐnst]; *(illness)* schwer [ʃveɐ]
serve servieren [zɛ'vi:ʀən/-'viɐn], bedienen [bə'di:nn], dienen [di:nn]
service der Dienst [de di:nst], die Bedienung [di bə'di:nʊŋ]
service charge die Bearbeitungsgebühr [di bɐ'ʔaɪbaɪtʊŋsgə byɐ]
set *(vb)* setzen [zɛtsn], hinstellen ['hɪnʃtɛln], aufstellen['ʔaʊfʃtɛln]; *(TV)* der (Fernseh)Apparat [de ('fɛɐnze) ʔapa ʀaːt]
set meal das Menü [das me'ny:]
severe *(wound, accident)* schwer [ʃveɐ]; *(judgement, winter)* streng [ʃtʀɛŋ]
severely handicapped person der/die Schwerbehinderte [de/di 'ʃveɐbəhɪndɐtə]
sexual harassment die sexuelle Belästigung [di sɛksu'ɛlə bə'lɛstɪgʊŋ]
shade der Schatten [de ʃatn]; *(colour)* der Ton [de to:n]
shadow der Schatten [de ʃatn]
shampoo das Schampoo [das 'ʃampo/'ʃampu]
shape die Form [di fɔɐm]
shaver der Rasierapparat [de ʀa'ziɐʔapa ʀaːt]
shaving brush der Rasierpinsel [de ʀa'ziɐpɪnzl]

shaving foam der Rasierschaum [de ʀaˈziːʃaʊm]

she sie [ziː]

shin das Schienbein [das ˈʃiːnbaɪn]

shirt das Hemd [das hɛmt]

shoe der Schuh [de ʃuː]

shoe brush die Schuhbürste [di ˈʃuːbʏstə]

shoe cream die Schuhcreme [di ˈʃuːkʀɛːm]

shoe store das Schuhgeschäft [das ˈʃuːgəʃɛft]

shoemaker's der Schuhmacher [de ˈʃuːmaxe]

shop das Geschäft [das gəˈʃɛft], der Laden [de ˈlaːdn]; shop window das Schaufenster [das ˈʃaʊfɛnstɐ]; go shopping einkaufen [ˈʔaɪnkaʊfn]

shore das Ufer [das ˈʔuːfe]

short kurz [kʊɐts]; at short notice kurzfristig [ˈkʊɐtsfʀɪstɪç]

short-circuit der Kurzschluss [de ˈkʊɐtʃlʊs]

short-cut die Abkürzung [di ˈʔapkʏɐtsʊn]

short film der Kurzfilm [de kʊɐtsfɪlm]

shorts die kurze Hose [di ˈkʊɐtsə ˈhoːzə]

shoulder die Schulter [di ˈʃʊltɐ]

shoulder bag die Umhängetasche [di ˈʔʊmhɛŋə taʃə]

shout (vb) schreien [ˈʃʀaɪn]

show (vb) zeigen [ˈtsaɪgn], vorzeigen [ˈfoɐtsaɪgn]; (exhibition) die Ausstellung [di ˈʔaʊʃtɛlʊn]; (entertainment) die Revue [di ʀeˈvyː], die Show [di ʃoː]

shower die Dusche [di ˈduːʃə]; (rain) der Regenschauer [de ˈʀeːgnʃaʊe]

shower gel das Duschgel [das ˈduːʃgeːl]

shower seat der Duschsitz [de ˈduːʃzɪts]

shrimp die Krabben f pl [di kʀabm]

shut (adj) zu [tsu(ː)]; (vb) schließen [ʃliːsn], zumachen [ˈtsuːmaxn]

shutter (camera) der Auslöser [de ˈʔaʊsløːze]

shuttlecock der Federball [de ˈfeːdebal]

shy schüchtern [ˈʃʏçtɐn]

sick krank [kʀaŋk]

side die Seite [di ˈzaɪtə]

sidelights das Standlicht [das ˈʃtantlɪçt]

sights die Sehenswürdigkeiten f pl [di ˈzeːnsvʏɐdɪçkaɪtn]

sightseeing tour of the town/city die Stadtrundfahrt [di ˈʃtatʀʊntfaːt]

sign das Schild [das ʃɪlt], das Zeichen [das ˈtsaɪçn]; (directions) der Wegweiser [de ˈveːkvaɪze]; (vb) unterschreiben [ˈʔʊnteˈʃʀaɪbm]

sign language die Zeichensprache [di ˈtsaɪçnʃpʀaːxə]

signature die Unterschrift [di ˈʔʊnteʃʀɪft]

silence (quiet) die Ruhe [di ˈʀuə], (personal) das Schweigen [das ˈʃvaɪgn]

silent ruhig [ʀuɪç]

silk die Seide [di ˈzaɪdə]

silk painting die Seidenmalerei [di ˈzaɪdnmaːlə ʀaɪ]

silly blöd(e) [bløːt/ˈbløːdə]

silver das Silber [das ˈzɪlbe]

similar ähnlich [ˈʔɛːnlɪç]

simple einfach [ˈʔaɪnfax]

simultaneously gleichzeitig [ˈglaɪçtsaɪtɪç]

since (time) seit [zaɪt]; (as) da [daː], weil [vaɪl]

sincere herzlich [ˈhɛɐtslɪç]

sing singen [zɪŋn]

singer der Sänger/die Sängerin [de ˈzɛŋe/di ˈzɛŋəʀɪn]

single ledig [ˈleːdɪç]

singles das Einzel [das ˈʔaɪntsəl]

sink das Geschirrspülbecken [das gəˈʃɪʀəspyːlbɛkŋ]

inusitis die Stirnhöhlenentzündung [di 'ʃtɪʀnhøːlnˀɛn tsʏndʊŋ]

ister die Schwester [di 'ʃvɛstɐ]

ister-in-law die Schwägerin [di 'ʃvɛːgəʀɪn]

it sitzen [zɪtsn]

ituation die Lage [di 'laːgə]

ize die Größe [di 'gʀøːsə]; (paper) das Format [das fɔ'maːt]

kateboard das Skateboard [das 'skɛɪtbɔɐt]; (vb) Skateboard fahren ['skɛɪtbɔɐt 'faːʀən]

ki der Ski [dɐ ʃiː]; (vb) Ski fahren ['ʃiː 'faː(ʀə)n]

ki bindings die Skibindungen f pl [di 'ʃiːbɪndʊŋn]

ki boots die Skistiefel m pl [di 'ʃiːʃtiːfl]

ki goggles die Skibrille [di 'ʃiːbʀɪlə]

ki instructor der Skilehrer/die Skilehrerin [dɐ 'ʃiːleːʀɐ/di 'ʃiːleːʀəʀɪn]

ki poles die Skistöcke m pl [di 'ʃiːʃtœkæ]

kiing das Skifahren [das 'ʃiːfaː(ʀə)n]

kiing course der Skikurs [dɐ 'ʃiːkʊɐs]

kin die Haut [di haʊt]

kirt der Rock [dɐ ʀɔk]

ky der Himmel [dɐ hɪml]

led der Schlitten [dɐ ʃlɪtn]

leep der Schlaf [dɐ ʃlaːf]; (vb) schlafen [ʃlaːfn]

leeping pills die Schlaftabletten f pl [di 'ʃlaːfta blɛtn]

leeplessness die Schlaflosigkeit [di 'ʃlaːfloːzɪçkaɪt]

leeve der Ärmel [dɐ ˀɛɐml]

lender schlank [ʃlaŋk], dünn [dʏn]

lice die Scheibe [di 'ʃaɪbə]

light leicht [laɪçt]

lim dünn [dʏn], schmal [ʃmaːl], schlank [ʃlaŋk]; (vb) abnehmen [ˀapneːmm]

slow(ly) langsam ['laŋzaːm]

small klein [klaɪn]

small packet das Päckchen [das pɛkçn]

smell der Geruch [dɐ gə'ʀu(ː)x]; (vb) riechen [ʀiːçn]

smoke der Rauch [dɐ ʀaʊx]; (vb) rauchen [ʀaʊxn]

smoked geräuchert [gə'ʀɔɪçɐt]

smoked ham roher Schinken [ʀoːɐ 'ʃɪŋkn]

smoker der Raucher/die Raucherin [dɐ 'ʀaʊxɐ/di 'ʀaʊxəʀɪn]

smoking compartment das Raucherabteil [das 'ʀaʊxɐˀap taɪl]

smuggle schmuggeln [ʃmʊgln]

snack der Imbiss [dɐ ˀɪmbɪs]

snake die Schlange [di 'ʃlaŋə]

snapshot der Schnappschuss [dɐ 'ʃnapʃʊs]

snore schnarchen [ʃnaːçn]

snorkel der Schnorchel [dɐ ʃnɔɐçl]; go snorkeling schnorcheln [ʃnɔɐçln]

snow der Schnee [dɐ ʃneː]

so (adv) so [zoː]; (conj) also [ˀalzoː]

soaked nass [nas]

soap die Seife [di 'zaɪfə]

sober nüchtern ['nʏçtɐn]

soccer der Fußball [dɐ 'fuːsbal]

soccer match das Fußballspiel [das 'fuːsbal ʃpiːl]

socket die Steckdose [di 'ʃtɛkdoːzə]

socks die Socken f pl [di 'zɔkn]

soft weich [vaɪç]

soft drink die Limonade [lɪmo'naːdə]

solarium das Solarium [das zo'laːʀɪʊm]

sole die Sohle [di 'zoːlə]; (fish) die Seezunge [di 'zeːtsʊŋə]

solid fest [fɛst], hart [haːt]

soloist der Solist/die Solistin [dɐ zo'lɪst/di zo'lɪstɪn]

some einige [ˀaɪnɪgə]

somebody jemand ['je:mant]
something etwas ['ʔɛtvas]
sometimes manchmal
['manҫmaːl]
son der Sohn [dɐ zoːn]
song das Lied [das liːt]
Sonnabend ['zɔnaːbmt]
soon bald [balt]
sore throat die Halsschmerzen *m
pl* [di 'halfmɛɐtsn]
sort die Sorte [di 'zɔɐtə], die Art
[di ʔaːt]
sound der Klang [dɐ klaŋ], der
Ton [dɐ toːn]
soup die Suppe [di 'zʊpə]
soup plate der Suppenteller
[dɐ 'zʊpmtɛlɐ]
sour sauer ['zaʊɐ]
sour cream die saure Sahne
[di zaʊɐə 'zaːnə]
source die Quelle [di 'kvɛlə]
south der Süden [dɐ zyːdn];
south of südlich von ['zyːtlɪҫ fɔn]
souvenir das Souvenir [das
zʊvə'niɐ]
souvenir store der Souvenirladen
[dɐ zʊvə'niɐlaːdn]
space der Raum [dɐ ʀaʊm]
spare tire der Ersatzreifen
[dɐ ʔɛ'zatsʀaɪfn]
spark plug die Zündkerze
[di 'tsʏntkɛɐtsə]
speak sprechen [ʃpʀɛҫn]
speaker der Lautsprecher
[dɐ 'laʊtʃpʀɛҫɐ]
special speziell [ʃpɛ'tsjɛl], Sonder-
['zɔndɐ-]
special-issue stamp die
Sondermarke [di 'zɔndɐmaːkə]
special (of the day) das
Tagesmenü [das 'taːgəsme nyː]
specialist der Facharzt/
die Fachärztin [dɐ 'faxaːtst/
di 'faxʔɛɐtstɪn]
specialty die Spezialität
[di ʃpetsjaliˈtɛːt]
spectator der Zuschauer/
die Zuschauerin [dɐ 'tsuːʃaʊɐ/
di 'tsuːʃaʊəʀɪn]

speed die Geschwindigkeit
[di gə'ʃvɪndɪçkaɪt]
speedometer der Tacho(meter)
[dɐ ʁtaxo('meːtɐ)]
spell buchstabieren
[buxʃta'biːʀən/-'biɐn]
spend ausgeben ['ʔaʊsgeːbm];
(time) verbringen [fɐ'bʀɪŋŋ];
spend the night übernachten
['ʔybɐ'naxtn]
spice das Gewürz [das gə'vvɐts]
spinach der Spinat [dɐ ʃpɪ'naːt]
spine die Wirbelsäule
[di 'vɪɐblzɔɪlə]
splendid herrlich ['hɛɐlɪҫ]; *(fig)*
glänzend [glɛntsnt]
splint die Schiene [di 'ʃiːnə]
spoiled verdorben [fɐ'dɔɐbm]
spoon der Löffel [dɐ lœfl]
sport der Sport [dɐ ʃpɔɐt]
sporting goods store das
Sportgeschäft [das 'ʃpɔɐtgəʃɛft]
sports field der Sportplatz
[dɐ 'ʃpɔɐtplats]
spot die Stelle [di 'ʃtɛlə]
sprained verstaucht [fɐ'ʃtaʊxt]
spring der Frühling [dɐ 'fʀyːlɪŋ]
squid der Tintenfisch [dɐ 'tɪntnfɪʃ]
stadium das Stadion [das
'ʃtaːdjon]
stain der Fleck [dɐ flɛk]
staircase die Treppe [di 'tʀɛpə]
stairs die Treppen *f pl* [di tʀɛpm]
stalls das Parkett [das pa'kɛt]
stamp der Stempel [dɐ ʃtɛmpl];
(postage) die (Brief)Marke
[di ('bʀiːf-) ʁmaːkə]
stamp machine der
Briefmarkenautomat [dɐ
'bʀiːfma:kn̩ʔaʊto maːt]
stand stehen [ʃteːn]; *(bear)*
ertragen [ʔɐ'tʀaːgn]
star der Stern [dɐ ʃtɛɐn]
start der Anfang; *(vb)* anfangen
start (from) abfahren (von)
['ʔapfaːn (fɔn)]
starter *(engine part)* der Anlasser
[dɐ 'ʔanlasɐ]; *(food)* die Vorspeise
[di 'foɐʃpaɪzə]

startle erschrecken [ʔɛˈʃʁɛkn̩]

state *(country)* der Staat [deˈ ʃtaːt]; *(condition)* der Zustand [deˈ ˈtsuːʃtant]; *(vb)* feststellen [ˈfɛ(st)ʃtɛln̩], aussagen [ˈʔausˌzaːɡn̩]

statement die Aussage [diˈ ˈʔausˌzaːɡə]

station der Bahnhof [deˈ ˈbaːnhoːf]

stationery store das Schreibwarengeschäft [das ˈʃʁaɪpvaːʁənɡə ʃɛft]

statue die Statue [diˈ ˈʃtaːtuə]

stay der Aufenthalt [deˈ ˈʔaufntalt]; *(vb)* sich aufhalten [zɪç ˈʔaufhaltn̩], wohnen [voːnn̩], bleiben [blaɪbm̩], übernachten [ˈʔyːbeˈnaxtn̩]

steal stehlen [ʃteːln̩]

steamed gedämpft [ɡəˈdɛmpft], gedünstet [ɡəˈdʏnstət]

steep steil [ʃtaɪl]

steeple der Kirchturm [deˈ ˈkɪʁçtʊem]

step die Stufe [diˈ ˈʃtuːfə]

steps die Treppe [diˈ ˈtʁɛpə]

steward/stewardess der Steward/die Stewardess [deˈ ˈstjuaːt/diˈ ˈstjuadɛs]

stick der Stock [deˈ ʃtɔk]

still *(quiet)* still [ʃtɪl]; *(mineral water)* ohne Kohlensäure [ˈʔoːnə koːl(ə)nzɔːʁə]; *(adv)* noch [nɔx]

still life das Stillleben [das ˈʃtɪleːbm̩]

sting der Stich [deˈ ʃtɪç]; *(vb)* stechen [ʃtɛçn̩]

stink stinken [ʃtɪŋkn̩]

stitch (up) nähen [nɛːn̩]

stock der Vorrat [deˈ ˈfoːʁaːt]

stockings die Strümpfe *m pl* [diˈ ˈʃtʁʏmpfə]

stomach der Bauch [deˈ baʊx], der Magen [deˈ maːɡn̩]

stomachache die Magenschmerzen *m pl* [diˈ ˈmaːɡn̩ʃmɛetsn̩]

stone der Stein [deˈ ʃtaɪn]

stony steinig [ˈʃtaɪnɪç]

stop *(train)* der Aufenthalt [deˈ ˈʔaufntalt]; *(bus)* die Haltestelle [diˈ ˈhaltəʃtɛlə]; *(vb, stop doing sth.)* aufhören [ˈʔaufhøen]; *(car)* anhalten [ˈʔanhaltn̩], *(person)* stehen bleiben [ˈʃteːnblaɪbm̩], *(break off)* abbrechen [ˈʔapbʁɛçn̩], *(bus, train)* halten [haltn̩]; **stop!** **halt!** [halt]

stopover die Zwischenlandung [diˈ ˈtsvɪʃn̩ landʊŋ]

store *(shop)* das Geschäft [das ɡəˈʃɛft], der Laden [deˈ ˈlaːdn̩]; *(supply)* der Vorrat [deˈ ˈfoːʁaːt]

storm der Sturm [deˈ ʃtʊem]

story die Geschichte [diˈ ɡəˈʃɪçtə]

stove der Herd [deˈ heːt]

straight gerade [ɡ(ə)ˈʁaːdə]; **straight across/through** quer durch [kveeˈ dʊeç]

straight ahead geradeaus [ɡʁaːdəˈʔaʊs]

strange eigen [ˈʔaɪɡn̩], fremd [fʁɛmt]

stranger der/die Fremde [deˈ/ diˈ ˈfʁɛmdə]

straw der Strohhalm [deˈ ˈʃtʁoːhalm]

strawberries die Erdbeeren *f pl* [diˈ ˈʔeetbeːʁən]

street die Straße [diˈ ˈʃtʁaːsə]

streetcar die Straßenbahn [diˈ ˈʃtʁaːsnbaːn]

strenuous anstrengend [ˈʔanʃtʁɛnnt]

stroke der Schlaganfall [deˈ ˈʃlaːkanfal]

stroll der Bummel [deˈ bʊml̩], der Spaziergang [deˈ ʃpaˈtsieɡaŋ]; *(vb)* spazieren gehen [ʃpaˈtsiːʁənɡeːn/-ˈtsien-]

strong stark [ʃtaːk], kräftig [ˈkʁɛftɪç]

studio couch die Schlafcouch [diˈ ˈʃlaːfkaʊtʃ]

study *(vb)* studieren [ʃtʊˈdiːʁən/ -ˈdien]

stuffed gefüllt [gə'fʏlt]

stupid dumm [dʊm], blöd(e) [blø:t/ 'blø:də]

style der Stil [dɐ sti:l (ʃti:l)]

subject to duty zollpflichtig ['tsɔl(p)flɪçtɪç]

subtitles der Untertitel [dɐ ʔʊntɐtɪtl]

suburb die Vorstadt [di 'foɐʃtat], der Vorort [dɐ 'foɐʔɔɐt]

subway die Unterführung [di ʔʊntɐ'fy:ʀʊŋ]; (US) die U-Bahn [di ʔu:ba:n]

success der Erfolg [dɐ ʔɐ'fɔlk]

suddenly plötzlich ['plœtslɪç]

sufficient genug [gə'nu:k]

sugar der Zucker [dɐ 'tsʊkɐ]

suggestion der Vorschlag [dɐ 'foɐʃla:k]

suit (for men) der Anzug [dɐ ʔantsu:k]; (for women) das Kostüm [das kɔs'ty:m]; (vb) passen [pasn]

suitable for the disabled behindertengerecht [bə'hɪndɐtngə ʀɛçt]

suitcase der Koffer [dɐ 'kɔfɐ]

sum die Summe [di 'zʊmə]

summer der Sommer [dɐ 'zɔmɐ]

summit station die Bergstation [di 'bɛɐkʃta tsjo:n]

sun die Sonne [di 'zɔnə]

sun cream die Sonnencreme [di 'zɔnnkʀɛːm]

sun hat der Sonnenhut [dɐ 'zɔnnhu:t]

sun protection factor der Lichtschutzfaktor [dɐ 'lɪçtʃʊts faktoɐ]

sunbathing area die Liegewiese [di 'li:gəvi:zə]

sunburn der Sonnenbrand [dɐ 'zɔnnbʀant]

Sunday Sonntag ['zɔnta:k]

sunny sonnig ['zɔnɪç]

sunroof das Schiebedach [das 'ʃi:bədax]

sunstroke der Sonnenstich [dɐ 'zɔnnʃtɪç]

suntan lotion die Sonnenmilch [di 'zɔnnmɪlç]

suntan oil das Sonnenöl [das 'zɔnnʔøːl]

supermarket der Supermarkt [dɐ 'zu:pɐma:kt]

suppository das Zäpfchen [das 'tsɛpfçn]

sure sicher ['zɪçɐ]

surf (vb) surfen ['sœɐfn]

surfboard das Surfbrett [das 'sœɐfbʀɛt]

surgeon der Chirurg/die Chirurgin [dɐ çɪ'ʀʊɐk/di çɪ'ʀʊɐgɪn]

surgery die Operation [di ʔɔpəʀa'tsjo:n]

surprised, be ~ (at) sich wundern (über) [zɪç 'vʊndɐn ʀʏy(:)bɐ]

surroundings die Umgebung [di ʔʊm'ge:bʊŋ]

sweat (vb) schwitzen ['ʃvɪtsn]

sweater der Pullover [dɐ pʊ'lo:vɐ]

sweet (adj) süß [zy:s]

sweetener der Süßstoff [dɐ 'zy:ʃtɔf]

sweets die Süßigkeiten f pl [di 'zy:sɪçkaɪtn]

swelling die Schwellung [di 'ʃvɛlʊŋ]

swim (vb) baden [ba:dn], schwimmen [ʃvɪmm]

swimmer der Schwimmer/ die Schwimmerin [dɐ 'ʃvɪmɐ/ di 'ʃvɪmərɪn]

swimming lessons der Schwimmkurs [dɐ 'ʃvɪmkuɐs]

swimming pool (public) das Schwimmbad [das 'ʃvɪmba:t]; (private) der Swimmingpool [dɐ 'svɪmɪŋpu:l]

swimming trunks die Badehose [di 'ba:dəho:zə]

swimsuit der Badeanzug [dɐ 'ba:də ʔantsu:k]

swindle der Betrug [dɐ bə'tʀu:k]

wiss francs Schweizer Franken *m pl* [ˈʃvaɪtsɐ ˈfʁaŋkn̩]
wiss (man/woman) der Schweizer/die Schweizerin [deɐ ˈʃvaɪtsɐ/di ˈʃvaɪtsərɪn]
witch der Schalter [deɐ ˈʃaltɐ]
witzerland die Schweiz [di ʃvaɪts]
wollen geschwollen [ɡəˈʃvɔln̩]
wordfish der Schwertfisch [deɐ ˈʃveɐtfɪʃ]
ymbol das Wahrzeichen [das ˈvaːtsaɪçn̩]
ymphony concert das Sinfoniekonzert [das zɪmfoˈniːkɔn tseɐt]

T

able der Tisch [deɐ tɪʃ]
able tennis das Tischtennis [das ˈtɪʃtɛnɪs]
ablecloth das Tischtuch [das ˈtɪʃtuːx]
ablet die Tablette [di taˈblɛtə]
ail light das Rücklicht [das ˈʁʏklɪçt]
ilor der Schneider/die Schneiderin [deɐ ˈʃnaɪdɐ/di ˈʃnaɪdərɪn]
ake nehmen [neːmm]; *(time)* brauchen [bʁaʊxn̩]; **take part (in)** teilnehmen (an) [ˈtaɪlneːmm (ʔan)]; **take place** stattfinden [ˈʃtatfɪndn̩]
ake-off der Abflug [deɐ ˈʔapfluːk]
aken *(seat)* besetzt [bəˈzɛtst]
alk das Gespräch [das ɡəˈʃpʁɛːç]; *(vb)* reden [ʁeːdn̩], sich unterhalten [zɪç ʔʊntɐˈhaltn̩]
all groß [ɡʁoːs]
ampons die Tampons *m pl* [di ˈtampɔŋs]
ap der Wasserhahn [deɐ ˈvasɐhaːn]
aste der Geschmack [deɐ ɡəˈʃmak]; *(try food)* versuchen [fɛˈzuːxn̩]

tasty lecker [ˈlɛkɐ]
taxi driver der Taxifahrer/die Taxifahrerin [deɐ ˈtaksifaːʁɐ/di ˈtaksifaːʁərɪn]
taxi stand der Taxistand [deɐ ˈtaksiˈʃtant]
tea der Tee [deɐ teː]
tea bag der Teebeutel [deɐ ˈteːbɔɪtl̩]
tea towel das Geschirrtuch [das ɡəˈʃɪʁtuːx]
teach unterrichten [ʔʊntɐˈʁɪçtn̩], lehren [ˈleːʁən/leːən]
team die Mannschaft [di ˈmanʃaft]
teaspoon der Teelöffel [deɐ ˈteːlœfl̩]
teat der Sauger [deɐ ˈzaʊɡɐ]
telephone das Telefon [das ˈteːləfoːn]
telephone directory das Telefonbuch [das teləˈfoːnbuːx]
telephoto lens das Teleobjektiv [das ˈteːləʔɔbjɛk tiːf]
television lounge der Fernsehraum [deɐ ˈfɛɐnzeː ʁaʊm]
telex das Telex [das ˈteːlɛks]
tell erzählen [ʔeˈtsɛːln̩], ausrichten [ˈʔaʊsʁɪçtn̩], sagen [zaːgn̩]
temperature die Temperatur [di ʁtɛmpəʁaˈtuɐ]; *(fever)* das Fieber [das ˈfiːbɐ]
temple der Tempel [deɐ tɛmpl̩]
temporary vorläufig [ˈfoɐlɔɪfɪç], vorübergehend [foˈʁyːbɐɡeːent], provisorisch [pʁoviˈzoːʁɪʃ]
tender zärtlich [ˈtsɛɐtlɪç]; *(soft)* zart [tsaːt]
tennis das Tennis [das ˈtɛnɪs]
tennis racquet der Tennisschläger [deɐ ˈtɛnɪʃlɛːɡɐ]
tent das Zelt [das tsɛlt]
terminal das Terminal [das ˈtɜːmɪnəl]
terminus die Endstation [di ˈʔɛntʃtatsjoːn]
terrace die Terrasse [di teˈʁasə]
terracotta die Terrakotta [di tɛʁaˈkɔta]

terrible fürchterlich ['fʏeçtelɪç], schrecklich ['ʃʀɛklɪç]
tetanus der Tetanus [de 'tɛtanʊs]
than als [ʔals]
thank danken ['daŋkŋ], thank you danke schön ['daŋkə ʃøːn]
that diese(r, s) ['diːzə/'diːzɐ/ 'diːzəs]; jene(r, s) ['jeːnə/'jeːnɐ/ jeːnəs]; *(conj)* dass [das]
theater das Theater [das teʔaːtɐ]
theft der Diebstahl [de 'diːpʃtaːl]
then dann [dan], *(in the past)* damals ['daːma(ː)ls]
there da [daː], dort [dɔɐt], dorthin ['dɔɐthɪn]
therefore daher ['daːheɐ], deshalb ['dɛshalp]
thermometer das Fieberthermometer [das 'fiːbɛtɛemo meːtɐ]
these diese ['diːzə]
they sie [ziː]
thick dick [dɪk], *(crowd, fog etc.)* dicht [dɪçt]
thief der Dieb/die Diebin [de diːp/di 'diːbɪn]
thin dünn [dʏn]; mager ['maːgɐ], schmal [ʃmaːl]; *(sparse)* spärlich ['ʃpɛːɐlɪç], dürftig ['dʏɐftɪç]
thing das Ding [das dɪŋ], die Sache [di 'zaxə]
think denken ['dɛŋkŋ, meinen [maɪnn]; think (of) denken (an) ['dɛŋkŋ ʔan]
third dritte(r, s) ['dʀɪtə (-tɐ, -təs)]
this diese(r, s) ['diːzə/'diːzɐ/'diːzəs]
this morning/this evening heute Morgen/heute Abend [hɔɪtə 'mɔɐgŋ/hɔɪtə ʔaːbmt]
those diese ['diːzə]; jene ['jeːnə]
thriller der Kriminalroman [de kʀɪmiˈnaːlʀomaːn], der Thriller [de 'θʀɪlɐ]
throat der Hals [de hals]; die Kehle [di keːlə]
throat lozenges die Halstabletten *f pl* [di 'halsta blɛtn]
through durch [dʊɐç]
Thursday Donnerstag ['dɔnɐstaːk]

thus so [zoː], also [ʔalzoː]
thyme der Thymian [de 'tyːmiaːn]
ticket die Karte [di 'kaːtə]
ticket machine der Fahrkartenautomat [de 'faːkaːtnʔaʊto maːt]
ticket office die Kasse [di 'kasə]; *(transport)* der Fahrkartenschalter [de 'faːkaːtn ʃaltɐ]
tie die Krawatte [di kʀaˈvatə]
tight *(clothes)* eng [ʔɛŋ]
till bis [bɪs]
time die Zeit [di tsaɪt]; *(occasion)* das Mal [das maːl]; in time *(adv)* rechtzeitig ['ʀɛçtsaɪtɪç]; on time pünktlich ['pʏŋktlɪç]
time of arrival die Ankunftszeit [di ʔankʊnf tsaɪt]
timetable der Fahrplan [de 'faːplaːn]
tincture of iodine die Jodtinktu [di 'joːtɪŋktuɐ]
tint *(vb)* tönen [tøːnn]
tip *(information)* der Tipp [de tɪp] *(gratuity)* das Trinkgeld [das 'tʀɪŋkgɛlt]
tire der Reifen [de 'ʀaɪfn]
tired müde ['myːdə]
to zu [zu(ː)], nach [nax]; *(time)* bi [bɪs]
toast der Toast [de toːst]
toaster der Toaster [de 'toːstɐ]
tobacco der Tabak [de 'tabak]
tobacconist's/tobacco shop der Tabakladen [de 'tabaklaːdn]
toboggan der Schlitten [de ʃlɪtn]
today heute ['hɔɪtə]
toe die Zehe [di 'tseə]
together zusammen [tsʊˈzamm]; gemeinsam [gəˈmaɪnza(ː)m]
toilet die Toilette [di to'lɛtə]
toilet for the disabled die Behindertentoilette [di bəˈhɪndɛtnto lɛtə]
toilet paper das Toilettenpapier [das toˈlɛtnpa piɐ]
tomatoes die Tomaten *f pl* [di toˈmaːtn]
tomb das Grab [das gʀaːp]

omorrow morgen ['mɔɐgn];
tomorrow morning/tomorrow
evening morgen früh/morgen
Abend [mɔɐgn 'fʀy:/mɔɐgn
'ʔa:bmt]; the day after
tomorrow übermorgen
['ʔy:bɐmɔɐgn]

one der Ton [dɐ to:n]

ongue die Zunge ['tsʊŋə]

onight heute Nacht [hɔɪt(ə)
'naxt]

onsilitis die Mandelentzündung
[di 'mandl̩ʔɛn tsʏndʊŋ]

onsils die Mandeln f pl
[di 'mandln]

oo auch [ʔaʊx]; (with adj) zu
[zu(:)]; too much zu viel [tsʊ'fi:l];
zu sehr [tsʊ zeɐ]

ools das Werkzeug [das
'vɛɐktsɔɪk]

ooth der Zahn [dɐ tsa:n]

oothache die Zahnschmerzen m
pl [di 'tsa:nʃmɛɐtsn]

oothbrush die Zahnbürste
[di 'tsa:nbʏʀstə]

oothpaste die Zahnpasta
[di 'tsa:npasta]

oothpick das Zahnstocher
[dɐ 'tsa:nʃtɔxɐ]

op station die Bergstation
[di 'bɛɐkʃta tsjo:n]

orn ligament der Bänderriss
[dɐ 'bɛndeʀɪs]

ouch (vb) berühren [bə'ʀy:ʀən/
-'ʀyɛn]

ough (not tender) zäh [tsɛ:]

our die Tour [di tuɐ], die
Rundfahrt [di 'ʀʊntfa:t]; (of
museum, palace) die Besichtigung
[di bə'zɪçtɪgʊŋ]

ourist der Tourist/die Touristin
[dɐ tu'ʀɪst/di tu'ʀɪstɪn]; der/die
Reisende [dɐ/di 'ʀaɪzndə]; tourist
information office das
Verkehrsbüro [das fɐ'keɐsby ʀo:]

ow (away) abschleppen
['ʔapʃlɛpm]

ow rope das Abschleppseil [das
'ʔapʃlɛpzaɪl]

tow truck der Abschleppwagen
[dɐ 'ʔapʃlɛpva:gn]

towel das Handtuch [das
'han(t)tu:x]

tower der Turm [dɐ tʊɐm]

town die Stadt [di ʃtat]

town center die Innenstadt
[di 'ʔɪnnʃtat]

town hall das Rathaus [das
'ʀa:thaʊs]

town walls die Stadtmauern f pl
[di 'ʃtatmaʊɐn]

toy store das Spielwarengeschäft
[das 'ʃpi:lva:ʀəngə'ʃɛft]

toys die Spielsachen f pl [di 'ʃpi:l
za:xn]

traffic der Verkehr [dɐ fɛ'keɐ]

traffic jam der Stau [dɐ ʃtaʊ]

traffic light die Ampel [di 'ʔampl]

tragedy die Tragödie
[di tʀa'gø:diə]

train der Zug [dɐ tsu:k]

training die Ausbildung
[di 'ʔaʊsbɪldʊŋ]

tram die Straßenbahn
[di 'ʃtʀa:snba:n]

tranquilizer das Beruhigungsmittel [das bə'ʀʊɪgʊŋsmɪtl]

transfer die Überweisung
[di 'ʔybɐ'vaɪzʊŋ]

translate übersetzen ['ʔybɐ'zɛtsn]

transmission das Getriebe [das
gə'tʀi:bə]

transmission (engine) das
Getriebe [das gə'tʀi:bə]

trash can der Abfalleimer [dɐ
'ʔapfal 'ʔaɪmɐ]

trash can liner der Abfallbeutel
[dɐ 'ʔapfalbɔɪtl]

travel reisen [ʀaɪzn]

travel agency das Reisebüro [das
'ʀaɪzəby ʀo:]

travel bag die Reisetasche
[di 'ʀaɪzətaʃə]

traveler's check der Reisescheck
[dɐ 'ʀaɪzəʃɛk]

treat (injury) behandeln
[bə'handln]

tree der Baum [dɐ baʊm]

trekking bike das Trekkingrad
[das 'trɛkɪŋra:t]
trial *(court)* die (Straf)
Verhandlung [di
('ʃtra:f)fɛ handluŋ]
trip die Tour [di tuɐ], die Fahrt
[di fa:t], die Reise [di 'raɪzə], der
Ausflug [dɐ ʔaʊsflu:k]
tripod das Stativ [das ʃta'ti:f]
trousers die Hose [di 'ho:zə]
true wahr [va:]
trunk *(case)* der Schrankkoffer
[dɐ 'ʃraŋk kɔfɐ]; *(US)* der
Kofferraum [dɐ 'kɔfɐraʊm]
try *(vb)* versuchen [fɛ'zu:xn]; try
hard sich bemühen [zɪç bə'my:n]
Tuesday Dienstag ['di:nsta:k]
tumbler das Wasserglas [das
'vasɐgla:s]
tumor die Geschwulst
[di gə'ʃvʊlst]
tuna der Thunfisch [dɐ 'tu:nfɪʃ]
tunnel der Tunnel [dɐ tʊnl]
turn back umkehren
[ʔʊmke:rən/-keen]
turquoise türkisfarben
[tyɐ'ki:sfa:bm]
twice zweimal ['tsvaɪma:l];
doppelt [dɔplt]
typhoid der Typhus [dɐ 'ty:fʊs]
typical typisch ['ty:pɪʃ]

U

ugly hässlich ['hɛslɪç]
ulcer das Geschwür [das gə'ʃvyɐ]
umbrella der Schirm [dɐ ʃɪɐm]
unbearable unerträglich
[ʔʊnɐ trɛ:klɪç]
unconscious bewusstlos
[bə'vʊstlo:s]
under unter [ʔʊntɐ]
underground die U-Bahn
[di ʔu:ba:n]
understand verstehen [fɛ'ʃte:n]
underwear die Unterwäsche
[di ʔʊntɐvɛʃə]

unemployed arbeitslos
[ʔa:baɪtslo:s]
unfit ungeeignet [ʔʊngəʔaɪknɐt]
unfortunately leider ['laɪdɐ],
unglücklicherweise
[ʊʔʊnglʏklɪçɐ'vaɪzə]
unimportant unwichtig
[ʔʊnvɪçtɪç]
university die Universität
[di ʔuniveɐzi'tɛ:t]
unpleasant unangenehm
[ʔʊnangəne:m], *(news)*
unerfreulich [ʔʊnɛfrɔɪlɪç]
unsuited ungeeignet
[ʔʊngəʔaɪknɐt]
until bis [bɪs]
unusual ungewöhnlich
[ʔʊngəvø:nlɪç]
up aufwärts [ʔaʊfvɛɐts], nach oben
[nax ʔo:bm], oben [ʔo:bm]
urgent dringend [drɪŋnt], eilig
[ʔaɪlɪç]
urine der Urin [dɐ ʔu'ri:n]
us uns [ʔʊns]
use die Verwendung [di
fɛ'vɛnduŋ], der Gebrauch [dɐ
gə'braʊx], die Anwendung [di
ʔanvɛnduŋ]; *(vb)* anwenden
[ʔanvɛndn], verwenden
[fɛ'vɛndn], gebrauchen [gə'braʊx
benutzen [bə'nʊtsn]; be used to
s. th. etwas gewöhnt sein [ʊʔɛtvas
gə'vø:nt zaɪn]
usual gewohnt [gə'vo:nt],
gewöhnlich [gə'vø:nlɪç], üblich
[ʔy:plɪç]
usually normalerweise
[nɔ'ma:lɐvaɪzə]

V

vacation die Ferien [di 'fe:riən
('feɐjən)], der Urlaub [dɐ ʔuɐlaʊp
vacation home das Ferienhaus
[das 'fe:riənhaʊs]

vacation property die Ferienanlage [di 'fe:Rɪən'anla:gə]

vaccination die Impfung [di 'ʔɪmpfʊŋ]

vaccination record der Impfpass [dɐ 'ʔɪm(p)fpas]

valid gültig ['gʏltɪç]

valley das Tal [das ta:l]

valuables die Wertsachen [di 'veɐtzaxn]

vantage point der Aussichtspunkt [dɐ 'ʔaʊsɪçtspʊŋt]

variety theater das Varietee [das vaRɪə'te:]

vase die Vase [di 'va:zə]

vault(s) das Gewölbe [das gə'vœlbə]

veal das Kalbfleisch ['kalpflaɪʃ]

vegetables das Gemüse [das gə'my:zə]

vegetarian der Vegetarier/die Vegetarierin [dɐ vegə'ta:Rɪɐ/di vegə'ta:RɪəRɪn]; *(adj)* vegetarisch [vegə'ta:Rɪʃ]

vending machine der Automat [dɐ ʔaʊto'ma:t]

very sehr [zeɐ]

vest die Weste [di 'vɛstə]

video camera die Videokamera [di 'vi:deo kaməRa]

video cassette die Videokassette [di 'vi:deoka sɛtə]

video film der Videofilm [dɐ 'vi:deofɪlm]

video recorder der Videorekorder [dɐ 'vi:deoRe kɔɐdɐ]

view die Sicht [di zɪçt], die Aussicht [di 'ʔaʊszɪçt], der Blick [dɐ blɪk]; *(opinion)* die Ansicht [di 'ʔanzɪçt], die Meinung [di 'maɪnʊŋ]

viewer der(Fernseh)Zuschauer/die (Fernseh)Zuschauerin [dɐ ('fɛɐnzeɐ) tsu:ʃaʊɐ/di ('fɛɐnzeɐ) tsu:ʃaʊɐRɪn]

viewfinder der Sucher [dɐ 'zu:xɐ]

village das Dorf [das dɔɐf]

vinegar der Essig [dɐ 'ʔɛsɪç]

vineyard der Weinberg [dɐ 'vaɪnbɛɐk]

virus das Virus [das 'vi:Rʊs]

visa das Visum [das 'vi:zʊm]

visit der Besuch [dɐ bə'zu:x]; *(vb)* besuchen [bə'zu:xn], *(sights)* besichtigen [bə'zɪçtɪgn]

visiting hours die Besuchszeit [di bə'zu:xstsaɪt]

volleyball der Volleyball [dɐ 'vɔlɪbal]

voltage die Stromspannung [di 'ʃtRo:m ʃpanʊŋ]

vote die Stimme [di 'ʃtɪmə]; *(vb)* wählen ['vɛ:ln]

voucher der Gutschein [dɐ 'gu:tʃaɪn]

voyage die Seereise [di 'ze:Raɪzə], die Seefahrt [di 'ze:fa:t]

vulgar ordinär [ʔɔdi'nɛ:ɐ]

W

wading pool das Planschbecken [das 'planʃbɛkn]

waistcoat die Weste [di 'vɛstə]

wait (for) warten (auf) [va:tn (ʔaʊf)], erwarten [ʔe'va:tn]

waiter/waitress der Kellner/die Kellnerin [dɐ 'kɛlnɐ/di 'kɛlnəRɪn]

waiting room das Wartezimmer [das 'va:tətsɪmɐ], der Wartesaal [dɐ 'va:təza:l]

wake wecken [vɛkn]; wake up aufwachen ['ʔaʊfvaxn]

Wales Wales [wɛɪls (vɛɪls)]

walk der Spaziergang [dɐ ʃpa'tsiɐgaŋ]; *(vb)* gehen [ge:n], laufen [laʊfn]; go for a walk spazieren gehen [ʃpa'tsi:Rən ge:n], einen Spaziergang machen [(ʔaɪn)n ʃpa'tsiɐgaŋ maxn]

wall *(external)* die Mauer [di 'maʊɐ]; *(internal)* die Wand [di vant]

wallet die Brieftasche [di ˈbʀiːftaʃə]

want wollen [ˈvɔln]

ward die Station [di ʃtaˈtsjoːn]

warm warm [vaːm]; *(regards)* herzlich [ˈhɛɐtslɪç]; *(vb)* wärmen [vɛɐmm]

warning triangle das Warndreieck [das ˈvaːndʀaɪɛk]

wash *(vb)* waschen [vaʃn]

washbasin das Waschbecken [das ˈvaʃbɛkŋ]

washcloth der Waschlappen [dɐ vaʃlapm]

washroom der Waschraum [dɐ vaʃʀaʊm]

wasp die Wespe [di ˈvɛspə]

watch die (Armband)Uhr [di (ˈʔaːmbant)ˈʔuɐ]; *(vb)* zuschauen [ˈtsuːʃaʊn], *(observe)* beobachten [bəˈʔoːbaxtn]

watchmaker's der Uhrmacher [dɐ ˈʔuɐmaxɐ]

water das Wasser [das ˈvasɐ]

water canister der Wasserkanister [dɐ ˈvasɐkanˌɪstɐ]

water consumption der Wasserverbrauch [dɐ ˈvasɐfɛbʀaʊx]

water ski der Wasserski [dɐ ˈvasɐʃiː]; go water skiing Wasserski fahren [ˈvasɐʃiː ˈfaːʀən]

water wings die Schwimmflügel *m pl* [di ˈʃvɪmflyːgl]

watercolor (picture) das Aquarell [das ˈʔakvaˈʀɛl]

waterfall der Wasserfall [dɐ ˈvasɐfal]

way *(manner)* die Weise [di ˈvaɪzə]; *(path)* der Weg [dɐ veːk]

way in der Eingang [dɐ ˈʔaɪngaŋ]; way out der Ausgang [dɐ ˈʔaʊsgaŋ]

we wir [viɐ/vɐ]

weak schwach [ʃvax]

wear tragen [tʀaːgŋ]

weather forecast die Wettervorhersage [di ˈvɛtɐfoɐ heːɐzaːgə]

wedding die Hochzeit [di ˈhɔxtsaɪt]

Wednesday Mittwoch [ˈmɪtvɔx]

week die Woche [di ˈvɔxə]; weekly wöchentlich [ˈvœçntlɪç]

weekend rate die Wochenendpauschale [di ˈvɔxn̩ʔɛntpaʊʃaːlə]

weight das Gewicht [das gəˈvɪçt]

weight training das Krafttraining [das ˈkʀaftʀɛːnɪŋ]

welcome *(adj, interj)* willkommen [vɪlˈkɔmm]; *(vb)* empfangen [ˈʔɛmpˈfaŋŋ], begrüßen [bəˈgʀyːsn]

well der Brunnen [dɐ bʀʊnn], *(oil)* die (Öl)Quelle [di (ˈʔøːl)ˈkvɛlə]; *(healthy)* gesund [gəˈzʊnt], wohl [voːl]; *(adv)* gut [guːt]

well-done durchgebraten [ˈdʊɐçgəbʀaːtn]

well-known bekannt [bəˈkant]

Welsh walisisch [vaˈliːzɪʃ]

Welshman/Welshwoman der Waliser/die Waliserin [dɐ vaˈliːzɐ/ di vaˈliːzəʀɪn]

west der Westen [dɐ vɛstn]

western der Western [dɐ ˈvɛsten]

wet nass [nas]

wetsuit der Neoprenanzug [dɐ neoˈpʀeːn ˈʔantsuːk]

what was [vas]

wheel das Rad [das ʀaːt]

wheelchair der Rollstuhl [dɐ ˈʀɔlʃtuːl]

wheelchair cabin die Rollstuhlkabine [di ˈʀɔlʃtuːlka biːnə]

wheelchair user der Rollstuhlfahrer/die Rollstuhlfahrerin [dɐ ˈʀɔlʃtuːl faːʀɐ/di ˈʀɔlʃtuːl faːʀəʀɪn]

whether ob [ˈʔɔp]

while *(conj)* während [ˈvɛːʀənt (veːnt)]

whipping cream die Schlagsahne [ˈʃlaːkzaːnə]

white weiß [vaɪs]

white bread das Weißbrot [das ˈvaɪsbʀoːt]

white wine Weißwein [ˈvaɪsvaɪn]